S0-BFB-216

'STAND BY YOUR BEDS!'

A Novel

by

CORDELL CROSS

© Copyright December 1990
Vanbrugh Management Ltd.
All rights reserved

Second Printing November 1992

Published by:
Aggie Blinkhorn Organization Inc.
P.O. Box 88549
101-13753 72nd Avenue
Surrey, B.C., Canada
V3W 0X1

ISBN 0-9696248-0-8

Cover art by Peter Lynde–Ganges, B.C.

FOR MARY, MR. CHIPS, AND ALEX MALCZYNSKI

Alex, you would have made it to the top. Being the Cadet Parade Commander at Camp Vernon was only the start. The 2290 British Columbia Regiment (DCO) Cadet Corps and the Vernon Army Cadet Camp were indeed blessed because you were there. Thanks for sharing what few years you could.

I NTRODUCTION

This book is about teenaged boys who joined army cadets and decided to spend the greater part of their summer holidays at the Vernon Army Cadet Camp.

I would like to think that these lads were not the norm for teenagers. In my opinion they were one step above the norm because they made a personal decision to allow the army to discipline them and teach them how they should conduct themselves in this tumultuous tunnel of adventure called life.

The era, like the town of Vernon in the interior of Canada's province of British Columbia, was beautiful and innocent. Crack Canadian Troops returning from the Korean War were posted to Vernon to train these cadets. When they arrived, they were surprised to find that the average age of the boys was fourteen. The boys, in turn, were surprised to find that age didn't count. They were there to be trained and trained they were.

Now, for those of you who might go on the offensive and deny some of the antics these boys get themselves into, you can relax…they really did happen. I'm referring to the few who always force themselves to view the world through rose-coloured glasses and say the right thing at the right time. To those who don't believe boys should be boys, I would ask that you think back to your youth. Remember? It was the time when you were young and you never had to put on the act. It was the time when you offered your real opinion, not the opinion you thought your superiors wanted to hear.

I suggest that you take off those glasses, sit back, think, read and smile. If you can't, then you've made life far too complicated for yourself. If you can only remember doing the 'proper' things, without recalling the whole story, then no one will ever remember you.

In September of 1952, David Flater, a tall, lanky kid about fourteen years of age, asked me if I wanted a hand delivering my newspapers after school. At first I thought he was joking because no one ever volunteered to help deliver newspapers.

As it turned out, he wasn't joking. He was new to the neighbourhood and wanted to meet new friends and find his way around the West End of Vancouver.

About halfway through the route, he asked me if I had ever heard about, "The Tankers."

"The Tankers? What are they, ships of some sort?"

He grinned. "No, army cadets. I joined them last April. They've shut down for the summer, but they start up again next Wednesday night. Wanna join?"

"Army Cadets? Have you gotta wear a uniform and salute and do all the stuff they do in the army?"

"Yeah, it's really neat. We go to Nanaimo once a month on a training exercise. Last May I actually drove a tank."

The word 'tank' excited me. "Wow! They've got tanks?"

"They've got five of 'em and all the guys get a chance to ride around in them and drive 'em."

"Whew, you bet. I'll go with ya."

The next Wednesday evening, I met Dave at his house. One look at Dave and I wanted in. He was wearing his uniform and looked like a completely different person. I didn't know what to say at first because I felt shy and envious at the same time. He actually looked like an adult.

"The pants itch like hell, but you'll get used to them," he said.

Just after we got off the bus and arrived at the Drill Hall on Beatty Street, Dave handed me four pieces of thick cardboard.

"Stick these in the heels of your shoes. It'll add an inch or two to your height. You've gotta be five-foot-two to get in."

When we entered the building, another hundred-and-eighty cadets just like him were getting ready to get on parade. Itchy pants or no itchy pants, they all looked sharp.

I lined up outside of the recruiting office with another fifteen guys who were joining. Eventually, a cadet about 16 years old and wearing three stripes, called me into the room and filled out a recruiting form on me. He then asked me to stand up against a measuring tape on the wall.

"You just made it," he said. "WELCOME TO THE 2290 BRITISH COLUMBIA REGIMENT, DUKE OF CONAUGHT'S OWN, CADET CORPS. CORPORAL HILL, TAKE THIS MAN TO 'C' SQUADRON."

A week later, I talked some of my friends into joining. The group of us were quite a team until Dave opted out for no apparent reason. If I knew where he is today, I couldn't thank him enough for mentioning the word, Tankers.

I paraded in the Drill Hall three times a week, for lectures, shooting and band-practices. Then in 1953 I was offered the opportunity to spend the summer at the Vernon Army Cadet Camp. What I was taught there has benefited me for the rest of my life and I want to share some of those experiences with you.

At first, I didn't quite know how to tackle writing STAND BY YOUR BEDS! I had to write it to get a message across; aiming it at numerous cadets who took advantage of 'the system,' but have never given anything back.

These are the boys who all had a friend like David Flater to get them interested. They joined cadets, used the knowledge they received as a stepping stone and advanced through the ranks to eventually become Junior and Senior Non-Commissioned Officers, Junior Officers, Senior Officers and yes, even General Officers in the Canadian Army.

Talking the project over with a friend of mine who knows the publishing business, she said, "Canadian novels are hard to sell. Why don't you write a memoir?"

"I can't do that," I replied. "I have got to get through to the people who participated in the cadet movement, but somehow forgot other youngsters were following them. Young Canadians who would benefit by the same kind of training, but for illogical reasons, had the rug pulled from under them and are now limited to serving in a mere shadow of the original army cadet organization of yesteryear. To do that, I've got to take the former 'forgetful souls' back in time and tug at their heartstrings by rekindling their recollection. I want to put them on the hot seat and let them ask themselves how they allowed such a tragic transformation to occur in the army cadet system. I have to write STAND BY YOUR BEDS as seen through their eyes."

"But your book will be fiction if you do that?"

"Only fractionally," I replied. "Although some of the antics took place over a four year period, it'll be 99 percent fact. There's no other way I can do it."

She smiled. "Like the pureness of Ivory Soap?"

"Oh much purer than that."

This book should have been written many years ago, by countless people. I'm really surprised it wasn't, because over a million Canadian youths have served in various cadet corps throughout this country and hundreds of thousands of them have had the opportunity to spend the summer at the many cadet camps across Canada.

Since the turn of the century, when some forms of army cadet corps came into existence, boys and now boys and girls put on a uniform to participate in a youth program that was at one time second-to-none in the world.

They lived and still do live in the small towns of logging areas in British Columbia; in the farming villages of the prairies; in the fishing communities on the east coast; and in every major city across this great country.

Initially it is the excitement of joining cadets which gets them involved. Little do they know that by participating, they will become better prepared for what lies ahead in their lives.

Over the year and a half it took me to write this book, I laughed and I cried because the memories of the past were so intensely overpowering.

With each page, I was reminded how fortunate I was to be part of it. At the age of fourteen, I had the opportunity of visiting places, making new friends and meeting many prominent people that other Canadians only dream about meeting.

During that time, language was never a barrier. I bunked with French Canadian cadets who never spoke English and it didn't matter that I didn't speak French, because we were part of a national team. We understood each other and nothing could tear us apart because we were Canadian. Today, the youth in this country could indeed teach our 'politicians' something about getting along with each other, but that's another story.

Many books have been written about how Paul Hellyer, as Minister of Defence in the Trudeau government, ruined the traditional military system in Canada. That system also included the army cadet organization.

Let there be no misunderstanding about what Hellyer did. Whether or not it was done through pure ignorance, or through blind obedience to a Prime Minister who was totally oblivious when it came to matters of the military, Hellyer, in effect, dismantled the Canadian Armed Forces.

Personally, I do not believe Hellyer was ignorant. The Prime Minister's cunning determination to smother the military and, in particular its traditions, was evident throughout.

The totally irresponsible and irrational changes that took place in the military after Trudeau's election forced thousands of loyal soldiers, airmen and sailors to leave. It didn't matter who complained, if they disagreed with the changes, they were gone. You see, the military, at that time, did not fit in with the lifestyle of a so-called self-anointed intellectual such as Pierre Trudeau. Historians in the future will discover that Trudeau really didn't want a military at all. Well, whether some people admit it or not, the Canadian military today still exists in the predicament created by Trudeau and Hellyer. The results of the dilemma they created have been disastrous. Again, that is another story.

As I have mentioned, the cadet organization was also affected. Trudeau and Hellyer weren't just happy ruining a tried and tested armed forces, they did their best to eliminate the Royal Canadian Sea Cadets, Army Cadets and Air Force Cadets.

The main character in this book, Lieutenant-General Douglas Brice, is fictitious, but hundreds like him stood aside and looked the other way when Trudeau and Hellyer's carnage started. They had already taken advantage of the system of the past, now they closed their eyes when these two gold-dust twins 'rearranged' army cadet training. After all, they didn't need it anymore, so they allowed the bleeding hearts who were always in the minority, to dictate to a Prime Minister who was a bleeding heart himself.

"We're training our youths to kill," was one of the expressions voiced by these people.

Nothing could be further from the truth. Cadets were never forced to join the Regular Force. As a matter of fact, only about ten percent of them did. But that didn't matter, so Trades-Training was cancelled, cut-backs affected and three-quarters of a reliable youth training process smothered.

My God, if some of the boys or girls who are in trouble with the law today had undergone the Trades-Training and discipline courses that used to exist, they would be leading entirely different lives.

Sometimes I wonder why the silent majority never speaks up. Unlike the forces, where if someone speaks up, a notation appears on his or her Personal Evaluation Report depicting that they are too much of an individual, the silent majority of citizens don't have that enigma to deal with.

I have written this book to jog hundreds of thousands of memories. It will remind the public, politicians and all members of the military, including General Officers, that it's time to put the meaning of the word, 'army' back into army cadets.

This is really going to be a tough job, because many of the 'real' men and women of the forces, *God bless them,* have gone. They fought the changes regardless of what appeared on their Personal Evaluation Reports. They spoke up and were told to leave, or left on their own accord. The people who stayed, in numerous cases, were too young to understand what the government was doing, or were enthralled with the possibility of a rapid rise in rank, filling the vacancies of the traditionalists.

It should be pointed out however, that even now, some of those who stayed speak out now and then, but they do it age fifty-four, one year prior to retirement.

Canada's youth hasn't changed over these many years. They have new interests to distract them, but basically they are the same youth described in this book. The only difference is, they do not have the same opportunities as the youth of yesteryear.

Many parents will say, "Such language." Well, I would ask them to look back to their youth. Children will always be children and what they say inside the house, in many cases, is not the vocabulary they use outside. There would be a few hard smacks across the face, if the reality was discovered. Maybe I'm wrong in that regard because these days, straps have disappeared from schools and if a parent smacks a kid, the 'child' is on the phone to the Minister of Human Resources. Oh Pierre, I wonder if you ever have sleepless nights, realizing what you started with so many of the 'gobbeldygook' things you initiated? Probably not.

When my best friend Wayne Banks returned home from Camp Vernon, he was having supper when it slipped out.

"Please pass the fucking sugar."

Wayne put his hand to his mouth, too late. His dad's arm came across the table and gave him a smack. One of the same arms which had hugged him moments before because he had returned home after being away for six weeks.

As Wayne's best friend, I only ever heard him use that word twice, and he tried to correct himself both times. Wayne was growing up.

There are those who will say that life in the fifties was entirely different than it is today. That is not true at all. Granted, the influence of television wasn't there, however the pace was fast and kids had to be a little smarter because life wasn't handed to them on a silver platter. The economy wasn't the greatest, so kids of the fifties had to think to survive, which included getting jobs, before and after school.

The historians of the future will write about our current era. The era of the silent majority, bleeding hearts and goody-two-shoes people who have nothing better to do than to interfere in other people's lives. Unrealistic people, who plan twenty-four-hours-a-day how to sway incompetent self-indulgent politicians to their way of thinking. The unfortunate fact is, the squeaky wheel does get the grease. It's about time we let the wheel wear out.

When writing STAND BY YOUR BEDS, I decided to only use a few real names. I also asked myself, wouldn't it be wonderful if I had access to the hundreds of thousands of personal stories about cadets who attended Vernon. Better yet, what if I had access to the half million personal stories of cadets who attended camps similar to Vernon. Oh, what a book *that* would make.

THEY ARE A GRAND AND EXCLUSIVE GROUP. GOD BLESS THEM ALL.

Cordell Cross
December 1990

D EDICATION

This book is dedicated to all those cadets who attended an army cadet camp in Canada, especially all members of the 2290 British Columbia Regiment (DCO) Cadet Corps, who attended the Vernon Military Camp from 1953 through 1956.

Good Senior Non-Commissioned Officers are hard to come by. Camp Vernon was fortunate to have Sergeant Bill Crawford, a gentleman who never tired of imparting all his years of knowledge and attention to fair play on his younger charges.

It is also dedicated to: Lieutenant-Colonel Arthur Lungley; Lieutenant-Colonel L.J.L. St. Laurent (although the cadets thought otherwise, he *was not* a relative of the then Prime Minister of Canada, the Hon. Louis St. Laurent); Brigadier W.J. Megill; Major-General George Kitching; Lieutenant-Colonel C.V. (Vince) Lilley; Lieutenant-Colonel Archie Steacy; Captain Len Vaness; and in particular, to Major Roy Forbes. Roy dedicated a great deal of his life to Camp Vernon, but regretfully, he was never recommended to command. It is the author's opinion that had Major Forbes commanded Camp Vernon, he would have been one of the finest Commanding Officers the camp ever had.

• • •

Many people assisted me in writing this book. My thanks go out to Ken Gourley, Dave Rae, Doug McLean, Gord Cunningham, Jan Terrien, Gerald McCaughey and especially to Val Wilson, who said, "My God, Cordell, I've got to edit this thing! When did you forget the Queen's English?"

"I didn't, " I replied. "I know she was born there."

Thanks go out to Moriah, Bonita, Sparkie, Earl Jackson, Tony McClennan, Richard Tong, and to my business partner Walter Passaglia, for being so patient with me over these few years. I haven't told them yet, I'm working on a follow-up. I'm afraid to.

I also want to thank the *Vernon Daily News* and the Vernon Museum for providing what pictures I could find of the era. Most of the pictures were taken by Doug Kermode, and a grand gentleman and an officer, Major Cam LeBlond.

• • •

Lastly, I must apologize to the people who owned Hop Sing's Laundry and the proprietors of the Silver Grill Cafe for some of the insinuations that cadets made of those establishments in the 50s. Rumors are hard to stop, however, there was never any doubt that Hop Sing's was just another laundry and the Silver Grill Cafe was just that, a cafe. Deep down inside, I feel certain the boys of the 50s knew that as well.

GOD'S COUNTRY

If a person ever wanted to visit what is referred to as God's Country, all one would have to do is travel to the City of Vernon in British Columbia, Canada.

Nestled against lakes, mountains and rolling hills, Vernon, for some reason, has kept its early village charm probably more than the other two beautiful cities in the Okanagan Valley, Penticton and Kelowna.

Named after the Vernon brothers, Forbes-George and Charles Vernon, in approximately 1887, this steadily growing city can boast about having two of the most spectacular lakes in the world right on its doorstep, Kalamalka Lake and Okanagan Lake.

In bygone days, the city was the end of the line for steamers that moved both freight and passengers on the lakes that caress the shores of what the Duke of Connaught referred to as, "The most magnificent setting I have ever seen. Absolutely stunning!"

Kalamalka Lake is the smaller of the two. At the Lookout above the lake, there used to be a sign which read, Kalamalka Means Lake of Many Colors. It indeed may mean that , but officially it was named after Kalamalka, an elder in the Okanagan Indian Band.

The population of Vernon in 1953 was approximately eight thousand friendly people. Then, like today, they were closely tied to 'The Camp' as they referred to it.

'The Camp' has been a part of Vernon for seventy-eight years, starting when a Drill Hall was built in 1912. That Drill Hall marked the beginning of the 'Mission Hill' Camp, which Ottawa officially established in 1915. Canadian soldiers trained there in two World Wars.

Not many years after the Second World War, it was designated as a summer training camp for Royal Canadian Army Cadets.

These days, it is used during the summer by cadets and personnel from the militia.

CHAPTER I

Military staff cars all look about the same. They are black and plain. The bureaucrats who buy them never seem to consider amenities such as air conditioning, comfortable seats, or radios. At least that's what the Major sitting in the back seat was thinking as the car sped south along Highway 97 toward the Kelowna Airport in British Columbia's Okanagan Valley.

Although the car windows were open, the incoming air didn't help matters; it was scorching as it discovered the bodies of the Major and his driver.

"Would you mind if I lit up a smoke, Sir? This heat is driving me up the wall. Maybe a cigarette will help cool me down."

The Major could see the perspiration rolling down the back of the driver's neck.

"No, go right ahead Corporal. If you've got a spare one, I'll join you."

Without taking his eyes off the road, the Corporal lit a cigarette and passed the package and a lighter to the officer.

"Do any of these cars in the auto pool have air conditioning in them?" the Major asked, as he passed back the cigarettes and lighter.

Wiping the sweat from his eyes with his arm, the Corporal winced. "No, Sir. As a matter of fact, this is one of the better cars. It's difficult to open the windows in the others. I was driving one yesterday and only the driver's window would open."

The officer smiled. "Who was your passenger?"

"None other than Colonel Forbes, Sir. He wasn't very happy and informed me that he would speak to the Transportation Officer."

"You can bet he'll do that," said the Major, sitting forward and pulling his sweat-soaked shirt away from his chest. The instant he released it, the cloth sucked his body again.

"Not only that, Sir. He wanted this car today, but he was informed it was being used to pick up General Brice."

"Any qualms when he was told that?"

"None whatsoever, Sir. The minute General Brice's name was mentioned, everything was cool. What's he like Sir?"

"Who?"

"General Brice. Everyone at the camp has been talking about him. Was he here as a cadet?"

The Major sat back again and took a long hard draw on his cigarette.

"I've never had the honour of serving with him. Apparently he was here as a cadet in the 50s and this is the first time he's returned. You've probably heard the same runours that I have. I hear he's tough, real tough. He never smiles; he's been nicknamed the iceman. Colonel Forbes says General Brice is very fair with his soldiers and when Brice is at the helm, battles are won before they're fought."

The driver turned the car off the highway into the Kelowna Airport parking lot.

"But if he was here as a cadet sir, I mean at the camp, how come there's not a plaque about him or even a street named after him?"

The officer reached for his tunic and tie next to him on the seat. "You've got me there, Corporal. I don't think too many General Officers with his stature, originated their military careers at the Vernon Army Cadet Camp."

The young officer looked at his wrist. "Damn it. I've left my watch at camp. What time is it?"

"We're twenty minutes early, Sir. It's 1430 by my watch."

"Good!" The Major looked pleased as he got out of the car and put on his headdress. He knew his pants were wrinkled, but his tunic would look sharp when he introduced himself to the General.

"Should I return to the car while you're waiting, Sir?"

"God no! Not in this heat. You can get the car while the General is waiting for his luggage."

For most of the short trip from Vancouver to Kelowna there had been nothing to see but clouds. When the pilot mentioned that the City of Penticton was below, Lieutenant-General Douglas Brice leaned forward in his seat to get a better view. The clouds had parted and Douglas knew he was nearing his destination.

"We'll be landing in Kelowna in a few minutes. Is there anything I can get you, General?"

Douglas almost didn't hear the stewardess. His mind was totally absorbed by the beautiful scenery below.

"No thank you," he replied as he tore his eyes from the window for a fraction of a second, returning his gaze as if he were mesmerized.

As the plane's wing dipped on the final approach, Douglas' eyes were glued to the clear-blue water of the lakes nestled in the sunburnt hills of the Okanagan Valley below. He could see endless rows of fruit trees woven into the ground, rising up from the lakes like giant green carpets. Here and there, a few head of cattle hid under a copse of evergreens, trying to escape the heat of the blazing, midday sun.

Douglas didn't feel excitement very often, but with this picture-postcard view, it was all coming back to him. As a youth, he referred to the Okanagan Valley as his little piece of paradise. Other people called it God's Country. They even called Kalamalka Lake the Eighth Scenic Wonder of the World. The names didn't matter. The Okanagan and in particular, Kalamalka were special to him and he had made a personal vow that he would do his damnedest to keep this area as pure and pristine as The Creator had sculptured it.

When the seatbelt sign came on, Douglas' mind raced as he looked at the sprawling city. The population of Kelowna couldn't have been more than seven thousand people when he was last here. Now it had to be over seventy thousand. He shook his head slowly, wondering why everything couldn't remain the same.

The lake below hadn't changed, he thought. Okanagan Lake, which runs a hundred miles from Penticton to Vernon, looked as appealing as ever. The boat traffic on the lake looked a lot like he remembered it, except something seemed different. The bridge. He had read about the bridge. One of the first floating bridges built, connecting Kelowna to the highway coming in from Vancouver, approximately 300 miles to the southwest. He wondered what had happened to the old ferry that chugged across the lake, carrying only a few cars. It seemed like yesterday, but it was 34 years ago.

Douglas sat back in his seat. Had it really been that long? Although he hadn't forgotten his training experiences at the Vernon Army Cadet Camp, the adventure didn't seem important anymore. He was only a kid then. Certainly, this is where his military career started, but time had taken away the significance of the event. He wouldn't be here now if he hadn't mentioned his military cadet past to the Chief of Defence Staff while they were having a coffee, three days ago in his office at Defence Headquarters in Ottawa.

"We've received a request from a Member of Parliament to send a General Officer to Vernon for the Graduation Parade."

"Good Old Vernon. Who are you planning to send?"

"I thought we'd send Murray Crabtree. He can get a few games of golf in while he's there. He says the Vernon Golf Course is one of the best. Douglas, I haven't heard you laugh like that in along time. What's so funny?"

"I was cadet at Vernon. The camp overlooks the golf course. We'd walk across it taking a shortcut to the beach. I can still see people swearing and waving their clubs at us. One weekend afternoon, the Commanding Officer was playing and he saw our group walking past the ninth hole. Believe me, the whole camp heard about it that night."

"Did it stop you from taking the shortcut?"

"Not on your life. To walk around it would have added a few extra miles. It's hot as hell there."

"Good memories, eh?"

"Now that I think about it, I wouldn't trade that time in my life for anything in the world."

"Good! Pack your bags."

"What? Harley, you're joking? I thought I just heard you saying you were going to send Murray Crabtree? I can't go now. You know I have to be in Europe in two weeks."

"You've got plenty of time. The trip will do you good and help take your mind off the European Conference. Take your clubs with you."

"I don't play golf."

"Then take a walk across the course again. The Commanding Officer won't give you shit this time, will he?"

"You sneaky bastard. What about Crabtree?"

"I've assigned him to inspect the Quadra Sea Cadet Camp. Apparently, he was there as a cadet."

"Jesus Christ! You had it all figured out, didn't you?"

"Have fun, Douglas. Report to me when you return."

"Thanks Harley, you're all heart."

There was an slight bump as the tires of the aircraft touched the runway and the jet engines were reversed to slow the plane down. As it taxied to the terminal, Douglas opened the upper compartment, retrieving his tunic and beret. His uniform looked immaculate.

A blast of red hot air hit him as the plane's door opened.

"What's the temperature?" he asked the smiling stewardess.

"The pilot told us it's 32 degrees celsius. Thank you for flying Canadian."

The sun's rays found Douglas' six-foot-two frame inviting, as he walked down the stairs, moving aside to get out of the way of other passengers walking the short distance to the terminal.

"My God, it's great to be back," he murmured as he filled his lungs with the dry, sweet air and looked around at the hills stacked on both sides of the landing strip.

As he walked to the terminal, the combination of the heat and scented air tugged at his memory, prying open a memory file that had been closed long ago.

The Major stood at attention, saluting, as General Brice entered the terminal.

"Good afternoon, Sir. I'm Major Henderson, your aide during your visit with us, Sir."

Douglas smiled and wondered if he had looked that young when he was a Major.

He returned the salute and held out his right hand to shake the young officer's hand.

"Thank you, Major Henderson. I hope you haven't been waiting long in this heat?"

"Not at all, Sir. May I suggest that you wait here while I retrieve your baggage? The driver is bringing the car around now."

Douglas nodded and within minutes the car was brought to the entrance of the terminal.

"If I recall this trip, I think it might be wise if we removed our tunics and headdress," Douglas said, with a wink.

"Thank you, Sir," the officer replied.

Before the car left the terminal driveway, Major Henderson joined the driver in the front seat. Soon, they were winding north along Highway 97 towards Vernon.

For the first few minutes, no one spoke. This suited General Brice just fine. His eyes were peeled on the surrounding countryside. He had been on this road many times before. The trip was beautiful and with every passing mile, unfolding memories were gaining momentum.

Major Henderson spoke. "Did you have a pleasant flight, Sir?"

"Very pleasant, thank you," replied Douglas. "I guess the only thing I wasn't prepared for was the heat. How long has it been like this?"

"Most of the summer," replied the officer. "The Commanding Officer shut down training this afternoon."

"Has he had to do that often?"

"About twice a week, Sir."

"How much rain have you had?"

"It rained twice in the first week, Sir, but since then, we haven't had a drop."

"How are the cadets taking it?"

"Pretty well, Sir, considering. I think if they had their way, training would be shut down every afternoon.

Douglas smiled. "How many cadets are in camp this year?"

"Just over a thousand, Sir," Henderson replied.

Douglas noticed the driver looking at him in the rear view mirror.

"Do you ever get tired of this trip, Corporal?" He asked.

"Not really Sir. It gives me the chance to get out of camp. If I hadn't been assigned to pick you up today, I'd be up in the hills driving trucks along dusty roads."

Douglas laughed at the driver's response. "I understand what you mean. When I was your age I was in the Militia. I spent two summers driving up here."

"What was your rank, Sir?"

"The same as yours Corporal. If the Tech-Sergeant was in a good mood, he'd assign me to pick up visitors at the airport or the train station. The problem was, he was hardly ever in a good mood."

Both the Major and Corporal chuckled.

Major Henderson turned around and looked at the General. "We've heard that you were a cadet up here, Sir. Do you mind if I ask you when that was?"

Douglas thought for a moment. "From 1953 to 1956. How did you learn I was a cadet here?"

"We've heard of you, Sir," the young officer replied. "The whole camp has heard of you. A lot of stories have been going around this past week."

"Good yarns, I hope?"

The Major chuckled. "The best, Sir."

Douglas lit up a cigarette and gave permission for his co-passengers to do the same as the car navigated the winding road of Highway 97. They had stopped talking and Douglas could not take his eyes off the spectacular landscape outside the car. Even the new houses blended in with the scenery.

As the car rounded the shores of two small lakes where families were frolicking, he found himself searching to catch a glimpse of Kalamalka Lake, the Eighth Scenic Wonder of The World. He had travelled all over the globe and had seen many beautiful sights, but nothing compared with his memory of Kalamalka's breathtaking vista.

"Major Henderson, how far are we from Kalamalka Lake?"

"You'll be able to look down on it as soon as we climb the next hill," Henderson replied.

Suddenly there it was and Douglas was entranced once again. The lake lay like a fine piece of aqua-green jade. A water skier on the far side was skimming the surface close to the shore. His actions cut a channel that rippled the mirror-like reflection of the neatly-lined orchards.

"Corporal, please stop at the Lookout, up ahead. I wish to take a good look at Kalamalka."

"The position of the highway has changed since you were here, Sir. I'll take you to the old location."

When they arrived, Douglas walked over to the edge of the Lookout while Major Henderson and the Corporal lit cigarettes by the car. With the magnificent scene of his boyhood years stretched out below him, Douglas was overwhelmed. The surroundings instantly took him back to 1953.

Kalamalka wasn't just a lake, it was more like a kindly old Grandfather who always had time to listen. When his character was being developed and everything went wrong, he would come to the Lookout and somehow, the lake would soothe his mind.

Douglas shrugged. What problems? What seemed like problems then were just the mixed-up feelings of a growing teenager in puberty learning about fair play and discipline. But they felt real then. My, did they ever.

Memories continued to surface as he stood there. It was all coming back to him. Smelling the air and seeing the lake had torn open a memory-closet of those long, lost, forgotten years. He could see Kal Beach, packed with people that looked like insects from where he stood. Yes, and there was Rattlesnake Point and Cosens Bay.

Looking down, a nostalgic smile came over his face. It had taken a lot to convince him to come to camp when he was fourteen. Yet at the end of six weeks training, he hadn't wanted to go home.

As Douglas walked slowly back to the car, he wondered why he hadn't returned to Vernon before now. Although he had spent some of the loneliest, most mixed-up days of his life here, he had really loved every minute of it. Deep inside he knew why. If he had come back, he would never have wanted to leave.

The car made the final turn in the highway and Douglas saw the City of Vernon below, about a half-mile north. Every metre of the trip had brought back old memories. Now Douglas' eyes were fastened to the camp, which straddles both sides of the highway.

"Pull over please, Corporal."

Leaving his tunic and headdress in the automobile, he walked about twenty feet and stopped. His eyes scanned one-hundred-and-eighty degrees in front of him and stopped at the old parade square. The concrete for that landmark had been poured in 1955 or 1956. Before it was built, it was just a giant dust bowl where the cadets did their drill.

He smiled as he thought of the time he was standing there at attention and a spider crawled up his military shorts and bit him. If he had moved or screamed, the wrath of his Company Sergeant-Major would have come down on him like a bolt of lightning. It took two injections of penicillin to halt a red line of blood poisoning encroaching the area his friend Wayne Banks referred to as, "The family jewels."

A fond look appeared on Douglas' face. This was the first time in over twenty years he had thought of Wayne Banks. Wayne had been his best friend; they had been inseparable. Wherever Banks went, he went and vice versa.

My God, he thought to himself. Have I been so wrapped up in my career and myself that I couldn't find the time to contact Wayne? What's happened to me? We were closer than brothers.

The fact that he hadn't looked up Wayne weighed heavily on his mind as he perused the buildings he could see. Some of the huts and been taken down, but most of them were still standing. They were now covered in a white material, or brown wood, instead of thick black tarpaper.

The few roads Douglas could see had been paved, including the one connecting the upper camp on the west side of the highway, to the lower camp on the east.

Douglas' lips formed a lost smile when he saw that road. Every morning after inspection, his platoon used it to head to the upper camp for training. By the time they reached the other side, dust covered them from boots to pith-helmets. Although they weren't allowed to talk when they marched, Wayne used to murmur from the corner of his mouth.

"I can't see, I can't see. Doug, where are you? Are you there, Doug? I'm blind. The army has blinded me. My future is selling pencils out of a tin cup. Halt the platoon Doug, I've got to call my lawyer. When the hell are they ever going to pave this bastard?"

The smile was still on Douglas' lips, as he thought of the other guys in the platoon. The cadets within earshot of Wayne would start chuckling and before long the whole platoon was roaring with laughter. They knew it meant extra duty if they got caught laughing, but it didn't matter. It was contagious enough that even the platoons in front and following joined in the merriment.

"BANKS, I'LL HAVE YOUR ASS FOR THIS," the Company Sergeant-Major would scream.

"Wouldn't you love to?" Banks would reply, making certain the Company Sergeant-Major couldn't see his lips moving.

Douglas walked back to the car.

"Major, are there any plans scheduled for me tonight?"

"The Commanding Officer has asked if you would join him and his officers for dinner in the Officers' Mess tonight, Sir. We've got you booked into the Village Green Inn during your stay. The CO thought you might like to freshen up and then join him?"

Douglas looked at his watch. "What time is Graduation Parade tomorrow morning?"

"It's at 0830 tomorrow, Sir. The cadets will be on parade at 0800."

Still looking at his watch, Brice said, "It's 1600 now. Please inform the

Commanding Officer I will not be joining him for dinner tonight. Tell him I'm a little tired after my trip. Pick me up tomorrow at 0815 sharp."

"Yes, Sir," Henderson replied. "Should we now proceed straight to the hotel?"

Brice nodded and the three of them departed, past the camp and down the hill, through the City of Vernon.

The journey through town took ten minutes and Douglas noted the many changes that had taken place. They blended in well with the Vernon he knew so well.

As they drove past the Vernon Jubilee Hospital, located halfway down the hill, flashes of memory kept returning. How he hated having to walk up the hill on Saturdays and Sundays, the cadets' days off. The group he was with would sing songs to make the climb seem easier. Passing motorists would yell disparaging remarks. When the cadets yelled back, the Military Police would take their names and once again the wrath of their Company Sergeant-Major would be upon them the minute they stepped back in their barracks.

This was like being born again, Douglas thought to himself. Although the adventure had happened so many years ago, it seemed like only yesterday. Faces from the past were returning and he was experiencing a storybook visit which should never end. It was great to be back.

Douglas Brice had never heard of the Village Green Inn. When he was a cadet, the spot where the hotel now stood was a farmer's field on the outskirts of town. Now there were shopping-malls, car dealerships and restaurants everywhere.

Major Henderson took the bags up to the large and well-furnished room and left. A basket of local fruit containing a bottle of complementary white Okanagan wine waited on the writing table. The note read, 'With the compliments of the management to Lieutenant-General Douglas Brice...welcome back.'

Douglas unpacked and poured a glass of wine. It was still chilled so it must have been placed there recently.

The trip had tired him a little, but after a hot shower and shave, Douglas felt new life entering his body. Combing his hair, he noticed the grey that had started coming in about a year ago, spreading first along the temples. In the past, he had commented to others that grey hair made a person look distinguished; now he wasn't so sure.

After a meal in the hotel's restaurant, Douglas picked up the Vernon Daily News. He wasn't really interested in what was happening in the world. Articles of local interest seized his attention. A Vernon lady by the name of Elsie Hathaway had won an annual pie-baking contest and she looked so proud in the picture. On the next page, an article about a local cow, caught his eye. The headline read, 'All of Vernon proud of Mugs.' Apparently, Mugs had produced more milk in a shorter period of time than any other cow in the Okanagan Valley.

Douglas stopped reading for a moment and stared out the window at the passing traffic. Those two articles, like many others in the newspaper, made him think of how nice it would be to live here. An Ottawa newspaper would be filled with articles of blood and guts and politicians pushing their gibberish.

It was seven o'clock when he walked outside the hotel. The air was cooler now with a breeze coming in from the west. He knew the sun would be setting shortly. The hills in the near-distance looked like they were breathing a sigh of relief as they waited for the sun to gently slip behind them.

Although he had been tired earlier, the shower and dinner had given him new life. He knew he wouldn't be able to sleep even if he did go bed. The traffic on the highway in front of the hotel was busy and now and then he saw a taxi drive by. In the old days, Vernon only had two taxi cabs and most of the time they were parked by the theatre, their drivers waiting for a call.

When a cab dropped a couple off at the hotel, Douglas asked the driver if he would show him around town and then let him off at the bottom of the hill. He decided he would walk up to the camp. Not only would the exercise do him good, he could look at the changes that had taken place since he was last here.

The driver was a congenial fellow about Douglas' age. Although he had never been in cadets, as they drove around, he informed Douglas of the various stories he had heard about the camp. Most of them were hilarious and it warmed Douglas' heart that some of the camp traditions set in earlier years were still being adhered to today.

Douglas couldn't believe how Vernon had grown. The driver showed him many new sights and let him know which clubs he should visit and those he should avoid. The driver mentioned that crime was increasing each year. The statement surprised the General, because in the 50s, the residents of Vernon never used to lock their doors. Crime and rowdiness were rare and most people knew the two-man Mountie patrol. This was a religious valley, with hard-working, church-going citizens. Douglas sighed. He never thought that the big city syndrome would come to the Okanagan.

A motel had been built on the A&W property. As they passed, Douglas remembered the girls who wore roller skates to wait on cars. One Sunday, a couple had been married there and the bride and groom also sported roller skates.

Along the main drag, some names had changed, but the buildings remained the same. The Hudson's Bay Store had been replaced with an office building. Across the street, a shiny new Bank of Montreal had a sign that read, 'Air Conditioning Inside.'

He remembered the way the main drag came alive on Saturday nights. Young guys in dragsters revved up their engines to show off their cars to the local girls. The jalopies would cruise the streets into the night, until some girls were sweet-talked into a ride. The cadets were always there, asking the girls to go for a walk, but usually the cars won out.

The air was cooler when the driver let Douglas off at a shopping mall that contained the new A&W Drive In. The site used to house the Fruit Exchange warehouse where cadets went around the back to hide from the Provost and neck with the local girls. This time, there wasn't a cadet to be seen. Where were they all? This was the time of night the cadets used to wait for, before taking on the hill in their trek back to camp.

With the memory of the stomp of hundreds of bootsteps with him, Douglas started up the hill, but stopped outside Polson Park. It was quiet, very quiet. There were no voices screaming, "WHERE WILL I MEET YOU TOMORROW? HEY, I DIDN'T GET YOUR PHONE NUMBER, ARE YOU IN THE BOOK? I DON'T EVEN KNOW YOUR NAME! WHAT COMPANY ARE YOU IN?" Polson Park used to be full of cadets, taking the short-cut up the back hill. Now, as he continued walking, there wasn't a sound.

As he passed the hospital, Douglas chuckled to himself. For some reason this was the area the Military Police patrolled the most. Cadets in uniforms looking so sharp you would cut yourself on them if you touched a crease, were given the once-over as the police drove by. If anyone was out of step, he would be told quickly to get in step and if the Military Police were bored, they would stop cadets and inspect them. He could hear it all now.

"IS THAT A BEARD YOU'RE GROWING SOLDIER?" The Military Police-man screamed, nose to nose with a young cadet standing to attention, trying not to wet himself or pass out.

"No, Sir! It's only......"

"SPEAK UP SON, I CAN'T HEAR YOU!"

"NO, SIR! IT'S ONLY ONE HAIR GROWING SIR!" The cadet replied, knees wobbling.

"IT SURE AS HELL LOOKS LIKE A BEARD TO ME. DO YOU THINK YOU'RE IN THE GOD-DAMNED NAVY? WELL, DO YOU?"

"NO, SIR! I...I...IT'S ONLY ONE HAIR, SIR!"

"DON'T YOU KNOW BETTER THAN TO CALL ME SIR? MY PARENTS WERE MARRIED...CAN'T YOU SEE I'M A CORPORAL?"

"YES, CORPORAL!" The young cadet looked straight ahead at the Corporal's shirt buttons, as the Military Policeman towered over him.

"THAT'S BETTER! WHAT'S YOUR NAME?"

The cadet was starting to gain some control of himself. "MY NAME IS HARRINGTON, CORPORAL!"

"WHAT COMPANY ARE YOU IN, HARRINGTON?"

"DOG COMPANY, CORPORAL!"

"RIGHT!" The Corporal then made a note of the cadet's name in his 'little black book.'

"NOW GET THAT GOD-DAMNED THING OFF THE MINUTE YOU REACH CAMP. IF I SEE YOU WITH A BEARD AGAIN, YOU'LL END UP IN THE NAVY. IS THAT CLEAR?"

"YES, SIR!"

"ARE YOU A PONGO SOLDIER?"

"NO, SIR!"

"DO YOU WANT TO BE A PONGO?"

"NO, SIR!"

"WELL, GET IT OFF! AND STOP CALLING ME 'SIR'!"

When the Military Police truck had driven out of sight, the cadets rallied around the person in question, straining their eyes, trying to find the hair on the boy's face. "I CAN SEE IT." Someone screamed. "YOU DO HAVE A HAIR GROW-ING."

Although a magnifying glass would be required to check the exact size of the hair, the owner was now as proud as punch. That hair would not be coming off. It would be prized and admired each time the cadet looked in the mirror trying to find it.

"Why did you tell him your name was Harrington? Do you know someone in Dog Company by that name?" Another cadet asked.

The cadet with the 'beard' smiled.

"Yeah. I owed him one for the time he flicked his towel at me down at the beach."

"The poor bastard," someone said. "I wouldn't want to be in that guy's shoes when his Company Sergeant-Major hears from the Provost-Sergeant."

Douglas had actually laughed out loud as he continued his climb. He wondered how anyone could yell at someone so innocent. Although he didn't know it at the time, he knew now that the Corporal wasn't serious. The act was perfectly played out by the Junior NCO. All of the Junior and Senior Non-Commissioned Officers at camp had that special quality about them. They would bellow and shout and have cadets shaking in their boots. But after it was all over, the cadet on the receiving end would notice a slight wink of the eye, or an incomplete smile, indicating that nothing would happen this time. If the cadet got caught for the same offence again, there would be no wink, no smile. Then he knew he had a problem.

Such great memories, thought Douglas.

At the top of the hill, General Brice entered the road leading in to the camp. The Military Police shack was deserted and the lights were out. He had never seen it like that before. It had been the centre of activity, with cadets being inspected as they left camp or were escorted back, for creating a disturbance downtown.

As he walked toward B-3, the large hangar, his eyes surveyed a four-foot fence that had been erected around the lower camp. It wasn't there before, but suggestions had been made about building one. It would keep out the dragsters from visiting the camp in the middle of the night. The noise of squealing tires could be heard everywhere and cadets couldn't get back to sleep.

Because the gate had no lock on it, Douglas was able to enter the camp. He walked a few paces up the main road. The lights were on in the hangar but it was silent inside and the end door was open. He entered. Rows upon rows of chairs had been neatly set up facing the stage. Probably for an upcoming movie, he thought.

The sound of his feet echoed everywhere as he walked around the grand old structure. This was the first building he had entered when he arrived here at age 14. The only changes he could see were that the old tar floor had been replaced with cement and a few new beams had been added to the roof.

He climbed the stairs onto the stage and then down into the washroom, or the 'jon' as it was called. Wayne Banks' initials were still carved in the wall over the urinal. Next to Wayne's were Bergie's and Rothstein's initials. Even after all those years, everything looked the same.

Douglas sat down on an old folding military bench sitting next to a bucket of sand by the closed main doors. Leaning back against the wall, he lit up a cigarette and watched the smoke rise toward the ceiling. Although it was so long ago, it just seemed like yesterday when he set off to come here as a cadet. The year was 1953 and he was packing. He could hear his mother calling him.

CHAPTER II

Mary Brice stood at the bottom of the stairs and looked up. "HURRY UP SON, THE TAXI WILL BE HERE IN A FEW MOMENTS. IF YOU MISS THE TRAIN YOU'LL HAVE TO SPEND THE SUMMER IN VANCOUVER."

Mary was a small lady of forty-five years. She had divorced her husband in England and decided to take her son to Canada at the request of her sister who had emigrated many years before.

Her sister suggested that since Douglas was only eight, if she immigrated now, he would have the opportunity of getting a good education along with all the other amenities the country had to offer.

It was a big decision for Mary. For one thing, her age was against her and it wouldn't be easy finding a job and settling down. Still, after more and more pestering by her sister, she decided to do it.

Mary was a good mother and had saved enough money to rent an old house in Vancouver's West End.

When they arrived, they were both homesick. Douglas longed for his dad and his brother Norman, who was thirteen years older. Norman had just been married. Douglas idolized him and missed him greatly.

Getting a job was tough at first, but Mary had been trained as a chocolate-dipper when she was young, so it didn't take her long to relearn her trade.

Night after night in this new land, Douglas and his mother yearned for The Old Country. Still, she wouldn't go back. She was determined this is where they would live. As discovery replaced homesickness, it wasn't long before they considered themselves Canadians.

At age fourteen, a couple of friends talked Douglas into joining the Royal Canadian Army Cadets. He wasn't really keen on it at first, but after one year's training, he started to like the comradeship and the monthly weekend exercises.

When attending Vernon for the summer was mentioned, the same two friends talked him into going.

"I'M COMING, MOM," Douglas replied, as he came down the stairs, dragging his duffel-bag behind.

"My, don't you look like the cat's meow in that uniform," his mother said. "You'll have all the girls in Vernon trying to meet you."

"Aww, c'mon Mom." He turned a pale shade of red.

Mary laughed as she picked a piece of lint off the front of his tunic. "Well, just remember now that I'm too young to be a mother-in-law. If you get any offers of marriage in Vernon, tell them you'll have to wait until you're a little older."

"What if the girl is worth millions of dollars?" he asked, smiling.

Mary thought for a moment. "Money doesn't really count when you're in love with someone, but if she is worth a few million, maybe you should consider it." They both laughed.

"Now are you certain you've got everything?" She was looking at his shiny face and neatly combed dark brown hair.

"There's no more room to pack anything even I have forgotten something."

"Well, here comes the taxi. Say goodbye to Major before you leave."

Douglas bent down and stroked the ears of his dog, who sensed he was going away.

"I'd give anything in the world to take you with me, old fellow, but the Joining Instructions said not to bring any pets. You're going to stay here and look after Mom and I'll bring you back a great big army bone when I come home. Alright? That a boy!"

As the taxi pulled in front of the Canadian Pacific Railway Station, there were cadets everywhere. Mothers and fathers alike were shaking the hands of their departing 'soldiers' after giving them a farewell hug.

Douglas had never seen so many cadets. All of them were neatly turned out in their various uniforms and it looked like every regiment in the area was represented.

Mary told the taxi driver to wait until she had seen her son join his regiment's group.

"There they are," said Douglas, after he saw more than eighty black berets, queuing up on the right hand side of the station. Each had his duffel-bag on his shoulder, or under the right arm. In many cases, fathers carried the bags and sons directed them as if they were Porters.

"WHY DID YOU ASK THE TAXI TO WAIT?" Douglas yelled over the noise.

His mother didn't reply. She stayed by his side until he reached his contingent.

An announcer over the loudspeaker said, "IT WOULD BE MOST APPRECI-ATED IF ALL PARENTS, RELATIVES AND FRIENDS OF CADETS WOULD PLEASE STEP TO THE BACK OF THE STATION." The announcer had to say it again because hardly anyone could understand him over the din.

"KISS HER AND GET IT OVER WITH, BRICE," someone at the front of his group bellowed.

"Who is he?" his mother asked.

Douglas looked over. "God, I didn't know he was going with us. It's Sergeant-Major Genova."

"Is he your Commanding Officer?"

"Mom, that man couldn't command an apple to drop, even if the stalk was rotten. Everyone hates his guts."

Mary smiled. "Well, whoever he is, he wants you over there. I'm going to leave you now, Doug."

Douglas put his duffel-bag down and wrapped his arms around his mother. There were tears in Mary's eyes as he kissed her on her forehead.

"Don't worry about me, Mom. I'll be alright."

His mother forced a smile as she opened her purse to find her handkerchief. "Please look after yourself, Son."

"I will, Mom, I promise. I'll write to you the minute I arrive."

His mother held his right hand in both of hers, before she turned away and left for the taxi. In a moment, she was gone.

As Douglas picked up his bag, Wayne Banks, his best friend, walked into the station. No one accompanied him. He said he was a bit late because he had to wait for the bus. His dad was working and couldn't make it.

Douglas' head and eyes made a motion. "Take a look at who's coming with us."

Wayne looked at the man who was staring at them. "Oh Christ," he said. "Everyone told us this was going to be fun!"

"BRICE AND BANKS! GET YOUR ASSES OVER HERE!" Genova had a sneaky smile on his face, as he glared at them with his beady eyes. The nostrils of his giant beaked nose, opened and closed every time he exerted authority.

The boys knew that the only people Genova liked were those who sniveled up to him. In most cases, it was the Cadet Junior and Senior Non-Commissioned Officers.

"Coming, ya big prick," Wayne whispered, as he picked up his duffel-bag.

Douglas could hardly help but laugh, but he had to muffle it, because he knew Genova had a sixth sense when he thought someone was making fun of him.

"DID YOU SAY SOMETHING, BANKS?" Six feet and two-hundred-ten pounds, stared at Wayne.

Wayne gave him a concerned look. "Not me, Sergeant-Major."

When the boys joined the rest of the cadets who had formed three ranks, Douglas looked around at the diverse uniforms. Everyone was dressed in khaki, with khaki web-belts around their waists and khaki puttees wrapped around their ankles. There were red berets, khaki berets, blue berets and maroon berets. Some cadets were even wearing forage-caps, the kind that officers usually wore. The Scottish cadets were wearing odd types of hats, kilts, hose-tops and spats. They also wore shoes, instead of boots.

As a member of the British Columbia Regiment (Duke of Connaught's Own) Cadet Corps, Douglas had been taught he should be proud to be part of an armoured regiment and wear the black beret. In addition, his regiment wore black ties, black web-belts and black puttees. Black ties and black puttees were not the norm for armoured regiments in Canada, however, the British Columbia Regiment had once been a rifle regiment. They had been given permission by Ottawa to wear items of that color. Every member of an armoured regiment, however, always wore a black beret.

The announcer had difficulty quieting everyone down, but bit by bit the noise subsided. An officer stood on a chair in front of them.

"PAY ATTENTION HERE! I SAID PAY ATTENTION HERE! YOU'RE GOING TO VERNON BY TRAIN, IN CASE SOME OF YOU DIDN'T KNOW."

A few laughs were released by the crowd, but it was Wayne who started the BCR cadets laughing when he said, "Gee, I thought this was an airport!"

'Old beady eyes' turned around and looked straight at Wayne, while the officer who was speaking looked straight at old beady eyes.

"IF YOU CAN'T CONTROL YOUR PEOPLE, SERGEANT-MAJOR GENOVA, I'LL FIND SOMEONE WHO CAN!"

Genova said something under his breath and instantly looked at Banks.

"YOU SEE ME ON THE TRAIN! DO YOU UNDERSTAND?"

Wayne looked a little sheepish. "YES, SERGEANT-MAJOR!"

The officer continued. "WE'VE NEVER HAD A PROBLEM ON TRAINS WITH THESE SUMMER MISSIONS AND WE DON'T EXPECT ONE THIS YEAR. YOU WILL BE ASSIGNED A RAILCAR, AN UPPER-BERTH, OR A LOWER-BERTH. UNDER NO CIRCUMSTANCES WILL YOU CHANGE CARS OR BERTHS."

At that point, a few cadets made disgruntled noises, but the officer continued.

"EACH BERTH WILL HAVE A NAME SCOTCH-TAPED TO IT. YOU WILL FIND YOUR BERTH AND STAY THERE UNTIL YOU ARE TOLD THAT YOU CAN MOVE AROUND. THERE WILL BE NO LOUD NOISE, NO FOOLING AROUND AND NO VISITING OTHER CARS. AT MEALTIMES, YOU WILL BE TAKEN TO THE DINING-CAR IN GROUPS. NOW IS THAT CLEAR?"

Approximately a quarter of the group answered, "YES SIR!" That wasn't sufficient for the officer.

"I CAN'T HEAR YOU! I ASKED IF THAT WAS CLEAR?"

Without hesitation, seven hundred voices gave him what he wanted.

"YES SIR!"

The officer winced when he heard the tumultuous response.

Wayne leaned over to Douglas. "Christ, is he deaf, or what?" Unfortunately, his comment was heard by other members of the 'black-hats' who started laughing.

Genova went beet red and turned around, but Banks was staring straight to his front and Genova didn't know who the 'smart ass' was.

Douglas had heard the expression 'hurry up and wait' many times during his regular training year. Now, the phrase turned into reality. They had waited over an hour since the officer spoke to them and the only activity taking place was cadets fidgeting and officers and Non-Commissioned Officers running around with an endless array of paperwork, attached to clipboards.

During their wait, the cadets had been allowed to 'stand easy.' This meant that they couldn't move their feet, but they could move their arms and talk quietly to those around them.

It was at this time that Douglas continued to hear the rumours of what would happen at camp. There were plenty of rumours, originating from the 'old boys,' the cadets who had attended Vernon before. They were one or two years older than Douglas and they delivered their sermons as if they had been baptized at Camp Vernon.

"I've got mine, have you got yours?" one of the old boys asked his buddy.

"Here in my pocket," his friend replied. "But I wonder how many of the first-timers have them?"

"What do you need?" asked a young cadet within earshot.

"Your masterbation papers," the 'pro' replied, keeping a straight face. "They won't let you on the train without them."

Douglas saw the worried look on the young cadet's face. He knew all about this ruse because he and Wayne and been caught before, when they first joined.

"What do they look like?" The young fellow was holding out his Joining Instructions along with other papers he had to produce when he got to camp.

"That's your problem to figure out," said the pro. "If you don't know what masturbation papers are, I suggest you ask Sergeant-Major Genova."

The cadet was flustered now, checking the headings of each piece of paper in his pocket. He used his finger to ensure he didn't lose his place as he read line after line of small print. When he couldn't find the word masturbation, he decided he'd better ask.

"Excuse me, Sergeant-Major Genova, Sir," he said in a low voice, not realizing at least thirty cadets were watching with their tongues in their cheeks.

Genova walked over to him. "What is it, Johnston?"

Johnston held out all his papers, as serious as a lawyer walking to the bench to see the judge.

"Which of these is my masturbation papers?" he asked.

"WHAT?" Genova's face turned red again, his beady eyes scanning the cadets who were now looking anywhere but at him and talking about anything other than masturbation papers.

"I want to know which one of these is my mas...........?"

"I heard you the first time, Johnston. When was the last time you played with your prick?"

Johnston didn't understand and appeared insulted by the Sergeant-Major's question. He pushed his glasses further up his nose and looked inquisitively at Genova. "I don't see what that's got to do with...........?"

Genova didn't give a chance to finish; neither did the other cadets, they were laughing so hard.

Cadet Johnston was mortified. He knew he had done something wrong because the cadets around him were hysterical.

Wayne came to Johnston's rescue. Standing next to him, he tapped him on the shoulder, cupped his hands around Johnston's ear and whispered into it.

Johnston looked shocked and embarrassed. It took a few seconds before the beginning of a smile appeared and then his eyes started to well up. He didn't know quite what to do with himself as the light-hearted verbal harassment continued.

Douglas felt sorry for him. Johnston was a good kid who was very scholarly. He was surprised that Johnston hadn't read about the subject in one of the many books he was always into.

"Don't let those jerks get you down, Tommy," he said. "If it's any comfort, they've pulled the same thing on most of us."

Douglas' solace seemed to help Johnston. Even though Genova had made a few additional wisecracks to him, it didn't take long before he was clowning around like everyone else.

Finally the long wait ended. The cadets marched in three ranks with their duffel-bags over their shoulders, past the roped-off barrier that had just been lifted and past railcar after railcar. Genova was at the side of their group. "WE'RE IN CARS NUMBER FOURTEEN AND FIFTEEN. COUNT THE NUMBERS ON THE CARS AS YOU PASS THEM!"

"Have you ever seen a bigger train in your life?" Douglas asked Wayne. It reminded him of the train he had taken to cross Canada, after sailing from England. Wayne couldn't hear him because of the noise on the platform, but Genova did and he thought it was Wayne who was talking.

"WHAT WAS THAT YOU SAID ABOUT MY NOSE, BANKS?"

Wayne was quick. "I SAID YOU'VE GOT A LOVELY NOSE," he replied, shrugging to Douglas as if to ask what the hell that was that all about.

"I think the guy has a nose guilt complex," Wayne said.

"BCR CADETS, HALT!" Genova's voice could be heard all over the platform even though pandemonium prevailed.

"THIS CAR AND THE NEXT CAR ARE OURS. PEELING OFF FROM THE LEFT IN SINGLE FILE...QUICK MARCH!"

Shortly, Douglas found himself climbing the stairs of the railway car. At the top, following the cadets ahead of him, he turned left past the smoking-room which was loaded with spittoons and sinks, and down the narrow aisle. The smell of the car instantly reminded him of the train he had travelled on from Halifax to Vancouver when he was eight.

The aisleway was clogged from top to bottom with cadets looking for their names on the sides of the seats. He was about to ask Wayne if they were in the right car when he heard a voice he recognized. It was Don Lyons, a good friend of theirs.

"DOUG, WAYNE, YOUR SEATS ARE OVER HERE ACROSS FROM MINE."

Although their seats weren't far away, the aisleway was full of cadets, duffel-bags and tunics.

Douglas had been assigned an upper berth. Wayne was in the berth below him.

"You lucky stiff, you've got a lower berth," he said to Wayne.

Wayne unslung his duffel-bag and threw it on the seat. "Being on Genova's shit-list has its privileges. What are you complaining for? At least the upper bunks are made up."

Wayne was right in that sense, Douglas thought, as he dumped his bag on the upper bunk and climbed up after it. His berth had been made up, but the curtains hadn't yet been hung.

For the next half hour, the railcar was like a circus. Cadets were piling gear on each others' berths, searching for theirs. When the rightful occupant arrived, the kit would be dumped in the aisle. Duffel-bags, tunics, berets and web-belts were everywhere. Arguments had even started because some cadets had switched the names on the seats.

Douglas took off his tunic and tie and was taking off his boots when he heard music coming from the upper berth across from him. Don Lyons had brought a portable radio and the song, Harbour Lights, was playing.

Although the bedlam was deafening, Douglas lay on his upper bunk, oblivious to it all. This would be his first lengthy trip away from home since arriving from England. He didn't want to think about homesickness, but he was close to his mother. Both of them had been through hell just trying to survive in this new country. Now each of them would have to make it alone.

Many things came to Douglas' mind as he lay there. The train reminded him of their six-day trip across Canada after they walked down the gangplank of the steamship Aquitania in Halifax. He hated that journey because the train was crowded with war brides, soldiers and young children making their way to the New World. His mother had purchased tickets for berth accommodations to cross the country. When they arrived in Winnipeg, a Conductor took her tickets away and never returned them. She complained and a different Conductor gave her coach-class tickets. The both of them had to complete the route with an immigrant family of five, packed into seats meant to hold a maximum of four people.

On that trip, Douglas had tasted his first banana. England was still on food rationing in 1947 and it was easy to recognize British children because they were so skinny.

A black porter had felt sorry seeing the seven of them crammed in the seats. Douglas remembered the porter picking him up and carrying him around the car on his strong shoulders. The porter was a great guy. He loved Douglas' Liverpool accent. "Talk to me in Scouse," he would say every time he saw him. Then he would hand Douglas a banana.

This train-ride wouldn't be like that one, he thought. That trip took six days. This was only an overnight jaunt to Vernon, approximately three-hundred-and-thirty miles away.

As Douglas lay reminiscing, he knew his friends were as apprehensive as he was. They would miss their loved ones also. After all, Vernon was a long way from home. This wasn't like a weekend visit to his regiment's Nanaimo Military Camp, on Vancouver Island where they trained on tanks. No, this was entirely different; six weeks of military training. It was going to be tough, because the 'old boys' said it would be. One even told Douglas, "You're going as a boy, but you'll come back as a man." Another said, "If you want to get rank, you've got to attend Vernon." Douglas smiled. These 'old boys' or seasoned professionals, were about fifteen and in most cases, it was only their second year.

The Royal Canadian Army Cadet organization had a rank structure similar to the Regular Force, so most of the old boys were either Lance-Corporals, Corporals or Sergeants.

Rank was taken seriously in cadets. Responsibility came with promotion.

Douglas' Squadron Sergeant-Major had told him on their last regular parade night, that if he kept his nose clean and got good marks at Vernon, he would most likely be promoted to the rank of Lance-Corporal.

The prospect excited him. He knew he had the brains to pass the course, but this was his first time away from home. Douglas also knew about his tendency to become a little lazy and sloppy from time to time. What kid didn't? But then he heard the voice of his Cadet Squadron Sergeant-Major again. "There's no room for slackers in Vernon, Cadet Brice. You'll realize that when you get there."

"Doug, Doug, what the hell are you doing up there?"

It was Wayne's voice that awakened him from his trance.

Douglas stuck his head over the top of his berth and looked down. Wayne had opened the window. The smell of engine smoke filled Wayne's seating area, so did the noise from the platform outside.

"C'mon down and get a load of these chicks crying their eyes out."

Douglas climbed down to join Wayne at the window. At least a hundred girls had gained access to the platform. Some were crying and others were reaching up to the windows trying to grab the offered hands of their departing soldier-boys. Parents were there as well, passing up food parcels, cases of pop, packets of potato chips and chocolate bars.

Wayne leaned out of the window. "HEY SWEETHEART, IF HE DOESN'T WRITE TO YOU, I WILL. PASS ME UP YOUR NAME, MEASUREMENTS AND ADDRESS."

"Look at the food," Douglas murmured to himself. Someone had told him he would hate army food and that he should bring decent food to camp, which he hadn't.

Wayne brought his head back into the car, still laughing at the remark he made to the girl.

"Where's your beret?" he asked Douglas

"Up top on my berth."

Wayne jumped up, retrieved it and passed it to him.

"What's the matter with you, Doug? Don't you remember the lecture we had about losing our capbadges?"

Douglas smiled but he was embarrassed. He had been told a capbadge lasts only seconds on a beret that isn't being watched.

"Keep it in your pocket or in your epaulet, Doug."

A loud voice emerged from the upper berth across the railcar. "JESUS, I WISH THEY HAD ALLOWED US TO BRING CIVILIAN CLOTHES. OUR UNIFORMS ARE GOING TO LOOK LIKE RAGS WHEN WE ARRIVE!"

"YOUR UNIFORM LOOKS LIKE A RAG AT THE BEST OF TIMES," said a Cadet Sergeant, from the berth below Lyons.

Lyons looked down at the Sergeant. "OH YEAH? HOW COME YOU DIDN'T READ THE JOINING INSTRUCTIONS ABOUT NOT BRINGING PETS ALONG?"

"I DIDN'T BRING ANY PETS," replied the Sergeant.

"THEN HOW COME I'VE BEEN SCRATCHING MYSELF EVER SINCE YOU CAME ON BOARD?" Lyons shot back.

"I'LL HAVE YOUR NUTS FOR THAT, LYONS!" the Sergeant shouted.

Lyons continued getting undressed. "YEAH, THEN AT LEAST YOU'D HAVE A PAIR, WOULDN'T YOU, SERGEANT?"

Douglas knew Lyons wouldn't normally talk that way to the Sergeant, but everyone had been told rank didn't exist while they were away. They were all the same rank now.

A whistle blew and the train slowly started moving out of the station. A chorus of cheers could be heard inside the car and more sounds of exuberance came in through the open windows, from the station platform.

"Thank God, we're getting some air in here now," said Wayne, referring to the fact that all of them had taken off their boots.

It was dusk as the train picked up speed. The street lights and lit windows sped by faster and faster. Before long, the brightness of the lights within the car made it difficult to see outside.

"WHO'S FOR STARTING A STUKE GAME?" screamed a cadet named Cunningham.

At those words, at least fifteen cadets managed to squeeze into Cunnigham's lower berth. The porter had gotten around to making up the lower berths and Cunningham's had been first.

As Douglas and Wayne wedged themselves in, Cunningham said, "Let's see the colour of your money."

Everyone brought out as many coins as they had in their pockets, but it wasn't long before paper money replaced the coins and the game was going full-blast.

With at least seventeen or eighteen cadets now crammed into Cunningham's berth, Don Lyons lit up a cigar. Instantly, the colour of most faces turned green, matching the tone of the eye-shade Lyons was wearing. Don called the cigar a 'Cuban' and it was gigantic. He must have been used to them because while everyone else coughed and gasped, Lyons looked as relaxed as a pensioner on a lawn bowling pitch.

The train was really moving as screams of "HIT ME!" and "I'LL TAKE THAT POT!" rang out from Cunningham's berth.

After an hour, there were only five cadets left in the game, including Douglas and Wayne. Lyons had left quickly after joining. It was as if he knew he could not beat Cunningham's luck. Later in the journey, others would learn Cunnigham's luck couldn't be beaten. He didn't cheat, he just had a knack of knowing where the cards were and when to go for the pot. Banks had whispered to Douglas that they would have to keep an eye on him.

When Douglas left the game and the only remaining card players were Cunningham and Banks, a cadet by the name of Foster rushed into the car.

"THAT GENOVA IS A REAL ASSHOLE. ALL OF THE CORPORALS AND SERGEANTS ARE IN HIS PRIVATE ROOM HAVING A BEER."

Everyone heard him except Cunningham, who was ending the game by taking the pot from Wayne.

"YOU BASTARD, YOU'VE CLEANED ME OUT!"

"It's been a business doing pleasure with you guys," Cunningham retorted. "Next time, I'd appreciate a little more talent at the table. This was like taking candy from babies."

Lyons was listening to Foster. He gave Cunningham the finger. "UP YOUR NOSE, CUNNINGHAM. NOW FOSTER, WHAT WERE YOU SAYING?"

Foster started again. "I said Genova........."

Lyons didn't allow him to finish. "Is that what you're worried about? My boy, Uncle Don can provide anyone here with the necessary comforts of life. It just takes money!"

Douglas laughed because he knew when Lyons called himself 'Uncle Don,' he was about to bring out the L.P.B., or 'Lyons Portable Bar,' as it was called.

"What will it cost us this time?" Foster asked.

Lyons appeared hurt, but then his face took on a more serious look. "The usual, my boy, the usual. Fifty cents for a beer and a quarter for a sip of the hard stuff."

"That's highway robbery," said Douglas.

Foster was nose to nose with Lyons. "Your bar's a gyp, Lyons. What the hell do you do with all the money you rip off from us?"

Lyons was cool. "I save it. Haven't you guys ever figured out why you're always broke? You're broke because I've got your money. If you don't spend it with me, you'll just end up losing it to Cunningham."

"Enough, enough! What have you got?" asked Foster.

Lyons put a hand into a box and mentally started counting.

"I've got seven Old Style beer and a 'mickey' of rum."

Douglas was surprised to hear Wayne say, "Let's have one then." He knew that Wayne was broke after losing all of his money to Cunningham.

Wayne gave Douglas a quick glance. "Better yet, make it two. I'm going to buy my buddy, Doug, a beer."

Lyons pulled two beer and a weird contraption out of his box.

Foster couldn't believe his eyes. "What the hell is that?"

"For the sake of you ignorant people around me, I'll tell you what it is. It's an abacus," said Lyons, moving some of the balls along a piece of wire. "That will be one dollar, Banks."

Douglas knew what was coming next. "Er, Doug," Wayne said, feeling into his pocket. "Any chance of borrowing a couple of bucks off you?"

Douglas smiled and handed Wayne two one-dollar bills. It had happened many times before, but he knew Wayne would always pay him back.

In the meantime, Foster was looking at the abacus, "Let me get this straight," he said. "Do you mean to tell me you needed that thing just to add up one dollar?"

Lyons flipped up his eye-shade. "I'm not telling you nothin'! The last time I had the bar out in Nanaimo, I was accused of cheating the customers. With this, the customers know I'm not cheating them."

Foster forced a grin. "It was me who accused you. If you can recall, you were charging me sales tax. Now how in the hell is that thing going to convince me you're not cheating? I can't read it."

In this own eccentric way, Lyons said, "Maybe not, but you won't accuse me of cheating, will you? NEXT!"

Douglas and Wayne were both laughing, listening to the familiar exchange of words between Foster and Lyons. They both knew that Lyons always came out the winner, but at least Foster tried to keep him in check.

Within minutes, the bar was cleaned out. Lyons was lying on his berth counting his money on his abacus, while some of the guys joined Wayne and Douglas in Wayne's berth.

"Keep that stuff out of sight," Lyons whispered. "If you get caught, you don't know me."

"I'll know you, you crook," replied Foster. Douglas knew Foster would never forget the sales tax episode.

After finishing his beer, Douglas lay on his berth reading as the train stopped at a station to pick up more cadets. The stop was short and once again the engineer poured on the coals.

Douglas wondered what the parents of cadets who frequented Lyons' bar would say, if they saw their sons drinking and smoking. His mother allowed him to have the odd glass of beer now and then, but he knew Lyons' mom and dad. If they found out about their son, he'd be yanked out of cadets and grounded for a year. The Lyons family was religious, never missing a Sunday in church. Neither Don's mother, nor his father took a drink or smoked. Now their son was the regimental bartender and racketeer supreme.

Douglas noticed his head was spinning a little. The beer was actually having an after-effect. He couldn't believe it. One beer? He thought it must be from the excitement of the trip, or the fact that he hadn't eaten since noon.

"FIRST CALL FOR DINNER IN THE DINING CAR! THIS IS FIRST CALL FOR DINNER!" The Conductor walked through the car, bouncing, because of the speed of the train.

Everyone was up and heading toward the door until someone who had read the schedule spoke up. "WE'RE SECOND CALL, YOU GRUNTS!"

As cadets from other cars were running through, heading for the dining car, Lyons' voice could be heard saying, "You're true; next! Yes, you're true; next!"

Douglas looked over his berth. Lyons was lifting up the backs of the kilts on the passing Scottish cadets. The cadets were from the Seaforth Highlanders of Canada and the Canadian Scottish Regiment. The kilts looked a little peculiar to Douglas at first, but he soon realized in Vernon that the Scottish cadets got girls first. Non-kilted cadets had to settle for the 'leftovers.'

'True' meant that they had no shorts on underneath their kilts. A strict rule in Scottish regiments was that nothing was to be worn beneath the kilt.

"Ah, got ya! You're cheating," Lyons said to a small cadet he had caught from behind.

"He might be, but I'm not!" said the voice of a large Cadet Sergeant who was following the line, "Why not try to lift my kilt?"

Facing a fist, Lyons thought better of it. "No, no, no, that's alright, Sergeant......sorry."

"You had better be," said the Sergeant. "The next time I catch you lifting kilts, I'll get down and put my bare ass on your face."

Wayne had to get into the act. "HE'D LIKE THAT, IT WOULD BE BETTER THAN THE ORIGINAL MOLD."

A bellow of laughter was heard throughout the car. Foster was laughing the hardest. He loved seeing Lyons humble himself. It made up for the sales tax rip-off.

Douglas said to Wayne. "It must be uncomfortable not wearing shorts under those things."

"Foster would have to wear shorts, otherwise his balls would be shining his spats," quipped Lyons.

A smile came to Foster's face. "Why thank you Don, but, er, how did you know?"

Once again, everyone was laughing. Now all cadets, rookies and veterans alike, were listening with intense interest to the banter coming from the area of Lyons' berth.

"SECOND CALL FOR DINNER! SECOND CALL FOR DINNER IN THE DINING CAR! SEC......" The Trainman couldn't get it all out the third time because he was almost trampled by the crush of cadets coming from all directions in the car.

Douglas watched Wayne pick on a rookie cadet who was in the 'jon' when the announcement was made. He had rushed out, trying to squeeze into line while still pulling up his pants.

"Did you flush the toilet and wash your hands?" Wayne asked.

"I flushed the toilet, but I haven't washed my hands," the cadet replied, expressing a bit of embarrassment.

"Then go back and wash them!"

"But I'll end up at the back of the line, Sir."

"Get back and wash 'em!"

"Yes, Sir."

Foster had seen the whole thing. "You've got no rank. You can't treat him like that."

Banks smiled and nodded. "I know, but it's more for us."

Foster thought for a minute. "Well, under those circumstances, you were quite correct, Cadet Banks," he said, placing his hand on Wayne's shoulder.

"Shall we dine?" asked Douglas.

"After you, Sir," Wayne replied.

Douglas was about to say 'after you' again, but the trio was pushed through the door by the waiting throng behind.

Douglas was impressed with the sterling silver service and the starched table-cloths. Dining on trains in 1953 was splendid. A small candle flickered at each table and the lights were dimmed so travelers could see outside.

Through a stroke of luck, Douglas, Wayne, Lyons and Foster managed to find a table to sit together.

Foster grabbed a menu. "I think I'll have a very large steak, smothered with onions and mushrooms."

Foster's words started Lyons drooling. "Sounds good, better make that two." He was a heavy-set boy who liked his food.

Douglas read the menu. "You should read this before you start getting your hopes up. There's only one choice, Wiener Supreme."

Lyons' jaw almost hit the table. "Wiener Supreme? How in the heck can they make Wiener Supreme? Do you guys know what that is?"

The three looked at each other. No one knew.

"It means breast of wiener," Lyons said with his head in his hands.

All of sudden Foster was at Lyons again. "How do you know it means breast of wiener? You wouldn't know what a breast looks like."

Lyons sat upright in his chair. "My good fellow, Chicken Supreme is breast of chicken, so I assume that Wiener Supreme means breast of wiener."

Foster belly-laughed. "Ahh, there you are then. You assume that Wiener Supreme means breast of wiener. You know what assume means, don't you, smart ass?" He took a pen and a piece of paper out this pocket and wrote down the word, 'assume.' Then, putting a stroke between the last 's' and the 'u' and another stroke after the 'u,' he showed it to Lyons. "It means never assume, because it makes an ass out of you and me." He then sat back with his chest out and a silly smile on his face.

"WELCOME TO ARMY FOOD!" The voice came from the front of the car. It was Genova, and Douglas noticed that he was actually smiling.

"Did you see that? Genova was smiling at us," he said.

Lyons turned his body so that he could see Genova. He gave the Sergeant-Major a small wave. He knew his action would bug Genova, but because he was returning the smile while waving, there was nothing Genova could do about it. "Douglas, don't ever say that Genova smiles. It wasn't a smile, it was a gas pain. The only time that guy smiled was when he popped out of his mother at birth and noticed the look of astonishment on her face. She thought she had given birth to a giant nose."

The four of them had to muffle their laughs.

When everyone had read the menu, the waiter arrived.

"What's the soup?" Lyons asked.

"I think it's fish soup," replied the waiter.

"Fish? Surely to God there's got to be a better description than that?" asked Lyons. "Is it salmon, or oyster or......?"

"The cook thinks it's shark."

When the waiter received four disgusted looks, he indicated he was getting annoyed with the delay. He looked at Genova's table. If he complained to Genova, there would be no supper at all.

Douglas reacted fast. "I think we should order, guys. What'll it be?"

It was a choice of Genova or less discussion on the meal. Four shark soups and four Wiener Supremes arrived quickly.

When the waiter moved on, Banks asked, "If the main course is this, what's for dessert?"

"I can tell you," said Douglas. "It's bread with warm milk poured over it at the table. You can add your own sugar."

Banks nearly choked on the water he was drinking.

"What?" What kind of.........?"

"Just joking. I'm trying to get you used to the food you can expect at Vernon. I think it's ice cream."

"It is ice cream," said a cadet sitting at the next table.

Wayne looked at him. "You again? Did you wash your hands like I told you?"

"Yes, Sir, and I wiped them on the back of your shirt as we were coming through the door."

Wayne didn't know what to say, so he joined in the laughter. Then he looked at Genova's table and whispered, "No, we're not talking about your nose."

Genova nodded with a 'gas pain.' He hadn't heard the comments.

With dinner over, everyone returned to their cars. All the beds had been made but the curtains weren't up. Some cadets were getting undressed, while others just lay on their beds reading, as the train swayed back and forth, winding its way through the Fraser Canyon of British Columbia.

The car was quiet as Douglas joined Wayne in his lower berth. They cupped their hands on the window, trying to see into the blackness outside. Nothing could be seen but a lonely light on the other side of the canyon. Then it disappeared. "It's pitch black out there," he said to Wayne.

Wayne still had his hands cupped to the window. "Yeah, I know and just think, we're on the edge all the way."

At the other end of the car, a Cadet Sergeant from the Seaforths asked the porter why the curtains weren't up. Apparently the cadet was having difficulty going to sleep with the car's upper lights on. The porter replied that Sergeant-Major Genova had told him to leave the curtains off.

Lyons jumped in the conversation and said something about the situation being 'barbaric' but Douglas and Wayne both knew that he was only worried about selling his 'merchandise.' If he had 'stuff' left, he couldn't sell it if the curtains weren't up. Any officer or NCO passing by would see it.

As usual, luck was with Lyons. An officer appeared.

"What's the problem here?"

"The boys can't sleep with the curtains down," the porter replied.

"Well, why aren't they up?" he asked.

When the porter explained, the officer could be heard loud and clear. "TELL SERGEANT-MAJOR GENOVA THAT I MAKE THE DECISIONS AROUND HERE. PLEASE PUT THEM UP. HAVE A GOOD NIGHT'S SLEEP FELLAS

AND DON'T FORGET, YOU'VE GOT A BIG DAY AHEAD OF YOU TOMORROW. GOOD NIGHT."

Although a good many cadets were sleeping, applause was heard throughout the car, followed by, "Good night Sir!"

Douglas was almost ready to climb up to his berth when Lyons appeared. "My berth in one hour. Pass it on!"

Douglas climbed up top and took off his clothes. He was tired; the movement of the train was putting him to sleep. The porter had put up his curtains and although he couldn't see what was happening in the aisle, he could hear Lyons' voice apologizing to the Cadet Sergeant sleeping below his berth. Apparently, the Sergeant was asleep with his arm outstretched when Lyons climbed up and accidently stepped on his hand. He heard the Sergeant's scream, followed by the words, "JESUS CHRIST, JUST HOW HEAVY ARE YOU?" Shortly thereafter, he heard Lyons murmur, "You swore at me, no beer for you."

He smiled to himself about what a guy Lyons was. With him around, there was never a dull moment. The car was quiet and a few people had heard the Sergeant and Lyons. Wayne was laughing below in his berth, the Sergeant's howl having jolted him from dozing off.

Douglas felt a little lonely as he lay on top of the covers. He was apprehensive about Vernon and he was concerned, too, about his mother. His mother wasn't young and he knew she had to work hard to support the two of them. Now she would have the whole house to look after.

He also thought of his dog. Major had been with them for only two years, since the day they picked him up from the pound. The dog was really one of the family. Every day in all kinds of weather, Major would accompany him as he delivered *The Vancouver Sun* newspaper. Major knew he had to do his share of the work, so when a paper was put into his mouth, he dropped it off on the porch Douglas pointed to.

Douglas wondered how his mother could handle the household expenses without the money he gave her from delivering newspapers. He had suggested to her that it would be missed, but she had laughed and said it didn't matter because the experience he received at Vernon would be worth his giving up the route.

Douglas took his wallet out of the pocket of his pants which were swaying on a hanger. He removed a picture of the two of them with Major. With memories racing through his mind, he turned on his side and the next minute, fell asleep.

It must have been more than an hour later when Douglas felt someone slapping him gently on his face, trying to wake him up. Banks was saying, "Wake up, you pongo!"

Before he opened his curtains, Douglas could hear the ruckus. Cadets were everywhere. The activities weren't limited to Lyons' area; other groups had decided to party after 'lights out' as well.

Cadets wearing shorts and pajamas were running up and down the aisle, pillow-fighting. Someone had brought a water gun and Douglas was splattered in the face as soon as he looked out. Pandemonium raged like the collapse of the New York Stock Exchange in 1929.

Amid the water fights, pillow-fights, wrestling, tag, loud stuke-games and cigar smoke, Douglas had difficulty recognizing anyone he knew.

A group of Royal Canadian Signals Corps cadets had gathered in one upper berth singing 'raw' army songs. There must have been 20 of them stuffed together. The smoke billowing out indicated that Lyons had opened his bar and sold each of them a cigar.

With arms and legs swaying like entwined tentacles, this opera-motivated group of untrained choristers were 'singing' the song, 'Lulu.'

"Lulu had a baby, she named it Tiny Tim, She threw it in the pisspot to see if it could swim. It swam to the bottom, it swam to the top. Lulu got excited and grabbed it by the cock. Oh bangin' away on Lulu, bangin' hard and strong. What'll we do for bangin' when Lulu's dead and gone."

As Douglas climbed down from his berth, he felt some cadet pull down his shorts and fire two squirts from a water gun, hitting him in the rear end. He knew he should have jumped across to Lyons' berth, but it would have been impossible. The 'patrons' were hanging out of the berth as it was.

When he finally clawed his way in, Banks handed him a beer.

"WHERE DID THIS COME FROM, I THOUGHT HE WAS OUT?"

"JUST TAKE IT," WAYNE BELCHED. "DON'T WORRY WHERE IT CAME FROM, IT'S ON THE HOUSE."

Douglas couldn't believe Lyons was actually giving the stuff away until he saw him lying on his back with his feet touching the ceiling. One hand was waving a mickey of rum to the tune of Lulu, while the other hand tried to hold on to a cigar. How he managed not to burn the cadets playing stuke around him, was a miracle.

"He's not a pretty sight, is he?" Wayne asked, through blurry eyes. He had his arm around Douglas, holding him into the berth. The cigar he had in his hand kept getting pushed into Douglas' ear.

"He's not pretty? Have you seen yourself? How long has this been going on?"

"Don't worry about it, pally of mine," Wayne replied. "I've only had three and would you believe I didn't have to pay for them? The son of a bitch broke his own rules and started drinking the hard stuff the second his curtains went up. Can you imagine what he'll feel like tomorrow?" Wayne could hardly control himself, he was laughing so hard.

"BUT HOW DID HE GET IT? JESUS WAYNE, MY EAR DOESN'T SMOKE!"

Douglas had just got the last word out when he was nearly shoved out of the berth by a winner reaching for the pot. "STUKE, YOU BASTARDS! GIMMEE IT ALL!" The winner was of course, Cunningham. He placed his lit cigar behind his ear when he grabbed the money.

It was Foster who saved Douglas from falling out. He was rubbing his hands together. "WE'VE GOT OUR OWN BACK FOR THE SALES TAX. THE SNEAK PAID SOME MILITIA CORPORAL FIVE BUCKS TO BUY THE BOOZE FOR HIM WHEN THE TRAIN MADE ITS LAST STOP. I KNEW I'D GET HIM."

Although the radio had been turned up, Ghost Riders In The Sky wasn't drowning out the choir singing Lulu. The combination of the music made it hard for Douglas to hear some cadet asking, "HEY, WHAT BEATS A ROYAL FLUSH?" The cadet thrust his card-hand into Douglas' face. They were now playing poker to Cunningham's rules.

Douglas shrugged him off. "Jeez," he said to Banks. "If Genova comes in here, he'll throw the book at us!"

Wayne wasn't the slightest bit worried. "Oh, screw old beaky. He's had his nose in the bottle since we came on board........."

Wayne was going to say something else but he got hit in the head with a pillow. Feathers went flying everywhere.

"IT'S CHRISTMAS. HEY GUYS, IT'S SNOWING. JINGLE BELLS, JINGLE BELLS, JINGLE ALL........." Lyons never got the chance to finish his carol.

"STAND BY YOUR BEDS! I SAID STAND BY YOUR BEDS!" Genova had entered the railcar when the 'snow' started. His nostrils were wide open, which meant trouble, anguish and now, misery. Douglas noticed Genova's beady eyes were nearly popping out of his head.

Every cadet in the car, except those who had managed to sleep through the melee, stood to attention in the aisleway, the best that he could.

Genova's eyes scanned the scene of the car, up one side and down the other. The silence was staggering, until Lyons, who was still in his berth, offered an interval of good-natured unselfishness.

"WHO WANTS TO BUY A DAY-OLD SUGAR AND CELERY SAND-WICH? STEP RIGHT UP, THIS IS THE LAST ONE LEFT. I CALL IT A GENOVA SANDWICH BECAUSE IT'S GOT A BIG PIECE OF CELERY IN THE MIDDLE. NO BIDDERS? C'MON, YOU GUYS. O.K., IT'S FREE."

Lyons had one leg out of his berth and he was waving the arm which held the sandwich wrapped in waxed paper.

The veins in Genova's neck and forehead nearly burst as he walked down the aisle. He was dressed in just a robe with slippers. Every cadet in the car knew Genova had been drinking because while the train was rocking, he was rolling and staggering against the movement.

Just as Genova neared Lyons' upper berth, the train turned a tight corner and the Sergeant-Major flew through the unbuttoned curtains of the Cadet Sergeant with the sore hand. How he had managed to sleep with the bedlam going on above him was a wonder.

"JESUS CHRIST, LYONS!" The Sergeant was now wide awake trying to push Genova off himself. In the meantime, Genova was trying to get up, but the bottom of his robe was caught around his head and his bare bottom stuck out into the aisle. The 'onlookers' couldn't take it. Howls of laughter rang out as they watched the Sergeant and Sergeant-Major trying to untangle themselves. At one point, the Sergeant threw a punch at the round object at the top of the robe. He thought it was Lyons' head. Unfortunately his blow connected with Genova's rather large proboscis.

When Genova finally straightened himself out, and the Sergeant saw whom he had slugged, he couldn't apologize enough.

Lyons still didn't know what was going on. "HEY, WHOEVER YOU ARE, YOU'RE SUPPOSED TO COVER YOUR BARE ASS WITH A KILT."

That did it. Everyone in the car collapsed laughing. Everyone except Genova. He was ready for war.

"GET DOWN HERE, NOW!"

The smile on Lyons' face disappeared instantly as soon as he realized who the 'bare-ass' was. With great difficulty, he climbed down, but once again, he stepped on the Cadet Sergeant's hand.

"JESUS CHRIST, LYONS," the Sergeant roared, rushing away to get a wet cloth for his hand.

Lyons did his best to stand at attention with Genova's nose stuck in his face.

"HAVE YOU BEEN DRINKING, LYONS?"

"NO, SIR, I HAVE NOT, SIR!" Although he was swaying a little, Lyons looked straight to his front.

Spittle shot from Genova's mouth as he continued to 'talk' to Lyons.

"I CAN SMELL IT ON YOUR BREATH, YOU LITTLE PONGO!"

Lyons belched. "THAT'S YOUR OWN BREATH YOU'RE SMELLING, SIR. SAY, YOUR NOSE IS A LITTLE RED."

Once again, the whole car erupted in laughter.

"LYONS, I'M GOING TO HAVE YOUR BALLS FOR BOOKENDS!"

"FOSTER'S THE ONE WITH THE BIG BALLS, SIR." Lyons belched again.

Genova must have thought better of it than to continue his conversation with Lyons. For all he knew, it was his own breath.

"I'LL SEE YOU IN CAMP, DO YOU HEAR ME, LYONS?"

"YES, SIR, I HEAR YOU, SIR."

Genova moved back to the entrance of the car. The cadets had stopped laughing and were standing at attention, eyes straight ahead.

"NOW GET THIS GOD-DAMNED MESS CLEANED UP AND GET TO BED! I'LL BE BACK IN TEN MINUTES. IS THAT CLEAR?"

"YES, SIR!" The response was loud.

Douglas knew Genova wouldn't be back, so did the rest of the BCR cadets. Nevertheless, all cadets who were awake pitched in, and soon the car looked presentable again. Even the porter assisted. He had enjoyed the whole performance. He said it reminded him of his journey overseas.

Lyons tried to climb back up to his berth, stepping on the Sergeant's hand for the third time. After the familiar, "JESUS CHRIST," the Sergeant grabbed Lyons' legs and threw him head-first into the upper compartment.

A few seconds after the thud, Lyons' voice said, "UP YOUR ASS, SERGEANT. THERE WILL BE NO SANDWICHES FOR YOU AT THE PARTY TONIGHT."

The Sergeant, who was only about sixteen, looked at Douglas. "How in the hell do you put up with him?"

Douglas smiled. "He's our procurer, that's why."

The Sergeant shook his head and closed his curtains. Although he thought his problems with Lyons were over, he was wrong. Lyons snored loudly and the sound reverberated into the Sergeant's berth all night long.

When Douglas got into bed, the sheets were so hard, they must be starched, he thought to himself.

Lying there, Douglas remembered friends who always had difficulty sleeping on trains. He wondered if he would have the same problem. He didn't. He drifted off quickly and was awakened from a wonderful dream by the voice of the Trainman. "FIRST CALL FOR BREAKFAST IN THE DINING CAR. FIRST CALL FOR BREAKFAST." The Trainman's voice trailed off as he walked through the car.

Douglas stretched. His dream had been about him and his dog Major running through golden sand and diving into waves of crystal-blue water on some Caribbean island.

There was some activity in the car as Douglas popped his head into the aisle-way. The porter was making up beds; some cadets were already up and dressed, and Wayne was walking down the aisle with a towel wrapped around his neck, soap and toothpaste in hand.

"What time is it, Wayne?"

Wayne looked at his watch. "It's almost seven o'clock. Some of us have been up since six. Get out of bed and check out this scenery; it's fantastic."

Not bothering to get dressed, Douglas grabbed his towel, soap, toothpaste, toothbrush, and comb. Wearing only his shorts, he headed for the sinks in the smoke-room. He was lucky to get a sink, because a line-up formed behind him as he went in.

While he was brushing his teeth, he looked out the window to his left. The train had left the Fraser Canyon and was making its way through rolling, brown, sun-drenched hills, toward the City of Kamloops. Some local children were waving at the train, so he waved back.

"What beautiful scenery," he said to Foster, who had just taken over the sink.

Foster looked like he had a bit of a hangover. "Yeah, but it looks like an egg could be fried on the ground."

After washing, Douglas experienced the 'fun' of getting dressed in an upper berth of a moving train.

After tugging on his woolly socks and pants, he had to roll his weights up to his knees. Normally, he did this by putting his foot on a stool at home. Now, he was cramped on his back with his legs bent.

The boot part was a bit labourious. Finally, when they were tied, he rolled on his puttees and climbed down to the floor. The weights, which he made to keep the bottom of his pants folded neatly over his puttees, dropped automatically. Douglas looked down and wondered how he had managed to make both pant-legs even. At home, it took him half an hour trying to get his pants to hang evenly over his puttees. He was amazed at himself for getting it right the first time, on the upper berth of a moving train.

Wayne was looking out the window, while Douglas put on a clean shirt.

"It looks hotter than a furnace out there," he said to Douglas.

"Yeah it does, but it's gorgeous."

The two of them were discussing the scenery, as Lyons' head appeared from the upper berth across from them.

"Who wants to buy a day-old sugar and celery sandwich?"

Banks said, "Get out of bed, ya lazy jerk."

"Please," pleaded the Cadet Sergeant whose hand was still wrapped up in a wet towel. "Can't we just leave him there until the train arrives in Vernon?"

Lyons put on his eye-shade and started rooting through his gear. "Where's all the profits from last night?"

Foster appeared. "WE GAVE THEM TO THE GOD-DAMNED SALES TAX DEPARTMENT!"

Douglas and Wayne laughed at Foster's remarks. He was never going to forgive Lyons.

It was Wayne who broke the news. "You gave everyone a free night at the bar. Don't you remember?"

"WHAT?" Lyons put his hand to his head to stop the pain. "I DID WHAT?"

Now the Sergeant got his 'digs' in. "AND THAT'S NOT ALL YOU DID. AFTER YOU GET BACK FROM WASHING UP, WE'LL TELL YOU ABOUT GENOVA."

Lyons didn't hear the Sergeant's last few words. He jumped out of his berth like a high jumper and rushed toward the toilet.

Douglas wondered how Lyons could finish off a mickey of rum, all by himself. "It's a wonder he's still alive," he said to Wayne.

"Who says he is?" Wayne replied.

It didn't take long for everyone to make a move when the second call for breakfast was announced. Everyone that is, except Lyons. He was still in the toilet making portentous noises, which could be heard through the door.

As they passed, Foster said, "That's Lyons wailing into the big white telephone."

When the boys arrived in the dining car, they were fortunate to sit together again. A chair was kept for Lyons; however, he never turned up, so they gave it to the Cadet Sergeant with the sore hand.

Everyone was served the same breakfast; bacon, eggs, toast and coffee.

"Hey, this is neat; they're serving us coffee," said Wayne. "The last time I asked for coffee, the waitress asked me how old I was."

When Genova arrived with some of the Senior NCOs he instantly glared at the group of four.

"WHERE'S LYONS?"

Foster smiled and waved. "HE'S IN THE BACK GETTING THINGS OUT."

"HE'D BETTER BE DOING SOMETHING RIGHT!"

Wayne leaned forward on the table and whispered. "God, look at Genova's eyes. They look like two pee-holes in the snow."

"That's how they normally look," Foster murmured out the corner of his mouth. Once again, Genova looked over at the table where the laughter was the loudest. Following breakfast, it was quiet in the car. Most cadets were staring out their window; others were involved in stuke games.

"NEXT STOP KAMLOOPS! THIS WILL BE A FIFTEEN-MINUTE STOP AND YOU CAN STRETCH YOUR LEGS. PLEASE DON'T LEAVE THE PLATFORM!"

Some cadets went outside to get a breath of fresh air. Those foolish enough to take their tunics with them realized how hot it was and took them off in a hurry.

When he stepped onto the platform, Douglas felt how dry the air was. The temperature must have been in the high eighties and it was only ten o'clock in the morning "Is it this hot in Vernon?" he asked the Sergeant.

"My boy, this is cool compared to Vernon," the Sergeant replied.

Douglas got a kick out of the fact that the Sergeant was only a few years older than he was, but he used the words, "my boy."

When they walked up front to the steam engine, everyone noticed, Last of The Iron Horses, printed on the side.

"These old workhorses won't be around much longer," said Wayne. "They're gradually changing over to diesel.

The thing I'll miss the most is the sound of the whistle. Did you guys hear the whistle as we were going through the canyon, last night?"

"Yeah, it's a real lonely sound," replied Foster.

Douglas gave him an enquiring look. Foster never appeared to be the type of person who could get melancholy, yet he was thinking of home also.

They were heading back to their car, when, "ALL ABOARD" was called. To be safe, they boarded the nearest car and started to walk through the train.

"Who the hell is that running out there?" asked Banks.

"It's Lyons!" replied Foster, watching him run over the adjacent tracks with one arm loaded up with packets of potato-chips and cookies and the other waving.

The train was moving and was picking up speed, but a porter noticed Lyons and kept the stairs down on his car, before closing the door.

As the porter held out his hand to help Lyons board, some cadets helped out verbally. "C'MON, C'MON, C'MON!"

Foster watched the episode, leaning out the half-door in between cars. "I DON'T THINK HE'S GOING TO MAKE IT!"

Douglas and Wayne wedged in with Foster. Wayne was more confident. "HE'S MADE IT. THE BASTARD HAS MADE IT!"

All three of them ran back to their car. By the time they got there, Lyons had set up shop. Although he was breathless, he managed to say, "Get your money out; the bar is open!"

The trip from Kamloops to Vernon was short. Some cadets packed their gear; others read their Joining Instructions. A few sat at the windows, their faces revealing fond thoughts of loved ones left behind.

"VERNON IN TEN MINUTES......TEN MINUTES TO VERNON!" The announcement jolted the 'window dreamers' back to life.

Douglas and Wayne were two of those dreamers. Very little had been said since leaving Kamloops. The fact that they were nearing their destination created some apprehension. As well, some of them were still trying to get over the night before. Particularly Lyons.

"C'mon, you lazy bums, let's shine our badges and get our boots in shape before we get there," Foster said, as he nudged Lyons, snoozing against the window.

"You should be doing my stuff for me," Lyons responded. "When have you ever had a free night on me before?"

Foster patted Lyons on his head. "NEVER, AND WE PROBABLY NEVER WILL AGAIN EITHER!"

Lyons cringed. "Not so loud!"

As the train slowed to a stop at the Vernon station, Douglas had never seen so many three-ton trucks in his life. Some had tarps over their frames, but the majority just had open frames. They had wooden bench-like seats on both sides in the backs, and standing beside each truck's cab was a driver.

Foster grabbed Wayne's arm. "GET A LOAD OF ALL THE BROADS! THIS IS GOING TO BE A BLAST!"

Foster was right. Douglas couldn't get over the number of girls who had turned up to meet the train. Some shy ones were looking for cadets they had met the summer before, but most were just staring, waving feverishly with eager smiles on their faces.

Lyons recovered quickly. "LOOK AT THE BAZOOKAS ON THAT ONE!"

Foster was on him like a bee ready to sting. "Those aren't bazookas, you dummy, she's just fat. HEY BABE, I'VE GOT SOMEONE HERE YOU SHOULD MEET. HIS NAME IS DON LYONS."

Foster grabbed Lyons' arm and waved it at the girl. Lyons tried to wrestle his arm away. Although his face was beet red, he still managed a smile for the girl.

When the train had stopped, a Regular Force Sergeant entered their car. "RIGHT! CHECK YOUR SEATS FOR ANYTHING YOU MAY HAVE LEFT BEHIND AND STAND IN THE AISLE WITH YOUR DUFFEL-BAGS!"

Douglas noticed that the Sergeant's voice had a serious mood to it. The kind he hadn't heard before. Other cadets thought the same; the aisle promptly filled with cadets, all standing at attention.

"YOU'VE GOT SIX SECONDS TO EXIT THIS CAR. MOVE NOW!"

It didn't take six seconds. The Sergeant's order was perfectly clear. There would be problems if it took more than six seconds.

The Sergeant left the car first and a Regular Force Corporal entered the car from the other end. While he was checking the seats, he herded the cadets off like cattle.

The Sergeant waited outside. His face looked serious.

"RIGHT! FORM THREE RANKS! THIS CAR, RIGHT DRESS! EYES

FRONT! STAND AT EASE! THIS CAR, ATTENTION! STAND AT EASE...STAND EASY!"

The heat hit Douglas like an open blast furnace. Even though the Sergeant had formed them up with the sun on their backs instead of in their eyes, the warmth was insufferable. Sweat started to run down the back of his neck.

"AS OF THIS MINUTE, YOU'RE SOLDIERS. YOU WON'T SMILE, YOU WON'T LOOK AROUND, AND YOU WON'T SCRATCH YOUR ASS! IN FACT YOU WON'T DO ANYTHING UNTIL YOU'RE TOLD TO DO IT! RIGHT NOW I'M GIVING YOU PERMISSION TO BREATHE! IS THAT CLEAR?"

A thunderous reply, "YES, SIR!" echoed against the train. Cadets from others cars were yelling the same thing, as other Sergeants administered their 'welcome.'

"DO YOU SEE THESE STRIPES? I AM A SERGEANT! YOU WILL REFER TO ME AS SERGEANT, NOT SIR! IS THAT CLEAR?"

"YES, SERGEANT!"

Douglas noticed that some girls standing off to the side, were giggling. Others were waving to cadets and pointing them out to parents. Although there weren't many parents there, the ones who had come, seemed quite interested and were also waving.

"RIGHT! PAY ATTENTION HERE. YOU WON'T HAVE MUCH TIME TO LOOK AT THE GIRLS TODAY, SO TAKE A GOOD LOOK AT THEM NOW! IS EVERYONE FINISHED?"

"YES, SERGEANT!"

"GOOD! OUR TRUCKS ARE NUMBERED FOUR AND FIVE. YOU ARE GOING TO PLACE YOUR DUFFEL-BAGS ON YOUR SHOULDERS AND MARCH TO THOSE TRUCKS. YOU'LL NOTICE I SAID THE WORD, MARCH! THIS GROUP, ATTENTION...PICK UP YOUR BAGS! RIGHT TURN! QUICK MARCH!"

As the Sergeant barked out the step, Banks murmured out of the corner of his mouth. "Jeez, I think I've had it with this place already."

"THIS GROUP, HALT! LEADING OFF FROM THE LEFT IN SINGLE FILE INTO THE TRUCK...QUICK MARCH!"

Douglas had learned at his regiment's camp in Nanaimo, that when you enter a truck, you make certain you get on last. That way, you were first off. The Sergeant didn't notice the black-hats holding back and sneaking to the end of the line.

Within minutes, the trucks were loaded and heading in a convoy toward camp. Looking back, Douglas saw that half of the cadets had to wait until the trucks went back for them.

"Those guys are going to look like wet mops when they finally get to camp," he told Wayne.

Because the convoy was large, the lead truck didn't go through the downtown streets of Vernon. Instead, the trucks took the side streets, behind Polson Park, passing the high school before turning left up the hill to the camp.

As they passed, groups of girls were waving, and some local boys were giving everyone the finger and making 'remarks.'

"YOU'RE JUST ENVIOUS," Lyons yelled back.

"You've got to watch out for those guys when you go to Polson Park." remarked a Seaforth cadet. "They'll gang up on you if they know you're alone."

"You mean they don't like us?" asked an Irish Fusilier cadet.

"You've got that right," the Scottish cadet replied. "Each summer they lose their girfriends for six weeks."

"Are they all like that?"

"Not all of them, but a good number."

It was hot going up the hill. Douglas could smell the heat from the road.

As the trucks turned left, a sign read, *Vernon Military Camp-Royal Canadian Army Cadets. All visitors must report to the guardroom.*

The Military Police building was a small shack on the road entering camp. Four red-capped policemen stood outside, each wearing a sly smile.

"I don't like the look of them," said Foster. "My dad has told me if I stay out of their way, I'll have it made."

The trucks came to a stop in front of a large hangar. The Sergeant who had been riding in the front of their truck came back with the driver to help open the tailgate.

"UNLOAD! QUICKLY THERE, GET A MOVE ON! FORM THREE RANKS WITH YOUR DUFFEL-BAGS ON THE GROUND TO YOUR RIGHT!"

As truck after truck dropped off the cadets, at least three hundred of them formed up in three ranks on the dusty brown grass facing the front of the hangar.

"RIGHT! STAND EASY AND PAY ATTENTION HERE! WELCOME TO CAMP VERNON. WE'VE GOT A LOT TO DO TODAY SO DON'T LET YOUR MINDS WANDER. WE'VE PREPARED A LITTLE SURPRISE FOR YOU INSIDE THE HANGAR, SO WE'RE GOING TO MARCH IN THERE AND YOU'RE GOING TO KEEP YOUR MOUTHS SHUT! IS THAT CLEAR?"

"YES, SERGEANT!

"GOOD! THIS GROUP, ATTENTION. MOVE TO THE RIGHT IN THREES, RIGHT TURN! QUICK MARCH! LEFT WHEEL!"

Marching toward the hangar, Douglas noticed rows and rows of huts with black tarpaper covering. The asphalt roads leading to them were cracked open with grass growing up through. All of the grassy areas Douglas could see were brown and dusty.

As they marched into the hangar, it was hard to see. Although the lights were on, the hangar was dark and the glare of the sun made it virtually impossible for them to see more than a few feet in front of them.

Slowly the hangar filled up with cadets. As their eyes got accustomed to the light, Douglas looked around. A Captain stood behind a microphone, in the middle of a large stage.

"YOU PROBABLY FEEL LIKE SARDINES AT THIS POINT," said the Captain. "HOWEVER, WE'RE GOING TO MAKE THIS AS PAINLESS AS POS-

SIBLE. NOW, I WANT ALL OF YOU TO STRIP!"

The cadets could not believe what they were hearing. Each looked around at the others, wondering if he had understood the Captain, correctly. But not for long.

"DID YOU HEAR ME? I SAID, STRIP! TAKE OFF YOUR UNIFORMS, INCLUDING YOUR SOCKS AND YOUR UNDERWEAR!"

"How in the hell can we strip?" asked Banks. "There's no room for a mouse to strip in this place."

In the next few minutes, the hangar looked like the aftermath of a Christmas bargain day at a department store. Every cadet occupied about one square foot of space and clothes went flying everywhere.

Foster pinched his nose. "Christ, this place stinks!" No sooner had he spoken, he was pushed into the cadet in front of him. Someone in the back had started pushing, activating the domino effect. Foster's private parts pressed against the bare buttocks of the cadet in front of him. Foster backed off quickly, pushing his rear end into the crotch of the cadet behind him. The furious cadet in front apologized to the cadet ahead of him and turned to face Foster.

"GET AWAY FROM ME, YOU HOMO!"

Everyone laughed when Foster got a blast from both cadets. He started to explain, but Lyons said, "Don't you believe him. He's never been sorry in his life."

As the domino effect continued, some cadets kept one hand protectively behind them, and the other hand in front. Suddenly the domino effect stopped along with the laughter, when someone said, "Get a load of the Nursing Sisters!"

The cadets in line moved their heads, trying to see. Sure enough, ten Nursing Sisters were lined up across the side of the hangar; next to each of them was a set of weighing scales and a male Regular Force Medical Orderly. A Regular Force Captain stood behind the scales. Douglas thought that he must be the Medical Officer.

Lyons cupped both of his hands over his 'lower parts.' "THEY HAVE GOT TO BE JOKING!"

Lyons wasn't the only one in distress. Douglas could see many embarrassed faces and a lot of 'cupping.'

"What's the matter, Lyons?" Foster said, laughing. "Are you afraid to show the 'one-incher' to the redhead?"

Lyons was in full form. "You should talk. The blonde is going to have a fit when she sees your balls hanging below your knees."

The banter between Foster and Lyons eased the dilemma of the cadets who were abashed by their nakedness. Laughter rang out throughout the building.

As Douglas was being slowly edged forward to one of the cutest girls he'd seen in his life, he noticed some shy cadets sneaking to the back of the line. They were hoping somehow to get out of the medical inspection. No such luck, because Regular Force Sergeants got them back to their original places, 'quickly.'

"Hey, get a load of Danyluk!" Wayne said, pointing to a another 'black-hat' from their corps; a good friend, who had been stuck in Genova's car on the train.

Danyluk had an erection a mile long and both hands on top of his head. Ever since Danyluk joined the corps and had been seen in the showers in Nanaimo, he was nicknamed Stud, or Moose. He wasn't one of the 'cuppers,' he was smiling and looking forward to reaching the front.

Lyons was still complaining as they neared the scales. "This is embarrassing. I don't want some broad grabbing my balls."

"They're not going to do it, you idiot," said Foster. "The medical orderlies do that. Personally, I'd rather have the blonde fondle these gems."

"She'd have a problem, her hands are too small," quipped Lyons.

Foster chuckled. "That would suit me just fine."

Although Danyluk was in the next line just a few cadets ahead of them, Douglas, Wayne, Lyons, and Foster, strained their heads to watch as he approached the scale like a stallion approaches a mare. With both hands still on his head, he never took his eyes off the Nursing Sister. His smirk didn't faze the Sister one bit. She checked his height and weight and told him to step off the scales and report to the orderly. The orderly wasn't amused either. He hit Danyluk's penis with a small rubber hammer and it reacted like a balloon does after being stuck with a pin. The *"OUCH!"* was loud, then the orderly simply asked him to cough and proceeded to investigate Danyluk's chest and back with a stethoscope.

Danyluk wasn't smiling when he picked up his clothes to get dressed. Although he was still trying to get her attention, the Nursing Sister was too busy processing other cadets.

As Douglas got to the front, the cadet ahead was referred to the doctor, because of a rash under his arms.

"Please lay your clothes down and step up on the scales," said the Nursing Sister. After she recorded his height and weight, she asked him to step down. A Corporal asked him to cough, checked his upper body with a stethoscope and told him to get dressed. In less than a minute, he was through.

Cadets who had been medically inspected had a small area behind the scales in which they could get dressed. If one of them took too much time, a Regular Force Sergeant was there to 'prod' him along. "YOU, YEAH YOU! GET YOUR ASS IN GEAR AND GET MOVING. WE HAVEN'T GOT ALL DAY!"

Douglas knew the Sergeant wasn't talking to anyone in particular. By scanning everyone when they spoke, Sergeants had a way of making each cadet believe he alone was the recipient of the 'blast.'

Walking out of the hangar with Wayne, the sun hit them like a flame-thrower.

"Where am I?" asked Banks, keeping his eyes closed and holding his hands out front of him as if he were sleepwalking.

No one formed them up outside. The same Sergeant was there, waiting until all of his group came out.

They all had their tunics off, but were still wearing ties as they stood in the shade at the back of the hangar. Everyone except Danyluk. He was sitting with his back against the hangar, having a cigarette and boasting to his buddy, Cadet Chan.

"The Nursing Sister should have asked me to cough. Hey, you gearboxes, why was I the only one with a hard-on?"

Lyons smiled. "You get a hard-on when a female dog passes ya. How come you never took Sergeant Laidlaw's suggestion and submitted your measurements to the book of records?"

Wayne put a hand on Lyons' head. "Because he needed Foster's balls to complete the oddity."

Douglas laughed. He remembered that event on a training exercise in Nanaimo. When their officer was away, a group of them had stripped off and gone swimming 'bare-balls' in the town's water reservoir. As Danyluk was about to jump in, Laidlaw warned, "If you bring that thing in here, there won't be any water left."

Danyluk gave everyone a disgusted look. "Jealous pricks," he said.

Everyone laughed. They liked Danyluk. Although not too swift, at the age of fifteen, he was six feet tall and weighed a hundred-and-sixty pounds. He always had a smile and if there was a fight going on, Danyluk broke it up. He was a good guy.

CHAPTER III

Lieutenant-General Douglas Brice was awakened from his daydream by the sound of footsteps entering the hangar. He looked at his watch. He'd been there only a short time, but it seemed like hours. The remains in the sand bucket indicated he had smoked three cigarettes as he allowed his memory to take him back to his younger days.

He hadn't wanted to stop reminiscing. His recollection had been so real. Many times before he had tried to remember what happened at Vernon, however only scanty images emerged. This time, because he was in the hangar, the whole scene had come back to him, like it had just happened.

"Excuse me, Sir, I'm closing the building," a female officer said to him. She was about twenty-eight years old, with one-and-a-half gold bars on her epaulets.

"Thank you, Lieutenant. I'm just leaving," he replied.

"Are you on camp staff, Sir?"

"No, I'm just visiting the camp for a few days. I was here as a cadet a long time ago and, well, this seemed the right place to sit down for a few minutes."

The Lieutenant turned off the lights. "You picked a good spot. Other than the wards in the hospital, this building is the coolest in camp."

Douglas walked outside with the officer. She pulled the door until it locked.

"Have a nice evening, Sir", she said from about ten feet away.

"Thank you," he replied. "You, too."

It was getting dark as Douglas walked up the main street of the camp. Passing the Sergeants' Mess, he could hear singing. Someone was playing a piano that needed tuning, but it didn't seem to be bothering the male and female singers. Their singing sounded like they were having a grand old time.

Vernon is mixed now, he thought to himself. When he was here, the only females who lived in the camp were the Nursing Sisters. The hangar scene made him smile again.

No sounds were coming from the Cadet Canteen. A hut across the road had some activity, but the windows were closed. Windows were never shut in the old days unless there was a rainstorm. Now they would have to be closed at night because it was a mixed camp.

He turned left, past the chapel. There it was, good old Hut Twenty One. He stopped at the end of the road, looking at it. It had a white covering, not the black tarpaper he remembered. He murmured to himself, "My God, if that building could only talk."

All of a sudden, he felt sad. He knew why. Those great times would never return.

Douglas couldn't take it any longer, there were too many memories. He turned and started walking back to his hotel. Even passing the Provost Shack brought back more recollections: twelve hundred boys leaving camp to go home, singing and throwing pennies at the Provost.

It would take him about an hour to get back to his hotel, but he needed the walk. He could hear the voices of Wayne, Foster, Danyluk and Lyons.

"I wonder where they are now?"

"General Brice, I have been asked to inform you that your staff car is here, Sir." The voice on the other end of the phone was the desk clerk of the hotel.

"Thank you, tell them I'll be right down," he replied.

Douglas had been up early that morning, even though he hadn't managed to get much sleep. It had taken him a little over an hour to return to the hotel the night before. The walk had done him good, but there were too many memories. They stayed with him most of the night and he was actually thankful when his alarm-clock sounded, so that he could have a shower and go down to breakfast.

After breakfast, he returned to his room and was reading the *Vernon Daily News* when his telephone rang. His personal staff officer informed him that something big was happening at Defence Headquarters and that he would call him back in fifteen minutes.

Twenty minutes had passed. His phone rang again. Apparently, the current Chief of Defence Staff had resigned.

"My God, he's only had the job for six months."

"I know, Sir, but his wife has been quite ill and her doctor has recommended that she spend some time in a warm climate."

Poor old Harley, he thought, hanging up. Harley Jasquinelle was a good friend. Like himself, he was an armoured officer who never had the opportunity to attend Military College. After he finished grade twelve, Harley had made it up the ladder the hard way. He joined the Regular Army and, in relatively short time, had been promoted to the rank of Sergeant. He was one of the youngest Sergeants in the army and because of that, his Commanding Officer had suggested he take Officer Training and get his degree at night school. Harley accepted and the rest was history. A rapid rise and finally, Chief of the Defence Staff.

Douglas lit up a cigarette. He'd miss Harley. Chuck Watson from the Navy would probably get the job next, he thought as he picked up his cap and closed the door behind him.

General Brice butted his cigarette in the ashtray while waiting for the elevator. When he arrived at the lobby, Major Henderson was standing to attention. He saluted and Douglas returned the salute.

"Good morning, Major Henderson."

"Good morning, Sir. I hope you slept well?"

"So so," he replied. "Another beautiful day I see?"

"It's always like this in God's Country, Sir."

As Douglas entered the car, he thought to himself how true the Major's words were. Nothing could compare with the beauty and serenity of the surrounding countryside.

The staff car climbed the hill Douglas had walked up and down the night before.

"Colonel Forbes has respectfully requested that you join him in his office for coffee before we attend the parade, Sir?"

"Fine, thank you Major."

The staff car continued up Highway 97, passing the old guardhouse and the parade square. He noticed at least one thousand cadets formed up, all wearing long pants. At the top, the car turned left, heading toward the Headquarters Building.

"Aren't those pants terribly hot in this weather?" he asked.

"Yes, Sir. I understand Colonel Forbes has asked Ottawa to review summer camp uniforms numerous times. He's always requesting regulation short pants, but all they send is green P.T. shorts. It's the same old thing, Sir...cadets are low on the priority list."

The car proceeded straight for about seventy-five yards before Douglas noticed the cannon in front of the Headquarters Building. It looked like an old ship's gun. As they drove past, he started smiling. The cannon, like everything else, brought back a memory.

The car turned right at the end of the building and stopped in front of a side door leading directly into the Commanding Officer's office. The Major jumped out quickly to open Douglas' door, but Douglas was out already.

Colonel Forbes was standing on the veranda as Douglas approached.

"It's good to see you, Sir. Thank you very much for coming."

Douglas returned the salute. "It's good to be here, but more than that, it's good to see you again, Peter,"

Colonel Forbes opened the screen door and followed the General into the office. General Brice had known Peter Forbes for over twenty-five years. Although they had never served together, their paths had crossed many times and he liked him immensely.

They sat down on two chairs in front of Peter's desk and his secretary brought in some coffee.

"I trust you had a pleasant trip?" Forbes asked.

"Couldn't have been better. I can't get over this great weather," he replied, looking at the pictures on the walls in the office; pictures of nearly every graduation parade since the camp opened. Next to them were pictures of every Commanding Officer who had run the camp.

Forbes took a sip of his coffee. "We're honoured that you found the time to join us, Sir."

"I feel guilty about not coming sooner. Harley had to push me to come, don't ask me why. Like many of us who had the opportunity to come up through the cadet system, once we left, it seems we never gave the place a second thought.

Over ten generals served in this camp as cadets and, if I'm not mistaken, I'm the only one who has returned."

"You are the only one, Sir. Although two years ago we received a call from General Manning enquiring about a job for his son in our sports cadre."

General Brice looked into Peter Forbes' eyes. "Peter, I have more respect for you than anyone I know in the cadet system. You've worked damned hard for this camp for over twenty years. Tell me what it's like now. Are you having any problems getting uniforms or equipment, or whatever?"

Peter Forbes looked at Douglas with a lost smile. "I have been told not to bother you with our problems."

"That's nonsense. What are they?"

"Well, there are a number of things wrong. When I discuss them from my heart, I'm called a shit-disturber."

Brice said, "We're alone now Peter. Please call me Douglas and give it to me straight."

Colonel Forbes grinned. He had too much respect for General Brice to call him Douglas.

"Well, for one, it's the staff cutbacks, particularly Regular Force staff. It all started during the Trudeau era. For example, I'll bet you didn't know we are now using cadets in the staffing structure?"

The General frowned. "In what positions?"

"In almost all positions at the platoon and company level, We have to use senior cadets as Platoon Corporals, Sergeants, and Company Sergeant-Majors. We've even come to the point that we're using cadets in the various training cadres."

"Doesn't that work?"

"To an extent, however, there's a limit as to what we can do. It's impossible to replace ten or twenty years of experience with someone who parades at his own corps only once or twice a week."

"What happens when you ask for additional Regular Force Staff?"

"We're told they have too many commitments and that we must work with what's available. In addition, officer training courses for Cadet Instructors List personnel have been steadily cut back, particularly in this province. A civilian who comes off the street and attends a few Mickey Mouse courses is promoted so fast, he or she doesn't have time to get used to their first rank."

"What ever happened to the Cadet Services of Canada training system? I think they called it, oh what was it, C.S. of C.? If I'm not mistaken, Officer Cadets had to train here for a minimum of six weeks before they became a Second Lieutenant?"

"All gone, Sir." They don't look at cadet training the way they used to. That damned Trudeau era ruined everything. He very nearly managed to eliminate the cadet system completely. I'll bet you didn't know this camp came very close to closing twice. As a mater of fact, at one point, it was closed, then reopened very quickly?"

"Are you serious?"

"I couldn't be more serious, Sir. Quite a lot of lobbying took place to keep it open. Also, I guess you know we've lost Trades Training?"

"You mean no more Signals Training or Driver-Mechanics courses?"

"None whatsoever, Sir. At one time, we rented a few civilian cars and taught cadets how to drive, but they can do that at their high schools now. In fact, section-tactics have also been eliminated and we are finding it more and more difficult to get ammunition for our rifle programs. There are no more blank rounds. I think if Ottawa had its way, cadets would be the same as Boy Scouts. It nearly is now. The only reason we survived at all is because some genius had a heart and decided to call it Citizenship Training and the *powers that be* liked the terminology. Christ, we've always trained good citizens in army cadets."

General Brice shook his head. He hadn't realized it had come to this. The happiest days in his life had been spent here. In fact, this is where his military career had started.

"Peter, I remember when there would be a convoy of more than 50 vehicles heading out of camp. On the Driver-Mech course, cadets not only learned how to drive the vehicles, they learned how to fix them, as well."

"All gone," Forbes replied. "We had one of the best Signals Training courses in the world. Cadets used to actually install our camp telephones each summer. When they took the course, they knew more about radio sets than most Regular Force instructors did. Anyway, those days are gone and I guess all of us are to blame. We didn't lobby enough."

Douglas sighed. "You're dead right, Peter. All of us who had the opportunity of coming here washed our hands of it the minute we got what we wanted. We never thought of the kids coming up behind us. But I don't want you to think it hasn't effected the Regular Force and the Militia. They have the same problems. Off the cuff, you know as well as I do that Trudeau tried to smother the military. Before Hellyer, [Canada's Minister of Defence in Prime Minister Trudeau's cabinet] Canada never took second place to any country when it came to professional sailors, soldiers and airmen. Now we've got over a hundred bloody generals, myself included, and no troops or equipment."

They both smiled and shook their heads.

"How are the girls making out?" Douglas asked.

"Fine, actually," replied Colonel Forbes. "Girls should have been included in the system long ago. In many cases, they do a better job than the boys."

"Then it's working?"

"Yes, it's working, but only to a point. Surely to God, someone should have given some thought to the basic fact that between thirteen and sixteen years of age, boys want girlfriends and vice-versa. When a fourteen year old boy stands up to give a lecture on a rifle, he has to do it with authority. When the girl in the front row blinks her beautiful eyes at him, in most cases the lecture is shot."

Douglas laughed. "I don't know if the girls would have survived when I was here as a cadet. The guys were animals."

Forbes continued. "You see, Sir, boys want to be boys. They don't want to be ordered around by girls. It's affecting recruiting in most corps throughout Canada and everyone turns a blind eye to it and says it isn't the problem. The perfect case was the Commanding Officer of a cadet corps in Vancouver whose corps was mixed. For two years, he just couldn't get his strength over thirty-five cadets. This really boiled his ass, because when he was in cadets, the strength of his corps was in excess of 200."

"What was his solution?" Douglas asked.

"One day he transferred all of the female cadets to another corps that was all female. There were problems with Victoria, but he took the bull by the horns and did it. The result was that within six months, he had over 110 male cadets on parade. When Commanding Officers changed, his successor once again allowed girls to join and now the strength is back to thirty."

Douglas nodded.

"Sir, I'm not saying boys are better than girls. It's usually the other way around. But female corps worked very well in the old days. They trained hard and they usually got together with the boys on nights other than their own training nights. The boys were there like bees to honey. I believe male camps should be set up, along with female camps. In addition, cadet corps should not be mixed."

Douglas sat upright in his chair. "Wow. You're probably right, but you know as well as I do that the squeaky wheel gets the grease. The bleeding hearts have taken over the whole country. Do you know that we can't turn down homosexuals applying to get in to the service? If we do, it's a human rights matter and all hell breaks loose. The fact that it's not healthy and totally alien to anything the military stands for is not considered at all. I've got nothing against them, but damn it, we have to face reality. Do you remember John Purcell, the cadet who received the top prize here in the fifties?"

Forbes searched his mind. "Who doesn't? I believe he entered the Regular Force and everyone thought he would make it to the top."

"Well, he nearly did make it to the top, but rumours persisted for quite some time."

"What happened?" asked Forbes.

"He was a damned good soldier, but he was a closet homosexual and finally some of his men complained. That was after twenty some-odd years, mind you. We had to release him and he just died of *AIDS.*"

The conversation lasted another ten minutes when Colonel Forbes' secretary entered the room.

"Excuse me, General Brice. Ottawa is on the telephone for you, Sir. You can take it in the private office next to mine, if you would like?"

Douglas excused himself and left Peter Forbes for about ten minutes. When he returned, he noticed that the staff car had been brought around.

"The cadets are ready for us, Sir," the Colonel said, holding Douglas' cap and passing it to him.

Both of them walked outside and entered the waiting car. As it passed the cannon, Douglas laughed out loud. "It's still here. You've kept the cannon?"

Peter Forbes looked at him and smiled. "You bet! That cannon has more history going for it than nearly anything else in camp."

Both men understood. They knew the history of the cannon and what it went through every year. Nothing else needed to be said.

The staff car didn't have far to go. The giant parade square was only about a hundred yards from the Commanding Officer's office. They stopped just by the reviewing stand on the centre edge of the square; rows of chairs were lined up ten deep behind it.

Two Guards of Honour of about fifty cadets each were formed up in two ranks across the front of the parade square, their rifles at the shoulder arms position. Behind them, approximately one thousand cadets were formed up in three ranks by company and platoon.

It was obvious to Douglas the parade had just been called to attention as he allowed the driver to open his door and then proceeded to walk with Colonel Forbes to the dais. The Colonel stood to the rear while Douglas walked up a few stairs and advanced to the front of it.

The seated guests who stood up when General Brice arrived remained standing while the Cadet Parade Commander, who couldn't have been more than fifteen, started the parade procedure.

"PARADE, GENERAL SALUTE, PRESENT ARMS!"

The massed bands at the rear of the parade started playing the General Salute the second the guards completed the last movement of 'present arms.' All of the cadets who held a position of authority brought up their right hands and saluted. Some held swords and saluted accordingly.

General Brice returned the salute.

After the General Salute, the Cadet Parade Commander continued with the ceremony.

"PARADE, SHOULDER ARMS! PARADE, ORDER ARMS!" He waited for the guards to get to the position of the order arms, before he marched forward toward General Brice. When he arrived, he saluted.

"CADETS OF THE VERNON ARMY CADET CAMP ARE READY FOR YOUR INSPECTION, SIR!"

Douglas promptly returned the salute and asked the Parade Commander to stand the parade at ease and have them stand easy.

The Parade Commander looked a little concerned when he was asked to have them stand easy, because it wasn't the norm. General Brice, however, remembered standing at ease in the hot sun at the camp. It was hell, so he decided to have them stand easy.

The Cadet Parade Commander saluted, turned, marched forward a few paces and halted. "PARADE, STAND AT EASE! PARADE, STAND EASY!"

A jeep arrived at the reviewing stand. It had been modified so that people could stand in the back.

Normally the reviewing officer would have boarded the jeep quickly. Instead, Douglas motioned to Colonel Forbes to join him on the dais.

"Peter, I know this is rather unorthodox, but I want to say a few words before I inspect them, do you mind?"

"Not at all, Sir," Forbes replied.

Douglas approached the microphone.

"I REALIZE THAT YOU ARE AWARE IT'S QUITE UNUSUAL FOR A REVIEWING OFFICER TO TALK TO YOU BEFORE THE INSPECTION AND MARCH PAST. HOWEVER, I THINK I KNOW, MORE THAN ANY-ONE, HOW MUCH HARD WORK AND EFFORT YOU HAVE PUT INTO PREPARING FOR THIS PARADE.

I WANT YOU TO KNOW THAT I AM PROUD FOR BEING ALLOWED THIS OPPORTUNITY TO INSPECT YOU AND I AM VERY PROUD OF ALL OF YOU.

YOU DON'T KNOW ME, BUT AT ONE TIME, I WAS A CADET STAND-ING WHERE YOU ARE NOW.

IT IS NORMAL FOR YOU TO SAY TO YOURSELVES. 'FOR GOD'S SAKE, LET'S GET THIS THING OVER WITH!' WELL, IN THIS CASE, I BEG YOUR INDULGENCE TO BE A LITTLE PATIENT WITH ME AND ALLOW ME TO TAKE MY TIME.

IF I HAD MY WAY, I WOULD WALK THROUGH YOUR RANKS AND TALK TO EACH AND EVERY ONE OF YOU. HOWEVER IF I DID THAT, I DON'T BELIEVE I WOULD BE ABLE TO TAKE THE DIRTY LOOKS I WOULD RECEIVE."

There was a loud chuckle and whispering in the ranks. Douglas smiled and continued talking. "YOU NEEDN'T WORRY, I'M GOING TO USE THE JEEP."

There was a loud sigh of relief. "HOWEVER, I'M NOT GOING TO RUSH. I ONCE AGAIN BEG YOU TO BEAR WITH ME. THANK YOU!"

When he had arrived, Douglas noticed the Cadet Parade Commander's name. It was Ninnis.

"Colonel Ninnis, would you join Colonel Forbes and me on the jeep, please."

The young man saluted and climbed on the back.

As the jeep began to slowly slalom in and out of the parade, each Cadet Company Commander called his or her company to attention as the vehicle approached.

Douglas was both excited and impressed as he reviewed the the cadets. These kids are very neatly turned out, he thought to himself. Their shiny faces were serious. They had their chins up, it was obvious that they were proud.

At one point he looked down at his own shoes. "I wish my shoes were as shiny as their boots," he remarked to Colonel Ninnis.

The boy grinned, as did Peter Forbes.

General Brice decided he would stop the jeep at least once per platoon during his inspection. When it stopped the first time, he disembarked and approached a young girl of about fourteen.

"Good morning, Cadet Halliday!" he said, looking at her nametag. The girl looked straight ahead, not moving her eyes.

"Good morning, Sir!"

"What's your first name?"

"Mary-Anne, Sir!"

"I see you're an artillery cadet. Where are you from?"

"Vancouver, Sir!"

"How long have you been in cadets?"

"About one-and-a-half years, Sir."

"Did you come here by train?"

"No Sir. They flew us here on a chartered plane, Sir."

"How was your flight?"

"A little rough, Sir. I nearly got air sick."

"Are you looking forward to going home?"

"I was a little homesick in the first week Sir, but now I'd like to stay here for a lot longer."

"Then you like it here?"

"YES, SIR!"

"Are you coming back next year?"

"If I get the chance, Sir!"

"What are your plans for the future?"

"I plan to attend Military College and become a doctor, Sir!"

Douglas smiled. "Good for you, Halliday. You are a very sharp-looking cadet. You'll make a good doctor. Thank you for talking with me."

"Thank you, Sir," she replied.

As Douglas boarded the jeep, he said to Colonel Forbes, "Very impressive, Peter."

The jeep continued around the parade square and had stopped about ten times, when Douglas spotted a little guy with white-blonde hair and freckles.

"How old are you, Simpson?"

"Fifteen, Sir,"

"What, fifteen? Do they call you shortly?"

"Yes, Sir, but I'm starting to grow now Sir."

"How do you like it here?"

"This is my second year, Sir. I love it!"

Although the boy wasn't looking at Douglas, he had a cute grin on his face.

"Well, Simpson, I think you're a bigger fellow than anyone else on this parade. Keep up the good work. By the way, what are your plans for the future?"

"I'm going to work with my dad on our farm, Sir."

"Where's the farm?"

"In Saskatchewan, Sir."

"Farm boy, eh? That work will put muscles on you. All the very best to you, Simpson."

"Thank you Sir, all the very best to you and thank you for coming back, Sir."

Douglas looked at Colonel Forbes who shrugged and said. "Rumours do get around, Sir."

All in all, he talked to about forty cadets and he was impressed with every one of them.

As they were driving toward the band, he noticed that some of the band cadets were of navy and air force persuasion. The band had been playing gently throughout his inspection and they sounded very good.

"Why are there so many sea and air cadets here?" he asked Colonel Forbes.

"In many cases, we take them to keep Vernon going, Sir. Their own camps are full and for some reason, navy and air cadet corps have more bandsmen. Most of the courses here have sea and air cadets in them, as well."

"How do they like doing all of this pongo stuff?" That was the first time in years he had used the word pongo and he was smiling at the thought of it.

"They're very good, Sir. Just as good as the army cadets. Our problem is we just don't have enough army cadets."

"Lack of Trades Training?"

"That's right, Sir. "The sea cadets have Trades Training, as do the air cadets. All we can really offer is map and compass and range."

Douglas inspected the brass band first. As he inspected them, he recalled that he had been in a drum and bugle band when he had first joined cadets.

"Do the sea and air types promote bands more at their home corps?"

"I don't know what it is, Sir? They do not seem to have a problem attracting young people who play instruments. As far back as I can remember, army cadets have always had difficulty interesting that type of a youngster."

"Are you saying they attract a more intelligent young person?"

Colonel Forbes smiled. "I don't think so. It's entirely possible that their Leagues have been in place so many more years than the Army Cadet League. That, combined with the fact that navy and air force associations promote cadets as well. They like recruiting bandsmen."

Douglas nodded.

Colonel Forbes knew that the General was taking it all in. He also knew that it wouldn't be forgotten, either.

"It takes six weeks to get them working together and we're proud of them, Sir," said the Drum Major, sticking out his chest. He was replying to Douglas' comment that he had heard a lot of military bands, but that this one was one of the best.

"I'll bet you are," Douglas replied.

"Anderson, what's your first name?" he asked a trumpet player whose lips were cracked from practising in the hot sun.

"Glen, Sir."

"You're navy? What sea cadet corps are you with?"

The young fellow stuck out his chest. "ROYAL CANADIAN SEA CADET CORPS BEACON HILL, SIR!"

"Where is it located?"

"On Vancouver Island, Sir. Near Esquimalt."

"How do you like it here, Glen?"

"It's great Sir, but......"

"But what?"

"Well Sir, I'd rather be in Quadra!"

Douglas had visited H.M.C.S. Quadra in his younger years, so he knew what Anderson was talking about.

"Quadra's a fine camp in a beautiful setting. Tell me Glen, do they still make cadets jump off the jetty?"

"YES, SIR!"

Well, I think you'll make it to Quadra next year. As a matter of fact, I'll guarantee it. Keep up the good work and the very best of luck to you, son."

"Thank you, Sir."

Moving through the band, he said to Colonel Forbes. "I'll bet you have to keep a good supply of lip-balm on hand?"

Forbes nodded with a wink. "We bring it in by the case."

"Make a note of Anderson's name, Peter. I'll speak to the Cadet Training Division about sending him to Quadra next year."

Arriving at the pipes and drums contingent, he spoke to a Scottish cadet. The boy was about fifteen years old and he was immaculately dressed.

"Aren't you hot in that kilt?"

"No, Sir!"

"Do you polish your skeandhu without drawing blood?"

The cadet grinned. "Well, I've cut myself with it a few times, but I try not to make a habit of it, Sir."

The grin was contagious because he was grinning with him now. "Tell me, do Scottish cadets still get the first pick of all the girls?"

"ALWAYS, SIR!"

"I know what you mean," he said as he started to walk away. Then he stopped and went back to the boy. The cadet's names was Banks.

"Was your father in the forces?"

"Yes, Sir."

Douglas knew it would be too much of a coincidence, but he asked him anyway. "What's your father's first name?"

"Wayne, Sir."

The boy's reply jolted Douglas. He put his hand on the cadet's shoulder and had to clear his throat. "Was he a Duke?"

"Yes, Sir. Did you know him, Sir?"

Douglas had to clear his throat again. Also, he had to try and stop his eyes from welling up. "I...Yes, I certainly did. Where is he now?"

The cadet who had been looking straight ahead, now looked at General Brice. "He's in Vancouver, Sir. He manages a liquor store."

As Brice looked at him, memories of his best friend started returning. It was all coming back to him. Young Banks was the spitting image of Wayne.

"I'll bet you I know what your first name is." he said to the cadet. "It's Doug, isn't it?"

"Yes, Sir. How did you know, Sir?"

Douglas had made an oath with his best friend when they were thirteen. If they had children, they would name them after each other.

"It's a long story," he replied, clearing his throat again. "If it's all right with Colonel Forbes and the Bandmaster, will you have dinner with me tonight?" He was looking at Colonel Forbes when he asked the lad. The Colonel smiled and nodded.

Young Banks had a surprised look on his face. "Thank you, Sir...I...would, Sir."

Douglas had to take a handkerchief out of his pockets to wipe his eyes. "Are those spats new?" he asked.

The boy sensed the General was trying to stop him from noticing the tears. "No, Sir," he replied.

"Well, they certainly look new," Douglas said, as he walked toward the jeep, looking back only once.

As the jeep neared the reviewing stand, Douglas was once again lost in memories. He didn't say anything to Colonel Forbes; he couldn't; he was speechless. He had met the son of his best friend. He had been closer to Wayne than anyone in his life except his wife and his mother. Even after all those years, he had never had a friend like Wayne. Many years ago, he gave up looking for him and now he had met his son and his name was Douglas. He and his wife had named their first son Wayne.

When the jeep stopped and Douglas walked onto the reviewing stand, images of his cadet years in Vernon appeared again. His mind was trying to take him back to where it had left off in the hangar. Memories were struggling to be freed, so he could nurture and cherish them for all time.

The Cadet Parade Commander called the parade to attention and marched up to the dais.

"May we proceed with the March Past, Sir?"

"Yes, please carry on!"

General Brice heard the Cadet Parade Commander give the order to shoulder arms, but did not pay attention to the combination of successive commands which followed. Although the band was playing and the companies were marching by, he was, once again reliving the past. As he raised his hand to return the salutes, his recollection became stronger and stronger with each passing footstep.

Although Lieutenant-General Douglas Brice was standing on the dais, Cadet Douglas Brice had just completed a medical examination and was standing next to the hangar known as building B-3 in the year 1953.

CHAPTER IV

When all of the cadets had gone through the medical inspection, or the first part of the 'sausage machine' as the 'professionals' called it, trucks started to appear carrying the balance of the cadets who had been left at the railway station. Foster decided to warn them.

"PUT AN ICE CUBE DOWN THE FRONT OF YOUR PANTS, GUYS, YOU'RE GOING TO NEED IT FOR THE SHORT-ARM INSPECTION! Many other remarks were yelled at them and Douglas thought the look of confusion on their faces was funny. He wondered to himself if some of them had been tipped off about the 'sardine tin' they were about to enter. The cadets were smiling so they obviously hadn't been.

Out of nowhere came a voice louder than thunder.

"RIGHT! PUT YOUR BUTTS OUT AND FORM THREE RANKS ON THE ROAD! COME ON, MOVE IT, MOVE IT! YOU THERE! YES, YOU! GET YOUR FINGER OUT OF YOUR NOSE AND GET A MOVE ON!"

The voice made the order quite plain and everyone hustled into three ranks on the road. A burly Regular Force Staff-Sergeant was standing in front of them.

"THIS MOB, ATTENT...TION! STAND AT...EASE! STAND EASY! MY NAME IS STAFF-SERGEANT ROSE! YOU WILL CALL ME STAFF! I JUST CALLED YOU A MOB BECAUSE YOU ARE A MOB UNTIL YOU CAN PROVE TO ME OTHERWISE THAT YOU ARE NOT A MOB!"

"I AM NOT YOUR MOTHER! AS FAR AS I AM CONCERNED, NONE OF YOU HAS A MOTHER. YOU WERE ALL HATCHED UNDER A ROCK AND I AM OF THE IMPRESSION THAT EVEN THAT WAS TOO GOOD FOR YOU!"

"WE ARE NOW GOING TO BOARD THE TRUCKS AND GO TO THE UPPER CAMP WHERE YOU WILL RECEIVE YOUR SUMMER CLOTHING AND EQUIPMENT. AFTER THAT, YOU WILL BE SEPARATED INTO YOUR VARIOUS TRAINING COMPANIES!"

"YOU WILL NOT SMOKE ON OR NEAR THE VEHICLES. YOU WILL NOT MAKE NOISE. I AM THE ONLY ONE WHO WILL TALK! GET YOUR JOINING CARDS OUT OF YOUR POCKETS AND GET READY TO HAND THEM IN. IS THAT CLEAR?"

Instantly, three hundred cadets screamed. "YES, STAFF!" The next minute, they were boarding the trucks.

"I'll bet *he* was hatched under a rock," said Douglas.

"Naah, he's the kind of stuff that sticks to the bottom of your shoes in a barnyard," the nearest cadet said.

Douglas chuckled as the other cadet introduced himself. "I'm Jack East. I think I've seen you at the Drill Hall a few times."

Douglas didn't recognize him. "Doug Brice," he replied.

Jack East was a big kid of 14. He had jet black hair and when he took off his beret to wipe his brow, his brush-cut revealed a one-inch scar on the top of his head.

"How'd you get the scar?" Douglas asked.

"A horse kicked me and sent me flying. My head came to rest against a barn that had a nail sticking out. I've only been in the Dukes three months since we moved from Chilliwack. What course are you on?"

Douglas had to think for a minute. The heat of the sun wasn't conducive to quick thinking. "I'm on the Instructor's Basic Training Course."

East was excited. "Hey, IBT? I'm on that course, too. I tried to get into Signals, but the course was full. Maybe we'll be in the same platoon?"

Douglas liked him. "Yeah, that would be neat."

As the trucks rolled over the 'road' to the upper camp, dirt and dust shot into the air, forming a giant brown cloud from which there was no escape. Their truck was somewhere in the middle of the convoy, making it impossible for them to see anything.

"Those lucky stiffs in the first truck aren't getting any of this stuff," said Lyons. Like everyone in the truck, his face was covered in caked mud. It was so hot that their sweat acted like a magnet.

"WHERE AM I? I CAN'T SEE! DOUG, I'M BLIND. WILL YOU BUY ME A TIN CUP AND PENCILS SO I CAN START A BUSINESS IN VERNON?" Banks was doing his sleepwalk act again.

Douglas roared out laughing when he looked at him. "You look like one of the Desert Rats."

"I FEEL LIKE ONE OF THE DESERT RATS," Banks replied. "ONLY WHAT YOU SEE ON THE OUTSIDE ISN'T NEARLY AS MUCH AS WHAT I'VE GOT IN MY MOUTH."

Five minutes later, the trucks stopped in front of another large hangar. Staff-Sergeant Rose was already there. This time, he had four Regular Force Sergeants with him and they were seated behind field tables lined up side-by-side, marked with letters, A to C, D to F, etc.

When the tailgates were opened, the Staff-Sergeant instructed them further.

"RIGHT! FORM THREE RANKS! QUICKLY NOW, QUICKLY! GET A MOVE ON YOUNG FELLOW, YES, YOU! YOU MOVE LIKE A SNAIL WHO CAN'T GET A PIECE OF TAIL!"

"YOU WILL NOTICE THAT WE HAVE LINED UP TABLES FOR YOU. THESE TABLES ARE NOT SET FOR DINNER, SO DON'T GET YOUR HOPES UP! WE ARE NOW GOING TO PROCESS YOU. IF BY ANY CHANCE YOU HAPPEN TO KNOW THE FIRST LETTER OF YOUR LAST NAME, GO TO THAT TABLE, NOW! GET A MOVE ON, THAT MAN!"

Douglas was lucky. He was already standing next to his table, so he was first in line. Cadets were quickly lining up behind him.

A Regular Force Corporal was assisting the Sergeants at each of the tables.

"Name?" asked the Sergeant.

"Brice, Sergeant!" he replied, noticing that the Corporal ticked off his name which appeared on the first page of a great number of pages.

"Joining Instructions, please!"

Douglas couldn't get over the fact that a Sergeant had said please to him. "Here, Sergeant," he said as he passed them over.

The Sergeant handed him a red ribbon and a large cardboard form. "This is for your epaulet and this is your clothing card. Move inside the hangar. "NEXT MAN!"

For the next hour, cadets received clothing and equipment they would require for the summer. Douglas and a line of cadets who followed him, moved along a counter in front of hundreds of shelves and thousands of boxes filled with items.

At the beginning of the counter, he was instructed to hand in his clothing card. It followed him as he moved along in front of civilian storesmen who looked at him and threw items of clothing and equipment in his direction.

One of the storesmen threw two pairs of short khaki pants on the counter. "TWO KHAKI SHORTS!" he yelled to an assistant, who repeated the transaction. "BRICE, TWO KHAKI SHORTS."

As he moved farther, a storesman threw him a pair of long khaki pants and two khaki shirts.

"ONE K.D. LONGS AND TWO SHIRTS," the storesman shouted, his assistant verbally confirming the 'deliverance' and marking the clothing card.

The same procedure followed him along the line. His clothing card moved with him. When he was finished, his hands were full with two pairs of khaki shorts; one pair of khaki longs; two khaki shirts; one pair of khaki puttees; three pairs of work socks; two white t-shirts; one pair of dark blue P.T. shorts; one pair of running shoes; one khaki pith-helmet; one pair of khaki hose-tops; two rubber elastic hose-top suspenders; one enamel cup; one combination knife, fork and spoon; two mess tins; one canteen bottle, and cover; one leather nametag; one khaki one-inch web-belt; one khaki two-and-a-half-inch web-belt; one small web-battle pack; one large web-battle pack; one regular knife, fork and spoon; two white sheets; one white pillowcase; three gray military blankets; one wash basin; two white towels, and one ground-sheet.

His 'mountain' of clothing, bedding and equipment was almost as big as Douglas as he heaped everything into a blanket and signed his clothing card and the newly acquired bedding card he received at the end of the counter.

Leaving via the other end of the hangar and walking around to where he left his duffel-bag and tunic, Douglas wondered how he would manage to get it all into the truck. The noise inside of the hangar had given him a headache. That, combined with the heat of the sun, made him feel like he'd already spent a year in Vernon.

It was hot and his trousers itched his legs. Dust completely covered him. His boots looked like they had taken on the Sahara, and lost.

Douglas watched cadets come staggering out. When he saw Banks, he had to chuckle because Wayne had taken off his beret and the top of his forehead was white while the rest of his face was caked in dark brown mud. He looked like a coal man all bent over ready to make his delivery.

Wayne spotted Douglas. "ARE YOU LAUGHING AT ME? HAVE YOU SEEN YOURSELF?"

The two of them roared when Douglas told his best friend he looked like he was down a quart.

Although Staff-Sergeant Rose had placed them with their backs against the sun, the heat was horrendous as they sat on their duffel-bags waiting for the rest of the cadets to complete the balance of the 'sausage machine.'

"That Staff-Sergeant Rose isn't such a bad guy, is he?" The voice came from the cadet who was next to them. He was native and his capbadge indicated he was from an artillery regiment.

"Are you from Vancouver?" Douglas asked.

"Victoria. Although I haven't lived there very long. I'm from Smithers."

He knew the cadet didn't know anyone because he looked a little lonely and had just started talking to them.

"I'm Doug Brice and this is my good buddy, Wayne Banks."

"Hi, I'm Earl Jackson. Are you guys in IBT?"

"We sure are," Wayne replied.

"So am I. Do you mind if I hang around with ya?" I don't know anybody up here."

Douglas and Wayne both looked at each other. "Sure, that's O.K. with us," said Wayne, holding his hand out to shake Jackson's which was already extended. Then Douglas shook his hand. They both thought he looked like a good guy, even though he wasn't a 'black-hat.'

"I knew you guys were from Vancouver because you're in the Dukes. I hear it's a great regiment."

Wayne smiled. "Doug, I like this guy already."

Jackson knew he had said the right thing because it felt like they had known each other for years.

Finally, when everyone had cleared clothing stores, Staff-Sergeant Rose reappeared. "WELL, FELLOWS AND I USE THE TERM LOOSELY. THAT WASN'T SO BAD, WAS IT?"

The cadets were still sitting on, or next to their duffel-bags. "NO, STAFF!"

Staff-Sergeant Rose was about to say something else when a cadet wearing a kilt, interrupted. "Excuse me Sergeant, excuse me Sergeant," he said in a timid voice.

"ARE YOU TRYING TO GET MY ATTENTION?" Rose bellowed.

"Yes, Sergeant," replied the cadet, standing there with his hand up.

"MY NAME IS STAFF-SERGEANT ROSE! DO YOU HEAR ME? I SAID

STAFF-SERGEANT ROSE! ARE YOU DEAF?"

"No, Sergeant, I mean Staff-Sergeant, I mean Staff," the cadet replied.

"PUT YOUR HAND DOWN. IF YOU WANT TO GET SOMEONE'S ATTENTION, YOUR LEFT FOREARM MUST SHOOT OUT, HELD PARALLEL WITH THE GROUND, FINGERS EXTENDED WITH THE THUMB ON TOP. WELL, WHAT IS IT? SPEAK UP, LAD!"

"What's a piece of tail...Staff?"

Everyone burst out laughing. It took them all by surprise. Someone had obviously put him up to it. The cadet had probably asked some older cadet and he'd been informed to ask the Staff-Sergeant.

"Why is there always one in every crowd?" asked Banks.

Staff-Sergeant Rose tried not to smile as he walked over to the cadet, but it was there and everyone knew it.

"WHAT'S YOUR NAME?"

"McGee, Staff."

"WELL, MCGEE. WHY, IN THIS HEAT, WOULD YOU BE THINKING OF A PIECE OF TAIL?"

"I wasn't Staff, you were. You mentioned the snail."

Rose grinned. "LOUDER SON, LOUDER! NOW, WHAT WAS YOUR QUESTION?"

"I SAID, WHAT'S A PIECE OF TAIL...STAFF-SERGEANT?" The cadet had now turned beet red, realizing that he had been set up.

Staff-Sergeant Rose played it to the hilt. "I STILL CAN'T HEAR YOU. WHAT'S A WHAT?"

"I ASKED, WHAT'S A PIECE OF TAIL, STAFF?"

Staff-Sergeant Rose was still grinning when he looked around at the group. Some cadets were laughing so hard, they had to lie down on the ground. Those out of control were wearing kilts, so they were probably the ones who had set McGee up.

"SETTLE DOWN, THERE! SETTLE DOWN! WE JUST MIGHT HAVE A SERIOUS QUESTION HERE."

The cadet who had asked the question now thought better of it. As far as he was concerned, he'd already made an ass of himself. "It's alright Sergeant, er, Staff, I don't need to know."

Rose wasn't about to let it rest there. "NO, THAT WAS A VERY GOOD QUESTION. ONE THAT DESERVES AN ANSWER. CAN ANYONE HERE TELL THIS LAD WHAT A PIECE OF TAIL IS?"

No one was going to get involved, but Lyons, who was perspiring heavily and wanted to get back onto the trucks. He stuck out his chest and said. "It's just a fuck."

That was all that Rose needed. "WHO SAID THAT? IT'S A WHAT? WHOEVER SAID THAT, COME OUT HERE. GET THAT GENIUS OUT HERE!"

Lyons walked out sheepishly as everyone clapped. He was probably wondering to himself how he got involved.

"EINSTEIN HERE IS NOW GOING TO STAND TO ATTENTION AND SCREAM OUT AT THE TOP OF HIS LUNGS, THE ANSWER TO THIS MAN'S QUESTION. AND ONCE AGAIN, I USE THE TERM 'MAN' LOOSELY."

Lyons was embarrassed. He stood to attention and screamed. "WHOEVER THE HELL YOU ARE, A PIECE OF TAIL IS A FUCK!"

"WHAT DO YOU MEAN, WHOEVER THE HELL HE IS? THIS LAD HAS A NAME. WHAT'S YOUR NAME AGAIN, SON? TELL HIM."

"MCGEE, STAFF."

"TELL HIM!"

The cadet looked at Lyons. "MY NAME IS MCGEE!"

"NOW, LET'S TRY IT AGAIN, USING HIS NAME."

Lyons could hardly be heard over the laughter. "CADET MCGEE, I HAVE BEEN ASKED TO INFORM YOU THAT A PIECE OF TAIL IS A FUCK. THAT'S ALL IT IS, JUST A FUCK!"

"You mean, just intercourse," said Rose, clearing his throat.

Lyons seemed puzzled. "What?"

Staff-Sergeant Rose tried to stop himself from laughing but he couldn't. He couldn't even speak as he motioned Lyons to get back to his duffel-bag. After about ten seconds, he managed to regain his composure. "NOW, DOES THAT ANSWER YOUR VERY INTELLIGENT QUESTION, CADET MCGEE? IS THERE ANYTHING ELSE WE CAN HELP YOU WITH WHILE WE'RE AT IT?"

"No Staff, thank you," McGee muttered lowly.

Rose was still smiling as he continued from where he left off earlier. "YOU HAVE BEEN ISSUED DIFFERENT COLOURED RIBBONS TO WEAR ON YOUR LEFT EPAULET. IF YOU ARE COLOURBLIND, YOU MAY HAVE A PROBLEM. NOW PAY ATTENTION HERE. BLUE IS FOR SIGNALS, RED IS FOR IBT AND GREEN IS FOR DRIVER-MECH! HAVE YOU GOT THAT?"

"YES, STAFF!"

Rose lowered his voice. "Now, I'm not going to fall you into three ranks because some of you will be bowled over with the weight of your packs. You will notice that the drivers of the trucks are holding different coloured cards. I want you to get into a truck that matches the colour of the ribbons you were issued with. MOVE!"

The seriousness of the Staff-Sergeant's voice had everyone moving quickly. It was hard to see the trucks because of the dust and it was difficult to get on them because some of the packs were bigger than the cadets carrying them.

"COME ON, GET A MOVE ON! SOME OF YOU LOOK LIKE LITTLE OLD LADIES PATIENTLY WAITING FOR THEIR PERIODS TO RETURN. WHERE'S MCGEE, OR WHATEVER HIS NAME IS? WHERE'S THAT CADET WHO WANTED TO KNOW WHAT A PIECE OF TAIL WAS?"

"HERE, STAFF!"

"I SUPPOSE YOU'D LIKE TO KNOW WHAT A PERIOD IS ALSO?"

The cadet was about to say yes, but he was literally lifted onto a truck by the cadets around him. He now knew better than to answer yes. "NO THANK YOU, STAFF."

"Now I know how Santa Claus feels," said Lyons as he passed Douglas, heading for a green-carded truck. His pack had opened a few times and he had to go back to pick up the gear he dropped.

"Don't tell me you still believe in him?" asked Douglas.

Lyons gave a puzzled look. "No, you dummy, I was just......" He realized Douglas was joking. With a grin and a wave, he headed for his truck.

Douglas stuck with Banks, East, Jackson and Danyluk. It was mayhem getting their gear on the truck. Cadets were everywhere, so was their equipment. Already, some of them were losing articles they had just signed for. The problem was with the dust; those who dropped things couldn't see to pick them up.

Douglas sat next to the cab of the truck. Banks was next to him, across from Danyluk, Jackson and East. They were tired, dirty and a bit bewildered and it showed.

All of a sudden Staff-Sergeant Rose jumped up on the back of their truck. Some cadets offered him their seats, but he turned them down. "You need them more than me, old chums," he said, still standing and holding on to the upper frame.

Once again the trucks rolled, disappearing into a cloud of dirt and dust.

"How are we all doing?" Rose asked them.

Half of them forced a smile and the other half said, "Good, Staff."

Rose gave them all a pathetic smile. "The worst of the first day is over now, fellas. All you have to do now is make your bed, wash up and head over to the mess hall. How's that sound?"

"Good, Staff!"

Staff-Sergeant Rose sensed they were a little astonished at the system. His job was to make them feel a little easier now. "IF WE HAD GUYS LIKE YOU WITH US IN KOREA, WE WOULD HAVE WON THE WAR IN THE FIRST SIX MONTHS! RIGHT?"

If Rose thought he was cheering them up, he was right.

"YES, STAFF!"

"That's the spirit. That's what I like to hear."

Driving to the main camp, the trucks drove over the long winding road, crossed the highway and passed huts shaped like the letter 'H.' The camp had been gridded with roads, just like grid squares on a map. There were two H-huts to a square.

They crossed one road, went to the next and turned left and then right again, stopping in a line that covered two of the H-huts.

The number on the first hut was B-21. Like all of the other huts, it was about forty yards long. It had two wings, and each wing had three entrances. There was an entrance at each end of a wing and one in the middle. The ground had been bulldozed so that half the building had storage space underneath it. As such, two entrances were even with a road on one side of the grid, and the other two entrances were above the road on the other side.

The centre entrances were similar. The front entrance on one wing was about three steps from the ground, facing a road, while the back wing's centre entrance was higher because of the storage space beneath. This entrance faced an identical H-hut about twenty yards away. The space in between was used as a smoking pit.

Douglas ascertained that the showers and toilets were located in the centre section of the building that joined the two large wings together.

When the tailgate opened, Staff-Sergeant Rose jumped down. "FORM THREE RANKS ON THE ROAD. MAKE CERTAIN YOU DON'T LEAVE ANYTHING BEHIND."

"NOW PAY ATTENTION HERE! YOU WILL NOTICE THAT THERE ARE TWO SIDES TO EACH BUILDING. INSIDE THE BUILDINGS THERE ARE DOUBLE BUNKS. I WANT YOU TO WALK, NOT RUN, INTO THE BUILDINGS AND FIND YOURSELF A BUNK. IT IS PREFERRED THAT SMALL CADETS SLEEP ON THE LOWER BUNKS!"

Some cadets started to make their move, but Rose wasn't finished yet.

"I'LL TELL YOU WHEN TO FALL OUT!" he barked, as he continued.

"IF YOU HAVE FRIENDS FROM YOUR HOME CORPS AND YOU WANT TO BE IN THE SAME PLATOON, MAKE SURE YOU ARE IN THE BUNKS CLOSEST TO THEM. PLATOONS WILL BE FORMED FROM A DIVISION OF BUNKS."

"INSIDE, YOU WILL NOTICE THAT EACH BUNK HAS ONE BARRACK-BOX IN FRONT OF IT. BUNK-MATES WILL SHARE THAT BOX!"

"NOW, WHEN I FALL YOU OUT, YOU WILL GO IN AND PUT YOUR GEAR ON YOUR BEDS. THEN, YOU WILL TAKE OUT YOUR WASH BASINS AND WASH UP FOR LUNCH. I WANT YOU FORMED UP ON THE ROAD AT THE OTHER END OF THE HUT IN THIRTY MINUTES! YOU WILL NOT CHANGE INTO YOUR SUMMER CLOTHING! IS THAT CLEAR?"

"YES, STAFF!"

"RIGHT! "INSTRUCTOR'S BASIC TRAINING, ATTEN...TION! FALL...OUT!"

All of the cadets made a smart right turn, paused for the usual silent count of 'two-three,' then the rush was on. Douglas made a dash for the large set of stairs closet to him. East, Jackson, Banks and Danyluk were not far behind. Other cadets were doing the same thing.

"I SAID WALK, DON'T RUN!"

There were cadets inside the building when Douglas entered, excited and puffing from carrying his 'load.' Immediately, he noticed three empty bunks next to each other at the far end of the wing. They looked out on the front road across from the Cadet Canteen and the Sergeants' Mess.

"HEY GUYS, OVER HERE," he yelled. Within seconds, they were deciding which bunk they would take.

Banks saw Douglas take a lower bunk, so he threw his bag on the upper. Jackson took the bunk below East and Danyluk, because of his size, elected to take the upper bunk above a cadet from the Royal Canadian Electrical and Mechanical Engineers (RCEME), by the name of Bergur. When Danyluk talked to him, the cadet said, "My nickname's Bergie."

It wasn't long before all five of them took a liking to Bergie. It was Bergie's second year and he informed them that he'd show them the ropes.

With their gear dumped on the bunks, they headed for the section in the middle that connected the two wings of the hut. Four rows of stainless-steel bench-like sinks occupied the main room in the centre section. Numerous taps were attached to pipes coming down from the ceiling. The cadet who happened to be at the drain end of one of the long sinks would receive all of the water from the other taps.

The frame holding the taps had mirrors attached to it. There was a mirror above each set of taps.

Three other rooms were also situated in the centre section. A shower room off to one side contained various shower nozzles coming out of two walls. There were no dividers between the showers and the room had a central drain in the middle.

Two rooms were across from the shower room. One was a drying room where wet clothes could be hung up on rope washing lines; the other contained seven toilets. Unlike the shower room, dividers stood between the toilets; there were, however, no doors. A large urinal with polished brass fittings and an old wringer washing-machine, also occupied the ablution room.

As the five washed up, a cadet doing a personal inspection of the place said. "Isn't this just great. The family that showers together, shits together."

Douglas came to life after he had washed. What he really wanted was a shower and to get out of his uniform, however, they had received instructions that they were only to have a wash.

After he combed his hair, he went back to his bunk and rolled down the mattress. His boots were filthy, so he took his shoe-rag out of his pack, wiped them off and lay down with his hands under his head.

The hut was like a madhouse. Cadets were running up and down the aisles; opening and closing windows and arguing as to who had the right bunk.

Douglas looked around. Forty sets of bunks lay across from one another in his wing. On both sides of the wing, two sets of bunks shared a window. With so many windows, the wing was bright with sunlight. He couldn't figure out what the wall covering was. It was some sort of hard cardboard, similar to plaster. The same material covered the ceiling which was six feet above the top of the upper bunks. The floor of the building at one time must have been hardwood, however, it had been scrubbed so often it was now just a mass of dirty-coloured slivers.

Wayne was on the top bunk looking around. "Hey Doug, who do you think sleeps in the cubicles?" He was referring to small cubicles at each end of the wing.

"Probably the Corporals," Douglas replied.

A continuous shelf, interrupted only by the windows, ran the full length of each side of the wing. Below that, behind each bunk, two coat racks were screwed into the wall. If a coat rack was missing, a couple of large nails had been hammered in.

Although all of the windows and doors were open, the hut was sweltering and a long lineup formed at the water fountain in the centre section. Cadets taking their time drinking had to put up with the 'comments' and pushing of those waiting behind them.

Douglas smiled when he saw one little cadet in the lineup turn around and look up at the cadet behind him. Apparently he had been shoved.

"Listen, Mac! If I have any more trouble from you, I'm going to cut off your nuts."

The cadet behind picked up the would be 'surgeon' and wrapped him around his shoulders. "You're going to what?"

Five feet off the ground allowed room for second thoughts. "O.K., I'll only cut off your left nut," the 'surgeon' said with a smile. "How's that?"

It must have been the start of a good relationship. They walked away talking, looking like an elephant and a mouse.

There were big cadets, small ones, fat ones, thin ones, lippy ones, quiet ones and trouble makers. Although no fights had broken out, Douglas saw them coming. Groups were forming and guys were starting to throw their weight around.

Wayne leaned over his bunk and peered down. "How many Dukes are on this course?"

"I think there's about thenty-five of us," Douglas replied. "We're the only ones in this hut. The rest are over in the far hut."

"O.K., O.K., who's the asshole?" said a cadet opposite them. "Where's my capbadge?"

They had only been in the hut twenty minutes and capbadges were starting to disappear. Apparently he had left his beret on his bunk and when he returned from washing up, it was gone.

Douglas felt his side pocket. His beret and his badge were safe. "YOU GOT YOUR BADGE?" he asked Wayne.

"You bet," came the voice from up top.

The cadet who had lost his badge was starting to panic, when one of the biggest men Douglas had ever seen walked into the hut. He was a Sergeant; the bush uniform he was wearing was spotless. It was starch-pressed to the point anyone touching the creases would have cut themselves, Douglas thought.

The Sergeant's boots gleamed, as did the pace-stick he carried under his arm. He walked over to the cadet who had lost his badge.

"What's your problem, son?"

The cadet told him his capbadge had been stolen.

WHAM! The Sergeant slammed down his right foot.

"PAY ATTENTION HERE, EVERYONE. ONE OF YOU HAS STOLEN THIS CADET'S CAPBADGE. BY THE TIME WE GET BACK FROM LUNCH, THE BADGE WILL BE BACK ON HIS BERET. You leave you beret on your bed," he said, looking at the cadet.

"THERE WILL BE NO STEALING ON THIS SIDE OF THE BARRACKS. I

WANT TO MAKE THAT PERFECTLY CLEAR. IF THERE IS STEALING, YOU WILL WISH YOU HADN'T BEEN BORN! IS THAT UNDERSTOOD?"

"YES, SERGEANT!" thundered the reply.

"GOOD! NOW GET YOURSELVES OUT ON THE ROAD, IN THREE RANKS. NOW!"

The sound of the Sergeant's voice was enough. Never in his life had Douglas seen people move so fast, himself included.

When they were on the road, the Sergeant 'introduced' himself.

"STAND STILL AND KEEP YOUR EYES TO THE FRONT! MY GOD, YOU'VE ONLY BEEN IN THE BARRACKS A FEW MINUTES AND NOW THE THIEVING STARTS. THAT MAKES ME ANGRY, VERY ANGRY, AND WHEN I GET ANGRY, HEADS ROLL. ALL OF YOUR HEADS, IF THAT'S WHAT IT TAKES."

"YOU!" he said pointing to a fat cadet in the front rank. "YOU LOOK LIKE A BLIFFY! DO YOU KNOW WHAT A BLIFFY IS? WELL, DO YOU?"

"No, Sergeant."

"IT'S TEN POUNDS OF SHIT, IN A FIVE POUND BAG! TUCK YOUR SHIRT IN AND PULL UP YOUR PANTS, MAN. BY THE TIME I'M FINISHED WITH YOU, YOU'LL LOOK LIKE A SOLDIER. NOW WHAT ARE YOU?"

"I'm a bliffy, Sergeant."

"I CAN'T HEAR YOU!"

"I'M A BLIFFY, SERGEANT!"

"YOU CERTAINLY HAVE THAT RIGHT!"

"MY NAME IS SERGEANT BECKFORD. MY REGIMENT IS THE PRINCESS PATRICIA'S CANADIAN LIGHT INFANTRY. IN MY REGI-MENT, THERE ARE NO BLIFFIES! I CAN'T STAND BLIFFIES! WHEN I'M THROUGH WITH YOU, YOU WON'T BE ABLE TO STAND THEM EITHER! IS THAT CLEAR?"

Every cadet screamed, "YES, SERGEANT!"

"STAND STILL! I SAID STAND STILL! CHARLIE COMPANY, ATTEN...TION! PICK YOUR BLOODY FEET UP. MY DOG LIFTS HIS LEG HIGHER THAN YOU PEOPLE DO WHEN HE PASSES A FIRE HYDRANT! MOVE TO THE RIGHT IN THREES, RIGHT TURN! BY THE LEFT, QUICK MARCH! LEFT, RIGHT, LEFT, RIGHT! LEFT WHEEL! GET YOUR ARMS UP, I SAID GET YOUR ARMS UP! IT'S CHEST OUT AND STOMACH IN, NOT THE REVERSE! LEFT, RIGHT, LEFT, RIGHT!......!"

While they were marching to the mess hall, Danyluk said. "I've never lifted my leg on a fire hydrant. Why would anyone want to lift his leg on a fire hydrant?"

The group around him laughed, knowing full well that Sergeant Beckford couldn't hear them. At least they thought he couldn't. They didn't realize that for some reason, Sergeants are gods and they possess many attributes.

"CHARLIE COMPANY, HALT! IF I HEAR ANYMORE CHATTER, WE'LL MARCH EVERYWHERE IN DOUBLE TIME! CHARLIE COMPANY, QUICK MARCH!"

The march to the mess hall wasn't very far. There were three mess halls in the lower camp and one mess hall across the highway in the upper camp. Their mess hall was only about forty yards away.

"CHARLIE COMPANY, HALT! WILL ADVANCE, LEFT TURN! WHEN I FALL YOU OUT, YOU WILL LINE UP IN TWOS TO ENTER THE MESS HALL! IS THAT CLEAR?"

"YES, SERGEANT!"

"CHARLIE COMPANY, FALL…WAIT FOR IT! OUT!"

After they turned to the right, Douglas was nearly knocked over by the rush as everyone headed for the mess hall stairs. It didn't take him long to get into the action either, because he nearly knocked Wayne over.

The line-up seemed to go on forever, but at last, the group of six entered.

Like the other huts in camp, the mess halls were H-huts. The centre portion was the kitchen. Cadets had to pick up a tray and walk past servers. The menu was listed on a small blackboard up on the wall and they could choose from three selections.

The wings of the mess hall were lined on both sides with typical military six-foot folding tables. They had plastic tablecloths and seated six cadets each.

The six managed to sit together at a table and it didn't take them long to dig in. Maybe it was the heat or the air, but everyone was famished.

"Hey, this is good grub," said East. For some reason, he seemed to have more than the others.

"How in the hell did you get all that food?" asked Danyluk.

"I just told them I was extra hungry."

Danyluk pouted. "Jeez, I gave her my best smile and all I ended up with is this." He looked at the small portions on his plate.

"Ya gotta have the knack," said East.

After they had finished the main course and dessert, cadets could help themselves to tea or coffee.

"Does anyone want tea?" Banks asked.

The other five of them indicated tea would be just fine, so Wayne got a stainless steel pot and six cups.

"You make a hellova good waiter," Bergie remarked.

"Just make sure you leave me a big tip," said Wayne.

When they had finished eating and were making their own way back to B-21, East said. "Let's call ourselves, the Six Musketeers."

After a bit of small talk on the subject, it was decided. The Six Musketeers it would be.

"We can't just walk like this; we should be marching," said Jackson.

He didn't have to say it the second time. They were proud. They had been told they could have won the Korean war sooner, so with chests out, chins up and arms straight, they marched the short trek back to their shack like soldiers.

As they entered, two Regular Force Corporals inside were demonstrating how beds would have to be made.

"Every one of you will have to learn how to put hospital corners on your beds," the Corporal said, showing them how it was done, pulling the upper sheet so tight that it nearly ripped.

Next, they put on the first blanket. "It's got to be as tight as the sheets. As a matter of fact, if it's made properly, you should be able to bounce a coin on it," the Corporal added, making certain the centre line of the blanket was perfectly centred on the bunk.

The second blanket was put on exactly the same way and then the pillow was placed at the head. The third blanket was then folded in half and wrapped around the pillow, ends tucked under the mattress. The Corporal made certain that the centre line on the third blanket lined up exactly with the centre line on the top blanket.

"In our regiment, the mattresses are squared on the sides," said the Corporal. "These mattresses are round, so if you want them to look squared on the sides, you can fold the edges of the first blanket inwards, before you put on the second blanket. Either that, or get some cardboard strips for the sides. This will give the impression that your mattress is square and the bed will look a lot sharper."

"Sounds good to me," said Danyluk.

"O.K., I want all of you to make your beds like the one we've just made," said the Corporal, ripping apart the 'work of art,' to the chagrin of the cadet who 'owned' it.

"If we can't bounce a quarter on your top blanket, you'll have to start all over again. Get to it."

Before long, all cadets on Douglas' side of the hut were bouncing coins on their beds. The Corporal were right; the coins did bounce. If not, the bed was tore apart swiftly and the cadet had to start from scratch.

Next, the Corporals showed everyone how to line up their bunks. They measured the distance between them and marked the spot. Then they used a piece of string to ensure they were in a straight line.

"I'm going to stand at the end of the hut and look down the row of bunks," said the Corporal. "If one bunk is out of line, it's twenty pushups."

There were no bunks out of line, nor were any of the dust covers (the third blanket), because the same piece of string was used to line them up also.

"The chart on the bulletin board will show you how we want you to place your boots and running shoes on the shelf. Those items will be cleaned, shined and laced when they are placed up there. In addition, when you hang your battledress up, every button will be done up and the bottom of your pants will not hang below the tunic. Your wash basin will be shined daily and placed in the centre of your dust cover."

Douglas heard Danyluk talking to Bergie. "Do they expect this everyday?"

"You haven't seen anything yet. Wait until it's Saturday," said Bergie, smiling.

"Your towel will be folded lengthwise and be hung like such on the end of your bunks; folds to the right," the Corporal continued. "Those towels will be spotless and at no time will there be more than two towels hanging there."

"You mean the only things we can put on the shelf are our boots, running shoes and pith-helmets?" East asked.

"During morning inspection and for the rest of the training day," the Corporal replied. "What you have up there in the evening or after inspection on Saturday morning, is up to you."

"My mother never told me it was going to be like this," Danyluk said, jokingly.

"You haven't got a mother. You here hatched under a rock. Remember?"

Douglas noticed that the Corporal who was speaking to Danyluk wasn't smiling. And for that matter, neither was Danyluk.

"STAND BY YOUR BEDS!" The words came out loud and clear as Sergeant Beckford entered the barracks once again.

"QUICKLY, WITHOUT PANIC, I WANT ALL OF YOU TO FORM THREE RANKS ON THE ROAD! CORPORAL, INFORM THE OTHER SIDE OF THE HUT AS WELL!"

The clamour of stomping boots shook the building as cadets from both sides of the hut rushed to form up on the road. Within seconds, the hut was empty.

"YOU, YES YOU...AND YOU! GET BACK IN THERE AND GET YOUR BERETS ON! NOW PAY ATTENTION HERE. I NEVER WANT TO SEE ANY OF YOU OUTSIDE THE BUILDING WITHOUT YOUR BERETS ON UNLESS YOU ARE IN P.T. STRIP! IS THAT CLEAR?"

Once again, a deafening, "YES, SERGEANT!" was heard.

"RIGHT! TODAY IS SATURDAY. FOR THOSE OF YOU WHO ARE SMART ENOUGH TO FIGURE OUT THAT TOMORROW IS SUNDAY, I HAVE SOME GOOD NEWS FOR YOU. THE CADETS WHO ARE COMING FROM THE PRAIRIES WON'T BE ARRIVING UNTIL TOMORROW. OVER 600 OF THEM WILL BE HERE AND THEY WILL BE GOING THROUGH THE SAME PROCEDURE AS YOU WENT THROUGH TODAY."

"Hey, maybe I can sneak into one of those short-arm inspection lines again?" Danyluk murmured.

"We should be calling you Stud instead of Moose," whispered Banks.

"SINCE THERE IS NOTHING ELSE PLANNED FOR YOU TODAY AND THERE IS NO CHURCH PARADE TOMORROW, THE COMMANDING OFFICER HAS DECIDED TO GIVE YOU THE BALANCE OF TODAY AND ALL OF TOMORROW OFF."

There was general approval throughout the company.

"I'M NOT FINISHED YET! IF YOU GO DOWNTOWN, YOU WILL BE BACK FOR SUPPER ON BOTH NIGHTS. TOMORROW BEING SUNDAY, THERE WILL BE A BRUNCH INSTEAD OF BREAKFAST. THAT MEANS YOU CAN SLEEP IN AND EAT AFTER YOU GET UP. THE MESS HALL WILL BE OPEN FROM 0800 UNTIL 1300 TOMORROW."

"NOW, I ONLY HAVE THREE MORE THINGS TO SAY. ONE...THIS WILL BE YOUR LAST DAY TO SLEEP IN EXCEPT FOR AN EXTRA FEW HOURS ON SUNDAYS. TWO...IF YOU GO DOWNTOWN, YOU WILL ENSURE THAT YOU CONDUCT YOURSELF IN A MILITARY MANNER AND LET THE FOLKS WHO LIVE HERE BE PROUD OF YOU.

THREE...FOR THOSE OF YOU WHO ARE ROMAN CATHOLIC AND WISH TO ATTEND SERVICE TOMORROW MORNING, TRUCKS WILL BE ON SICILY SQUARE AT 0700 TO TRANSPORT YOU TO ONE THE LOCAL CHURCHES! ARE THERE ANY QUESTIONS?"

Some cadets asked questions, but Sergeant Beckford referred them to the bulletin board in the barracks.

"HAVE A GOOD TIME. CHARLIE COMPANY, ATTEN...TION! DIS...MISSED!"

With Sergeant Beckford and the two Corporals gone, Douglas and the other Musketeers went back into the barracks and started unpacking. The notice on the bulletin board made it quite plain; everything they brought to camp was to be placed in the barrack-box along with items they were issued with. Suitcases and duffel-bags would be stored below the building on Sunday night.

When they were finished, their barrack-boxes were bulging; even so, they had to be locked. Douglas and Wayne got a cardboard box from the kitchen and cut a piece out of it, to use as a divider.

"An ant couldn't get in there," said Wayne, pushing the last of his clothing into the box.

"How come you brought so much stuff?" asked Douglas.

Wayne was perspiring, "I wanted to be prepared for the worst."

"Who feels like a shower?" Jackson asked, not knowing he would be last in. Clothes were removed fast and the meaning of'one for all and all for one' was discarded instantly with the thought of cool water hitting their bodies.

Wayne ran down the aisle with his towel wrapped around him. "HEY DOUG, BRING YOUR BADGE WITH YOU, OR LOCK YOUR BERET IN THE BARRACK-BOX!"

Jackson's idea of a shower was a little late. When they got there, the shower room was full, but in a few minutes they had it all to themselves.

"No wonder those guys left," said East. "The water's cold."

It didn't matter if it was cold, it was so hot in the barracks, the cold water was like rain from Heaven.

"Has anyone tried this soap? It doesn't foam and it stinks," said Danyluk, trying to get a giant bar of soap to suds up.

"It's called 'Sergeant-Major's soap' or 'Sergeant's Soap," said Bergie. "You should have brought your own. That stuff will take the skin right off you. Here, borrow mine."

East was standing in front of the room's open window, drying himself off. He slammed it shut. "HEY, WE'RE ALL BALLS-NAKED AND SOMEONE LEFT THE WINDOW OPEN!"

"There's no dames in the camp," Danyluk gurgled, holding his mouth under the nozzle. "If there were, I'd open it wider."

Douglas laughed. "You'd trip on your knob heading to the window."

"Jealous bastard!" he replied, grabbing his crotch.

Bergie was shampooing his hair. "If you guys want to go downtown, I'll show you around," he said.

Before long, it was agreed they would all go downtown to take in the sights. It was also unofficially agreed that they would use Bergie's shampoo, as well.

"What do you think I am, the Sally Ann?" he complained.

All of a sudden, Danyluk dropped Bergie's soap. "Banks," he said, "Will you grab that for me? I've got soap in my eyes."

Wayne was just about to bend over, when Bergie warned, "DON'T DO IT, THAT'S WHAT HE WANTS!"

The shower room was filled with howls of laughter. Even Banks joined in, but not before he showed Danyluk a fist.

Danyluk patted Wayne on the shoulder. "Just joking. I'm not in the Irish cadets, you know."

A shower and a meal was all it took to get the Musketeers back on their feet. After they dried off, they put on their serge pants and khaki shirts they had worn on the trip. But that didn't matter, they felt refreshed and ready for anything.

"Thank God, we don't have to wear tunics or ties," Wayne said, wrapping his web-belt around his waist.

"I didn't like the thought of having to wear those short pants, but this weather is starting to make them look mighty good," East remarked to Jackson.

Earl agreed. "The trouble is, we've got to wait until Monday to wear them," he replied, neatly rolling up his shirt sleeves.

Douglas was dressed long before the others. Since this was all new to him, he didn't want to have to wait in the barracks.

"I'm just going to walk around the camp; does anyone want to join me?"

Wayne had just finished shining his capbadge. "Hold on Doug, I want to see what this place looks like as well."

Douglas and Wayne left through the southwest door of B-21 and walked east, past another hut, until they reached a grassy area which ended on the upper edge of a hill. A wire-mesh fence had been erected, running north south.

Douglas suggested that they walk south along the fence and follow it around the camp, but Wayne said he had just spent fifteen minutes polishing his boots and would rather walk on the road. Since the road was following the fence anyway, they both agreed it would be more convenient.

To the east was a large valley with a golf course below. Douglas was overcome by the beauty of the valley and the hills on the far side. The golf course looked like a green billiard table set in the middle of the rugged, brown countryside. They both stopped to stare at the panorama view.

Douglas was the first to speak. "I've read books about how beautiful the Okanagan is, but I never dreamt it was like this. Those hills look so near, it's almost as if you could reach out and touch them, yet look at the size of the valley."

Wayne, who was never as sensitive as Douglas on matters such as these, was impressed as well. He removed his glasses and then put them on again as he viewed the small patches of trees sporadically spread along chasms running up and down the hills.

"I'll bet it's taken millions of years for water to create those," he said, his eyes following the hills from the blue sky, down to the highway which ran north-south along the base of them.

As they continued, they passed another set of H-huts and a clearing with a large asphalt parade square. Small pebbles had been spread on the surface, probably to stop the tar from sticking to the boots of anyone using it.

Wayne stepped onto the square and started doing drill. "Hey, this isn't so bad. It's easy to do turns on this stuff."

Douglas laughed. "It's alright for you to say that now, but what about when we're on it for hours at a time? There's also no shade."

They continued around the square until they arrived at a building with a sign on the front which read, Headquarters Building. Twenty feet in front of it, standing right in the middle of the road, was a cannon. They walked up to it and Wayne said, "This looks like it came from the deck of a submarine. What's it doing here?"

Douglas shrugged. His mind wasn't on the cannon; he had walked past the Headquarters Building and was looking south up the road at some horses grazing in the fields. Then he returned to the cannon and they proceeded south along the east side of the building. Another sign read, Commanding Officer.

Wayne stared at the rocking chair sitting on a small porch in front of the Commanding Officer's doorway. "I wonder if he sits on his porch in the evenings?"

Douglas climbed the few stairs and sat on the chair. "This isn't too bad. Yes, I think I'm going to like this."

Wayne ran up to him and grabbed his arm. "It'll be too bad if Beckford sees you."

Behind the Headquarters Building, they strolled through the outdoor chapel. It wasn't very big, but the weeping willow trees and neatly cut green grass made it look very serene and peaceful. The setting was ideal.

The altar was part of an old rowboat. When they stopped in front of it, a lonely look came over Wayne's face. "If we had a car and we drove south along that highway, we'd be in Vancouver in about eight hours." Wayne was looking at the winding road south-west of them.

Douglas too, gazed at the road. Just the mention of Vancouver made him think of his mom and Major. Although he was in the middle of six hundred cadets with his best friend, home was three hundred miles away. A feeling of loneliness was going through him. He knew Wayne felt the same way, but neither said anything to the other.

Wayne stopped them from reminiscing, when he slapped Douglas on the back. "We'd better head back and join the other guys."

Danyluk was standing at the door when they returned.

"Where the hell have you two been? We've been over to the cadet canteen looking for you and Jackson even checked the guardroom."

He didn't give them the chance to reply. "They're back, let's get our asses on the road."

There was a small line-up ahead of them as the six approached the guardroom. Each cadet leaving camp had to be inspected by the Provost. In five minutes, they were approved and marching down the hill, two abreast. Jackson and East were in front, followed by Bergie and Danyluk. Douglas and Wayne took up the rear.

"Christ, I don't mind walking down, but it's going to be a hell of a trip coming back up," Douglas heard Danyluk telling Bergie.

"You'll get used to it," was Bergies's response as he pointed to an old, one-floor corner building on the other side of the highway. "Do you see that building over there?" Bergie's question had stopped them; they were all glaring at the building.

"It looks like just another old building to me," said Banks.

Bergie glanced at him. "That's not just any old building. That's Hop Sing's Laundry."

"Ahh, so that's where we get our laundry done?" asked Jackson.

"You get more than your laundry done there." Bergie had a smile on his face from ear to ear. There are rumours that it's also a whorehouse. "You hand' em your tickee and you get more than the washee."

Danyluk was laughing and pumping his groin in and out. "Have you used it, Bergie?"

Bergie shook his head. "No, word went around that they throw in a dose if you're not one of their regulars."

"I'd become a regular," Danyluk said, as he started to saunter across the highway toward Hop Sing's. Bergie grabbed his shoulder and hauled him back. "If the Provost catch you walking by it, they'll nail you. You can come back to camp on that side, but when you get to Hop Sing's, you must cross the highway."

Douglas looked puzzled. "I know this might sound silly, but just what the hell is a dose?" He knew he shouldn't have asked the question, but it was better to be laughed at by friends than embarrassed by strangers.

Although all five gave him a weird look, he got the impression that a few of the Musketeers didn't know either.

Danyluk shook his head. "So you don't know what a dose is, eh?"

All of them were razzing him now. It was Wayne who came to his rescue. "Everyone knows what a dose is Doug. It's two baby deer."

Douglas turned a shade of pink. "Oh jeez, gimmee a break," he said.

Still laughing, Wayne slapped him on the back. "That's my buddy. I'll explain later what a dose is."

With the discussion about Hop Sing's over with, the six of them continued down the hill. East turned around and glanced at Banks. "I'll bet you don't know either?"

For the next two minutes, the group accused each other of not knowing. Bergie finally explained, but everyone, including Douglas swore he already knew.

The sidewalk was packed with cadets heading into town. It looked like the whole camp had decided to take advantage of the day off. Cadets were everywhere. Some were even walking back up the hill on Hop Sing's side. Vernon had been invaded by the army and local residents had decided to stay inside out of the military's way.

Two cadets wearing officer's epaulets walked by the six Musketeers. One of them said, "You people! Don't you know it's customary to salute an officer?" He was carrying an officer's swagger-stick and looked important to Douglas even though he was only about sixteen.

"Sorry, Sir, we didn't notice you," Douglas replied, looking at the green hackles sticking up from behind the capbadges on their carabineers.

Bergie stepped forward. "What are you talking about? We don't have to salute Cadet Officers while we're in Vernon. Try that on the ignorant ones. You should be worried more about your dress than a salute, Major. Your puttees are wrapped wrong."

As the Cadet Major's eyes dropped to his puttees, Bergie nudged the rest of the Musketeers forward. "Those snobs are at it again. They were here last year and they caught me on my first day. They try it on all newcomers."

Jackson was still looking back. "You mean we don't have to salute them?"

"Not at Vernon," replied Bergie. "Maybe at their home corps, but not here."

Douglas saw a familiar special expression on Wayne's face. "O.K., what are you thinking?"

Wayne's face lit up with a sneaky smile. "Oh, nothing. I've got an idea for the next time we come to town."

When Wayne had an idea, Douglas knew it would be a riot when it was put into action.

"Then I'm looking forward to it," he said.

They had talked about sports, the military, Korea, and Danyluk's girlfriends, when they neared the bottom of the hill. Hundreds of cadets had passed them on the way up, saying there wasn't much going on in town. Those returning had only been climbing for a few minutes and they were covered in sweat from the heat of the relentless sun. That, combined with the fact that all were dressed in long woolen battledress pants.

"What park is this?" Danyluk started to walk into a forest of large trees, green grass and a winding pathway leading to a narrow bridge that crossed a stream.

"It's called Polson Park. We passed it heading to camp in the trucks," Bergie said, walking a few paces inside the park to get him. "We'll go through it on the way back and and I'll show you a shortcut which leads to camp."

East took off his beret to wipe his forehead. "It sure looks mighty inviting right now," he said. No sooner had he wiped his forehead with his arm, a passing Provost truck stopped.

"YOU ! YES YOU! GET YOUR BERET ON!" A red-capped military policeman shouted at him. The truck paused only for a moment then continued on its way.

East couldn't get his beret on fast enough. "Christ, those guys are everywhere. Do they ever sleep?"

"I don't think so," Bergie replied. "They even patrol the camp after lights out. Many a cadet has sneaked a girl into camp, only to be sent home the next day."

Danyluk liked the part about sneaking a girl into camp. "If I did it, I wouldn't get caught. They're like all cops; they appear when you don't need them. Just pretend you need them and they won't be there. That's my secret."

The five just shrugged, especially East, who nearly had a heart attack when he heard the Provost's voice. His nerves were still on edge. "Are you for real, Danyluk?" he asked.

After passing the Park and the Fruit Exchange, they found themselves at the centre of town, where Highway 97 crosses the main street of Vernon.

"This is the main drag," Bergie pointed out. "We'll turn right here because I want to show you guys a restaurant next to the movie theatre. You can get a neat banana-split there."

After walking two-and-a-half blocks past small shops and hotels, they entered the restaurant. The air-conditioning hit them like an arctic storm.

"You're never gonna get me out of here," Jackson said, as a waitress came over to the booth which was built to seat four, but had the six of them crammed into it.

"WHAT'LL IT BE, SOLDIERS?" She had to speak loudly because the place was packed with cadets and the voice of Guy Mitchell was blurting from the juke box.

Danyluk liked what he saw and he decided to make his play. "Any girl who calls me *soldier* has stolen my heart. We'll have six banana-tits, er I mean splits. But really, I'd rather have you."

The girl wrote out the order on her pad. "Six banana-splits coming up," she said confirming the order without giving him a second look or acknowledging his remark.

While they were waiting for the ice cream, a Rosemary Clooney record began at exactly the same time that Lyons and Foster entered and sat in the next booth.

"We thought you guys were going to wait for us? We went to your hut and it was empty." Lyons appeared a little upset. "How soon you forget your best friends," he added, putting his beret into his epaulet.

Foster didn't say anything, he was sitting under the air-conditioning fan with an expression of utter joy on his face. "I'm not going back to camp. I'm sitting under this thing all summer."

The six banana-splits arrived, and the two newcomers decided to have the same.

"If you sit there all summer, your Company Sergeant-Major might have something to say about it," said Bergie.

Foster leaned over the back of his booth, breathing down Douglas' neck. "Guess who my Company Sergeant-Major is?"

Banks looked at him. For some reason, he knew without asking. "It can't be?"

Foster wore a look of despair on his face. "It fucking well is. I've got none other than Casanova Genova. You know, I think the guy's a homo?"

"Why's that?" Douglas asked, sticking his spoon into a giant piece of banana.
Foster was hurrying to get it all out. "Well, you guys both know Lance-Corporal Scheaffer from our corps, don't you?"

"Yeah, we know him," replied Wayne.

"Well, he keeps going into Genova's cubicle fully clothed and he comes out nude, and I mean nude. No shorts, no socks, no nothing; NAKED!"

"How do you know that?" asked Douglas.

"How do I know it? I keep seeing it! Genova's moved into a cubicle in our barracks, can you imagine that? The guy gives up a perfectly good room elsewhere, to sleep in the same hut as us. Genova yells out, "IT'S TIME FOR YOUR RUBDOWN, ROGER," and Scheaffer comes out smelling like Vicks Vapo-Rub or whatever it's called."

"You dummy," said Wayne. "Roger Scheaffer's got a cold and Genova is trying to help, that's all."

Wayne's statement only made Foster more upset. "Oh yeah? Well, let me tell you something, Doctor Banks. Roger Scheaffer comes out with Vicks on his chest, his back, his legs, and his ass. I'm surprised it's not all over his head and his feet as well. It must be one fuck of a cold!"

"Maybe he's got the flu," offered Banks.

Danyluk laughed. "I don't think he's got the flu. I think it's a case of dicktheria."

Sounds of laughter, stomping feet, and hands banging the tables brought the waitress over to ask them to quieten down. Lyons was convulsing. He had his head resting on both arms on the table and he nearly knocked over his banana-split.

When they finished eating, they haggled over how much each they would have to pay and how large the tip should be. The pot was short by the amount of one banana-split.

"Alright, alright," said Bergie, assuming the role of bookkeeper. "Who's shorting us here?"

After a few minutes' discussion, the unanimous decision was that it was Lyons. Sheepishly, he put his hand into his pocket and paid his bill, plus his portion of the tip.

"I wish there was sales tax on this so you'd have to divvy up a little more," Foster said, still thinking of the sales tax affair. "Jesus, you're cheap, Lyons!"

A burst of hot air surrounded them as they left the restaurant and checked out the movie playing at the theatre next door. Then they crossed the street and headed back to Highway 97.

Before long they were marching up the hill, two by two, swinging their arms and keeping their chins up. Danyluk had made certain they were marching on Hop Sing's side of the highway.

"Let's sing it, guys!" Lyons said, turning and leading off the song like he was conducting a choir with an imaginary baton. Everyone joined in except Jackson and Bergie, but it didn't take them long to learn it.

"You guys are honorary Dukes now" said Lyons. "O.K., one, two, three..."

We come from the west by the sea;
And a mighty battalion are we;
We will add more fame, to our glorious name;
And the province of old B.C.!"

"We're the Duke of Connaught's and we're damned good shots;
And we're out to help the Tommy beat the hun;
And while we're over there, you bet we'll do our share;
An we'll stay in the battle till it's won, won, won."

"Every morn, we hear reveille blowing;
We are one day closer to the foe;
They must fall, but we will always be;
The Duke of Connaught's from old B.C.!"

By the time they had finished the last verse, they were across from Polson Park.

"Hey," said Jackson. "I thought we were going in there to learn the shortcut up the back hill?"

"Let's do that tomorrow," Danyluk said, grabbing his crotch again. " I think we should take a look in Hop Sing's window."

"Let me tell you something else," said Bergie. "If you walk in Polson Park at night, make sure you're with someone. Some of the local punks hang around in there and they'll grab you if you're on your own. But if you are on your own and they do grab you, just yell out 'ARGO'!"

"You mean like ARGO FUCK YOURSELF?" asked Danyluk.

Bergie smiled. "I don't know what it means, but it sure brings cadets to the rescue."

Seven of the eight crossed the road before they arrived at the forbidden Hop Sing's. They watched Danyluk cup his hands on the window, trying to look inside.

"YOU! GET ACROSS THE HIGHWAY!" screamed a Provost Corporal who 'just happened' to be passing in his jeep.

"What did you see?" they asked Danyluk as he joined them.

"Just laundry," Danyluk answered. "Maybe the girls are underneath it. If they are, they must stink like hell."

The eight turned left past the guardroom, marching and looking straight ahead. They knew they were being scanned by the Provost Sergeant. He didn't say anything, so they kept on marching, turning right onto the main camp road.

Shortly, Lyons and Foster went their own way and the remaining six turned left past the Sergeants' Mess and headed for their hut.

"GIVE MY REGARDS TO CASANOVA," Douglas yelled, as Foster walked away.

Foster turned. "THE ONLY REGARDS I'LL GIVE HIM IS A SWIFT BOOT UP THE ASS."

The barracks was boiling as they entered. Only half the cadets had returned from town. The others were lying on their beds reading, or sitting talking to one another. The Regular Force Corporals were walking the floors explaining to cadets about training and how they should prepare for daily camp life. They weren't very old themselves, Douglas thought. One was about nineteen and the other twenty.

"It's five o'clock; anyone for chow?" East had been steadily looking at his watch, waiting for the mess hall to open.

"You'd better get used to the twenty-four-hour clock," said Bergie. "It's now 1700."

The heat in the mess hall was worse than the barracks and it was only half full as the six entered.

The menu listed roast pork, roast potatoes, brussels sprouts, peas and gravy. The second choice was roast turkey, mashed potatoes, stuffing, and corn. The third choice was ham sandwiches.

East rubbed his stomach. "I'm going to like it here. This food is better than the stuff I get at home."

He must have said the magic words, because the girl who was serving him heaped up his plate. He got twice as much as anyone else.

After East had finished, he went back for seconds and followed that up with three desserts.

"You haven't got an ounce of fat on you, so where are you putting that stuff?" asked Jackson.

"My dad says I'm just a growing boy," East replied, eating a cookie, one of six he had stuffed into his pocket when he went back for his last dessert.

Danyluk put his arm around East's shoulder. "But you're not growing in the right place."

East laughed. "I don't think I'd like to be growing like you, Danyluk. I'd get tired of tripping on it."

Jackson was killing himself laughing. "When are you guys going to give us a break?"

"Oh, he doesn't want to break it," Wayne remarked, forcing a massive piece of turkey into his mouth. "If he broke it, he wouldn't be able to stick it into the top of his boot when he puts on his puttees."

The whole table broke up.

"I can't get over what Foster told us about Roger Scheaffer and Genova," Douglas said, sipping a hot cup of tea. He had been raised on tea, so it didn't matter how hot the weather was, he always had a cup of tea after meals.

"I think Foster's blowing the whole thing up," replied Wayne. "I know Genova's weird, but I don't think he's a homo. If he is, how did he manage to stay in the army this long? The RSM (Regimental Sergeant-Major) would have noticed it long before now."

The subject was dropped after East decided he was going back for another dessert. When he stood up, he was grabbed by Bergie and Danyluk. They dragged him out of the door.

B-21 held its full complement of cadets when they arrived back. Everyone was busy ironing or working on their boots. Some cadets didn't like the smell of moth-balls on their summer clothing, so they were washing them in the machine.

Danyluk took out his radio and placed it on his area of the shelf. Johnny Stanley was singing, It's In The Book, so Danyluk joined in. "MRS O'MALLEY, DOWN IN THE VALLEY, SUFFERED FROM ULCERS, I UNDERSTAND. SHE SWALLOWED A CAKE OF GRANDMA'S LYE-SOAP, NOW SHE'S GOT THE CLEANEST ULCERS IN THE LAND."

As Douglas lay on his bunk, the next song on the radio was dedicated to some girl in Vernon from her boyfriend Bill, who was working in Vancouver. Jo Stafford was belting out her current hit single, You Belong To Me.

Because it had been a long train ride and a long day, everyone within earshot of the radio went into a somber mood. They were thinking about home. Before long though, cadets went back to running up and down the aisle of the barracks chasing each other and fooling around. The flick of towels could be heard coming from the shower room followed by the usual, "Ouch!"

Douglas took out his shoe kit and started working on his boots. Banks found a comic and was up on his bunk reading and chuckling to himself. East had managed to slip a turkey leg into the pocket that wasn't full of cookies and was eating it while he watched Bergie shine his RCEME capbadge. Jackson, in the meantime, was trying to bounce a quarter on his top blanket, and Danyluk had found a broom and was practising rifle drill in the middle of the aisle. He didn't care if a passing cadet nearly got hit in the head with his broom. As far as he was concerned, he was patrolling his territory.

At seven thirty, the group of them and some other cadets went over to the Cadet Canteen. About two hundred cadets sat in the canteen and the adjoining garden which was closed off with a high wooden fence. Douglas bought Wayne a Kik-Kola and a Creamsicle and they walked out of the room because the jukebox was blaring so loud they couldn't hear each other talk.

It was getting cooler now as they sat at a picnic table. The sun was making its way further to the west and the first breeze they felt since arriving started to waft through the garden.

"It seems like we've been here a year," Wayne said, looking up and staring blankly at the sky.

Douglas didn't answer. He was thinking of his mom as she left the train station. He knew she had tears in her eyes and she really didn't want him to go. He didn't want to come to camp either, but the pressure of his friends combined with the fact that she had told him it would do him good, made it a fait-accompli. Now he wondered who would look after the place and take Major for a walk. Major liked to run on the beach and fetch the stick that Douglas would throw into the water. Ever since they had rescued him from the pound, the dog knew he had found someone who loved him and would care for him.

"What are you thinking about?" Wayne asked.

"Home, I guess."

"Me, too." Wayne's voice was almost a whisper.

The barracks was still a madhouse when they returned and decided to have another shower. This time, there was plenty of hot water and the ones who hadn't brought soap had purchased some at the Cadet Canteen.

The Musketeers had formed a close relationship in the short period they had known each other. They used the democratic system to make decisions and there wasn't a mean person among them. Even Bergie, who in effect was a second year 'pro,' didn't toss his weight around. He was one of them and that's all there was to it.

The shower felt great and when they were back at their bunks, Sergeant Beckford entered the barracks.

"THOSE OF YOU WHO ARE NOT IN BED, STAND BY YOUR BEDS!"

As he went from bunk to bunk, the Sergeant made certain every set of bunks had two people on them, or standing next to them.

"Who's in this bunk?" he asked, stopping at the first set.

"It's Robinson, Sergeant. He's in the shower," a cadet answered.

Then he moved to the next set of bunks. "And who's in this bunk?"

"I don't know his name; he's in the 'jon,' Sir."

"DON'T CALL ME SIR, I HAVE TO WORK FOR A LIVING!"

"Er, he's in the 'jon,' Sergeant."

"THAT'S BETTER!"

Sergeant Beckford checked all the bunks on Douglas' side of the hut, questioning where some cadets were and answering questions that were put to him.

"RIGHT, PAY ATTENTION HERE. LIGHTS OUT IN TEN MINUTES. CARRY ON!"

After the Sergeant stomped out, cadets scurried everywhere. Those who were in the drying room, jon or showers were told by their bunk-mates that the lights were going out in ten minutes. Some who rushed out of the showers still had wet hair. That didn't matter because wet hair was better than the wrath of Sergeant Beckford.

It was exactly 2230 when the two Regular Force Corporals who lived in the hut came in and turned off all the lights except for the one in the shower room. That lit up the centre area and shone through the inside window of the shower room, providing a glimmer of light at the other end of Douglas' wing.

As the two Corporals went up and down the aisles, they answered various questions and sat on the bunks of younger guys who seemed apprehensive of the magnitude of camp life.

"You come and see me if there's a problem," Douglas heard one of the Corporals say."

When everyone had settled down, one of them left the building, while the other stopped at the exit.

"THAT'S IT FELLAS. HAVE A GOOD NIGHT'S SLEEP! TRY AND KEEP IT DOWN TO A DULL ROAR! GOODNIGHT!"

The words, "Good night, Corporal," were screamed, shouted, whispered, yelled and sung to him as he walked out.

"I wonder where they're going?" East asked anyone who could hear him.

"They're probably going to the Junior Ranks Club," Bergie replied. "One of them will be back at 2300 and the other will be back at midnight."

It didn't take long for the noise to die down. Some cadets were snoring just after the Corporals left. Although a breeze entered the barracks through all the open windows, it was still hot and most cadets were just lying on top of their blankets. In the night, when it was cooler, they would subconsciously cover themselves up.

Wayne's head appeared over the side of the bunk. "Are you going to sleep in tomorrow, Doug?"

"You bet!"

"Same here. Good night?"

"G'night buddy!"

When Wayne's head disappeared, the bunk swayed as he turned onto his side.

Douglas lay on his back with his hands behind his head. The breeze coming in from the window behind him was fabulous. It was the first time all day he had felt cool. The light on the road outside allowed him to count the coils connecting the springs to the frame on Wayne's bunk. He didn't know why he was counting the coils; his mind was recalling the feel of Major who normally would have been on the foot of his bed. But there wasn't enough time to think of Major, because after he counted coil number fourteen, he was asleep.

CHAPTER IV

Douglas didn't know if he was having a nightmare or if he was awake. Voices were yelling, "HEY YA FARMERS, WHERE'S YA TRACTOR? AW, DID YOU GET YOUR BALLS SQUEEZED TOO HARD? WELCOME TO GOD'S COUNTRY, IT'S ABOUT TIME YOU SAW HOW THE BETTER HALF LIVES."

Army truck engines make noise and when Douglas finally opened his eyes, the voices and the clatter going on around him made him think the Third World War had started right outside his window.

A cadet, without clothes and dripping wet, stood at Douglas' window with his hands cupped around his mouth. "ALLEN, HEY ALLEN, I'M OVER HERE!"

The boy was in the shower when he heard the trucks, so he had rushed out to see his friend from last year.

"YAHOO! WE'LL MEET AT THE CADET CANTEEN LATER, O.K.?"

Douglas looked at his watch. It was only eight o'clock and nearly the whole barracks was up and at the windows, 'welcoming' the truckloads of prairie cadets who were arriving.

To make matters worse, the cadets in the trucks were shouting back and giving the finger to everyone stretching out of the windows.

Wayne looked over the side. "Good morning, Mr. Brice, I see you're finally awake. This has been going on for over half an hour. You must have been beat?"

The noise in the barracks was deafening. Cadets who had been up awhile were running up and down. The showers were going full blast, and with the showers, the yelling, toilets flushing, barrack-boxes slamming shut, and the washing-machine whining, Douglas was amazed he could have slept through it all.

After a few seconds, he flung his legs out of bed and sat up in the middle of the action.

Rags to Riches, with Tony Bennett was blaring from Danyluk's radio and Jackson and East were practising rifle drill with brooms, right next to Douglas' head.

Wayne said. "Let's grab a shower and go and eat."

The two of them yanked their towels off the end of the bunks and headed to the shower room. It was full of steam.

Douglas had his face to the wall and was just letting the water pour over his head. "Jeez, they call this being allowed to sleep in?"

Wayne had shampoo in his eyes but he still had a sense of humour. "This could only happen in Vernon, old buddy..."

Douglas laughed because he saw Wayne groping for a towel near the open window. One of the kitchen girls was looking at him as she passed by. She even whistled. Wayne had soap in his eyes, and with his glasses off, he couldn't get a good look at who it was.

"HEY, WHO'S THE HOMO THAT'S WHISTLING?"

When Douglas told him, he never saw his friend move so fast in his life. In one second, he was back under his shower, forgetting he had his towel with him.

"Where are the others?" Douglas asked, referring to Bergie and Danyluk.

"They're over in the mess hall. They were up at six-thirty."

After their shower, they made their beds and got dressed. The mess hall was full of prairie cadets. They had their berets off and the tops of their foreheads were white. Unlike themselves the day before, these cadets hadn't been given the opportunity to wash. They had just completed the sausage machine and looked really tired. When Wayne repeated Douglas' line about being 'down a quart,' the prairie cadets within earshot only managed a slight grin.

Foster and Lyons were waiting in B-21 when Brice and Banks got back from breakfast. The eight of them were together again and had decided to go downtown to try and "find some dames."

As they left camp, Douglas was told by a Provost Corporal that he would have to go back and get a clean shirt on. Back in the barracks, he discovered both shirts he was issued with were wrinkled; he had to iron one. The other Musketeers waited for him and before long, they were making their way down the hill toward the city.

Passing Hop Sing's on the other side of the highway, Lyons gave the appropriate command. "Eyes left!" Each of them automatically cut their arms to their sides and paid the small wooden building their respect by turning their heads sharply in unison as they marched by.

"We've got to get in there, we've just got to," said Danyluk, licking his lips.

Bergie had his tongue in his cheek. "If you get in there, you may never want to come out."

Danyluk stuck out his crotch. "Suits me just fine. Drag out my worn and ravished body and send it back to my mother with a note saying I died for Queen and Country."

Bergie screamed. "YOU'VE GOT NO MOTHER; YOU WERE HATCHED UNDER A ROCK, REMEMBER?"

For the next two hours, the Musketeers sat in Polson Park and talked army. Bergie gave them the royal tour and showed them the famous short-cut route. Some of the local kids were playing baseball so they stopped to watch them from the covered stands.

It was cool in the park and since they were out of sight of Military Police, they took off their berets and flopped down next to a stream. It was Lyons, of all people, who suggested that if they wanted to pick up dames, they wouldn't get them in the park. "The women will be where the action is, on the main drag."

After a short discussion, they devised a plan. It was decided that they would split up into pairs and meet back at Polson Park at three-thirty. "That's fifteen-thirty," Bergie pointed out.

Danyluk had his arm around Jackson's shoulders. "If me and Jackson aren't here, you'll know we're in the sack."

Jackson opened his eyes wider and wider. "Jesus, I sure hope you're right, Moose."

Wayne leaned over to Douglas. "It's all talk, you know. He wouldn't know what to do if it was staring him in the face."

Although Wayne whispered, Danyluk heard him. "I HEARD THAT BANKS. I'LL HAVE YOU KNOW THAT BACK HOME, I'VE GOT A PUSSY STARING ME IN THE FACE EVERY DAY!"

As Wayne and Douglas walked away, Wayne responded, "THE ONLY PUSSY THAT EVER STARES YOU IN THE FACE IS YOUR CAT, GERTRUDE."

Douglas thought he must be stupid, moving around in this heat with itchy pants. It was Sunday and not too much was happening in town. The stores were shut and because the sun was scorching, even the locals weren't hanging around.

After about an hour, Douglas and Wayne had decided to head back to Polson Park, when Wayne said. "Get a load of those two!" He was pointing across the street at two girls who appeared from nowhere. They were standing in front of the radio station, giggling as the boys looked at them.

"This is it, buddy," said Wayne, grabbing Douglas' arm to start him off crossing the street. When they got to the other side, although still giggling, the girls started strolling away.

Wayne stopped. "What kind of girls are these? I know they wanted to meet us because of the way they were acting."

"Maybe they want us to follow them," said Douglas, as he started after them. He'd never had a girlfriend before and he was getting a little bit excited at the thought of it.

They had walked ten blocks in circles and still the girls hadn't stopped. "Christ, what are they, Amazons?" asked Wayne as he stopped to wipe his brow.

When the girls did stop, the two boys didn't waste any time in catching up to them.

Wayne smiled. "Can we talk to you for awhile?"

The girls giggled and the blonde said, "Sure, but you'll have to walk with us."

For some reason Wayne ended up walking with the blonde and Douglas took up the rear with the other one who was a brunette.

The blonde glanced shyly at Wayne. "Where are you guys from?"

"We're from Vancouver."

"I've never been to the coast," said the brunette. "What's it like?"

Douglas grinned. "O.K., I guess. It's a little cooler than here."

As they were walking, Wayne said. "Hey, would you guys like a soda?" He slipped his hand into the blonde's hand as he asked. When the brunette saw that, she put her hand in Douglas' hand. Douglas hid his delight. A feeling came over him that he'd never had before. The only thing bothering him now was who was going to pay. He knew Wayne didn't have any money and he only had a few dollars left. Oh, what the hell, he thought to himself. This doesn't happen every day.

The air conditioning at the Capital Café was on high when they entered and sat in the first booth.

Douglas thought the girls were cute. The blonde had short hair and the brunette had long hair. Neither was very tall and he convinced himself they would look great in bathing suits.

Two sodas led to four, and although they had talked about everything under the sun, they still didn't know the girls' names.

"I'm Doug," he said, looking into her eyes.

She turned her head shyly, " My name's Diane."

Wayne had his arm around the blonde whose name was Debbie. Giggling, she said Wayne is a "really nice name."

Douglas thought of the time. He looked at his watch; it was three-thirty already. "We've got to go," he said, standing up in a hurry.

Wayne took a pen out of his pocket and handed it to Debbie. "How about giving us your phone numbers?"

She wrote out both numbers and the three of them went to the door while Douglas paid the bill.

When they were outside, Debbie said, "We only live about eight blocks from here. When will we hear from you again?"

Wayne was trying to get a goodbye kiss but Debbie kept backing away. "Don't you worry, doll, we'll call you guys tomorrow."

After they separated and the two boys were rushing to get to Polson Park, Douglas said. "Doll? Did I hear you right? You did say doll?"

Wayne shrugged. "Well, that's what Humphrey Bogart says. I'm surprised you never said it because you're the one who keeps using the Humphrey Bogart accent. Besides, look what he gets?"

When they arrived at the park, the other six were waiting. Only Danyluk and Jackson hadn't met any girls and Danyluk couldn't get over the fact they had come away empty-handed.

Jackson said sourly. "We actually did meet two dames, but I told Danyluk after they took off, that you don't ask girls what size bra they wear before you get to know them."

"Well, I've never been one for beating around the bush," Danyluk said, looking a little let down. "Her tits were whoppers. They like to brag about those things."

The group of them were still laughing as they took the shortcut up the back hill. At the top, they started singing the "Dukes Song" and shortly they arrived back at camp, missing the guardroom with their new route.

"This is the road we should take when we leave camp," said East.

Danyluk gave him a sharp look. "What? If we did that, we wouldn't have the chance to check out Hop Sing's place."

Everyone thought supper was great that night, but when they returned to the barracks, it was chaos.

"Christ, this place looks like the main drag in Peking," quipped Bergie.

"No, there would be dames there," said Danyluk.

When the lights were turned off, Wayne leaned over his bunk and looked at Douglas.

"Just think, Doug. We may have met our first piece of tail today?"

Douglas just chuckled, but East heard Wayne, and he thought of Cadet McGee, the day before.

"Sir, Sir. What's a piece of tail, Sir?"

Everyone in their end of the barracks came to life after East's statement. Wayne threw a pillow at him just as one of the Regular Force Corporals came into the hut.

"What are you doing?"

"I'm just going to give him a good night kiss, Corporal," Wayne replied.

The Corporal walked into his cubicle shaking his head as he closed the door.

When the fun died down, Douglas rolled onto his side and went to sleep. Sunday had been a good day.

While being herded off the train, the photographer asked these young fellows to smile for the camera. Fifteen minutes later they were in B-3 bashfully smiling for the Nursing Sisters, coughing for the Medical Orderlies, and saying to themselves, "My God, where's my mother?"

The fun is about to begin. Cadets being picked up from the railway station after arrival in Vernon. Next stop, the sardine tin (B-3) with the Nursing Sisters......and, irregular heartbeats.

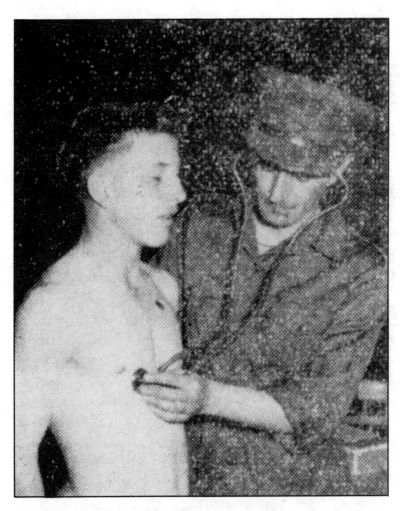

Starkers. Yes, this unfortunate individual had survived the sardine tin, Nursing Sisters, and even the Medical Orderlies. He was referred to the 'Doc' because of an irregular heartbeat. The Medical Officer's diagnosis: "You're perfectly healthy, my boy. Just keep your mind off the Nursing Sisters."

"O.K., now. Let me explain to you the ingredients in powdered-eggs."

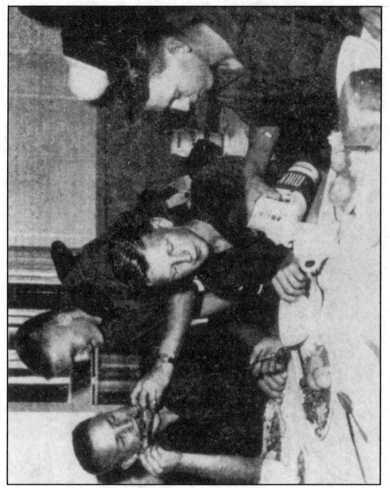

No. this isn't Jack East trying to grab a turkey-leg. It's some other company's equivalent of Jack East trying to grab a turkey-leg. If it was Jack, he would have had it.

A company of 'mushrooms' receiving a lecture on how to sit around the Commanding Officer.

No. that's not his finger. It's the bottom of a bayonet-scabbard. This young fellow was the last to respond to, "FROM THE RIGHT, NUMBER!" The cadet on his right is wearing running-shoes. The notation on his MIR slip, must have read, 'M&D.' Medicine and duty. I betcha he just loved that.

Ahhh, a break from the heat. Cadets participating in a swim-parade.

"GET IT UP, MAN! It's left arm parallel with the ground, not parallel with the mountain."

Aiming-rests being used in the upper camp.

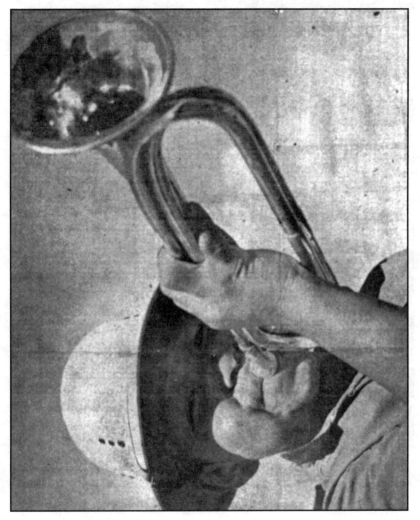

A Louis Armstrong in the making? Possibly. With the help of a box of lip-balm.

"There you are, son, five silver dollars. They'll have to last you for one whole week."

A pianist provides some entertainment just prior to a dance at the Arena.

CHAPTER VI

Although summer days in Vernon are extremely hot, it can be quite cool at night. When early morning comes along, it takes a few hours of the sun's rays to warm things up again.

Douglas and all other cadets in Vernon found this out on their first working day. The hut was quiet. Most cadets had kicked off their blankets in the middle of the night, leaving only their upper sheets to cover them. When morning came, they were curled up in the fetal position with their heads under the covers, subconsciously wondering why they were cold. The sun had been up an hour, but its full heat wouldn't be felt for another two hours.

It was six o'clock on Monday morning. A small man in P.T. strip entered the hut and rushed down the aisle turning over mattresses and pulling down the covers of the cadets who weren't up.

"STAND BY YOUR BEDS! COME ON...STAND BY YOUR BEDS! LET GO OF YOUR COCKS AND GRAB YOUR SOCKS!"

Within seconds, cadets were standing in pairs at the foot of their bunks. Most were still shivering; others were yawning, stretching and rubbing their eyes.

"I gotta pee...Jesus, I'm bursting," whispered Danyluk as he bounced from leg to leg trying to stand at attention with a monumental erection. Then he started whistling to take his mind off his predicament.

"I WANT ALL OF YOU ON THE ROAD IN FIVE MINUTES! YOU'LL WEAR ONLY A T-SHIRT, YOUR P.T. SHORTS, SOCKS AND RUNNING SHOES! MOVE!"

The hut came alive with the sound of barrack-boxes banging shut and cadets rushing to the urinal. The line-up was four deep and every one knew he only had five minutes.

Danyluk was second in line at the urinal. "If you don't hurry up, I'll pee in your back pocket."

"These shorts don't have pockets," the one in front replied.

"Really? It will be down your sock if you don't get a move on."

Cadets fell over themselves rushing out the south doors of the building. Some were still pulling up their shorts and trying to pull on their T-shirts as they arrived outside.

Gradually, Charlie Company was formed up in a hodgepodge of three ranks; the short person facing them.

"THAT TOOK SEVEN MINUTES! TOMORROW, WE WILL DO IT IN FOUR!"

"MY NAME IS SERGEANT SIMPSON. GOOD MORNING, CHARLIE

COMPANY?"

There wasn't much of a response from the cadets lined up in front of him.

"I SAID GOOD MORNING, CHARLIE COMPANY!"

"GOOD MORNING SERGEANT!" came a noisy, but somewhat sleepy reply.

"THAT'S BETTER. I GET LONELY WHEN I HAVE TO RUN BY MYSELF IN THE MORNING. I LIKE COMPANY, SO I'VE PICKED YOU PEOPLE TO JOIN ME! ISN'T THAT GOOD OF ME?"

"YES, SERGEANT!" A few other comments were heard as well. Particularly Danyluk's whisper, "He's got to be fucking joking!"

"GOOD! THIS MORNING, WE'RE GOING TO RUN UP TO THE UPPER CAMP AND BACK AGAIN. MOST OF YOU HAVE NEVER SEEN IT OTHER THAN BY TRUCK. I THINK THAT'S MOST UNFAIR, SO I WANT TO GIVE YOU A PERSONAL TOUR. ISN'T THAT KIND OF ME?"

"YES, SERGEANT!" Then Danyluk's whisper, "Who the hell is this creep?"

"RIGHT! CHARLIE COMPANY, ATTEN...TION! MOVE TO THE RIGHT IN THREES, RIGHT...TURN! BY THE LEFT, DOUBLE-QUICK, MARCH!"

For the next twenty minutes, Charlie Company jogged throughout the upper camp. The morning dew kept the dust down on the road as they ran. Other companies were everywhere and some were even singing.

"Those poor bastards have been ordered to sing," said Banks, who was limping with a rock in his shoe. "There's no way they would volunteer to sing at this time of the morning."

"Who's bright idea was it to come here?" Danyluk asked.

Douglas was out of breath when he replied. "You two talked me into coming."

"Well, the next time we come up with such a brilliant idea, kick us in the ass, will ya?"

Within minutes, they passed another company jogging in the opposite direction. "HEY LOOK, THERE'S FOSTER!" screamed East. "HEY FOSTER, WHERE'S GENOVA? DOESN'T HE LIKE RUNNING?"

Foster looked moody, like all of the other cadets in his company. "HE'S PROBABLY PUTTING SOME VICKS ON CORPORAL SCHEAFFER."

East was shocked. "CORPORAL SCHEAFFER? He was only a Lance-Corporal before we came."

Banks laughed. "I think we should all go for a rubdown. It seems to be the way to get promoted around here."

When they arrived back on the road next to B-21, they were halted and stood easy. Most of them were breathing hard and some were gasping for breath.

"A GAGGLE OF GIRL GUIDES COULD HAVE DONE BETTER THAN YOU PEOPLE TODAY, BUT I'M SURE WE'LL IMPROVE TOMORROW!"

"AS A MATTER OF FACT, I CAN SAY WITH COMPLETE CONFIDENCE, WE WILL IMPROVE WITH EACH PASSING DAY! ISN'T THAT RIGHT, CHARLIE COMPANY?"

"YES, SERGEANT!"

Danyluk whispered. "This guy's elevator doesn't go to the top floor."

"GOOD! NOW WHEN I FALL YOU OUT, YOU WILL HAVE A SHOWER, MAKE YOUR BEDS AND CLEAN YOUR HUT IN ACCORDANCE WITH THE INSTRUCTIONS ON THE BULLETIN BOARD, WHICH OF COURSE, EACH OF YOU HAS READ! BREAKFAST IS AT 0700! YOU WILL BE DRESSED IN YOUR SUMMER GEAR AND ON THIS ROAD AT 0800! IS THAT CLEAR?"

"YES, SERGEANT!"

"RIGHT! CHARLIE COMPANY, ATTEN...TION! FALL...OUT!"

Douglas didn't rush in with the other cadets. He was astonished at how sweet and fresh the air smelled. It had been cold when they first left the hut, but that abated after a few minutes. The sun was slowly rising over the hills across the valley to the east. In the distance he could hear roosters signalling the start of a new day. Never in his life could he imagine he would be in the middle of such peace and serenity. "God, I love this country," he murmured, as he walked into the hut.

As he entered, it was like Grand Central Station. The showers were running full blast, the toilet stalls were full and the washing up area was as busy as a beach on a hot day.

Cadets were everywhere. Some were lining up their bunks; others were brushing or mopping around their bed-spaces.

Douglas was slow. He wasn't used to a routine. Although the Regular Force Corporals were insisting everyone get a move on, he closed his ears to them, made his bed and went for a shower. Other cadets were ironing their shirts and pants, lining up their barrack-boxes and shining their boots. A group of cadets had organized themselves to line up the rocks which formed a circle in front and in back of the barracks.

Douglas was oblivious to it all. While he showered, some cadets were using scrubbing-brushes on their one-inch web-belts, on the steel shelving of the long sinks.

Bergie popped his head into the shower room.

"Jesus, Doug, you'd better get a move on. We're all going over to the mess hall and you're not even dressed yet."

"What's the rush, we're not on parade until 0800?"

Bergie frowned. "Yeah, but it's seven-thirty now and don't forget the Alberta and prairie cadets are here. The lineup for the mess hall is a mile long."

"What's Wayne doing?"

"Wayne is doing your share of the brushing and mopping around your bunk space. He could use a hand."

When Douglas left the shower and got dressed, the hut was empty. His barrack-box had been lined up but he inadvertently moved it. He also left his towel on his bed, instead of hanging it up.

By his watch, it was quarter to eight when he walked into the mess hall. It was nearly empty because most cadets had returned to the barracks.

"Where the hell have you been?" asked East, eating a piece of bacon as he rushed out the mess hall door.

"There's plenty of time," Douglas replied, walking past the servers to pick up his food.

Halfway through his meal, he looked at his watch and panicked. It was five after eight.

Forgetting the rest of the food on his plate, he rushed toward the door, but didn't get very far.

"YOU! DON'T YOU KNOW BETTER THAN TO LEAVE YOUR PLATE ON THE TABLE? CLEAN YOUR FOOD OFF THE PLATE INTO THE GARBAGE CAN AND PUT YOUR PLATE AND UTENSILS IN THE CONTAINERS!"

"But I'm late for parade," he said.

The Messing Sergeant wasn't sympathetic. "THAT'S YOUR PROBLEM, NOT MINE! DO IT!"

The company was on parade as he ran to B-21 to get his pith-helmet. Everyone could see him and he felt humiliated. Although they were at the position of attention, he saw smiles on faces that were supposed to be looking to their front.

Sergeant Beckford saw him. "YOU! ARE YOU IN THIS COMPANY?"

"Yes, Sergeant," he replied.

"I CAN'T HEAR YOU!"

"YES, SERGEANT!"

"WELL, YOU JUST STAND WHERE YOU ARE! FREEZE! I DON'T WANT YOU ON THIS PARADE OR IN THE HUT! IS THAT CLEAR?"

"YES, SERGEANT!"

"I CAN'T HEAR YOU!"

"YES, SERGEANT!"

Douglas didn't move. He felt completely abashed as he stood to attention and watched the four platoons of his company start the morning inspection routine.

The Regular Force Corporals had sized each platoon. The tallest cadets were on the flanks and the shortest ones in the middle.

Four officers were promenading in front of the company. As they marched the complete length of the four platoons, they turned inwardly, never showing their backs to the cadets. Each one was a Lieutenant.

Two new Sergeants had joined the scene. They were standing next to Beckford and Simpson.

The CSM (Company Sergeant-Major) was standing next to the Company Commander, who was a Captain in the Royal Canadian Regiment.

All of sudden, the Company Sergeant-Major marched to the front of the company. His name tag read *Walsh.*

"I WANT THE PLATOON SERGEANTS IN FRONT OF THEIR PLATOONS AND THE PLATOON CORPORALS IN THE REAR OF THEIR PLATOONS," he ordered.

The Company Commander moved to a position six paces to the centre-front of the company.

"CHARLIE COMPANY, ATTEN...TION!" The Sergeant-Major was now preparing to hand over the company to the Company Commander.

"CHARLIE COMPANY, STAND AT EASE!"

"CHARLIE COMPANY, ATTEN...TION! OPEN ORDER MARCH!"

The front rank marched forward two-and-a-half paces and the rear rank marched two-and-a-half paces backwards.

"CHARLIE COMPANY, RIGHT...DRESS!"

All cadets took one small pace forward except the Right Marker. He was on the extreme right of the first rank. Then all cadets, except the two behind him, turned their heads to their right. The front rank, except the Right Marker of each platoon, then extended their right arm and touched the next cadet with their fist. The two cadets on the extreme right of each platoon, behind the Right Markers, judged their position. Then all cadets shuffled back so they were perfectly in line.

Sergeant Beckford turned and faced his platoon as did all of the Platoon Sergeants. Then he marched to the side of the Right Marker and screamed commands, sizing the rank. He did the same with the second and third ranks. When the company was aligned, he returned to his position in front of his platoon.

The Company Sergeant-Major screamed, "CHARLIE COMPANY, EYES FRONT!"

All arms came down as the cadets faced their front.

The CSM then turned and faced the Company Commander and saluted. "CHARLIE COMPANY HAS ONE-HUNDRED-AND-EIGHTY-SEVEN CADETS ON PARADE AND FOUR CADETS ON SICK-PARADE, SIR. THE COMPANY IS FORMED UP AND READY FOR YOUR INSPECTION, SIR!"

Douglas knew the Platoon Corporals had called the roll earlier and that Sick-Parade cadets had to report to the camp hospital at 0730. He didn't know that the hour of 0730 had been picked so cadets going on Sick-Parade wouldn't have much of a breakfast. In this way, Sick-Parades were discouraged.

The Company Commander returned the salute. "Thank you Sergeant-Major, please fall in."

The Company Sergeant-Major saluted again, then turned to his right and marched to a position next to the Right Marker of the first platoon.

The Platoon Officers had now stopped promenading and were standing at ease behind the Company Commander, in front of their respective platoons.

Then the Company Commander took over.

"CHARLIE COMPANY, STAND AT...EASE!"

"CHARLIE COMPANY, ATTEN...TION!"

"CHARLIE COMPANY, STAND AT...EASE! FALL IN THE OFFICERS!"

The officers came to attention, saluted and proceeded to march in front of the Platoon Sergeants who had called their individual platoons to attention as their officer approached.

When the Sergeants' salutes were returned, the Sergeants marched behind the Platoon Corporals, in the rear of each platoon. The Platoon Officers stood their platoons at ease, called them to attention again, then stood them at ease. They then turned, faced their front and stood at ease themselves.

The Company Commander screamed. "CHARLIE COMPANY, ATTEN...TION! I WILL INSPECT NUMBER NINE PLATOON (THE FIRST PLATOON) THIS MORNING. COMPANY SERGEANT-MAJOR, YOU WILL JOIN ME. REMAINING PLATOONS, CARRY ON WITH YOUR OWN INSPECTION!"

For the next fifteen minutes, various commands were heard along with 'advice and punishment.'

Since Douglas was standing slightly behind his platoon, he could see the Company Commander go through the ranks.

"What's your name?"

"Cadet Smith, Sir!"

"Did you press that shirt, Smith?"

"No, Sir!"

"You were probably too lazy, right, Smith?"

Smith never had a chance to answer as the officer moved on to the next cadet. The Company Sergeant-Major who was now standing in front of Smith, said, "You're a bloody disgrace, Smith. Two days CB (confined to barracks).

East was now in front of the Company Commander.

"What's your name?"

"East, Sir!"

"What's that on your pants, East? Don't look down, man! What's that on your pants? I said don't look down! Well, what is it?"

"Sir, how can I tell you what it is, if I can't look down?"

Walsh got involved. "DON'T GET SMART EAST!"

The Company Commander then continued. "I'll tell you what it is, East. It's pancake syrup. Do always run around with pancake syrup on your pants, East?"

East never got a chance to answer that question either. The Company Commander had moved on to the next cadet and East was now facing the CSM, who wasn't as polite as the Company Commander.

"Answer the question, East!"

"What question, Sir?"

"The question the Company Commander asked you, East?"

"I can't remember the question, Sir!"

"The question was, do you always run around with pancake syrup on your pants?"

"NO, SIR!"

"Then what is it doing on your pants?"

"It's from breakfast, Sir."

"I know it's from breakfast, East. You dribbled it, didn't you? You dribbled like a baby didn't you, East?"

"NO, SIR!"

"DIDN'T YOU, EAST?"

"YES, SIR!"

"TWO DAYS CB!"

While the Company Sergeant-Major had been 'talking' to East, the Company Commander was looking at Danyluk who was the next to be inspected.

"SERGEANT-MAJOR, I'M NOT EVEN GOING TO BOTHER TALKING TO THIS MAN. TAKE A LOOK AT HIS DRESS!"

The CSM stood in front of Danyluk.

"How tall are you, Danyluk?"

Danyluk didn't get a chance to answer. "Let me tell you. You're too God-damned tall for those pants. They're crawling up your crotch, man. Those pants were meant for a two-year-old. How old are you, Danyluk?"

"Fifteen, Sir!"

"I said how old are you, Danyluk?"

"Fif...Two, Sir!"

"I've never seen a two-year-old like you, Danyluk. Your testicles are hanging below the legs of your pants. Don't look down! Are they not, Danyluk?"

"Yes, Sir!"

"I CAN'T HEAR YOU!"

"YES, SIR!"

"YES, WHAT?"

There was a pause. Then Danyluk 'spoke' again.

"MY BALLS ARE HANGING OUT THE LEGS OF MY PANTS, SIR!"

"TWO DAYS CB!"

"But Sir, these were the pants I was issued with." Danyluk was not only red in the face because he had been humiliated in front of the cadets in his platoon, he was mad as hell and it showed.

"Did I give you permission to speak?" The CSM was on him again. "Well, did I?"

"NO, SIR!"

"Well keep your mouth shut! IS THAT CLEAR?"

"YES, SIR!"

"CHANGE THAT TO THREE DAYS CB!"

Jackson was next to Danyluk. The Company Commander didn't call the CSM this time, he decided to talk to Jackson himself. "Good turn-out Jackson, but you've got your pith-helmet on backwards. The strap goes to the front. Do you know which direction your front is, Jackson?"

"YES, SIR!"

"Good. Don't let it happen again."

The inspection lasted half an hour. Although cadets were getting a blast in the other platoons as well, they weren't being treated like the CSM treated the cadets in Douglas' platoon.

In all, ninety-nine names were taken, which included all of the Musketeers, except Douglas. His name would be taken shortly.

After the inspection, the Company Commander stood them at ease and spoke to them.

"PAY ATTENTION HERE. NEVER IN MY LIFE HAVE I SEEN A WORSE TURN-OUT THAN I'VE SEEN TODAY. MOST OF YOU PEOPLE HAVE HAD A DAY-AND-A-HALF OFF AND YOU TURN UP LIKE THIS ON MY PARADE."

"WELL, THINGS ARE GOING TO CHANGE. IF THEY DON'T THIS WILL BE THE ONLY COMPANY THAT WILL BE CONFINED TO BARRACKS FOR THE BALANCE OF CAMP. IS THAT CLEAR?"

"YES, SIR!" The response was thunderous.

"WOULD YOU BELIEVE I ACTUALLY KNEW THIS WAS GOING TO HAPPEN? FOR THOSE OF YOU THAT REVIEWED THE TIMETABLE ON THE BULLETIN BOARD, YOU KNEW THAT REGULAR TRAINING STARTED AFTER LUNCH IN THE AFTERNOON ON DAY ONE. PERHAPS YOU THOUGHT THAT I WAS GOING TO GIVE YOU THE MORNING OFF? NO, I'M GOING TO GIVE YOU THREE HOURS TO GET YOUR DRESS AND YOUR BARRACKS IN SHAPE. BUT THERE WILL BE NO THREE HOURS TOMORROW MORNING. IF EVERYTHING IS THE SAME AS IT WAS TODAY, THEN YOU'LL BE WORKING ON YOUR SPARE TIME IN THE EVENING! IS THAT CLEAR?

"YES, SIR!"

"NOW, PLATOON SERGEANTS, GET THIS MESS STRAIGHTENED OUT, AND I WANT THOSE NAMETAGS WORN!"

After the parade was over, three platoons rushed into the barracks to work on their kit and straighten out their platoon areas. Not Douglas' platoon. Sergeant Beckford had told them to stand fast after the CSM had fallen them out.

He asked Douglas to fall in without his headdress and marched them over to a tree that provided a lot of shade.

He asked them to sit down and make themselves comfortable, before he spoke.

"When things go wrong with my platoon, I blame myself," he said.

"Instead of leaving everything up to the Corporals like I did yesterday and the day before, I should have stuck around and had a talk with you guys. I didn't and for that I apologize."

"I assumed that between the Corporals and some of you people that are in your second year, enough information would have been passed around so that everyone would know and understand what was expected of him."

"Well, fellas, I made a big mistake. But I'm big enough to accept my mistakes and I want to set everything right. I'll try not to assume again."

As he spoke to them, every person there thought Sergeant Beckford was looking at him and him alone. It was his unique method of scanning the group while looking into their eyes.

"Where's Danyluk and East?"

When he saw their hands, he said, "Good, thank you. I want you to know that I think you were treated a little unfairly back there. Not that I'm talking behind the CO's or the CSM's backs...I'll talk to them in the office. I just think that perhaps they should have been a little more lenient on you because it is your first day."

"Listen guys, this is an Instructor's Basic Training Course. We're here to teach you the tricks of the trade. No one ever gets things done by bullying. You get things done by properly teaching your men and earning their respect."

"Over the next six weeks, we're going to be working together. During that time I want to earn your respect and in turn I want to be able to respect each one of you."

"There are going to be times when you will think I'm the meanest son of a bitch you've ever laid eyes on. I hope that happens because then I know I'm doing my job properly."

"We're going to be having more talks like this. But before I let you go, I want to give you some food for thought. One day an officer was passing some men and they were bitching at each other about the system. He made a mental note of this and when he found the Regimental Sergeant-Major, he mentioned it."

"That's good, Sir," said the RSM. "It's when they're not bitching we have to worry about them. When they're not bitching, they're not happy."

Smiles started appearing on the faces in front of Sergeant Beckford. They understood.

"Now when you get back into the barracks, I want you to organize yourself into teams. Take turns cleaning your bed-space. Work together when you're doing laundry. Let's face it, you're going to study together, why not get together on most things that you do?"

"For the next six weeks, our platoon is going to be the best platoon in the company. To be the best, we have to be the happiest and work the hardest. That means lots of bitching, right?"

Grins were everywhere. "Right, Sergeant!"

"GOOD! WHAT'S THE BEST PLATOON?"

"NINE PLATOON!"

"O.K....away you go and I'll be over in a minute. Brice, I want you to remain here."

Douglas was nervous. He could have remained seated but he stood up when everyone else stood up.

Wayne and the other Musketeers were looking back, giving him the 'thumbs up.' They were worried too.

Sergeant Beckford faced him. "You didn't hang up your towel today and your barrack-box was out of line. In addition, your dress looks horrible. You were also late for parade, weren't you?"

"Douglas looked down. "Yes, Sergeant," he replied in a low voice.

"Look me in the eye, Brice. We all make mistakes and you've just made your first one. The secret to success in life is to never make the same mistake twice. You let your platoon down this morning. Can I count on you to ensure it doesn't happen again?"

"Yes, Sergeant."

Sergeant Beckford was smiling as he put his hand on Douglas' shoulder. "I'm supposed to ask your permission to put my hand on your shoulder. Do I have it?"

Douglas was also smiling. "YES, SERGEANT!"

"O.K., Brice. Get in there and let's show 'em how it's done. Alright?" Douglas had a smile from ear to ear. "Alright Sergeant," he beamed.

"GOOD!" Beckford said, as he marched away toward the Company office.

When Douglas entered the barracks, cadets were remaking beds, ironing clothes, shining boots, polishing belt-brass and scrubbing pith-helmets. Four Regular Force Corporals from the two platoons on Douglas' side of the hut were assisting and showing them what was expected.

"I'm sorry about the towel and moving our barrack-box," he said to Wayne, who was one of five Musketeers gathered in a circle around him.

"Don't worry about the barrack-box. We were just hoping you didn't get shit. What did Sergeant Beckford say to you?"

"He's actually a pretty good guy. He just told me to learn by my mistakes and don't make them again."

East spoke up. "We've decided we're not going to let him down, Doug. When he was talking to you, all of us guys in the platoon got together and had a meeting in the drying room. We want to earn his respect and we want him to respect us. To do that, we've got to work our butts off."

Douglas nodded. "Count me in. I learned a lot this morning."

"CSM Walsh is a bit of an asshole," Danyluk said. "I don't think he's ever worked with cadets before."

Jackson was washing the windows by his bunk and heard Danyluk's statement. "If anyone was hatched under a rock, it was him." he said.

Bergie laughed out loud. "There's lots of those guys around, Earl. Just say nothing and stay out of their way when they're around."

Over the next two-and-a-half hours, all the platoons in Charlie Company made a point of competing with each other to become the best platoon. It really wasn't a fair contest because the little talk Sergeant Beckford had with Nine Platoon gave them the edge.

Sergeant Beckford also backed up his words. He came into the building and pitched in, showing cadets how they should iron their clothes and how they should polish their boots. He even wore a pair of coveralls and climbed on the folding tables to clean the light shades and shine the windows. The fact that he was working with them made Nine Platoon work even harder.

"Remember the rule. It takes two million circles, one tin of shoe polish, lots of water and a ton of elbow grease to make boots gleam."

When he was showing cadets the military method of ironing, he told his platoon they shouldn't bother using the washing machine. Instead, they should use scrub brushes and scrub their clothes on top of the sinks. Then, they should take them outside and let them dry in the sun.

"They will dry in ten minutes, and make certain you take turns watching them," he said.

Then Beckford showed them how to iron with liquid starch and how to wet a bar of soap and rub it inside the creases of their summer pants. Afterwards, when a hot iron was applied on the outside, the creases looked as sharp as a razor blade.

Then it was time to learn how to dress. Sergeant Beckford and the Corporals showed everyone how to properly wear their summer shorts, shirts, hose tops, boots, puttees, and even their coloured ribbons.

The hose-tops were made of a mixture of wool and nylon. Although they itched a bit, they went from just above the ankles to just below the knees. Not too high and not too low. Every cadet had to ensure they were worn correctly and when they were folded over the elastic bands at the top, the amount of hose-top that folded over had to be exact, throughout the platoon.

Next came the puttees. They were shown how to roll the puttees on, starting at the top of the boot and finishing around one or two inches over the bottom of the hose-top.

There had to be three edges showing on each puttee and both puttees had to be rolled precisely the same. The ribbon was then tightly wound around the last roll of the puttee and then wrapped around itself at the end of the 'V' of the puttee which ended precisely above the centre of the ankle bone.

When they were finished and it was nearly time for lunch, Nine Platoon was ready. Not only did their quarters look like you could eat off the floor, but the cadets looked like they had been in camp for a month already, their dress was that immaculate.

When it was time to head over to the mess hall, Sergeant Beckford told his cadets to wear coveralls or their P.T. strip. That way, when they were inspected after lunch, their pants and shirts wouldn't be wrinkled.

Nine Platoon had the advantage in that respect, because when they were inspected after lunch, the Company Commander informed everyone that Nine Platoon not only had the best quarters, but they were the best dressed on parade, as well. He was pleased enough that he cancelled all CBs.

CSM Walsh wasn't on parade when they were inspected the second time. The cadets of Charlie Company didn't miss his presence, either.

Before training started after lunch, everyone was issued a notebook and a pencil. In addition, their names were written on a white cardboard sheet and it was firmly implanted in their leather nametags which hung from the left breast pocket button on their shirts.

With dust flying everywhere, they marched over to the upper camp. On the way, Danyluk still complained about how the CSM had treated him.

"He called me a two-year-old. Can you imagine that?"

All cadets needing a kit-exchange were driven over to the hangar before lunch. Danyluk had exchanged his "diapers" as Banks had called them, for two pairs of proper-fitting pants.

"Those pants were too short. Anyway, remember what Sergeant Beckford said about bitching? You must be happy," said Wayne, roaring his head off.

"Well, how the hell could I help it? The other pair was even shorter. The guy who threw them at me must have had a glass eye. Do I look like a fucking midget?"

"Keep it down to a dull roar, guys." The Corporal who was marching to the side of them was chuckling at Danyluk's remarks just as much as the cadets around him.

"Where am I? I can't see! Am I in a furnace?" Banks looked just like the rest of them. He was covered from head to toe in dust, as he started his blind act again.

Douglas looked and felt exactly the same way. Dust was in his eyes and his mouth and the temperature was at least ninety-five degrees.

"For all the work we did on our kit, two steps on this road and it's all for nothing," said Bergie.

"Look at it this way," Danyluk replied. "It gives us the opportunity to scrub them again tonight." This time, Danyluk was actually laughing and it was contagious.

As the Corporal called the step, Wayne said, "We'd better call the chicks tonight and tell them that we can't see them."

"Why can't we see them?" asked Douglas.

"Because, you dummy, although we're not confined to barracks, we are confined to the camp."

Douglas grimaced. "Sorry, you're right. "Let's give 'em a call after dinner. How old are they anyway? Did the blonde tell you?"

"Yeah, she said they were both fourteen. That means, they're probably twelve or thirteen."

"No, they look fourteen. That one of yours looks about sixteen. What a body she's got."

"You bet she has and she's mine, so keep your eyes off her."

A sly smile appeared on Douglas' face. "I don't think I could handle two of them. Get your arms up, you're starting to look like an Irish cadet."

"Up yours!" When Wayne smiled, the dirt in his mouth made him look like he had teeth missing.

"And see a dentist, too."

As the four platoons marched over the 'road,' Jackson said, "Thank God we're in the first platoon. I can't even see the one behind us."

The Corporal was marching next to them. "YOU'RE NOT SUPPOSED TO BE LOOKING BEHIND YOU! WHAT COMPANY ARE WE?"

"CHARLIE COMPANY," the cadets replied.

"AND WHAT'S THE BEST COMPANY?"

"CHARLIE COMPANY!"

"AND WHAT'S THE BEST PLATOON?"

"NINE PLATOON!"

"YOU'RE OUT OF YOUR MINDS, IT'S TEN PLATOON," the Corporal with the platoon following them yelled.

Everyone in Nine Platoon turned around but they couldn't see Ten Platoon. It was lost in a cloud of dust.

That afternoon, they attended lectures on map-reading for four hours. It was hot in the building as they sat through British World War Two films on the subject. At two-thirty, though, they had a break and were allowed outside. Some cadets lit up smokes, others rushed to the water-taps or bought tickets for a bottle of Kik-Kola which was delivered by the canteen-truck. It was ice cold and never in his life did Douglas appreciate a pop more than at that moment.

During the break, Banks asked Bergie when they got their first pay.

"In two weeks, on the morning of the third Saturday in camp," Bergie replied. "We get five dollars then and five dollars a week for the next three weeks. "

Wayne looked a little upset. "I thought we were supposed to get a hundred bucks?"

"After you get home, they mail a cheque to you for eighty dollars."

The concern left Wayne's face. "It's only been three days and I'm flat broke already. I lost all of my money to that God-damned Cunningham. I think I'll phone my dad and ask him to send me some."

"Borrow some money off the dames, that's what I'd do." Danyluk was standing there looking like he was holding court.

"Christ, we don't even know them, how the hell can we borrow money off them?" Wayne was going to say something else, but Danyluk retorted, "I get to know my women in the first five minutes."

Wayne laughed. "I've seen your women, Danyluk. They probably pay you just to let you take them out of their cages."

Smiling, Danyluk cocked his head. He was going to rebuff Wayne's statement but he was stopped by the sound of a scream coming from a cadet who was sitting close to them. The cadet emitted a loud "EEEOWWW!" and ran around in circles, slapping at his pants and jumping up and down.

Everyone in Nine Platoon laughed at him and Douglas thought the cadet was having a fit. It took two Regular Force Corporals to wrestle him to the ground. The next minute, they had his pants and his shorts down and he was lying on his stomach.

Everyone gathered around. "What the hell's wrong?" asked East.

"A whole buncha wasps crawled up his pants and stung him," someone answered.

The Corporals finally removed the stingers from the cadet's buttocks and he was escorted to the camp hospital, still rubbing his rear-end.

Danyluk started again. "That happened to me once. I got stung when I was having a piss and they had to lance it. One of the nurses fainted in astonishment. She'd never seen one so big."

East butted in. "Jesus, will you quit boasting! There are other people with dongs as big as yours, you know?"

"I was only talking about the size of the lump and the stinger they took out," Danyluk replied, smiling.

East winked at the rest of them. "Sure you were, Danyluk."

After the sting episode, the last lecture seemed to go quickly. When they were preparing to leave, Douglas, Wayne and Bergie made certain they were the first person in each rank. That way, there would be no one to kick up dust at them when they marched to the main camp.

The conversation on the way back wasn't about the heat or the fact they would hit the showers when they returned. It was mainly about hospitals and Danyluk's story about the nurse fainting. East told Danyluk that people "with long dongs, don't live as long as people who are built normally." Danyluk looked really worried until Jackson pointed out, that if what East said was true, people with "short dongs would live longer."

"You've all heard of Superman, well just call me Superdong," said Danyluk. "Bergie, you're going to live a long life."

"Maybe it's the other way 'round?" said Wayne.

The Corporal overheard the conversation and now he got involved. "Oh, for Christ's sake, let's change the subject!"

"Now see what you've gone and done, Danyluk," Douglas remarked. "You've got the Corporal worried."

"He'll live a long life, too." Those were Danyluk's last words as he grinned all the way back to camp.

As the platoon crossed the highway, the only person who wasn't laughing was the Corporal. He had a puzzled look on his face, like he was concerned.

"I'd check it out Corporal," East said, turning his head slightly and winking at the rest of them before looking at the sky with a smirk a mile wide.

Three other companies used the same mess hall as Charlie Company and they hadn't finished training when Charlie was dismissed. This gave everyone in the company an opportunity to have a quick wash and be first in line when it opened.

As usual, East was at the front of the line, keeping a space for the other Musketeers. When they arrived and butted in, Danyluk's job was to stop the bitching coming from the cadets standing behind them.

Being first in the mess hall meant the cadets from Charlie were first out. This gave them the privilege of being first in the Cadet Canteen after they had prepared their uniforms for the following day.

After dinner, B-21 was alive with activity. Cadets from all platoons were working as teams washing their clothes and finishing off various tasks that hadn't been completed earlier.

Douglas and Wayne had showers before they scrubbed their shorts and shirts, taking them over to the porch of a nearby signals lecture hut to dry. Before long, they were ironing and starching them for the following day. They took Sergeant Beckford's advice and only wore their P.T. strip in the evening. That way their personal gear would always be clean.

While Wayne shined their wash-basins, Douglas put Khaki-It on their one-inch web-belts and brushed them until they shone. Then he shined the brass buckles and the brass at the end of the belts.

They were both scrubbing their pith-helmets under the taps when Douglas noticed Jackson, limping.

"What happened to you?" he asked.

Jackson took off his running shoe. "I've got an ingrown toenail and I don't know if I can take this marching any longer."

Douglas and Wayne both looked at it. "Jesus," Wayne said. "You'd better report on Sick-Parade tomorrow, that looks pretty bad."

Jackson sat on the sink, blowing air on his toe. "I think I'd be O.K., if my boots fit. What if they send me home?"

Bergie was just coming out of the showers when he heard Jackson. "They won't send you home just for having an ingrown toenail. The torture of this place is worse than the torture you're going through. They won't deprive you of that."

Jackson smiled because of what Bergie said and the fact that everyone around him was starting to limp, including the Corporal who just happened to be passing by.

"STAND BY YOUR BEDS!" Sergeant Beckford was in the barracks and he was speaking to the whole wing.

"I HAVE PART ONE AND PART TWO ORDERS IN MY HAND. I'M GOING TO POST THEM ON THE BULLETIN BOARD AND I WANT ALL OF YOU TO READ THEM. IS THAT CLEAR?"

"YES, SERGEANT!"

"CARRY ON!"

"We could spend our whole lives reading the junk on this bulletin board. What the hell do we need a second set of Part One and Part Two orders for?" asked East.

"These are Company Orders," Bergie replied. "They list the responsibility our platoon has in the barracks."

East started reading. "Our platoon's got the washing area to look after this week until next Monday. Guess what our section has got, guys?"

The other Musketeers gave him a curious look.

"We've got the urinal to look after."

Danyluk pushed him aside. "Christ, are you serious? I'm not putting my hands in that."

East was nose-to-nose with Danyluk. "What's the matter, are you afraid of getting your lily-white paws dirty? We all know you've had 'em in worse places than that."

Banks couldn't resist the opportunity. "Yeah, like in your girlfriend's bra!"

Danyluk grabbed Bank's T-shirt and then let go. "I'll have you know my girlfriend's bra smells like the petals of a rose on a summer's day."

Douglas walked toward them still shining a belt buckle. He'd heard all the banter while sitting on his bunk. "I'll bet that's right. The closest you ever get to your girlfriend's bra is when you sneak it off her clothesline to show all your buddies."

"Jealous creeps," Danyluk muttered, as he headed for the 'jon' to check out the size of the job.

Later, after all the chores were done, the six of them went over to the Cadet

Canteen, and Douglas bought Wayne a Kik-Kola. They were surprised that the place was full already.

Wayne saw Lyons. "Hey, we had a head start working on our barracks, how come you Driver-Mech types are over here so early?"

Lyons was wearing his 'know it all' look. "Our officers and NCOs are not nearly as tough on us as yours are. They've given us every evening off for the whole week, just like Signals. We've also heard a rumour that you guys are going to be the guard."

Wayne looked amazed. "You lucky stiffs. Who told you that we're going to be the guard?"

"That's the rumor going around. You know what that means? It means hundreds of hours on the parade square and hundreds of hours preparing your kit."

Danyluk stomped his foot down and assumed the position of attention. "Christ, more work?"

All of a sudden, Foster ran in. "Hey guys, guess what?"

"Don't tell us, let me guess," said Bergie. "Scheaffer's pregnant?"

Foster tried to catch his breath. "No, but he's been promoted to Sergeant."

No one said a word for at least five seconds. They were all looking at each other. Banks was the first one to speak. "Promoted to Sergeant? He was only a Lance-Corporal two days ago?"

Foster nodded. "And he's still got his cold."

"I'll bet he has," said Banks. "Jesus, if he can manage to get pneumonia, he'll leave camp as a General."

"No, just the flu will do that," said Douglas.

Lyons laughed so hard, he knocked over Douglas' Kik-Kola and it ran down Danyluk's leg. Not one of them had seen Danyluk move so fast in his life. He was swearing to himself as he went to get a rag to wipe himself off.

"It would have been worse if you still had your diapers on," quipped Wayne.

When they left the canteen, Douglas and Wayne walked over to the east fence. The sun going down in the west was shining on the hills across the valley. Douglas couldn't believe how beautiful the landscape looked. The silhouettes were striking, and to him, the scene was absolutely magnificent.

A gentle breeze flowed through the barracks as they returned and started working on their boots. Shortly, the duty bugler could be heard playing The Last Post. Had they still been outside, they would have heard it echoing in the nearby hills.

Although some cadets were still running around, most of them were working. Everyone had had a shower and Danyluk stood guard next to the urinal. He had a broom at the slope arms. "Make it quick and keep it clean," he 'advised.'

"STAND BY YOUR BEDS!"

The command was loud as Sergeant Beckford walked down the aisle, checking the bed-spaces. The usual excuses could be heard by cadets who were covering for their buddies. Before leaving the barracks, he informed them of what was expected of them the next morning.

"DON'T LET ME DOWN! LIGHTS OUT IN TEN MINUTES! DANYLUK, TURN THAT DAMN RADIO OFF!"

After Beckford left, Danyluk said. "Did you guys hear that? He actually called me by my name. He knows my name." Danyluk stood there with his chest out. He was proud that Sergeant Beckford knew his name without having to read his nametag.

"Poor you," said Bergie. "Most people don't want their names to be known."

The next sound heard was Danyluk's chest deflating.

Bergie must have felt guilty saying that to Danyluk. "I was only joking. It's alright for him to know your name."

"Screw you, Bergie. Now I'm going to be up all night wondering if he should know my name. What's the matter with you, Bergie?"

"Oh, you'll get to sleep, quit worrying about it."

"No, I won't get to sleep."

"Quit worrying, you'll get to sleep!'

"No, I won't!"

After the lights were out, Wayne leaned over. "We forgot to phone the girls tonight."

"I thought you phoned them earlier?"

"I was going to but I had my hands in the urinal and I was enjoying my work so much, I forgot about it."

"Hey, did you guys know we missed mug-up? There's bread and jam and cocoa and......" East was thinking about food again.

Jackson butted in. "Jeez, East, don't you ever think of anything but your stomach?"

East was still rambling on. "I won't miss it tomorrow night!"

Douglas rolled on his side. "Good night, Wayne."

"Good night, Doug."

Douglas closed his eyes, but he couldn't get to sleep. Danyluk was snoring too loud.

It is said that only the army can bring people together and get them working as a team in a short period of time.

Over the next four days, that's exactly what happened to the cadets of Charlie Company. Cadets and company staff alike started to get to know each other by name. In addition, routines were set up so that everyone knew their individual responsibilities. Both staff and cadets worked very hard that first week to ensure that the remaining weeks ran smoothly.

Although Mail-Call was a little bit sparse at times, a few letters were distributed and enough money was received so that a Kik-Kola was always available. Danyluk, of course, started charging interest, but no one complained because the price of a Kik was only five cents.

When cadets complained that the weather was horrendously hot, they were told, "You ain't seen nothin' yet." This usually kept them on their toes. Rumours of temperatures as high as 120 degrees persisted throughout the camp. When East complained it was too hot to do any work in temperatures as high as ninety-five degrees, he was told to start getting grouchy if it rose by another thirty degrees. "Then someone might listen to you."

During the first five days of training, the whole camp, except Signals, was confined to the perimeter of the base. No one in Charlie complained, they thought Signals cadets dressed like slobs anyway.

The food was good and the Cadet Canteen was busy during lunchtime and evenings, serving pop, chocolate bars, popsicles, potato chips and whatever sundry materials the cadets required; i.e., shoe polish, soap, shampoo, etc.

Kit exchanges took place every day and all of the cadets looked decent on parade. At the start, improvement was still needed in the way they washed and ironed their clothes, but it didn't take long before everyone was using the 'Beckford system.'

Spirits were high in Charlie Company even though rumours persisted they were going to be the guard. Those rumours were quickly dismissed, because they only had two periods of drill a day. The rest of the time was taken up with lectures on Map-Using, Section-Tactics, Instructional Technique, Leadership, Military Writing, and Weapons.

The P.T. they received every morning included push-ups, sit-ups, nearly anything that would get city boys looking like their muscular country counterparts.

It was learned that Sergeant Simpson was the Drill and Discipline Instructor at Royal Roads Military College. Therefore, when he entered the barracks each morning at 0600 and softly said, "STAND BY YOUR BEDS," he didn't have to say it the second time. They wanted him to know they were just as good as the students at Royal Roads, if not better.

Every cadet also got used to the command STAND BY YOUR BEDS! The nighttime excuses heard at the start of the week disappeared. Now all of them stood at the foot of their bunks, or they were in bed. Even cadets using the toilets finished up and washed their hands within seconds, rushing to stand by their beds.

Time flew by so fast during the first week, that Friday morning rolled around fairly quickly. They were told that the whole camp was confined to barracks on Friday nights, so that their kit and barracks would be in tip-top shape for Saturday Morning Inspection. The parade would be held on Sicily Square, the parade square not far from their barracks. The Camp Commanding Officer, Lieutenant-Colonel St. Laurent, would inspect them for the first time, that day. Rumour had it that he was a brother or a relative of the present Prime Minister of Canada, Louis St. Laurent. They were also told that he was a good soldier, a very fair man, and that he was approachable.

It was the Camp Regimental Sergeant-Major they were concerned about most of all. His name was Gardiner. His regiment was the Princess Patricia's Canadian Light Infantry and the Musketeers heard that he ate cadets for breakfast, lunch and supper. "Probably Mug-up too!" East told Jackson.

It didn't matter if it was morning or afternoon, the heat on the hill in the upper camp took its toll on the cadets of Charlie Company, who had to sit on the burned grass and take lectures on the .303 rifle.

The only time they felt any breeze whatsoever was when they peeled through the rifle-stores and each cadet picked up a rifle and sling, two magazines, two clips of dummy-rounds and a cleaning kit.

The ground was cracked from the constant ferocity of the sun's rays as they sat in semicircles learning how to check the rifle, strip and clean it, and how to hold it properly for firing.

After only two periods, each cadet looked like he had crossed the Sahara on foot, until the pop truck rolled into the training area. At that point, they came back to life again.

The cadets who were broke lined up at the watertaps and it was surprising they didn't drink the city's reservoir dry.

Douglas borrowed some money from Danyluk and bought Wayne a pop. Then he looked at the surrounding countryside. He could see the hills in the distance and the large mountain to the north of them. Bergie told him it was Silver Star Mountain.

"You know, I'd like to live here," he said to Wayne.

Wayne took off his beret and wiped this brow with his arm. "In this heat? You've got to be out of your mind."

Douglas pointed toward the town. "Living here wouldn't be like this. The only reason we're hot is because we're stuck on this hill."

Wayne didn't bother answering him. He just shook his head and relished every drop of the cold pop, rhythmically holding the bottle against his forehead after each gulp.

While they were having their break, cadets from Signals Company were sitting in line-laying vehicles, making fun of the 'grunts' who had to dig trenches and crawl on the ground.

"Just look at those lucky bastards," said Banks. "Why in the hell did we sign up for this course?"

Douglas didn't answer. He spotted Foster climbing up a telephone pole.

"HEY, FOSTER, IT'S ABOUT TIME YOU STARTED EARNING YOUR KEEP."

Foster waved and cupped his hands to his mouth. "HAVE YOU GUYS HEARD THAT SERGEANT SCHEAFFER HAS BEEN AWARDED THE V.D. AND SCAR?"

Foster was spoofing the Victoria Cross decoration and Bar.

Wayne got involved. "THERE'S NO BAR ON THE VICTORIA CROSS! AT LEAST I DON'T THINK THERE IS?"

Foster shrugged. "You know what I mean!"

Both Douglas and Wayne waved. They knew only too well.

Danyluk approached them, drinking his Kik-Kola. "Scheaffer should be awarded a medal for having to put up with Genova."

"For Christ's sake," said Wayne. "He's been promoted to Sergeant. Foster's right though, he'll probably end up getting the V.D. and scar!"

"WHAT'S THE COURSE LIKE?" Douglas asked.

"I'M LEARNING MY CRAFT!" Foster replied.

Wayne looked puzzled. "WHAT THE HELL ARE YOU TALKING ABOUT? WHAT CRAFT?"

Foster was laughing so hard, the spikes attached to his boots nearly slipped out of the telephone pole.

"CRAFT MEANS, CAN'T REMEMBER A FUCKING THING!"

After the morning's lectures, the march back to camp for lunch went smoother than usual because they knew they were going to have their first swim parade that afternoon."

"There's two beaches," said Bergie. "We'll either be going to Kal Beach or Kin Beach."

"Is there a difference?" asked Wayne.

"There sure is. Kal beach is at Kalamalka Lake, where all of the dames are, and Kinsmen Beach is at the end of Okanagan Lake. There's no broads there."

Danyluk's ears perked up. "Jeez, I hope we go to Kal Beach."

The Corporal laughed. "For the first time since you arrived in camp, Danyluk, I actually agree with you."

Danyluk looked at the Corporal. "Stick with me, Corporal and you won't go wrong. I'll have all the dames waving their bras at you when we leave. Just think of it guys. Women, bras, legs, lips...? I can't stand it any longer," he said, raising his arms to the sky.

Wayne looked at Douglas. "When we find out which beach we're going to, let's phone Diane and Debbie. Maybe they can meet us there."

Danyluk grabbed his crotch. "Have they got any friends with bikinis? C'mon, say they have. SAY THEY HAVE!"

Wayne smiled. "They have. They're bringing a girl just for you. Her name is Hilda Schwartz and if you don't mind kissing a harelip, you'll have it made."

"I don't care if she's got three harelips as long as she's built." Danyluk was now out of step; it took him three tries to get in step when the Corporal gave him a blast.

Douglas whispered to Wayne. "Maybe we should ask them to bring some friends with them?"

Wayne nodded. He was still looking at Danyluk. Ever since he mentioned Hilda Schwartz, Danyluk had kept the usual silly smile on his face. When they arrived back at their barracks, he took fifteen minutes looking at himself in the mirror before they washed for lunch. Then at lunch, he was the perfect gentleman.

"It's amazing what the thought of a dame can do for Danyluk," East said, filling his pockets with cookies.

After lunch Sergeant Beckford entered the barracks.

"STAND BY YOUR BEDS AND PAY ATTENTION HERE!"
"RIGHT! THERE HAVE BEEN COMPLAINTS FROM THE CITY OF VER-
NON THAT THEY ARE FED UP WITH CADETS LEAVING THEIR UNDER-
WEAR AND SOCKS ALL OVER KAL BEACH!"
Douglas and Wayne both glanced at each other. They now knew which beach
they were going to.
"TO COUNTER THIS, YOU WILL NOT WEAR ANY UNDERSHORTS OR
SOCKS. ALL YOU WILL WEAR IS A T-SHIRT, YOUR P.T. SHORTS, AND
YOUR RUNNING SHOES."
"YOU WILL CARRY YOUR BATHING SUIT IN A TOWEL AND
CHANGE THERE. IS THAT CLEAR?"
"YES, SERGEANT!"
Jackson had his arm extended. He wanted to ask a question.
"YES JACKSON?"
"Sergeant, why can't we wear our swimsuits under our P.T. shorts?"
Beckford glowered down at him. "Do I look like a walking encyclopedia?"
"Yes, Sergeant...I mean...no, Sergeant!"
"WELL, DON'T ASK SUCH SILLY, IDIOTIC QUESTIONS! ISN'T IT
OBVIOUS?"
"I WANT THIS PLATOON ON THE ROAD AT 1325! THE TRUCKS WILL
BE HERE AT 1330!"
After Beckford left, Jackson walked over to Bergie. "What was silly about my
question?"
"I don't have a clue, Earl. Apparently in the past, companies have just been
dropping everything on the beach and running into the water. Maybe they want to
control it by having everyone use the changing rooms?"
As Jackson was taking off his socks, Douglas saw his ingrown toenail.
"Jeez, Earl, that's starting to fester. When are you going to go to the MIR?"
[Medical Inspection Room]
Jackson limped to open his barrack-box. "I was going to go on Sick-Parade this
morning but I don't want them to send me home."
"We told you. They won't send you home just because you've got an ingrown
toenail."
"But what if they do?"
"They won't! Go tomorrow, O.K.?"
Earl nodded. He wasn't too fussy about going, but he now realized he couldn't
let his toe get any worse.

As the trucks pulled up in front of B-21, Charlie Company was already on
parade and ready to board.
All of them were happy because they didn't have to wear any headdress. All
they had was a towel with their swimsuit wrapped inside.
Danyluk brought his portable radio with him, and Tony Bennett was singing
Rags to Riches. The cadets within earshot of Danyluk had to listen to his version

of the song, "Hags To Bitches."

As they climbed on board the trucks, Bergie boarded first. He had made certain of this, by being the platoon's Right Marker.

"DOUG, GUYS, TRY TO GET YOURSELF A SEAT!" he called.

It was too late. The rest of the Musketeers were in the middle rank, at the end of the platoon. When they boarded their truck, there was standing room only.

When the trucks passed the guardroom, cadets from Number Ten Platoon acknowledged the 'smiling' Provost Corporals, standing at the bottom of the stairs. "HI, MEATHEADS!" This started a chain reaction and other audacious comments were unleashed in the direction of the shack. When the Provost Sergeant appeared, there was instant silence. The cadets only had smiles on their quiet 'innocent' faces.

The ride to Kalamalka beach took only about ten to fifteen minutes. The trucks travelled the normal route, down the hill, turning right past Polson Park and then out to the winding highway which passed by the golf course that could be seen from the camp.

As the convoy drove by the high school next to Polson Park, summer students started to wave. A lot were girls so the sound of hoots and whistles coming from the trucks became louder.

Then it happened. The cadets sitting on the side benches of the trucks had organized a 'show parade.' On a given signal, they pulled down the P.T. shorts of the ones standing up. Each standing cadet now had his shorts down around his ankles, and he couldn't pull them up because boots were firmly implanted in the crotch. The trucks turned and there was chaos in the backs of them as the cadets let go of the overhead frames, to try to cover themselves up.

Danyluk went flying, bare ass to the breeze, and landed on a Chinese cadet who didn't assist him because he was too busy keeping his feet on the crotch of the shorts of the cadet standing in front of him.

Amidst the roar of laughter from within the trucks and from the students outside, Douglas tried like hell to pull his pants up. It was impossible, and he ended up on top of East, lying face down on the floorboards.

Banks stuck his bare bottom in someone's face and was pushed to the other side of the truck. The opposite cadet was fiercely trying to keep someone's pants down and received the full force of Wayne's crotch in his face. When he was pushed back, Wayne ended up sitting on Danyluk's bare crotch thus adding more weight to the Chinese cadet who sent both of them flying over to the other side again.

Jackson thought the whole thing was funny, until he got hit with the full force of a knee, against his 'covering' hand. With eyes crossed, he slowly sank to the floor.

After they had passed the high school, the 'shows' were allowed to pull up their P.T. shorts. Most of the cadets sitting were bent over with laughter. They couldn't care less about the cadets standing with red faces.

"SON OF A BITCH! East, take a look at my ass, will ya? I don't know what I hit but it's sore as hell." Danyluk was still on the floor of the truck next to the cab, trying to get up so that East could tell him what was wrong. He was upset for two reasons. The first being he had a sore behind and most of all, he'd missed seeing all of the girls.

East took a look. "You've got a lump the size of an egg on the left side of your ass."

That made Danyluk more furious as he pulled up his shorts, rubbing his rear-end at the same time. "YOU PONGOES MADE ME MISS THE ACTION!"

As the trucks wound their way along the highway, the occupants could see the huts of the camp on the hill across from the golf course. Some cadets wearing pith-helmets were taking bearings with their prismatic compasses.

Danyluk spotted them first. "EAT YOUR HEARTS OUT!" He was back to normal although he was still rubbing his backside.

When the trucks were unloaded, Charlie Company was formed into three ranks. It embarrassed the cadets a little because some of the children playing nearby made fun of them.

Danyluk licked his lips. "Look at all of the broads. This is smorgasbord!"

The cadets were formed up facing the water. As they looked around at the packed beach, there were girls everywhere. The colour of the water looked crystal green as it washed up on the white sandy shore.

"NOW PAY ATTENTION HERE! I DON'T WANT THESE CIVILIANS BOTHERED. ALSO, EVEN IF THERE ARE LIFEGUARDS ON DUTY, I WANT YOU TO USE THE BUDDY SYSTEM. KEEP YOUR EYE ON YOUR BUDDIES, PEOPLE. WE HAVEN'T SENT ANYONE HOME IN A COFFIN YET AND WE DON'T INTEND TO! IS THAT CLEAR?"

"YES, SERGEANT!"

"I'M NOT GOING TO FALL YOU OUT FORMALLY. GET IN THERE AND HAVE SOME FUN, YOU'VE EARNED IT!"

That's all they wanted to hear. Every cadet in Charlie Company ran for the changing rooms. In seconds the beach was crammed with 'battle weary' cadets running into the water. Douglas and the other Musketeers swam out to the float. Between pushing themselves off the sides of the float, and diving from the high board, it wasn't long before every memory of camp was behind them. As far as they were concerned, this was Heaven.

Five of them were lying on their stomachs getting a suntan when they heard East shouting. He was eating a hot dog waving, standing next to Diane and Debbie. The girls were waving as well, and as Wayne had asked, they had brought some friends with them.

Swimming to the beach, Wayne and Douglas pointed out that Diane and Debbie were 'out of bounds,' a military term meaning 'stay away.'

Douglas was a little shy when he saw Diane again; so was she. Wayne, however, grabbed Debbie's arm and they spread out the blanket she had brought.

Danyluk was introduced to a girl called Alma Thornton. No sooner had she said hello, he had his arm around her and was leading her away from the crowd. She was a tall girl, nearly bigger than Danyluk, but that didn't phase him a bit because he was more interested in Alma's 'fully stacked' bathing suit.

"Jeez, he sure doesn't waste any time, does he?" Bergie remarked.

Within minutes, four of the couples had gone their own way and Wayne and Douglas were lying next to Diane and Debbie.

"I like your bathing suit," Douglas said, mainly just for something to say.

Diane was still shy. She didn't know what to say and looked anywhere but at him. Finally, she gained her composure. "Would you like me to put some of this suntan lotion on your back?"

Douglas couldn't believe how good it felt. When she first squeezed it on, he shivered a little. But her hands were smooth and he thought he was in Shanri-La.

Facing Wayne, without making a sound, he moved his lips. "Is this really happening to me?"

Wayne smiled and nodded. He was getting the same treatment.

"Would you put some on me?" Diane asked and she lay on her stomach.

Although she was wearing a one-piece bathing suit, her back was open. It seemed to take him a lifetime to smooth out the lotion on it. During the operation he winked at Wayne who was already rubbing lotion on Debbie's legs and grinning like a Cheshire cat.

When Diane said, "Would you do my legs, too?" Douglas' elbow slipped from the shock of the question and his chin hit her back.

"I'm sorry," he said, trying to hide his anticipation.

"That's alright," she replied. Both girls were giggling as Wayne and Douglas tried hard to conceal their look of pure delight.

Nothing was said for the next half hour as the four soaked up the warm Okanagan sun; the same sun Douglas had cursed, less than three hours earlier.

Diane suggested that she and Douglas should go for a walk across the highway and sit on top of the hill. As they climbed, she took told of his hand and never let go.

The panoramic view was something to behold as they surveyed the lake and the surrounding countryside. Douglas was lost for words, the scenery was so beautiful. The closest thing he could compare it to was movies he'd seen about Jasper, Alberta.

"I've never seen anything like this before. You must love living here?" he asked.

Diane put on an astonished look. "Oh, come on? I've seen pictures of the coast. Do you really think this compares with that?"

"Nothing compares with this," he replied.

"See the Lookout up there?" she said, pointing to Highway 97 on the west side of the lake. "There's a sign saying from that point, the view from there is the eighth scenic wonder of the world."

Douglas nodded his head automatically. "I believe it," he said softly, staring at the highway and then into her eyes. They were blue and they matched the aqua-blue colour of her swimsuit. Her long, dark-brown hair glistened as it rested on her shoulders.

Diane turned her head away when their eyes met. "Do you have a girlfriend?"

Douglas shook his head. "No, I, er, I had a date with a girl once, but that's as far...no, no I don't. Do you have a boyfriend?"

"No. My mom and dad watch me pretty closely. I met this boy in school last year, but when I took him home, my dad didn't like him."

When Diane smiled, Douglas noticed she had a dimple. She was radiant and he felt so wonderful being with her.

"He was a creep anyway," she said.

"Why?"

"I think he was a bit like your friend Danychuck, or whatever his name is? All he wanted to do was to get me in the bedroom."

"What's wrong with that?" After he said it, he didn't know why it came out that way. "I, er...I didn't, I didn't mean it that way."

Diane squeezed his hand. "But that's what you said?"

"I think what I was about to say, is, er......"

Diane didn't let him finish. "That point over there is called Rattlesnake Point. Apparently there used to be a lot of rattlesnakes on it but they turned some pigs loose to clean them out."

Douglas breathed easier when she changed the subject.

"Also, there's a bay over there called Cosens Bay. It's difficult to get in there by land, but my dad has a boat and we go there to picnic sometimes."

He strained his neck to see the beach at Cosens Bay, but he couldn't.

"Would you like to come with us some weekend?" she asked.

"Sure, but what if your dad doesn't like me, either?"

"My dad will like you. Don't worry, silly," she replied, tickling him on his waist.

When he tried to grab her hands, his arms were around her. She was leaning back and looking into his eyes. He kissed her and she wrapped her arms around him.

Nothing else seemed to matter at that moment. The clatter coming up from the beach stopped, the sound of traffic stopped and the world stopped. The only thing Douglas could hear was the sound of his heart.

Diane nudged him up. "I think we had better get back to the beach?" Her shy smile revealed the dimple again as she held out her hand to help him up.

When they arrived back at the blanket, all of the Musketeer couples were there. Somebody had bought french fries and pop for everyone. Everyone except East. He and Shirley had never left the concession stand for more than a few minutes at a time. Shirley seemed to love eating just as much as East. Douglas chuckled at the thought of it being love at first bite.

Danyluk had his arm around Alma and he kept slipping it downward. Alma also had her arm around him, but her other hand lifted his arm up.

"This has got to be the greatest day of my life. I......"

The loudspeaker cut Danyluk off.

"ALL CADETS FROM CHARLIE COMPANY WILL BE ON THE ROAD IN

TEN MINUTES!"

Douglas looked at Diane. "We've got to go and get changed."

"When will I see you again?" she asked.

"We're confined to barracks tonight, but we've got Saturday afternoon and all day Sunday off."

"Would you like to come and meet my mom and dad?"

"Sure, if you don't think they'll bite my head off."

He was talking to her as he was walking to the changing room. She walked beside him, as if she didn't want him to go.

After the company had formed up, the girls stood watching them. When they boarded the trucks and started to pull away, Diane waved wildly. "WILL YOU CALL ME?"

"YOU BET! I'LL CALL YOU AFTER SUPPER, O.K.?"

Diane stood on the highway waving. Just before the trucks turned out of sight, she blew him a kiss and he caught it.

The ride back to camp was quiet. Each cadet in the truck was locked up in his own thoughts. Danyluk's radio was picking up the Theme From Moulin Rouge and the song didn't help matters any.

"What was the name of the girl you were with, Earl?" Douglas asked Jackson.

Earl winced. He had taken his running shoe off and he was looking at his toe. "Her name's Tammy."

Douglas looked at it. "Jesus, that's getting worse. We're going to the MIR when we get back.! Alright?"

Earl gave a slight nod. He didn't want to go but he couldn't stand the pain anymore.

As the trucks pulled up in front of B-21, Sergeant Beckford was standing there in civilian clothes.

"PAY ATTENTION HERE! YOU'VE GOT AN HOUR BEFORE SUPPER. I WANT YOU TO RELAX AND TAKE THE WEIGHT OFF YOUR FEET! BE ON THIS ROAD IN THREE RANKS IN P.T. GEAR AT 1800!"

While the rest of the cadets were running into the barracks, Douglas and Jackson walked up to the Sergeant. "Excuse me please, Sergeant. Jackson, here, has a really bad ingrown toenail. Can I take him to the hospital?"

Sergeant Beckford was going to ask him why Jackson couldn't go by himself, but he noticed the sincerity in Douglas' voice.

"Is it bad?"

"Yes, Sergeant," Douglas replied. Jackson's face showed the pain he was in.

"You'll be O.K., son. Alright, get to it but I want you back here shortly!"

When Douglas returned to the hut, not much was going on. Some cadets were lying on their bunks reading, while others were having a shower or washing and ironing their clothes.

Danyluk was once again guarding the urinal as Douglas walked in. The washing machine was full. Cadets in the other platoons still hadn't learned that the best method was to scrub them and then take turns watching them dry. Any other process didn't work, because cadets who hung clothes in the drying room usually returned to find them missing. Danyluk found that out. He had washed his three pairs of undershorts and hung them in the drying room. When he returned, there were three pairs of undershorts hanging there alright, but they weren't his and they were dirty. Some cadet had exchanged his dirty shorts for Danyluk's and left a note saying, 'Thank You.' In most cases a note wasn't left, but this thief must have had a sense of humour.

"SON OF A BITCH," echoed throughout the barracks. Wayne noticed Danyluk's plight and loaned him a new pair he had brought from home. He told Danyluk he wanted them back, and then on second thought told him to keep them.

Stealing was now going on in the barracks and it was hard to stop. It wasn't happening with Nine Platoon though, because Sergeant Beckford had them working as a team. As far as the other three platoons were concerned, the barracks was an open house. The cadets in those platoons hadn't heard Sergeant Beckford's lecture about how they treat 'barrack-room thieves' in the Regular Force.

"We cover their heads with blankets and then walk them down the aisle, or through 'the gauntlet' as it is called. Not too many of them end up on their feet afterward and if officer asks them what happened, they usually tell him they fell down a flight of stairs. You may think we're cruel, but it sure cures the problem."

When the company was formed up in three ranks on the road at 1800, the CSM no one liked called them to attention.

"TOMORROW MORNING, CHARLIE COMPANY WILL BE THE BEST TURNED OUT COMPANY ON THE COMMANDING OFFICER'S PARADE. IN ADDITION, YOUR BARRACKS WILL BE THE BEST IN CAMP!"

"TO ACCOMPLISH THIS, YOU WILL ENSURE TONIGHT THAT ALL OF YOUR CLOTHING IS WASHED, PRESSED AND LOOKING LIKE IT WAS BRAND NEW! YOUR PITH-HELMETS WILL BE SCRUBBED AND I WANT YOUR BOOTS LOOKING LIKE MINE!"

Bergie got a kick out of the CSM's last statement. "Everyone knows he has them shined by the cadets who are incarcerated in the guardroom," he said.

"FURTHERMORE, THE CADET CANTEEN WILL BE CLOSED UNTIL 2100 AND ALL OTHER AREAS OF THE CAMP ARE OUT OF BOUNDS UNTIL THIS COMPANY IS FINISHED!"

Douglas thought he had better phone Diane during the supper hour if the phones were off limits until 2100.

"EACH INDIVIDUAL PLATOON HAS BARRACK RESPONSIBILITIES, SO I'LL KNOW WHO LET US DOWN IF THE INSPECTING OFFICER GIVES US DEMERIT POINTS IN CERTAIN LOCATIONS TOMORROW MORNING!"

"IS THAT CLEAR?"

"YES, SIR!"

"GOOD! CHARLIE COMPANY, DIS...MISSED!"

"That creep is the only one who leaves us at attention when he talks to us," Danyluk said showing his fist to the back of the Sergeant-Major who was walking away. "He should attend some of the lectures we've been taking on Man-Management."

Banks also gave the Sergeant-Major's back a sign, only it wasn't a fist, it was a finger. "He probably wouldn't be able to because he can't read or write. He's just an ignorant man and you know what Sergeant Beckford says we should do about ignorant people? We should ignore them."

"How do you know he can't read or write?" asked East.

Wayne gave East his know-it-all look. "I was only joking. But does he look to you like he can read or write?"

"No."

"Well then?"

East had his arm around Danyluk's shoulder as they rushed back into the barracks. The two of them were laughing, making other remarks about CSM Walsh.

The CSM's 'talk' made Charlie Company the last company to enter the lineup for meal parade that night. Although East was bitching there wouldn't be any good food left, he held spaces for Douglas and Wayne in the never-ending line, until they returned from phoning the girls.

"Hello, is Diane there please?"

"Who's calling?" a very pleasant female voice asked.

"Er, it's er...Doug Brice, from the camp."

"Just hold on Douglas, I'll get her."

Douglas heard the phone being put down and a voice saying, "Diane, Douglas is on the phone."

Within seconds Diane lifted it up.

"Hello?"

"Hi! It's...it's Doug."

Her voice was soft. "Hi. I was waiting for your call."

Douglas smiled. "We're confined to the camp tonight, but I just thought I'd call and ask if we can get together tomorrow?"

"Sure. I told my mom and dad about you."

"What did they say?"

"My mom said she wants to meet you and my dad just grunted. That's his way of saying he probably wants to meet you. When the trucks left the beach, I missed you."

"You did? I guess...I...well I missed you, too."

Diane laughed. "I also couldn't stop thinking about you," she said.

"Me, too!"

There was a pause before Diane spoke again. "Do you know what Alma told me?"

"Who's Alma?" he asked.

"You know? The girl I introduced to Danychuck."

"Oh her? You mean Danyluk?"

"Yeah. Anyway, she said he told her he was the best cadet in the company and that he has to help everyone else out."

"He told her that?"

"Yes. Isn't it true?"

"Well...he's pretty good, but...I don't know if he's...!"

"He also said he was going to buy her a ring and now she wants to get him one as well."

"He'd only wear it in his nose."

"You're just protecting him, aren't you?"

"No, er...well I'd better be going now."

"Where should we meet you guys?" she asked.

"How about Polson Park at one o'clock?"

"O.K. I'll be thinking of you again tonight, Doug."

Wayne was outside the booth, looking in. He was the next one to use the phone in a lineup of twenty cadets. Douglas turned away so that Wayne couldn't hear him.

"I'll be thinking of you, too," he said in a low voice.

"Bye, Doug."

"Bye, Babe."

As he hung up he murmured to himself, "Babe? Why did I call her Babe?"

Walking back to the mess hall, he was still mad at himself for calling Diane, Babe. He couldn't understand where it came from, because he'd never used the word before.

He shrugged. Now she probably thinks I'm some sort of a frump, he thought, as he put his hands in his pockets and kicked a stone.

"YOU! YOU THERE! GET YOUR HANDS OUT OF YOUR POCKETS AND MARCH!"

Wayne laughed. "I've got a feeling someone I know is in love," he said.

When they returned to the mess hall, East was nearly at the bottom of the stairs. There were a few 'comments' from the cadets standing behind him when he let his friends into line.

The conversation at supper was a little more active. Although East was complaining about the food, the rest of the Musketeers missed Jackson and were wondering what was going to happen to him.

"I still say they won't send him home," Bergie said, pointing his fork at Douglas. "Remember, they want us here. We're the future of this country, you've got to recognize that."

Douglas changed the subject. "I hear along the grapevine that you're the best cadet in Charlie Company?" He was looking at Danyluk, who nearly choked when he heard the statement.

Danyluk went red in the face as he cleared his throat. "Well, I didn't want to tell her that I was in charge of the urinal," he said. "What was I supposed to say?"

"You should have just said casually that you were the Sergeant At Arms of the ablution facilities," Bergie said, now pointing his dinner knife at Danyluk.

Danyluk's face lit up. "That's what I'll tell her tomorrow," he replied.

"Do you know what ablution means?" Wayne asked Danyluk.

"No, but it sounds good," Danyluk replied, sticking out his chest. "Ablution sounds like solution, so she'll think I'm the one who solves all the problems. What would I do without you guys?"

No one answered. They all looked amazed. When East said, "Yeah, that's a great idea," three of them broke up.

When the Musketeers entered the barracks, the rest of the guys in the platoon were already at work. They had moved all of the bunks in their platoon from one side of the barracks to the other and were scrubbing the floors. It didn't seem to matter how much soap and water was smeared, the floor was still a dirty brownish-black colour and a mass of slivers.

"Nobody could get these floors clean," Wayne said, picking up a scrub brush and getting down on his knees. "Too many people have lived here."

Bergie was down next to him. "It doesn't matter. All of the huts are the same way, so we've got to get ours cleaner than the rest."

After they finished one side of their platoon area, all bunks were moved to the other side and the scrubbing process started over again.

After the floors, three sections from Nine Platoon climbed ladders and cleaned the windows outside and in. The other section cleaned the light shades, polished the light fixtures, the fire extinguisher and washed down the shelves.

With their platoon area looked after, they had the centre part of the building to do. That was their 'listed' responsibility, but it was agreed they wouldn't clean the shower room, washing-up room, drying room and toilets until early the next morning. If those areas were cleaned that night, they would be dirty for inspection.

Time flew for everyone. While Nine Platoon was working, the other platoons were cleaning their own platoon areas and their 'listed responsibility areas' such as the smoke pit, the 'gardens,' the inside walls and the outside windows of the centre section.

When B-21 was clean, all of the cadets on Douglas' side of the hut were shown how to fold their bedding, Saturday Morning Inspection Style.

The Corporals showed them how to fold their mattresses and then form a 'sandwich' with their sheets, pillow, pillow-case and blankets.

A blanket was folded so that three folds were facing the front. It was then placed on the folded-up mattress, which held the pillow inside.

Next, each sheet was folded and placed on top of the blanket, with the pillow case folded in between them. Each item had three folds facing the front.

The second blanket was then folded exactly the same as the first and placed on top of the sheets and pillow case. Then the sandwich was completed by folding the third blanket lengthwise and wrapping it around the others, fold to the front.

For the next hour they practised making their beds in this manner. Doing it per-

fectly was painstaking but the Corporals informed them what the inspecting officer would be looking for.

"The sandwich has to be flawless, otherwise they'll knock points off us."

East looked at the Corporal.. "If you ask me, the whole thing is ridiculous."

"Nobody asked you. Have you worked in Ottawa?"

"No, and I don't think I'd want to either."

The Corporal tried to hide his smile after he saw the expression on East's face,
but he couldn't. He was laughing when he told East to get back to work 'folding.'

After the Corporals were certain every cadet knew how to make his bed, they
all worked on their personal kit.

The fuse box would blow now and then, but no one thought of reducing the
number of irons which were being used. Cadets were ironing upon barrack-boxes,
folding tables, folding benches and the floors. The smell of liquid starch filled the
hut.

At nine o'clock the cadets of Nine Platoon were allowed to go over to the canteen. They tripped over each other, trying to be first out the door, but were called
back.

"HOLD IT! YOU KNOW HOW THIS PLACE LOOKS! IT'S UP TO YOU
PEOPLE TO KEEP IT THAT WAY! DON'T BRING ANY FOOD BACK WITH
YOU AND KEEP THE DIRT OUTSIDE! IS THAT CLEAR?

"YES, CORPORAL!"

"O.K., GET OUT OF HERE!"

The Canteen was nearly empty when Charlie Company arrived. Other huts
weren't as well organized. When Douglas and the rest of the Musketeers were sitting having a pop, they could hear NCOs screaming in the huts across the way.
Really to no avail, because cadets were running up and down the aisles, just having fun.

"I'm not sleeping in my bed tonight," said Danyluk.

Wayne looked at him. "Well, you're not sleeping in mine. What do you mean
you're not sleeping in your bed?"

Danyluk looked insulted. "I don't mean that I'm going to sleep in somebody
else's bed, you dummy. I mean I'm going to leave my bed made up and sleep on
the floor. That way I won't have to make it tomorrow."

East stopped eating his chocolate bar for a moment.

"Danyluk, that's the best idea you've had since we arrived! Well, nearly the
best."

Danyluk loved praise. "I know," he said sticking out his chest and smirking.
"I'm not just another pretty face, you know?"

"You can say that again," East shot back. The next sound they would hear was
Danyluk's chest deflating.

Quite a few cadets were already in bed when they returned to their quarters.
Danyluk woke up a cadet who was sleeping on a lower bunk across from him.

"WAKE UP, WAKE UP!"

"What's, what's the matter?" the cadet asked, rubbing his eyes.

Danyluk planted his face inches from the cadet's face. "You've only got eight more hours to sleep."

"Oh, go fuck yourself, Danyluk," the cadet said, rolling over on his side.

Danyluk yielded. "Ya see what ya get for trying to help people?"

"You're a mean bastard," said Wayne.

"Yeah, but I'm a nice mean bastard."

Sergeant Beckford had given his usual speech and was walking out of the barracks when he said, "Good night, guys!"

The cadet who had been woken up, replied, "GOOD NIGHT, MOTHER!"

Instantly, the Sergeant turned the lights back on. "WHO SAID THAT? DANYLUK...DANYLUK, WHERE ARE YOU? STAND BY YOUR BED!"

Although Danyluk had been on the floor asleep and snoring, he stood at the foot of his bunk wiping his eyes.

Sergeant Beckford looked at him, then after realizing it wasn't he who had said it, turned around and switched off the lights again.

"Why me?" Danyluk asked.

Bergie laughed. "Because he knows your name."

After the usual quiet small talk, Danyluk was snoring again. Wayne looked at him. "He's going to wake up in the middle of the night freezing his nuts off."

"No, he won't," East said. "He'll just wrap his foreskin around himself. I just hope he doesn't smother."

Another round of laughter rang around Nine Platoon, but after a few minutes, other snores drowned out Danyluk's .

Douglas got up and threw one of his blankets over Danyluk. Then it wasn't long before he was snoring also. It had been a long day.

Reveille was blown early on Saturday morning. The bugler had barely finished when Sergeant Simpson stomped into the barracks. Most cadets jumped out of bed when they heard his footsteps. They knew if they didn't, their blankets would be pulled down or they would be dumped on the floor along with their mattresses.

Sergeant Simpson fooled them. Instead of marching down the aisle, he stood at the door and never moved.

"STAND BY YOUR BEDS!"

"JUST LOOK AT YOU LAZY LOT! LET'S GET THIS SHOW ON THE ROAD. BREAKFAST IS AT SIX-THIRTY THIS MORNING AND THERE'S A LOT TO DO BEFORE THE PARADE! I EXPECT THIS BARRACKS TO BE IN SHIPSHAPE CONDITION BY THE TIME I RETURN!"

Wayne yawned and stretched as he looked out the window. "We should learn how to play the bugle. I hear the bugler goes back to bed after he sounds Reveille."

Douglas was going to say something about the bugler, but Bergie spoke first.

"Christ, look at Moose!" he yelled.

Danyluk had taken off his undershorts and was straddling down the aisle heading to the showers, with his towel draped over his usual morning erection.

All the cadets in Nine Platoon were laughing at him, so he turned around. "Haven't you ever seen a towel holder before?" he asked.

East could hardly control himself. "We're not looking at that Moose, we're looking at your lily-white ass."

Danyluk was wearing his sneaky smile. "You like it, eh?"

"Not really. Go take a look at it in the mirror."

Danyluk turned and strolled into the washing area. Then he climbed up on the sink-ledge to look at his backside.

"SON OF A BITCH!" The erection disappeared quickly, as he came out with his towel wrapped around his waist.

Although he was smiling, he was trying to see everyone on his side of the wing. "WHO'S THE WISE ASSHOLE?"

Despite the fact it had happened to others, Danyluk had always managed to pick a toilet seat that wasn't covered with shoe polish. This time he had a black horseshoe mark completely covering his rear-end.

Howls continued for about five minutes and got even louder when the rest of the Musketeers and most of Nine Platoon discovered that they had also fallen prey to the 'mad toilet seat painter.'

It took scrub brushes and Sergeant's soap in the showers to correct the situation.

"I'm certain it's someone from Ten Platoon," Danyluk said rubbing his buttocks. "We'll have to get even."

Everything went smoothly that morning. After they had made their beds Saturday Morning Inspection Style, the Musketeers cleaned the centre area of the hut before they went to breakfast. They wore their P.T. strip so their uniforms would look sharp on parade.

Following breakfast, the company formed up on the road and received a lecture from CSM Walsh.

"YOU PEOPLE ARE GOING TO RUN THE SHOW THIS MORNING. IN OTHER WORDS, THERE WILL BE NO REGULAR FORCE STAFF WITH YOU ON THE PARADE. THAT SHOULDN'T BE TOO DIFFICULT BECAUSE YOU HAVE BEEN WATCHING THE PROCEDURE ALL WEEK."

"I WANT EVERYTHING TO COME OFF WITHOUT A HITCH THIS MORNING. THAT MEANS WE'RE GOING TO DO IT WITH CHARLIE COMPANY FLAIR! IS THAT CLEAR?"

"YES, SIR!"

The CSM then started passing out rank insignia which would be worn on the right upper arm. Douglas was made the Cadet Company Sergeant-Major; Banks, a Platoon Sergeant and Bergie was the Company Commander. The rest of the platoon and company positions were filled by other cadets in Nine Platoon and the other three platoons.

Before long, all of the companies in camp were marching on to the parade square behind the band of The Royal Canadian Engineers which had been brought up from Chilliwack for the occasion. The march they were playing was The Standard of Saint George.

The parade square was hot and it was a miracle 1200 cadets managed to form up on it. Actually, there was an overflow and the first platoon of each company ended up standing on the road, with the rest of the company behind them on the parade square.

Within minutes, a long line of Cadet Officers appeared. They had been receiving instructions at the Headquarters Building.

The Battalion Commander for that day was picked from the Driver-Mechanics Company, as was the Second-in-Command and the Battalion Regimental Sergeant-Major.

With the preliminaries over with, the Battalion Commander called the parade to attention and carried on.

"BATTALION, STANDAT...EASE!

"BATTALION, ATTEN......TION! GENERALS SALUTE...SALUTE!"

Although the cadet band was in attendance, the band from Chilliwack played the General Salute and the formalities of the parade continued.

Douglas was standing on the right side of Charlie Company when it was brought to attention for inspection. He was allowed to join and walk behind the inspecting party, which was in pairs: Lieutenant-Colonel St. Laurent and the Cadet Battalion Commander; The Cadet Second-in-Command and the Cadet Company Commander; the Cadet Battalion Regimental Sergeant-Major, and the Cadet Platoon Commander.

As they walked down the front rank, Colonel St. Laurent stopped in front of Danyluk.

"What's your name, son?"

"Cadet Danyluk, Sir!"

"Where are you from, Danyluk?"

Danyluk looked straight to his front. "Vancouver, Sir!"

"What regiment are you with?"

"The British Columbia Regiment, Sir!"

Colonel St. Laurent thought for a moment, before he spoke. "The Dukes?"

"Yes Sir, The Dukes!"

"A fine regiment and a fine turnout. Keep up the good work, Danyluk!"

"Thank you, Sir!"

As the Inspecting Party moved down the rank, Douglas glanced at Danyluk, who winked, keeping his head and eyes straight to his front.

Colonel St. Laurent showed some pity for the cadets standing on the hot parade square. He only stopped about ten times inspecting Charlie Company. When he moved on to the next company, Douglas returned to his position on the right side of the Right Marker of the company.

The total inspection took forty-five minutes. During that time, many cadets passed out because of the heat. They were taken to the sidelines and checked over by personnel from the MIR These cadets were told to remove their pith-helmets and to sit down with their legs drawn back. Then they rested their heads on their knees.

When the inspecting party had completed its tour, Colonel St. Laurent returned
to the Reviewing Stand, so the march-past procedure could begin.

Douglas felt proud marching past the dais. Everyone in the company had been
told to look the Reviewing Officer in the eyes when they were given the command
'Eyes Right'! The Reviewing Officer, in turn, looked each of them in the eye.

After the march-past, the parade was ordered to Stand at Ease and Stand Easy.

Colonel St. Laurent grasped the large microphone stand and said, "GATHER
AROUND ME!"

It only took seconds for the cadets to form a semicircle around him.

"I HAVE HAD THE OPPORTUNITY OF INSPECTING BOTH REGULAR
FORCE AND MILITIA TROOPS AROUND THE WORLD. CONSIDERING
THE SMALL AMOUNT OF DRILL YOU'VE HAD, YOUR PARADE TODAY
WAS ONE OF THE BEST I'VE SEEN.

"THIS IS THE FIRST TIME I'VE TALKED TO YOU SINCE YOU
ARRIVED LAST WEEKEND AND I HAVE BEEN LOOKING FORWARD TO
IT. ALTHOUGH I HAVE MET SOME OF YOU WHILE YOU WERE TRAIN-
ING, IT IS HERE WHEN I SEE THE EXPRESSIONS ON YOUR FACES
THAT I CAN SEE YOU ARE ENJOYING YOUR STAY AT CAMP VER-
NON."

A few grumbles came from the crowd and the Commanding Officer smiled.

"MY STAFF HAVE INFORMED ME THAT ALL OF YOU ARE WORKING
HARD TO ACHIEVE THE AIM OF THE TRAINING PROGRAM. I'M
PROUD OF YOU FOR THAT AND I'M ALSO PROUD THAT THIS GREAT
COUNTRY ALLOWS YOU TO PARTICIPATE IN ONE OF THE FINEST
YOUTH PROGRAMS IN THE WORLD.

"WHILE I WAS INSPECTING YOU, MEMBERS OF MY STAFF HAVE
BEEN INSPECTING YOUR BARRACKS. I HAVE LEARNED FROM THEIR
COMMENTS THAT YOUR QUARTERS ARE ALSO EQUAL TO THIS
SPLENDID PERFORMANCE I HAVE JUST WITNESSED.

"SHORTLY, RSM GARDINER WILL TELL YOU WHICH COMPANY IS
THE BEST IN CAMP SO FAR. I'M GLAD I DIDN'T HAVE TO MAKE THAT
DECISION. THE MARKS ALLOCATED ARE THE TOTAL FOR DRESS,
DEPORTMENT, BEARING, YOUR DRILL AND GOOD INTERIOR-ECONO-
MY IN THE QUARTERS.

"SPEAKING OF QUARTERS, I WOULD LIKE YOU TO KNOW THAT I
HAVE ASKED THE CARPENTERS TO PUT DOORS ON THE TOILETS."

A roar of approval rose from the cadets.

"I PROMISE YOU THAT WE ARE GOING TO MAKE THESE QUARTERS
MORE LIVEABLE. IT MAY TAKE TIME, BUT WE HAVEN'T FORGOTTEN
YOU. PLEASE BEAR WITH US!

"THANK YOU VERY MUCH, CADETS!"

Mister Gardiner stepped forward. "RIGHT! BACK INTO YOUR FORMA-
TIONS!"

After the Advance in Review Order, all cadets were allowed to Stand Easy as the Commanding Officer left the parade square, and Mister Gardiner, grabbed the microphone.

"JUST BECAUSE THE COMMANDING OFFICER SAID NICE THINGS TO YOU, DON'T EXPECT THE SAME FROM ME!"

He took hold of both ends of his handlebar-mustache as he spoke and he looked like he was smiling.

Douglas chuckled as Wayne looked at him and moved his lips. "It's a gas pain, not a smile."

"ACTUALLY, THE PARADE WAS GOOD, HOWEVER, THERE IS ALWAYS ROOM FOR IMPROVEMENT! THEREFORE, WE ARE GONG TO PRACTISE THIS PARADE EVERY MORNING FOR A HALF-HOUR NEXT WEEK!"

More grumbles rolled through the ranks.

"My feet are flat, already," Danyluk said in a low voice.

"THERE HAVE BEEN RUMOURS GOING AROUND THAT CHARLIE COMPANY IS GOING TO BE THE GUARD FOR THE BALANCE OF CAMP. THAT'S NEWS TO ME, BECAUSE I NEVER MADE SUCH A DECISION. AS FAR AS I AM CONCERNED, THE BEST COMPANY ON PARADE TODAY WILL BECOME THE GUARD!"

He glanced at Charlie Company. "SO CHARLIE COMPANY, YOU DON'T HAVE TO WORRY WHEN YOU HEAR SILLY RUMOURS!"

A sigh of relief came from the cadets in Charlie Company as an envelope was passed to the RSM. When he opened it, he once again began playing with the ends of his mustache.

"THE BEST COMPANY ON PARADE TODAY...AND THE BEST COMPANY IN CAMP THIS WEEK, IS......!"

RSM Gardiner's pause was long as he looked around. Every cadet was straining to hear the results. Although a few cars were driving along the highway a hundred yards away, you could hear a pin drop.

"CHARLIE COMPANY!"

Although they knew what they were in for, every cadet in the company cheered and held his helmet in the air. They had done it and they were proud of themselves.

While the cadets from Charlie Company congratulated themselves, on the side of the parade square, the company staff were shaking hands also. Each of them looked like the cat who swallowed the canary. Everyone, that is except Walsh. He just stood there with a smirk that resembled one of Wayne's 'gas pains.'

Danyluk, who had been complaining about his flat feet just minutes before, was jumping up and down.

"THANK YOU. WELL DONE! NOW CARRY ON!"

Douglas' chest was out and his chin was in the air when the company marched back to their quarters. The Regular Force Corporals had joined them now and every so often one of them would speak up.

"WHO ARE WE?"

"CHARLIE COMPANY!" WAS THE RESPONSE.
"WHAT ARE WE?"
"THE BEST!"
Back on the road next to B-21, all of the Officers and Non-Commissioned Officers, congratulated them. The cadets were also informed that they could have a midnight pass if they so desired and there would be a sheet exchange and a Mail-Call after lunch.

As Douglas walked into the barracks to remake his bed, Sergeant Beckford and the Platoon Officer of Nine Platoon were standing side by side, shaking the hands of the cadets who entered. The expressions on their faces said it all. They were proud of their charges.

Charlie Company was allowed into the mess hall first that afternoon. It was a perk they appreciated, because after the Prairie cadets arrived, the lineup was long and winding, and for some reason, Charlie Company always arrived last. East had said many times that the reason for this was that Charlie worked harder in the barracks and most of the Musketeers agreed with him.

Although Camp Orders said cadets must eat in their own respective mess halls, Lyons and Foster joined them for lunch that day.

"Our company was so thankful that we weren't chosen as the guard, we thought we'd come and celebrate with you," Lyons said, patting Banks on the back.

"That was good of you," replied Wayne. "It wouldn't be because we're having roast beef, would it?"

Lyons knew that was the real reason they had come, but he had some other information, also.

"One of our cadets just got back from the MIR and he heard they're sending Jackson home tomorrow."

The news shocked everyone, especially Douglas and Bergie. They were the two who had convinced Jackson that he wouldn't be sent home.

Douglas looked at Lyons. "Are you sure?"

"Of course, I'm sure! Jackson told him to tell us, so that we'd pass it on to you guys."

Douglas stood up and took his beret out of his pocket. "Bergie, would you scrape my plate off? I'm going up there to see for myself."

"Sure, but why don't you finish eating? It's lunchtime; no one will be able to answer your questions."

Douglas was mad and everyone at the table knew it. When he got that way, they didn't push him because they knew he was as stubborn as an ox.

"How in the hell can they send him home just because he's got an ingrown toenail? Jesus, if we were in a war this wouldn't happen."

Wayne agreed with his best friend. "Hold on Doug, I'm coming with you."

As they were marching past the Headquarters Building, Wayne said, "If it's final and they are sending him home, I don't think there's much we can do about it."

"I don't think so either, but we can try. At least we can try. DAMN IT, THAT'S THE LEAST WE CAN DO! Let's see what Earl has to say."

When they entered the ward, Earl was sitting on his bed in his pajamas. His eyes were red and it was obvious he had been crying. When he saw them, he turned his head away and wiped his eyes.

Douglas sat beside him. "Is it true? Are they planning on sending you home?" He put his hand on Earl's shoulder.

Two tears slowly rolled down Earl's face. "They've fixed up the toe, but the doctor says if I do any drill it will get infected. He told me they're going to put me on tomorrow's train."

All three were sad now. Wayne sat on the other side of Earl. "We're the best company. They shouldn't send guys home from the best company. You're one of us and we're a team. Ya don't break up a team. We've got to stick together."

Earl tried to smile. "What can I do? I've tried talking to the doctor but he won't listen."

Douglas stood up. "It's not what you can do, it's what we've got to try and do. C'mon Wayne, let's go."

Douglas and Wayne had never been in Charlie Company's office before. The only person there was a civilian typist who told them they could wait, that everyone would be back after lunch.

The first person to return was Sergeant-Major Walsh. He spotted them right away. "What do you two want?"

Douglas cleared his throat. "Sir, we've come about Jackson. They're going to send him home tomorrow."

"So I hear. What's that got to do with you?"

"We're his best friends, Sir. We're a team and...well, he's one of us."

"So you don't want him to go? Is that what you're trying to tell me?" Walsh looked at Douglas' nametag. "Where did you get your medical degree, Brice?"

Douglas tried to respond, but Walsh cut him off. "Besides what the hell are you two doing here? You've been told to use the chain of command. GET OUT!"

Sergeant Beckford had entered the hallway and heard part of the conversation, especially the last words of the Company Sergeant-Major.

"They did use the chain of command. I told them to come up here and see the Company Commander. Our Platoon Officer has gone to Kelowna. Besides, I think they've got a good point."

Walsh glared at Beckford, but there was nothing he could do to him. "Alright, you take them and fuck up the OC's day."

The three of them walked down the hall into an open area where Sergeant Beckford had his desk. He motioned to them to sit down.

"Now, just why are you here?" he asked with a smile.

Douglas and Wayne explained the situation. They also told him that they were only doing what he had been teaching them. "We're watching our buddy's back. There's teamwork and loyalty in Nine Platoon."

The Officer Commanding Charlie Company had returned and was in his office when Sergeant Beckford told them to wait a few minutes while he talked to the OC first. When he walked out of his office, both boys showed their crossed fingers to each other. Five minutes later, they were called in.

The OC's face was stern when they entered. "Take off your berets and stand to attention," ordered Sergeant Beckford. "Now tell the Company Commander what you told me."

Douglas did the talking. "Well, Sir, Jackson is our buddy and in Nine Platoon we watch out for each other. He's only got an ingrown toenail. If he had a new pair of boots, it would heal in no time. In the Leadership periods, we were taught to speak up when there's problems and......"

"Hold on. Hold on Brice. Even if I agreed with you, there are procedures. We can't just break the rules."

"But Sir, sometimes rules are meant to be broken."

"Who taught you that?"

Douglas looked at Sergeant Beckford, who was now moving his neck around inside his collar. Beckford now had to clear his throat before he spoke.

"In certain circumstances."

"Yes, Sergeant, that's what I meant. In certain circumstances."

The OC smiled. "I think this is an extraordinary case, don't you, Sergeant?"

"Most definitely, Sir," Beckford replied, his face a little flushed.

The OC stood up. "Well, you two head back to the barracks and I'll look into it."

The boys replaced their berets, saluted, turned about and marched out.

As they were passing Walsh's office, they heard him yell, "SERGEANT BECKFORD, I WANT TO SEE YOU!"

"SERGEANT BECKFORD IS STILL WITH ME!" The OC's words made it quite plain he was upset with the CSM.

"Oh, sorry Sir." Walsh muttered.

Both Douglas and Wayne gave Walsh's office the finger as they left the building. The typist smiled and winked at them.

Fifteen million questions were thrown at Douglas and Wayne when they entered the barracks. Half an hour later, they had answered them all, and everyone in Nine Platoon was anxiously awaiting the verdict.

Sergeant Beckford walked in the door. He showed no emotion, so a few hearts started beating faster.

"He'll be staying with us," he said with a smile. Then he walked out.

Nine Platoon cheered so loudly they could probably be heard on Silver Star Mountain, a few miles to the north. It was the second time that day that the news had been great.

With the help of Sergeant Beckford, Douglas and Wayne had won the battle and the Musketeers were back to six.

A few minutes later Earl walked into the barracks. His face beamed enough to make everyone want to pat him on the back. He told them he had to report to the

MIR every morning for the next week to have his dressing changed and in his right hand, he held a new pair of boots.

Earl put his new boots on his bed then walked over to Wayne and Douglas. He extended his arms around their necks, and gently pulled them in towards him. "Thank you," he said softly.

Neither replied. They couldn't because each had a lump in his throat.

With their arms around each others' shoulders, the Musketeers headed toward the Cadet Canteen with other members of Nine Platoon, in tow.

When Mail-Call arrived, Wayne had gone to phone Debbie to tell her they wouldn't be able to meet until two-thirty. Before leaving, he asked Douglas to pick up his mail.

The Corporal's voice rang out loud and clear as he called out the names of cadets who had received a letter. Over the next ten minutes, envelopes were tossed to eager outstretched hands. In many cases, this was the first letter from home. News from the outside would be welcomed.

"Danyluk...Danyluk...Rothstein...Danyluk...Stanley...Wesson...Danyluk... Banks...Passaglia...Gourley...Danyluk......Danyluk...East...Danyluk......Danyluk......Jackson.......Brice...Danyluk...Conradi...Danyluk...Cohen... Danyluk...Thornton..."

The Corporal was getting sick of hearing the name Danyluk as Mail-Call continued.

"Christ, what the hell have you got? A harem?"

"THEY'RE PROBABLY BILLS," screamed East.

"Eat your hearts out, you jealous virgins. They don't send out bills with perfume on 'em."

With all the letters distributed, cadets went to their bunks and read the news from home. It was quiet in the barracks for the next few minutes until Danyluk broke the silence.

"SON OF A BITCH! HILDA VISITED THE DOCTOR!"

There was laughter throughout the platoon, but Douglas didn't hear it; he was engrossed in the letter he had received from his mother.

"Dear Doug:
I don't know how long it might take this letter to reach you, but I'm sure the enclosed ten dollars will help.
I've been reading about how hot it is in Vernon, so now at least you will be able to buy yourself a few cold pops.
I hope everything is going well for you and that you are enjoying it up there. You must be, otherwise, I'm sure you would have telephoned by now.
Major and I are fine. He was going to enclose one of his favorite bones, but it looked too delicious so he ate it instead.
I do hope you understand why I didn't wait in the station until you boarded the train. You see Douglas, I couldn't. When you were just a toddler, I saw your brother off at Lime Street Station in Liverpool. He was only about eighteen and he wore a uniform quite like yours. In those days, everybody kept up a brave front, because we never knew who was going to come back. When his train went out of sight, I stood in the

station for a half an hour somehow thinking it would return. I wasn't alone, there were hundreds of mothers and wives standing there thinking the same thing. In the taxi going home, I couldn't stop crying. I know it was silly of me to think of those memories, but well, you are growing up Doug and it all came back to me.

The house is quiet now that you're gone. At first I thought it was nice to have peace and quiet around, but after you left, I changed the sheets on your bed and sat down waiting, as if you were coming home. Major jumped up on your bed next to me and our cat Mickey just paced the halls. I guess they miss you just as much as I do.

The two of us have been through a lot together, Doug. I guess we've fought the world and won so far, son, and I don't know what I would have done without you.

I've been working nights, lately. Although I hate coming home at that time of the night, it at least allows me to do some shopping during the day.

I was going to buy you a pair of pants and a shirt yesterday, but I had second thoughts. I'll wait until you come home because you'll probably grow and gain some weight at camp. That is if the food is good. I know how fussy you can be at times.

Tomorrow I'm going over to visit your Auntie Florrie. I know that you don't care for her after the way she treated us when we arrived in Canada. But she is my sister and maybe she was right, rushing us out of her house a month later.

It's funny what went through my mind when I was sitting on your bed. I remembered how you went home with a boy you met on your first day in school and told his mother that I had no friends and was sitting home alone, night after night. I remembered when she invited me over the next day and how we became good friends.

The other day, I did the most foolish thing. I had just dusted the living room and I heard a noise in your room. Although it was only Major jumping off your bed, I yelled up and asked if you were doing your homework. It was an automatic reaction and before I finished saying it, I realized you'd gone away. Silly. wasn't it?

Well son, there's not too much more to say, except that I hope you're enjoying yourself and that you're staying out of trouble. You know I love you very much and all three of us miss you. I'm certain in my next few letters I won't be reminiscing as much.

Love, Mam

P.S. Major and Mickey send their love. Major keeps looking at his ball. He knows you're away, but he's guarding it until you return. I'm going to take him down to the beach right now and throw it for him."

Douglas read and reread the letter as he lay on Wayne's bunk. Memories kept coming back to him about the trip from Liverpool, his brother Norman and his dad. It seemed like yesterday that he started his first day of school in Canada and all of the kids made fun of his short pants. They didn't like his Liverpool accent either. Many a day, he came home with a black eye from a fight he'd gotten into because he was different from the others.

He grinned. Five fights a day finally convinced his mother that if her son was going to survive, he had to have long pants.

Douglas placed his hands behind his head and stared at the ceiling, trying to remember it all. The letter had made him homesick and he didn't quite know how to deal with it.

Wayne had entered the barracks and was reading his letter. He looked a little lonesome, as well.

"AH, HILDA ONLY WENT TO THE DOCTOR'S OFFICE WITH A COLD. SHE HAD ME WORRIED THERE." Danyluk's last statement got everyone back on track.

The trip to Charlie Company's office was the second that day for Wayne and Douglas. This time, however, they were with the rest of the Musketeers, picking up their midnight passes.

On their way through camp, they joined Lyons and Foster and the group headed down the hill to meet the girls. This time, they all had money in their pockets and it was nice to be 'rich.'

After the usual 'eyes left' across from Hop Sing's, Wayne said, "There's a dance at the Arena tonight and cadets get in free." The others thought the idea was fantastic, and they all agreed to go.

Douglas had never been to an organized dance before, all he had ever attended were 'sock hops' at his school during lunch hours.

Two cadets walking back to camp passed them and Wayne stopped them. He was pointing to two silver bars on both of his epaulets. "YOU, THERE! YES, YOU! DON'T YOU KNOW YOU SHOULD SALUTE AN OFFICER WHEN YOU SEE ONE?"

"Er, sorry Sir. We didn't see, er, we didn't notice you were an officer."

Wayne glared at them. "Well, I'm waiting!"

Although perspiration oozed out from under their berets and they looked tired, both cadets stood to attention and saluted.

"CARRY ON NOW AND PAY ATTENTION IN THE FUTURE. AND GET THOSE PUTTEES TIED CORRECTLY!"

The cadets saluted again and started marching up the hill, each trying to explain to the other how it was that they missed seeing the officer.

Bergie was the only person who didn't find it humorous. "Jesus Wayne, we're trying to stop that sort of thing. Don't you remember last week I stopped us from getting nailed?"

Banks smiled. "I had to try it, Bergie. I was going to do it when we first arrived but I couldn't find any silver cigarette paper."

Bergie gave him an inquiring look. "That's cigarette paper?"

"Sure is!"

He slapped Banks on the back. "Well, if it's that easy, why don't we all become Colonels tomorrow?"

Danyluk was now into the act. "Hey, I think I'd rather become a General."

"You mean you'd rather be a general fuckup, just on general principles," said Lyons.

Danyluk scratched his head. "No, we've got enough Generals with no principles, I'll settle for being a Field Marshal."

Douglas butted in. "There are no Field Marshals in the Canadian Army."

Danyluk thought for a moment and then said with a straight face, "In that case,

I'll settle for being a Court Martial."

East and Jackson were holding their stomachs, they were laughing so hard. "You'd have no trouble making that," said East.

It was quiet in the park that afternoon. The girls were waiting for them in the stands, watching a junior baseball game. Alma rushed over to Danyluk like she hadn't seen him in years. The rest of the girls casually walked towards them.

Everyone had a different idea of what they should do.

Danyluk wanted to go bowling, but East didn't like the idea. "Let's go for a banana-split?"

"Christ, all you ever think of is your stomach."

Bergie suggested they go swimming.

"We've got no bathing suits, you silly twit," said Foster.

That made Danyluk speak up again. "What's wrong with that?" Then he whispered. "We could go bare-balls."

Alma didn't know what was going on, but she was smiling and nodding anxiously. Finally, she said, "We can all go to my house, my parents have gone shopping."

Danyluk put his arm around her waist. "That's the best idea I've heard all day. But, er, well, how about just you and me!"

At that point they decided to split up and meet at the dance at eight o'clock.

Wayne and Douglas went with the two girls to Diane's house. When they arrived, Diane suggested the boys wait outside while she and Debbie went in to talk to her parents.

Within five minutes, the girls came back to the porch and asked the boys to come inside. Diane's mom and dad were standing in the living room. Although Diane's mother was small, Diane's father was about six feet tall and built like a wrestler. He eyed the boys over.

"Which one of you is Douglas?"

Douglas swallowed and took his beret off. "I am, Sir."

Diane's dad held out his hand. "I'm Tom and this is my wife, Ellen."

Ellen shook Douglas' hand, then Douglas introduced Wayne to the both of them.

Diane's mother said, "We're going out to Grandpa's farm this afternoon. Would you boys like to come with us?"

Douglas didn't hesitate in replying. "You bet, I've only been on a farm twice in my life."

After one week of military life. the boys enjoyed just being in a car and talking to people who weren't wearing uniforms.

Douglas was mesmerized by the beauty of the countryside they were passing. The varied shades of green blending in with the blue of the lakes reminded him of picture postcards. Cattle and horses grazed in the fields and the sky was so clear, Douglas wanted to reach out and touch it to see if it was real.

The four teenagers were sitting crammed in the back of the car but the boys didn't mind; for that matter, neither did the girls. Every so often when one of her parents made a statement Diane thought was funny, she would take hold of Douglas' right hand and squeeze it. Then she would take her eyes off the road and look into his eyes. When their eyes met, they both smiled shyly.

"How are they treating you at the camp?" Tom asked.

"Pretty good, Sir," Douglas replied. "We're starting to get the hang of it now."

"Do you have to wear those khaki shorts everywhere you go?"

"Everywhere except swim parades, but there are a few rumours going around that they might let us wear our longs to the dances on Saturday Nights."

"Well, those short pants are pretty sensible. I guess you'd hate to be wearing your battledress pants?"

"Yes, Sir. The only time we wear those is when we arrive and when we leave."

When Douglas mentioned the word 'leave,' Diane squeezed his hand.

"Don't they let you wear civilian clothes?"

"No, Sir. We couldn't even bring them to camp."

When Diane's mother heard that, she thought it was unfair. "I wonder why they do that? Everyone needs a change now and then. Why does your whole world have to be khaki?"

Wayne answered. "It's probably done for control purposes. The meatheads wouldn't know who were cadets if we wore civilian clothes downtown."

"Such a word. What does meathead mean?"

Tom and the girls chuckled when Wayne explained. "It's a slang word meaning Military Police."

Diane's dad was looking at them in the rearview mirror. "Have the two of you ever been to Vernon before?"

Both boys replied they hadn't and Douglas said, "I wish I had. This is the most beautiful country I've ever seen."

"It truly is God's country," said Tom "There are rumours that a bridge is going to be built over Okanagan Lake connecting Westbank with Kelowna."

"What's there now?" asked Douglas.

"A small ferry. That's why there's not too much traffic on Highway 97. As far as I'm concerned, that's just the way it should stay."

Not too much was said for the next few miles and it didn't matter because Douglas couldn't tear his eyes away from the scenery.

Ellen asked, "Are both of you in the same grade at school?"

"We're in grade ten at King George High School," said Douglas. "We met in grade five."

"I understand you've got a CSM at camp by the name of Walsh?" asked Tom. His voice was a little harsher.

"He's our Company Sergeant-Major," Douglas replied.

"What do you think of him?"

"Well, Sir...he's, ...well, he's..."

"You don't have to tell me, I know what he's like. We had him in Korea. How he ever made Sergeant, I'll never know? And now he's a CSM?" Tom was shaking his head as he talked.

"You were in Korea, Sir?" asked Wayne.

"That I was," Tom replied. He didn't say anything more about it.

The car passed a large lake and then turned onto a dirt road, lined with apple and pear trees laden with fruit. It stopped beside an old farmhouse where an elderly grey-haired gentleman was down on his knees pulling weeds from a small vegetable garden. When he heard the car, he stood up and said, "Lordy, Lordy who's here."

When everyone was out of the car, Debbie rushed over and gave him a big kiss on his cheek. "Hi Grandpa," she said. Then she looked at Wayne. "I think of him as my Grandpa, too."

The boys were introduced to him and everyone walked into the old farmhouse where a short robust lady was baking pies. She put her rolling-pin down. "Well, it's about time," she said, kissing four of them and shaking the boys' hands. "Would you kids like a piece of hot apple pie?"

She didn't have to ask a second time. Instantly, the teenagers were sitting at the table, drinking cold milk and eating huge pieces of fresh apple pie.

"Don't look at it, eat it," she said to Wayne who was 'eyeing' the last piece of two pies. "You're a growing boy, aren't you?"

Wayne whispered, "I feel like East."

After their snack, the boys were watching the girls do the dishes, when Tom said, "Douglas, Wayne, come up to the attic with me."

The attic was as neat as the rooms below. It was loaded with bygone-era furniture and old trunks. Tom opened one of them.

"Here's some jeans for you and somewhere in here I've got a couple of old shirts. Ah, here they are. I think they'll fit you."

The boys put them on and Wayne looked at himself in a large old mirror that was standing against the wall of the slanted roof. "A little loose, but I feel human already."

When they came down, Ellen was at the foot of the stairs. "Why don't you girls show the boys around?"

"I don't know if that's wise, Ellen." Tom had a twinkle in his eye when he said it. "You know what I mean, eh guys?"

The boys grinned at each other. "Yes, Sir," Wayne replied with a smile.

Tom was grinning too. "Go on. Have a good time. Supper's at…what time is supper, dad?"

His mom answered. "Tommy, you know it's always at six."

"Be back by five-thirty," he said.

The four of them strolled hand in hand down to a small lake about two hundred yards from the house.

"You've got great grandparents," said Douglas.

Diane gave him a glazed smile. "I know. They bend over backwards every time someone visits. I feel guilty that I haven't been here in over two months."

"Why is that?"

"Well, I can't ride my bike out here and dad's working split-shifts at the mill. He's been after my mom to get her drivers' license, but she won't do it and I've got to wait two more years before I can apply for mine."

Wayne was trying to skip rocks as the four of them sat on the bank overlooking the lake. The reflection of the weeping willow trees swayed in the ripples created by the stones hitting the water.

Douglas lay on his back next to Diane. "If I lived here, I don't think I'd ever get anything done. The scenery would take up all of my time."

"What does your dad do?" Diane asked.

"My dad is in England. I just live with my mother, who is a chocolate-dipper at Purdy's Chocolates in Vancouver."

"How come you're not fat, then?"

"Fat?"

"Yeah, from all of the free chocolates."

Douglas smiled. "I used to be fat, but after awhile I got sick of them."

Wayne winked at Douglas as he and Debbie stood up.

"We're going up to the hayloft."

"I saw that," Diane said. "What are you going to do up there?"

Debbie looked a little flushed. "We're just going to swing on the bale-chains," she replied, trying hard not to laugh. "What did you think we were going to do?"

Diane smiled. "Oh...just swing on the bale-chains."

Over the next hour, Douglas and Diane walked all over the property, eating pears and apples and just talking. When they got back to the lake, Douglas saw an old rowboat and asked Diane if she'd like to go out on the lake.

Diane sat in the boat trailing her hand in the water while Douglas rowed.

"What do you want to do after you've finished school?" she asked.

Douglas stopped rowing for a second. "I think I'm going to join the army."

Diane giggled. "It won't be much of a home life for you. When my dad was in the forces, we were posted all over the place."

"I know," Douglas replied. "But I want to see the world anyway. How about you?"

"My dad wants me to be a nurse but my mom just wants me to get married and raise kids. I think I like the idea of being a nurse."

"Doesn't the thought of blood and guts bother you?" he asked.

"Naaaah, although I can't watch Grandpa slaughtering an animal anymore."

The boat was drifting and Diane had moved next to him on the seat. Shortly he got up enough nerve to put his arm around her shoulder, turn her head, and give her a kiss.

"You're kind of shy aren't you?" she asked.

"You mean Vernon guys put the make on girls faster?"

Diane just smiled as they slipped back on their seat, ending up on the bottom of the boat. His heart was pounding. This was the first time he had had an intimate conversation with a girl.

"No, I didn't mean that. It's just that you're different than the other boys."

"How many have there been?" he asked, thinking to himself that if Diane was used to this, he might look like a total idiot because he didn't have a clue what to do, or what to say.

He was relieved to hear her reply. "None, I've just heard stories from Debbie and Alma."

He gently rolled her over on her side and turned toward her. Their bodies were so close that he could feel her heart pounding. At least he thought it was hers; it could have been his.

As he kissed her, he brought his hand up to her breast. She didn't try to stop him and the most incredible feeling in the world shot through his body. He felt himself getting 'aroused.' It was embarrassing because he knew she would feel it through their clothes as he embraced her tighter and tighter. It was as if he wanted them to be one. Diane's hips were starting to move rhythmically against him and his mind was going wild.

Suddenly she moved his hand away and sat up on the seat, straightening her clothing.

"Did I do something wrong?" he asked. "I thought that's what you...well, I......?"

Diane took out her comb and started combing her hair.

"No, it was me. I mean...we'd better be getting back. Come on, I'll help you row."

Douglas couldn't get up. He had a sharp pain between his legs and it wasn't going away. "Just...just give me a minute," he said both grimacing and smiling at the same time.

Diane looked at him inquisitively and started laughing. "That's as far as you've ever gone, isn't it?"

Douglas' face was beet red. He had to stand up before he could sit down because the pain was so excruciating. Hesitantly, he replied, "Yes."

They were both smiling at each other now. "Well, if it's any consolation, I've never let a boy get that near to me before."

When they rowed back to the wharf, the trip seemed to take a lifetime. Neither of them wanted it to end.

The sun was falling as they drove back to town.

"How did you like the food, boys?" Tom asked.

"I told your mom it was the best meal I have ever eaten," Wayne said, licking his lips.

Douglas laughed. "It was obvious; you had three helpings."

"You should have taken the clothes with you so that you could sneak out some night."

"They'd probably just catch us." Douglas replied. "Thanks for letting us use them."

Tom looked in the rearview mirror. "You're welcome, but it might take a little while to get the straw off one pair of pants and one shirt."

Wayne was mortified. He tried not to connect his eyes with Tom's.

Tom spittled as he burst out laughing. The only person in the car trying to keep a straight face was Wayne.

When the laughter died down, Ellen said. "I hope the roll in the hay was just that?"

"Oh, it was, it was," Debbie and Wayne both replied in unison.

"Oh come on, Mother, you and I spent a lot of time in that hayloft," Tom said as he glanced at Ellen.

"THOMAS! How could you......?" Ellen turned around and winked. "We were older then."

When the car pulled up next to the arena, Ellen was digging Tom with her elbow, trying to stop him from laughing and telling stories of their courtship.

At least five-hundred cadets were outside the arena when Tom and Ellen dropped the kids off. All of the other Musketeers were there with their girls, patiently waiting.

"Jesus, what took you so long?" asked Danyluk as he and Alma herded Douglas, Wayne and the girls, in the direction of the door. Everyone else quickly followed and before long they were inside and Danyluk and Alma were on the floor, dancing.

"Moose sure doesn't waste any time, does he?" Jackson asked. But no sooner had he spoken, his girl took his arm and he was dancing as well.

Soon everyone was up. The record was Ebb Tide and the floor was full of slow moving couples.

"This looks like a scene from a war movie," Douglas said, looking at all the cadets in their short pants. Their berets were tucked into their epaulets, badges facing the front so that everyone could see in which regiment they were serving.

Diane didn't speak. She was resting her head on Douglas' shoulder as the music reverberated throughout the arena.

Douglas had never heard the record before and he liked it. "I'm going to think of this as our tune," he said.

She lifted her head and gazed into his eyes. "Me, too," she replied softly.

After a few dances, the group gathered in the seats and watched the dance floor fill up again.

"How's your foot?" Douglas asked Earl.

"Never been better. These new boots are beautiful. I should have got a new pair long ago."

East and his girl were eating hotdogs, when all of a sudden the foulest smell wafted into their nostrils.

East nearly choked. "Who died?" he asked, coughing.

The smell originated from an Irish cadet walking by.

Danyluk was killing himself laughing as he pointed to the cadet. "Do you remember him?"

East couldn't finish his hotdog because of the smell. He draped his arm around Moose.

"Yeah, he was that Cadet Officer that tried to nail us on the first day. O.K. Danyluk, what have you done now?"

Danyluk couldn't control his excitement. "I got 'em."

Douglas couldn't get the smell out of his nose, either. He looked puzzled. "What do you mean, you got 'em?"

"Well, when they first arrived, I watched them check their berets...sorry, their carabineers at the hat check. When the girl stepped out for a few minutes, I sneaked in and put a few drops of Apple Blossom Perfume on their hackles."

Bergie laughed. "Jesus, that stuff smells like rotten eggs and it takes weeks to disappear. Where did you get it?"

Danyluk couldn't control himself as he watched the two Irish cadets accuse each other of being the source of the smell.

"I got it from the joke shop in town. Have you noticed no one will go near them?"

Wayne screwed up his face. "I don't blame them; I wouldn't go near them, either."

"They're complaining that some Canadian Scottish cadet did it," Danyluk said, trying to keep his eyes on them but not wanting to be obvious.

East prepared two new hotdogs for himself and his girl. "If they catch him, they'll kill him," he said.

Danyluk grabbed Alma's hand, dragging her to the dance floor. "Oh, he's already headed back to camp. They won't catch him now."

When Glen Miller's In the Mood started playing, everyone in the arena headed for the dance floor except the two Irish cadets.

"I've got to go to Penticton tomorrow for a week," Diane said, as she jived around Douglas. "I've really been looking forward to this trip but now I don't want to go."

"Do you have to go?"

"Yes. I tried to get out of it today, but my dad would have no part of it. Debbie's going with me."

Douglas found himself yelling because of the loudness of the record. "WHY ARE YOU GOING THERE?"

"I'M GOING TO SPEND SOME TIME WITH MY MOM'S PARENTS," she yelled back, twirling under his arm. She was going to say something else but the music was too loud. They both smiled and kept dancing.

When the next break in the music came, the girls went to the ladies' room and the boys just watched the two Irish cadets. It didn't matter who they asked to dance. they were turned down.

"Poor buggers," Wayne said, feeling sorry for them.

Bergie took a slug of his coke. "Poor buggers, my eye. Have you forgotten what they tried to do to us?"

For the next half-hour, the Musketeers switched partners and were on and off the dance floor at least five times. Soon they started to separate in pairs, and they were lost in their own worlds. Ebb Tide started again and Douglas and Diane found themselves dancing closer than ever.

"You won't meet someone while I'm gone, will you?" Diane asked.

"There are no other girls. I don't want anyone else but you."

"Do you promise?"

Douglas noticed tears rolling down her cheeks. "I promise. What are you crying for?"

"Because I'm going to miss you," she said, placing her head back on his shoulder.

"I'll miss you, too, but it's only a week. We've still got four weeks left after that, haven't we?" He was smiling as he lifted her head up to look into her eyes. Diane smiled. "That's better," he said holding her tightly.

The air was cool and fresh when the two of them emerged from the crowded arena. It was dark out and this was the first time Douglas had been outside of camp at this time of night.

"Can I walk you home?" he asked.

"My dad's picking me up. Do you guys want a ride up the hill?" She had no sooner said it when her dad arrived, beeping his horn.

He took hold of her hand. "No, thanks. It's going to be great walkin' up the hill without the heat. So I won't see you for a week?"

Diane looked at the ground. "It'll be the longest week of my life."

Wayne and Debbie appeared. Tom had arranged with Debbie's parents to drive her home. As Wayne took her to the car, Douglas noticed her hair was all messed up and that Wayne had lipstick everywhere on his face.

Diane gave Douglas a small kiss on the cheek. "Well, I guess I'd better get going."

Douglas walked her to the car. "When will I know you're back?"

She sat in the car and opened the window. "I'll get word to you."

As the car started moving, Tom yelled something about giving them a ride, but Diane told him the boys wanted to walk. He waved, along with the girls, who were sticking their heads out of the car window, throwing kisses.

Although couples were all over the place, some pushing, some shoving, some screaming, the minute the car drove out of sight, Douglas felt alone. Both he and Wayne just stood there with their mouths open, staring at the disappearing taillights. Neither of them spoke and neither wanted to move.

Wayne was the first to speak. "We'd better get back." His eyes were still on the spot he had last seen the car before it turned the corner.

Douglas snapped out of his trance also. "If you think for a minute that I'm walking up the hill with you, you've got another think coming."

"Why, what's wrong?"

"You're covered in lipstick from ear to ear. If you walk in the barracks like that you're going to be in for one heck of a ribbing."

A smirk appeared on Wayne's face as he cocked his head and remembered the source of the lipstick. As he walked back into the arena to wash, the thought of the moment lingered with him.

Douglas was right, the walk up the hill was pleasant. It was only around eleven o'clock and since they had an hour left, they took their time.

"What time do we have to get up tomorrow?" asked Wayne.

Douglas tried to remember what he had read on the bulletin board. "I think we can sleep in until eight. There's no inspection of the barracks, but we've got a Church Parade at nine."

Wayne stopped. "A Church Parade?"

Douglas nudged him forward. "Yup, we gotta sing the hymns."

Although a lot of cadets were walking up the hill, none of them were Musketeers. Both Douglas and Wayne missed the regular banter that was the trademark of the group.

"Where are all the guys?" asked Douglas.

"I think they're walking their chicks home. I hope they make it back before bed-check," answered Wayne.

A Military Police truck drove by and they both felt the Corporal's eyes inspecting every inch of their clothing.

Wayne gave a finger to the back of the passing vehicle. "Jesus, don't those guys ever sleep? I think they're just a bunch of horses asses!"

Douglas laughed. "Well, you're probably right, because horses do sleep on their feet. But they're not good enough to be the whole horse though, just the rear end part. RIGHT?"

"RIGHT!" Wayne replied. "By the way, I'm not going to tell you about the hayloft."

"Good. I don't want to know about it anyway."

"Even if you asked, I wouldn't tell you."

"Good, because I'm not going to ask."

"You could get down on your hands and knees and I wouldn't tell you."

"Wayne, old buddy, old pal. I ain't gonna ask."

"You'll ask!"

"No, I won't and that's final. What happened?"

Wayne's smile kept stretching. "I got her bra off."

"You what?"

"I got her bra off. She's got nipples the size of thimbles."

"Don't bull-shit me, Wayne!"

"I'm tellin' ya, Doug, I did. Look at this."

Wayne took a bra out of his pocket and Douglas looked at it in amazement.

"Jesus, she let you keep it?"

Wayne cleared his throat. "Well, not exactly. When I was going to give it back to her, Gramps got on the ladder to get some chicken-feed and I had to shove it in my pocket."

"GET YOUR ARMS UP!" The Provost Corporal's voice was loud as they passed the guardroom. If he hadn't been looking at their arms, he would have seen the straps of a brassiere sticking out of Wayne's rear pocket.

"SSSHHHH," someone said as they entered the barracks. Most cadets were asleep and a Corporal was standing in the aisle. "Get into bed quickly, guys," he whispered.

After Douglas was in bed, he leaned up to Wayne and whispered. "I can still smell that Apple Blossom stuff."

"Me, too! That stuff's strong!"

A few minutes later, Danyluk, Jackson, East and Bergie stomped into the barracks. After they got the same warning from the Corporal, they crept, and Danyluk also stopped singing his version of an Eddie Fisher song with newly revised worlds. "LADY OF SPAIN, I EXPLORE YOU..."

For the next few minutes they all whispered together about how much they enjoyed the night.

"SON OF A BITCH!" Danyluk was sitting on his bunk in his shorts, sniffing his pillow.

A cadet across the aisle said, "Two Irish cadets came in and dumped some of that Apple Blossom stuff on your pillow."

"THE BASTARDS," he said as he took his pillow and the pillow case to the drying room. When he came out, he stood in the middle of Nine Platoon's aisle, "O.K., WHO FINKED?"

Nobody answered so he went to bed. As he was getting between the sheets, there was a loud 'RRRRRRRRRIP!"

"WHAT THE HELL?" Danyluk had pushed his foot through one of the sheets.

The cadet across the aisle said, "They also frenched your bed."

The next minute Danyluk was standing in front of his bunk with a dead fish in his hand.

"WHAT THE HELL IS THIS? WHAT AM I SUPPOSED TO DO WITH THIS?"

Banks was laughing into his pillow and almost fell off his bunk.

"SON OF A BITCH!"

The voice from across the aisle said, "They also left a fish."

CHAPTER VII

"IT'S COMPULSORY, EVERYONE'S GOT TO GO!"

Bergie was explaining to the rest of the Musketeers at breakfast that they must all attend Church Parade.

"But what if you're an atheist, or what's the other one, er, an agnostic?" asked East. "Besides, Cohen's not going?"

"Isn't an atheist a stone fitted into a ring?" asked Danyluk.

"That's an amethyst, you ignoramus." Bergie looked exasperated. "Cohen's Jewish, he can get out of going."

East leaned over the table and put his face in Bergie's face. Speaking slowly and softly, he said, "Well, if Cohen can get out of it by being Jewish, then I suggest we all become Jewish for the balance of camp."

"You can't just say you're Jewish. They'll check the Joining Cards."

Danyluk got an idea. "Alright, let's tell 'em we're Moslem and, er, we left our turbans at home."

Bergie laughed. Danyluk always made him laugh. "You dolt! Muslims don't wear turbans. At least I don't think they do."

Danyluk stood up. "They don't? Well, who the hell does?"

"Sikhs do, and don't tell me you now want to become a Sikh?"

"Well, why not, if it works?"

Bergie threw up his hands. "Listen, I don't give a fat rat's ass what you guys do. If you don't go, they'll nail ya. It's as simple as that!"

East picked up his plate. "I'm going back for more eggs."

Douglas gave him a weird look. "I thought you told us you hate powdered eggs?"

"I do, but all that dancing last night drained the nutrients out of my body."

"Jeez, you ate at least a hundred hotdogs."

East smiled as he walked away. "That don't count."

Danyluk was not about to give up. "Well, I'm informing the CSM that I'm a Jewish Atheist."

"What the hell is a Jewish Atheist?" asked Bergie.

Danyluk shrugged. "I don't know, but it sounds good. I don't even know what an atheist is."

With breakfast over, Charlie Company formed up on the road. All cadets had to wear their regimental headdress and sure enough, the roll was called. The cadets who were not Christian were allowed to fall out. Danyluk had his arm around

Cohen and walked away too, but that only lasted a second because the CSM spotted him.

"DANYLUK, YOU'RE NOT JEWISH?"

"I might be, my parents never tell me what's going on."

"GET BACK IN THE RANKS!"

With the Roman Catholics in one group and the Protestants in another, the cadets of Charlie Company marched in different directions to receive the lessons of the Lord.

The Protestants were the larger group and Hangar B-3 was used for their service. When they entered, it was cool inside and they were handed a military hymnbook.

Danyluk asked Bergie if they could keep the books and Bergie said no and told him they had to be returned at the end of the service. Then after a few moments, Bergie asked him what he wanted it for anyway.

"One of my girlfriends is a Jehovah's Witness and I want to send her a present."

A typical church service followed, but ninety-five percent of the cadets were not impressed and did not want to be there at all.

After a few hymns, the military Chaplain droned on and on, to the point Wayne couldn't take it any longer. He leaned over to Douglas. "This guy is giving me a headache, I'm going to the jon."

"That's where Danyluk has gone," Douglas whispered.

"Where's East and Jackson?" asked Wayne.

"They're R.C.s; they've gone to their own service," Bergie replied.

When the service ended and cadets were dropping their hymnbooks into a box, Douglas' jaw dropped. "May capbadge is gone!"

"Your what?" asked Wayne.

"My capbadge has been stolen. Jesus Christ...!"

"What, in church? Someone stole your badge in church?" Wayne was shaking his head.

Douglas was furious. "I put it on the bench next to me, instead of in my pocket like you did. I didn't think anyone would steal it in church. Now I'm going to have to walk around like one of those 'gormphs' without a badge."

Wayne smiled. "We'll find you one, don't worry. Did Bergie tell you the story about what happened to the Chaplain last year?"

Douglas shook his head.

"Well, apparently some cadet got his wallet stolen in church. When he went to complain to the Chaplain, the Chaplain was too busy trying to find the person who stole his pocket-watch."

Douglas smiled. Wayne had cheered him up.

"Maybe I should go back and steal the Chaplain's capbadge," he said.

After lunch, Douglas found himself alone in B-21. This was the first time he had been alone since coming to camp. Something was bothering him and he didn't know what it was.

During lunch, he and Wayne had been invited to join the other Musketeers but only Wayne accepted. Douglas had refused because he didn't feel right. Many things were going through his mind and he had never felt like this before.

It was warm in the barracks as he lay there. Even the quiet was now starting to bother him as he took out his mother's letter to read it again. Although it had only been a week, he knew he was partially homesick and at the same time, he never wanted to go home. He didn't know what was bothering him.

After he put the letter away, he thought of the last moments he had with Diane. She didn't want to go and now he missed her. Wayne had told him that girls break up men's relationships and if he didn't watch it, he'd be caught. He had laughed then, but Wayne's words kept coming back to him.

"Listen, Doug, you and I are best friends. We'll always be best friends, but if we're caught, it's possible we won't find time for each other anymore."

He smiled. He was lucky to have a friend like Wayne. Everything they did, they did together. When Douglas got sick, Wayne never left his side. When Wayne was sick, Douglas was there. They went to school together, set pins together, went swimming three times a week together, and they had joined cadets together.

"You and I are closer than brothers," Wayne had once said. And now Diane had entered his life and he didn't want her to leave. It was different with Wayne, he only toyed with Debbie. He wasn't serious and he knew that Debbie wasn't either.

Douglas got up and climbed up to Wayne's bunk. He knew he was in a rotten mood. He had lost his badge and everything else was bothering him, including the feeling that he had in the boat when he got up enough courage to put his hand on Diane's breasts. The passion that went through his body was overpowering.

He had heard some of the guys talk about masturbation but he'd never given it any thought. Sure, some mornings he knew something had happened during the night, but that had only started lately, just before he came to camp. Now things were different. He knew that if Diane hadn't pulled herself away, his body would have reacted like it never had before.

Two cadets coming into the other end of the hut disturbed his thoughts. They had just returned from town and both of them were complaining about the walk up the hill.

Douglas climbed down and opened up his barrack-box. He took out a writing tablet and pen before he lay on his stomach on his own bunk and wrote a letter home.

At first, he didn't quite know what to say. He hated writing letters and he felt guilty that he hadn't written home before now. Some cadets wrote home every day. Danyluk was always writing letters, but they probably weren't to his mom or dad. It must cost him a mint in postage stamps, Douglas thought.

Dear Mom:
    You're probably saying, 'who is this stranger that's writing?' I bet you can't even recognize my handwriting, it's been so long. I know I should have written before now, however, things seem to move so fast here at camp that I didn't find the time. That's a

lie. I did have some time but not much.

I received your letter yesterday and so far I've read it about five times. Thanks for the ten dollars. It saved my life. I want you to know that I miss you very much and I've been thinking of you a lot. The letter you sent reminded me of how lucky I am to have the best mom in the world. The part about you seeing Norman off on the train really got to me. I know you love Norman a lot and that's why you give me a blast when I don't live up to how Norman used to do things.

The train ride was really great. I've never seen such beautiful country in my life, but it's really hot. Right now the temperature must be in the high nineties. How is it on the coast? You've got to see this place, Mom. Do you think Purdy's would let you off for a few days? I know it would be expensive but I think it would be worth it.

The other day I met a girl. Her name is Diane. We went to her grandparents' farm the other day, Wayne and me. I like her a lot and I know she likes me. Don't worry, there are no plans to get married.

I got my badge stolen today. It happened in church, can you believe that? You know, I'm learning a lot up here, about people and how to treat them and respect their feelings and things. It's called Leadership and Man Management. We have Regular Force Officers and Non-Commissioned Officers and the guy who we like the most is Sergeant Beckford. He goes to bat for us. If he keeps teaching us like he does, we'll all be better people for it.

Well, there's not too much more to say, except that I miss you and love you. Please say hello to Major and Mickey for me and tell them that I miss them as well. I'm looking forward to throwing Major's ball to him when I come home.

Love, Doug xxxxxxx

P.S. I'm not a Field Marshal yet. But a buddy of mine said that if he can't make that, he'd settle for Court Martial.

Douglas addressed an envelope and slipped the letter underneath his dust cover. He was all alone again because the cadets who had entered the barracks earlier had left. Now, all the bunks were empty, and the silence in the barracks was mind-boggling. He never imagined it could be this quiet in camp.

After he had read a comic that was laying around, Douglas started to straighten out his half of the barrack-box. When that was completed, he did his and Wayne's military laundry and watched it dry outside the barracks. After that, he pressed his clothes and neatly folded them into his side of the barrack-box.

The day was dragging when Douglas decided he would walk around camp. He wore his pith-helmet because as far as he was concerned, no one was going to see him walk around without a badge on his beret.

Both the Signals and the Driver-Mechanics huts were just as quiet as his own. A few cadets were playing cards in the D&M hut but that was about it. The whole camp was deserted; like everyone had gone home.

As he passed the fenced-off area of the Officers' Mess garden, he heard laughter, and he decided to take a look through a knothole. Officers were sitting around a table under a giant weeping willow tree, drinking large cold drinks. The lawn looked like a golf course, it was so well kept.

"Jesus," he murmured to himself. "These guys live the life of luxury."

"YOU, THERE! GET AWAY FROM THAT FENCE! IT'S NONE OF YOUR BUSINESS WHAT GOES ON IN THERE. DO YOU THINK YOU'RE AN OFFICER?" The Camp Regimental Sergeant-Major's's voice boomed.

"NO, SIR!"

Douglas walked toward the Headquarters Building, the direction from which the RSM had appeared. He noticed the cannon had been moved from the centre of the road in front of the building, to the side of the building. Chirping sounds were coming from inside the barrel of the cannon and when he looked into it, he saw four baby birds with their mouths open, waiting for their parents. He tried to get a better look, but the barrel was so hot he couldn't touch it.

At its old location, two swallows were flying around feverishly trying to find their young. The cannon had only been moved about twenty-five yards and was in plain view, but for some reason the parent birds couldn't relate to it.

He didn't know what to do. If they didn't get water to the baby birds in a hurry, they would fry in the barrel.

It was at that point Douglas saw Colonel St. Laurent sitting on his porch reading a newspaper. He rushed over and saluted.

"Excuse me, Sir."

"What is it, son?"

"Sir, someone has moved the cannon, not knowing that some swallows have laid their eggs in there. They've hatched and for some reason the parent birds can't see them."

The Commanding Officer left his chair and walked over to the cannon with Douglas. "You're right. Can't they see where it is?"

"For some reason they can't, Sir. Why was it moved in the first place?"

"The Duty Officer has been complaining that the cannon was in his way when he raised and lowered the flag. What do you think we should do?"

Douglas really didn't know. "Well, Sir, if we can't move the cannon, we'll have to find a way of moving the babies and, er, put them into a box at the old location."

"Good idea," said the Colonel. "You wait right here until I come back."

The CO walked back to his office and returned with a small cardboard box and a leather-covered swagger-stick.

"Here," he said, passing the stick to Douglas. "Try to move them out with this, then we'll put them into the box."

Douglas soon got the birds out and into the box. He then put the box where the cannon had been, but even that didn't help. Although the babies were chirping, the parents were either too dumb or they just couldn't associate the box with the cannon. They continued flying around.

"We may be too close," the Colonel said. "Let's go into my office and watch them through the window."

Inside, the Colonel offered him a glass of cold lemonade and they both watched. It was fruitless; the parent birds did not go near the box.

Douglas went outside and put the baby birds on the ground, but that didn't help either. Even though they were chirping, their parents ignored them.

"It's not working is it, son?"

"No, Sir."

"Do you think it's possible those birds are air force or navy birds?" the Colonel asked, smiling.

"They're sure not army birds, Sir."

"Right you are son, right you are."

The bird episode had made Douglas completely forget his homesickness. He was totally wrapped up in the problem and didn't know what to do.

Finally the Colonel came up with a solution. "Well, we can't move the cannon, so I suggest we put them back into the box and put them on my porch. Perhaps sometime soon, the parents might recognize the sound of the chirps."

Douglas moved the box back. He knew if they didn't get food and water soon, they would die.

"What's your name, son?"

"Brice, Sir."

"Well, Brice, I'm placing you in charge of the Colonel's Birds. Will you make sure they're looked after?"

"I'll do my best, Sir."

"I'm sure you will. Thank you, Brice."

As Douglas left, he saw the Colonel looking at the birds. Then he picked up his newspaper and started reading again.

For the next two hours, Douglas tried to give the birds water from an eye-dropper he picked up from the MIR He also dug up some worms and tried to feed little pieces to the birds, but nothing worked and just watching the parent birds flying around only a few yards from the babies made him more frustrated.

At four o'clock, Douglas returned to his barracks to lay down on his bunk. He was beat and the earlier peace and quiet of the barracks would have been nice. However, the hut was more active now. About thirty cadets were at the other end making noise and just generally fooling around.

As he closed his eyes, he heard, "GRAB HIS ARMS, YOU DUMMY, HE NEARLY HIT ME!" The voice was loud and it made Douglas sit up and look through the spaces of the bunks to see what was going on.

A group of cadets had surrounded a bunk and although he couldn't see the activity, he heard enough to know what they were doing to the cadet they were holding down.

"O.K., GET HIS SHORTS DOWN. I SAID HOLD HIM! NOW WHERE'S THE SHAVING CREAM AND RAZOR?"

The cadet on the bunk was yelling for assistance and the large cadet who was giving the orders said, "HOLD THE TOWEL OVER HIS MOUTH!"

Douglas started to walk down toward them. "DON'T COME OVER HERE UNLESS YOU WANT SOME OF THE SAME," said the mouthy one. The sound of his voice made Douglas walk back to his bunk to lie down again. There were too many to argue with and he wasn't in the mood to get involved anyway.

There was silence as the shaving took place. The cadet who was being held down had stopped yelling because there was nothing else he could do.

About two minutes later, Douglas heard, "I WAS PROUD OF THOSE HAIRS, YOU HOMOS. I'VE BEEN NURTURING THEM."

"OH, WE'RE NOT JUST SHAVING YA," said the big one. "WE'RE GOING TO SPREAD THE SHOE POLISH."

Once again the victim started to yell and then the yelling stopped again as the shoe polish was applied.

When the action stopped, a cadet ran to the washing-up area trying to pull up his pants.

Douglas was glad it was over, but it wasn't. No sooner had it stopped, it started all over again. They had grabbed a little guy who was reading a comic on his bunk. The same procedure took place but this time it was different.

The mouthy one was still giving the orders. "HOLD ON TO HIM, YA DUM-MIES. AHHH, HE'S STARTING TO CRY, AND LOOK, HE'S GETTING A HARD-ON. LET'S WHACK HIM OFF."

That was it, Douglas had had enough. "HEY YOU HOMOS, WHY DON'T YOU GO AND CRAWL UNDER THE ROCKS WHERE YOU CAME FROM. ESPECIALLY YOU, FATTY."

There was silence at the other end. They stopped working on the small cadet and followed the large one toward Douglas' bunk.

"ARE YOU CALLING ME FATTY? I DON'T LIKE PEOPLE CALLING ME FATTY. PEOPLE WHO CALL ME FATTY END UP GETTING SHOE POLISH ALL OVER THEIR BALLS, AND THAT'S WHAT I'M GOING TO DO TO YOU, RIGHT NOW."

Douglas' heart was pounding so hard he could feel it in his throat. He'd seen kids like this when he came over to Canada from Liverpool. There was always one who was the ringleader and he was usually mean. If he could be taken out, the others went their own way.

The fat one walked closer with his entourage behind him. Douglas didn't have too many hairs on his legs and his opponent noticed this.

"SO LILY-WHITE WANTS TO GET INVOLVED, DOES HE?"

Douglas forced a smile as he got up and stood in the aisle.

"If you're planning on black-balling me, I want you to try to do it personally. You're fat enough to do it by yourself without any helpers. C'mon, you can do it. You're not just a bliffy, you ton of lard, you've even got shit for brains."

The fat one's 'friends' backed off now, leaving him to face Douglas alone.

As the fat cadet held out his arms to grab him, Douglas brought up his boot with full force and caught him square in the middle of his testicles.

Moaning and grabbing his crotch, the cadet started to go down in pain and Douglas hit him as hard as he could in the face. The cadet went flying backwards with one hand holding his crotch and his other hand covering his face.

"YOU'VE BROKEN MY NOSE, YOU'VE BROKEN MY NOSE," he cried. Douglas was so mad he was going to hit him again but his hand was sore and he though better of it. The cadet's nose was bleeding badly. There was blood all over the cadet's shirt and all over the floor.

"If I catch you doing that again I'm going to march you to the company office and you can tell them what you've been doing." Then he gave a disgusted look to the fat one's 'friends.' You homos better take him to the MIR and have his nose looked after. I hope they put some black ointment on his blue balls."

None of them wanted to help and the big one made his own way out of the hut holding his nose and making sure he didn't have to pass Douglas.

When it was over, the cadet who had been black-balled came over. "They put shoe polish all over my balls and my dink. It's starting to swell up."

"I saw that happen once in Nanaimo," Douglas replied. "Your balls will be alright, but if the swelling in your wang doesn't go down, you'll have to have it checked out by the doc."

"They got two on the other side before they got me," the cadet said. His nametag read 'Rothstein.'

"Just kick 'em in the nuts, that's all those bullies deserve," Douglas replied. "Hey, you're one of the guys that managed to get out of Church Parade."

"I'm Jewish so I didn't have to go. Want to go for a pop?"

After they grabbed their pith-helmets, Douglas and Harvey Rothstein headed for the Cadet Canteen. It was a half-hour later that Douglas realized the unhappy affair had allowed him to meet a new friend.

When suppertime came around, the mess hall was nearly empty because most cadets were still downtown. Douglas and Harvey Rothstein had a whole table to themselves and their plates had been heaped full with beef stew.

"I don't know how they expect us to eat all of this," Rothstein said, as he was 'digging in.'

"I guess they expected more cadets for supper than they got," replied Douglas. Then he explained to Harvey the problem he was having with the birds. Harvey listened intently and came up with what they both thought was a brilliant suggestion. They would get two boxes and lay a plank on them. The birds might think this was the cannon and if the baby birds were placed on the end of the plank, the parent birds might relate to them.

After supper, the boys tried out the idea, but their efforts were in vain. The parents were frantically flying around, but they still stayed away from the babies.

"It's no use," said Douglas, squirting water down the throats of the birds and shaking his hand. It was still sore from hitting the big cadet. "I don't know what we can try now, we've tried everything else."

Eventually they put the birds back in the box and returned them to the Commanding Officer's porch.

"There's a movie starting in ten minutes in B-3," said Harvey. "Do you want to go?" He knew Douglas was worried about what would happen to the birds and he was trying to ease his mind.

Douglas shrugged. "Sure, what's on?"

"It's Bird of Paradise with Debra Paget and Louis Jourdan."

Douglas put his arm around Harvey's shoulder. "With a name like Bird of Paradise, maybe we'll get an idea how to solve my bird problem."

Cadets were returning to camp by the hundreds and B-3 was full when they entered. It was dark inside, and hard to see. Eventually they found a couple of seats about halfway to the screen.

The movie was great but when the lights came on, Harvey noticed he was sitting next to the cadet with the bandaged nose. When their eyes met, 'the nose' as he was later called, found another chair.

At nine o'clock, when the rest of the Musketeers started dribbling into the barracks, B-21 was a beehive of activity. The showers were going full out, every sink in the washing-up area was running and the washing machine was whining Douglas' wing was full of cadets singing, jumping across bunks, ironing their clothes, cleaning barrack boxes, shining boots and squirting fire extinguishers at each other.

Danyluk was particularly happy even though he found it difficult ironing his clothes dry.

"Alma's parents weren't home today and we had the basement all to ourselves," he said, showing Douglas his new ring. "And what do you think of this?"

"Jesus, she must be pretty serious about you."

Danyluk smiled. "They all get serious when the Moose slips them ten pounds of sausage meat."

East was standing there eating a chocolate bar. "You had sausages for supper? I was there, why didn't you tell me?"

"I'm not talking about that, you creep. HEY, WHO SAID YOU COULD TOUCH THE RADIO?" he yelled at a cadet who had turned up the song Truly, Truly Fair, with Guy Mitchell. "Oh, that's O.K., I like that song."

"Guess what?" said Wayne.

"What?"

"Scheaffer's been promoted again."

Douglas was sitting next to Wayne, buffing his boots. "You've got to be joking? What is he now, a General?"

Wayne laughed. "To tell you the truth, I don't know what he is. Foster told us coming up the hill."

Danyluk stopped ironing his wet shirt, and said, "I got those two Irish cadets."

"What do you mean you got them?" asked Douglas.

"I found out what hut they live in and I put itching-powder in their sheets and frenched their beds.

He was about to say something else when all of a sudden they heard a loud CCCRRASH! BAAANG! BBOOOOOM!

The noise nearly made Jackson fall off his bunk. "What the hell was that?"

It was thunder. "Christ, that scared the shit out of me."

Danyluk smiled at Earl. "It just said on the radio that we can expect thunder, lightning, and heavy rain tonight and tomorrow."

Bergie stopped straightening out his barrack-box. "Thank God. It'll be a welcome change from all this heat."

It happened again. BARRRROOOOOM!

Wayne looked out the window. "You guys should have seen that one. Wow, what a sight!"

"How's your toe, Earl?" Douglas asked.

"Good, I..." He didn't have time to finish.

"STAND BY YOUR BEDS!"

Sergeant Beckford entered the barracks. He was wearing civilian clothes as he walked the aisle sniffing.

"What's burning in here?" he asked.

"We're trying to iron our clothes dry," Danyluk replied.

"You've had all bloody day to get your clothing dry. What have you been doing?"

Danyluk showed him his new ring. "We've been with the ladies, Sergeant."

Beckford laughed. "The day that I see you with a lady, Danyluk, I'll kiss your ass at high noon on the steps of the Headquarters Building and give you half an hour to gather a crowd."

This time Danyluk laughed. "Is that a promise, Sergeant?"

"RIGHT! PAY ATTENTION HERE! LIGHTS OUT IN TEN MINUTES!"

When the lights were finally out, Wayne leaned over his bunk. "I forgot to give Debbie her bra back before she left."

"Surely she has more than one?" Douglas whispered.

"She does, but this is the easiest one to get off."

BARRRRROOOOOM!

Danyluk hadn't gone to bed. He was still trying to iron his clothes dry. "They're all easy for me. I've got magic fingers," he said. Then he unplugged his iron and got between his sheets.

"SON OF A BITCH! I CAN'T STOP SCRATCHING!"

"I forgot to tell you that those Irish cadets visited your bunk before you got back." The voice was the same cadet from across the aisle.

Now everyone in Nine Platoon was alive with merriment. Danyluk thought he had outsmarted them. He was wrong once again.

"Good night, Wayne."

"Good night, Doug."

When the next bolt of lightening struck, it was as bright as daylight. Before the boom was heard, Douglas got up and closed their window.

The sound of pelting rain on the roof soon put them to sleep.

CHAPTER VIII

When a storm finds its way from the coast to the Okanagan, its magic elixir quenches the dry, cracked ground, freshens the air, and injects new life into everything it touches.

Sometimes Mother Nature just sends a short storm to tide things over for awhile. This wasn't one of those times, because the rain that started after the boys had gone to bed was still bludgeoning the area when Reveille was sounded. Joining the rain, a cold strong wind found every bunk inviting as it howled through the open windows of B-21.

The cadets in Charlie Company weren't prepared for getting out of their nice warm beds in this weather. When the bugle blared, some were huddled under their blankets like babies in a pram. Others had kicked off their blankets in the middle of the night and their bodies were wrapped like a mummy, shivering under only one sheet.

It wasn't surprising no one was up when Sergeant Simpson entered the barracks and screamed, "STAND BY YOUR BEDS!" Nor was it surprising when he walked the aisle dumping mattresses on the floor and stripping the cold and confused mummies by pulling down their shrouds.

"C'MON, C'MON! I'M NOT LETTING YOU OFF JUST BECAUSE OF A LITTLE RAIN! YOU LOOK LIKE A BUNCH OF GIRL GUIDES HIDING UNDER A TREE AT THE FIRST TOUCH OF A RAINDROP! LET GO OF YOUR COCKS AND GRAB YOUR SOCKS! OUT ON THE ROAD IN TEN MINUTES!"

"A LITTLE RAIN? DID YOU HEAR THAT? HAVE YOU SEEN IT OUT THERE?" Danyluk was shivering, trying to find his P.T. shorts in the 'maze' of his side of the barrack-box. "There's no doubt in my mind that Simpson is a sadist."

Douglas looked at him. No wonder Danyluk was shivering, he was soaking wet. The wind had blown the rain in through his window.

In ten minutes, Charlie Company was on the road running to the upper camp. With each step, mud that was caked on the soles of their running shoes flew everywhere and allowed no compromise. It was on their hair, all over their faces, in their mouths, on their legs, and as Danyluk put it, "We're going going to have mud up our asses, if we don't slow down our pace."

"Doug, thank God you closed our window, otherwise we'd look the same as these guys," said Wayne, breathlessly.

"Who's talking to me?" replied Douglas. He was cold, soaked, covered in mud, and the rain was blinding him.

After the run, twenty-five pushups and fifty sit-ups, the company was fallen out. The barracks looked like a trench scene from the First World War. Mud stuck to everything and they had no real place to hang their clothing. They couldn't stick their wet clothes in their barrack-boxes because all of their other clothes would get dirty.

The Musketeers were first in the showers along with Rothstein. They couldn't see each other because of the steam.

"Don't worry about the clothing," said Bergie. "I've got a secret place where it will dry."

"Where abouts?" asked Wayne.

"In the furnace room."

"You mean that little room with the steps outside?"

"That's the one. The caretakers don't mind us using it as long as we leave them room to stoke up the stove with coal."

"Bergie, you're a genius," said Wayne, allowing other cadets who were cold to share his shower. Soon the shower room held three times its normal capacity.

"I'm no genius, I was tipped off to it last year. You can tip someone off to it next year."

"NEXT YEAR?" screamed Danyluk. He had been singing "UNDER THE SHADE OF THE OLD APPLE TREE. THAT'S WHERE NELLIE FIRST SHOWED IT TO ME."

"You'll never get me back next year." Then he continued singing. "IT WAS WRINKLED AND BROWN AND HAD HAIR ALL AROUND AND IT LOOKED LIKE A BIRDS NEST, YOU SEE."

"You'll be back," said Bergie.

The song reminded Douglas of the birds. He dried himself off quickly. "I'VE GOT TO GO. I'LL SEE YOU GUYS AT BREAKFAST."

Douglas rushed back to his bunk and put on his shorts, sweater, running shoes and a ground sheet, before he ran out the door, heading toward the 'Colonel's birds.'

As he looked into the box, a voice came out from behind the screen door. "They didn't make it, son."

The Colonel came out. "It was a cold night and without their parents, they couldn't handle it. I guess nature wanted it to be this way."

Douglas was on his knees looking into the box. He hadn't stood up when the Colonel appeared. When he did stand, there were tears rolling down his cheeks.

"God, they never had a chance," he said, as the Colonel handed him a hand-kerchief.

Every inch of Douglas' face indicated the battle had been lost. The Colonel gave him a sympathetic smile. "I'm going to have the cannon moved back. They'll probably lay more eggs and raise their young."

Douglas didn't say anything, he just kept looking at the box.

Colonel St. Laurent put his hand on Douglas' shoulder. "They didn't suffer.

Would you like to help me bury them?"

He nodded and for the next few minutes, Douglas and the Commanding Officer stood in the pouring rain burying the birds close to a nearby tree.

When it was done, the Colonel thanked him and said that Douglas had better rejoin his company. The colonel didn't have a coat on and he was soaking wet.

Douglas handed him back his handkerchief. "Thank you, Sir," he said as he saluted. "At least we tried."

"Yes, we did and had they been a little older, they might have made it."

On his way back to his barracks, Douglas looked at the cannon. The parent birds were gone.

The weather made the hot breakfast taste better that morning. The cooks knew the boys were cold; there were extra helpings on everyone's plate.

A chair was placed at the head of the table for Rothstein and he and Douglas told the other Musketeers about the fight and the birds.

All of them wanted to get their hands on the large one, but Douglas told them it was over with. "I don't normally kick people in the nuts, but it was me or him."

After a few minutes, they agreed to let it be. The fat cadet had probably learned his lesson.

At inspection, it was raining so hard the Company Commander walked through the ranks quickly. There wasn't much to see anyway because the cadets wore their ground sheets. It was impossible to see their shorts or shirts.

"We look like large mushrooms," said Danyluk. He was bitching because he had ironed his clothes dry and now no one could see them.

"NOW PAY ATTENTION HERE! AS YOU ALL KNOW, CHARLIE COMPANY HAS BEEN PICKED AS THE GUARD OF HONOUR. THIS IS WHAT EVERY COMPANY IN THE CAMP WANTED, BUT YOU PEOPLE EARNED IT. THIS MEANS THAT THE TRADITION HAS BEEN PASSED TO YOU AND YOU KNOW WHAT WE WILL BE GOING THROUGH. NEXT SATURDAY, WHEN CHARLIE COMPANY MOVES, IT WILL MOVE AS ONE! IS THAT CLEAR?"

"YES, SERGEANT!"

Sergeant Beckford's voice was loud even in the rain.

"NOW, DANYLUK, YOU'VE BEEN COMPLAINING ABOUT NOT BEING INSPECTED. WHY?"

Danyluk didn't know what to say. "I...er...well. This is Nine Platoon, we worked on our kit."

"Alright. Take off your ground sheet and I'll inspect you. Come on, take it off."

Danyluk took it off. Now he was getting drenched just standing there as Sergeant Beckford looked him up and down.

"YOU'VE PRESSED THE FRONT OF YOUR PANTS, BUT THE BACK LEGS HAVEN'T BEEN TOUCHED! WHY?"

Danyluk now realized that when the lights were turned off, he had planned on pressing the back of the legs the next morning, but had forgotten. His mind was going at a mile a minute before he came up with an answer even Sergeant Beckford hadn't heard before.

"DO YOU REALLY WANT TO KNOW, SERGEANT?"

"YES I WANT TO KNOW! OF COURSE I WANT TO KNOW!"

Danyluk smiled. "Well, you keep telling us that there's always room for improvement. If I had pressed the back, there wouldn't be any room left. Also, you said that a good soldier always looks ahead of himself, never behind."

The smile on Sergeant Beckford's face turned into a roaring laugh they hadn't heard before.

Danyluk's chest stuck out a mile as he joined Nine Platoon in the laughter.

It took Sergeant Beckford two minutes to gain control of himself and have Danyluk put his ground sheet back on.

After Sergeant Beckford regained his composure, he informed the company what they could expect after being made the guard.

"WE ARE GOING TO BE ON THE PARADE SQUARE EVERY MORNING FOR THE NEXT TWO WEEKS. IN ADDITION, WE WILL BE ON THE PARADE SQUARE EACH AFTERNOON, AND IN THE EVENINGS, FROM 1800 TO 2000!

"EACH AND EVERY ONE OF YOU IS GOING TO WORK HARDER THAN YOU'VE EVER WORKED BEFORE IN YOUR LIFE. NOW, I KNOW AS WELL AS YOU DO THAT NONE OF YOU HAVE WORKED BEFORE. THIS IS THE FIRST TIME, ISN'T IT DANYLUK?"

"Not really Sergeant, I used to raise rabbits and..."

"WHAT?"

"YES, SERGEANT, IT IS!"

Sergeant Beckford had to look away for a minute, he was nearly going to break up again.

"Son of a bitch, why me?" Danyluk whispered to anyone within earshot.

"Because like I told you, Moose, he knows your name," Bergie whispered back.

Nine Platoon started chuckling again.

"SETTLE DOWN! WE'RE GOING TO START FROM SCRATCH! THIS LITTLE BIT OF RAIN SHOULDN'T BOTHER US BECAUSE WE'RE CHARLIE COMPANY...THE GUARD! FROM NOW ON YOU WILL BE REFERRED TO AS GUARD! IS THAT CLEAR?"

"YES, SERGEANT!"

"RIGHT! GUARD, ATTEN....TION!"

Sergeant Beckford wasn't fooling when he said they were going to start from scratch. Over the next four days, Charlie Company thought of the small parade square as their home. It was drill and more drill, in the morning and in the evening. They started on page one of CAMT 2-2 (Canadian Army Manual of Training) and worked their way through it.

During the afternoons, they attended lectures on various subjects and after supper they were on the parade square again.

Rifle drill was introduced on the second day and bayonets on the third day. This necessitated Sergeant Beckford obtaining additional help; Sergeant Simpson and two other Regular Force Sergeants were added to his staff of eight Regular Force Corporals.

If a cadet blinked, it was noticed. If an arm wasn't raised up to the right level, it was noticed. If their dress wasn't 'up to snuff,' names were taken and 'the lazy people' had to turn out in full summer dress every hour from 2000 until midnight, even after lights out.

Some cadets were slow to learn, but after awhile, the company started to look like a Regular Force Company on parade.

Every single day, they would start from scratch again. "ATTENTION...STAND AT EASE...STAND EASY...RIGHT DRESS...OPEN ORDER MARCH...CLOSE ORDER MARCH...RIGHT TURN...LEFT TURN...ABOUT TURN...LEFT AND RIGHT INCLINE...FORM TWO DEEP...FORM THREE RANKS...FORM SQUAD...LEFT FORM...RIGHT FORM...CHANGE STEP...ABOUT TURN ON THE MARCH...RIGHT TURN ON THE MARCH...LEFT TURN ON THE MARCH...OPEN ORDER MARCH ON THE MARCH...CLOSE ORDER MARCH ON THE MARCH...SALUTING AT THE HALT AND ON THE MARCH...EYES RIGHT...EYES LEFT...PROVING...SIZING...DISMISSED...FALL OUT...SLOW MARCH... CHANGING INTO SLOW AND QUICK TIME...GETTING ON PARADE...STANDING AT ATTENTION WITH THE WEAPON... STANDING AT EASE WITH THE WEAPON...STANDING EASY WITH THE WEAPON...SLOPE ARMS...ORDER ARMS...PRESENT ARMS...CHANGE ARMS...SHORT TRAIL ARMS...LONG TRAIL ARMS...FIX BAYONETS AT THE HALT...FIX BAYONETS ON THE MARCH...UNFIX BAYONETS AT THE HALT...UNFIX BAYONETS ON THE MARCH...PORT ARMS FOR INSPECTION...PRESENT ARMS ON THE MARCH...REST ON YOUR ARMS REVERSED..."

Sergeant Beckford's voice never wore out, but every cadet in the company was hoarse from calling out the time. It got to the point that cadets were calling out, "ONE, TWO THREE, ONE!" in their sleep, along with Sergeant Beckford's other comments.

"YOU, YES YOU, GET YOUR HEAD UP! GET YOUR ARMS UP, THAT MAN! GET YOUR BLOODY ARMS UP, HIGHER, HIGHER! MY DOG LIFTS HIS LEG HIGHER THAN YOU! I SAID CHEST OUT AND STOMACH IN, NOT STOMACH OUT AND CHEST IN! STAND STILL, YOU HORRIBLE EXCUSE FOR AN UNDERTAKER! STAND STILL! LOOK TO YOUR FRONT! THAT'S IT, THAT'S BETTER! GOOD, DON'T LOSE IT NOW! I SAID DON'T LOSE IT! PICK UP YOUR FEET! YES YOU, PICK UP YOUR BLOODY FEET! DID YOU BLINK?! DID YOU BLOODY WELL BLINK?! DON'T SCRATCH YOUR NOSE ON MY PARADE SQUARE! DON'T PICK YOUR ASS! DID YOU PICK YOUR ASS? WELL, DID YOU? DRIVE YOUR FOOT DOWN, MAN! DRIVE IT DOWN! BEND THE KNEE! I SAID, BEND THE KNEE AND SHOOT THE FOOT FORWARD! BRING YOUR FOOT UP! HIT THE RIFLE! HIT IT, HIT IT, HIT IT! AM I SEEING DAYLIGHT

BETWEEN YOUR ARMS?! FIX YOUR HANDS! CORPORAL, GET THAT MAN'S NAME! RELAX AND SHAKE YOUR HEADS! GET THE COBWEBS OUT! DON'T SCRATCH YOUR PRIVATE PARTS! DID YOU SCRATCH YOUR PRIVATE PARTS ON MY PARADE SQUARE?! IT LOOKS GOOD TO ME LADS, IT LOOKS GOOD! PERFECT, BUT THERE'S STILL ROOM FOR IMPROVEMENT!"

The guard didn't mind working for Sergeant Beckford. he had a way about him that made everyone want to do the best they could for him.

Although he shouted and yelled and tossed his pace-stick on the ground, he gave them a wink once in a while to show he was human.

Charlie Company was getting good, very good, and every cadet knew it. They were working as a team, thinking as a team and if one cadet screwed up, he heard about it. There wasn't room for individuals when it came to drill. It had to be perfect and eventually, they were just that, perfect.

"Between looking after my kit, studying for our exams on Saturday and working on the parade square, I don't know if I'm shitting or going blind," said Danyluk in the mess hall. It was noon on Thursday.

Bergie smiled. "Well, one good thing has happened."

"What's that?" Wayne asked.

"The rain has stopped."

Jackson rubbed his hands together. "Not only has the rain stopped, but we've got a swim parade this afternoon. Did you hear me guys? A swim parade."

They were tired, but the thought of a swim parade cheered them up.

Danyluk opened his eyes. "Swim parade? Hey, that means girls, girls, and more girls."

"That would be nice," said Bergie, "But we're going to Kin Beach, not Kal Beach. And, wait for it...guess which company is coming with us? Tarrarrah, Signals Company!"

Danyluk's face lit up. "You mean the chumps from the dit, dit, dit, dah, dah, dah, up the pole, down the pole, are you finished, finished, finished, company? Christ, I wonder if Genova is coming with them?"

Wayne gave him a cocky look. "If Scheaffer is there, he'll be there."

A piece of unchewed meat shot out of his mouth onto the middle of the table and even Danyluk wanted to barf when it happened.

East interrupted eating his third piece of cake. "We work our butts off; why can't we just be on our own?"

He was referring to the fact that while Charlie Company was sweating on the parade square, cadets from Signals and Driver-Mech took delight in giving Charlie the finger. Signals did it when they were up the poles and Driver-Mech did it when they drove by in their convoys.

"They just don't deserve to join us."

Bergie broke in. "Well, they're with us. You guys really don't like this Genova, do you?"

"He doesn't like himself," replied Danyluk. "I betcha when he gets up in the morning, he looks in the mirror and says, "AGGGGAGGHHH! God, I'm ugly!""

Bergie looked like he was in deep thought, before he spoke. "Well, I was thinking of a few things we could do tomorrow night that would get us in deep shit, but, er, we could also do a few things today."

During the next five minutes, the Musketeers were huddled together at their table. A cannon blast wouldn't have disturbed their train of thought as Bergie did the talking. Over belly-laughs and chuckles, plans were made for that afternoon.

When the trucks arrived for swim parade, the Musketeers made certain they had seats. If any shorts were going to be pulled down today, it wouldn't be theirs.

Jackson was sitting next to East. "Did you get the cookie?" he asked.

"Yup, three of them. Did you get the porridge?"

Earl nodded. "A whole canteen full and it's wet and soggy."

As the trucks lumbered out of Camp Vernon and down the hill, the cadets of Charlie Company were in high spirits singing, *"Old King Cole was a merry asshole and a merry asshole was Old King Cole. He called for his wife in the middle of the night, and he called for his privates three!"*

Before they reached the beach, they had finished all the verses of Old King Cole and a few other songs as well.

The drive to the beach was pleasant for Douglas. He was proud of himself for getting a seat, because before the trucks reached the bottom of the hill, some cadets were wearing their shorts around their ankles and the girls were whistling.

He noticed cadets holding up their pants with one hand and hanging onto the frame of the truck with the other. That was wise, but some cadets just plain forgot and they had to pay the price. This time the Musketeers pitched in and placed their feet on a few crotches.

Okanagan Lake splits like a snake's tongue at the north end, near the outskirts of Vernon. Kinsmen Beach is located at the extreme end of the east fork of the lake.

The ground in between is cattle country. Rolling, weather-beaten golden hills with very little vegetation, except at the top.

Douglas couldn't take his eyes off the land they were passing. Once again he was stunned by the beauty of it all. Even the noise of the truck didn't distract his attention as he tried to take it all in.

When they arrived and unloaded, he was still in a trance. The lake was gorgeous and the sounds of cadets yelling, flicking towels and pushing each other didn't disturb his gazing.

"This truly is God's Country," he murmured.

Kinsmen Beach is quite unlike Kal Beach, as the cadets soon realized. The main part of the beach is 200 yards long with very little sand near the water. Sporadic grass grew from the water's edge up to a road about seventy yards away which ran parallel to the beach and turned south to what is known as Adventure Bay.

In the middle of the beach in front of the road, there were two changing shacks open at the bottom with no roofs on them. They also didn't have doors, but the entrances were the wraparound type, making it totally impossible to see what was going on inside.

Charlie Company was halted in front of the shacks and because there were no girls, they were told they could use both buildings to change into their swimsuits.

When they were fallen out, a long lineup formed at each building, but that didn't bother Douglas. He was looking at a very old large wooden structure about a mile away on the east side of the lake. He asked Bergie what it was.

"That's the old Sutherland Arms Hotel. It was built around the turn of the century to look after passengers that embarked and disembarked from the paddle steamers travelling up and down the lake. The steamers aren't used anymore, but it's a nice old hotel. My parents visited last year and we stayed there. It's a riot on the wharf and at night, some kids and parents just sleep on the beach and jump into the water in the morning."

Douglas just stared at it thinking how much he'd love to see it.

"If you'd like, we could hitchhike there some Saturday or Sunday and I'll show it to you."

As Douglas was getting changed, he heard the sound of motors running on the back road behind the changing shacks. He knew it was Signals Company arriving.

"Is everyone sure of the plan?"asked Bergie.

The group of them nodded with eager smiles.

Nobody from Charlie Company was allowed to go near the water until everyone was out of the changing shacks. When they came out they all had to have their clothing and towels with them. Then they were formed up in three ranks and told to lay their clothing down. That way, they would always know where it was and the staff would know if a cadet went missing.

There were no lifeguards on the beach, so their Company Commander gave a pep-talk about water safety. The buddy system would be used.

When they were fallen out, the peace and tranquility of Kin Beach disappeared. In no time, cadets were all over the wharf, the grassy area and in front of the small refreshment stand at the end of the beach.

Cadets from Signals Company were lining up at the changing rooms and the voice of Genova could be heard everywhere.

Douglas just listened. He knew Genova never delegated tasks. He had to do it himself even though he had Regular Force Corporals along. Apparently, they were used to this and headed for the water as soon as they arrived.

The Signals cadets were formed up in three ranks behind the clothing of Charlie Company, then they were fallen out.

Genova took off his bush uniform and as Foster had predicted, he was walking around in his red bathing suit and a white T-shirt. Cadet Scheaffer was walking with him and it appeared they were discussing Morse Code.

Okanagan Lake soon made the cadets of Charlie Company forget the parade square and guard routine. The water was a miraculous cure for stopping the bitching. Although the temperature was in the high nineties, the coolness of the lake and the serenity of the surrounding countryside made all the cadets forget about camp. They were now having fun which they had earned and most rightfully deserved.

About an hour after they arrived, Bergie called the Musketeers together. They held their meeting in one of the changing shacks so they wouldn't attract attention.

"Wayne, your job is to get Scheaffer away from Genova. When that's done, Douglas, you get Genova into a conversation. East, have you ground up the cookies?"

East nodded. He had ground up the cookies and added water. The gooey mess was now in his right hand which he showed to them.

Jackson gave East a sour look. "Christ, it looks like shit."

Bergie laughed. "That's what it's supposed to look like. O.K., everyone knows what to do. Let's get at it."

It didn't take long for Wayne to get Scheaffer away from Genova. Not too many people talked to Scheaffer, so it was a pleasure for him to walk the beach expounding about the soft life in Signals.

Bergie had his hand on Douglas' shoulder. He watched Wayne take Scheaffer away and then said, "Go!"

As Douglas walked towards Genova, Danyluk headed for Genova's pile of clothing and East circled around behind Genova. East only had half of the 'paste' with him because he gave the other half to Danyluk.

When Douglas was about ten feet away from Genova, he said, "Excuse me Sergeant-Major, can I talk with you for a few minutes?"

Genova walked toward him. "What is it, Brice?"

Douglas had positioned himself so that Genova's back faced Jack East.

"A cadet in our company said he heard an officer saying you're going to be sent home because your wife is sick and someone has to look after your kids."

Genova gave him a weird look. "Don't be so damned silly; you know I'm not married. Who was the cadet?"

"I don't know his name but he said that wasn't the real reason you were going home."

Douglas now had Genova's attention because the Sergeant-Major walked up to him.

"Oh, really? And, er, what is the real reason?"

Genova's eyes were now bulging and he was starting to look annoyed.

"Come on, out with it, Brice!"

"I can't really tell you, Sergeant-Major. It's pretty embarrassing."

Douglas could almost feel the breath coming out of Genova's giant nostrils. "Well, get it out man! Just what did he say?"

Douglas looked nervous. "I shouldn't be the one to tell you. That cadet there heard it as well." He was pointing to Bergie who just 'happened' to be walking by.

Genova looked at Bergie. "You there, come here. I understand you heard some cadet saying I was going to be sent home? What reason did he give?"

Bergie nodded and said something very low and unintelligible.

"Speak up man, what did he say?"

"HE SAID YOU GOT A DOSE AT HOP SING'S PLACE!"

Genova was now pumping his hands up and down toward the ground, trying to get Bergie to lower his voice.

"He said what?"

Genova was now madder than hell. This gave East the opportunity to spread the 'shit' all over the bottom of the back of Genova's T-shirt without his feeling it. Then East walked away casually.

"HE SAID YOU GOT A DO....."

Genova interrupted him. "Not so loud."

"HE SAID YOU GOT A DOSE AT HOP SING'S PLACE!"

Genova was furious. "Whoever he is, I'll have him for this. That is the most ridiculous thing I've ever heard. Ha, ha, ha. I'll be over to your company. I'll have that son of a bitch, wait and see!"

As Genova stomped away, Douglas, East and Bergie were splitting their guts, looking at the stain on the back of Genova's T-shirt. Nothing could look more real.

"God, that looks real," said Bergie. "If I didn't know any better, I'd say he caught his T-shirt up with some toilet paper when he wiped his ass."

As they were laughing, Jackson and Danyluk joined them. They had completed their 'job' as well.

For the next hour, as Genova strolled the beach, cadets didn't go near him. When he approached them, they left, making a wide swath around him with a look of plain disgust on their faces.

The Musketeers forgot about Genova and were now in the water around the wharf. The 'sand' in the water at Kin Beach is a brownish-black color and when a handful is thrown at someone, it sticks to their skin like glue.

The Signals cadets were on the receiving end of the 'delivery' and it was difficult for them to locate the culprit who threw it because once released, the elusive individual ducked under water to resurface in another location.

Soon everyone got into the act. Throwing mud was the unofficial order of the day; trying to elude it became more and more difficult. It was a fun afternoon and although there weren't any civilians on the beach, the cadets of Charlie Company didn't miss them. They deserved this small respite and made good use of it.

Genova walked up and down the beach and onto the wharf, but no one spoke to him. Finally he got into the lineup at the refreshment stand and even there, the nearest cadet stood five feet away.

He tried to force a smile. "WHAT THE HELL'S THE MATTER WITH YOU PEOPLE? DO YOU THINK I'VE GOT LEPROSY OR SOMETHING?"

The closest Signals cadet said, "Well, Sir, its ahhh, it's your ah..."

The Musketeers were watching, holding towels in their mouths to stop anyone from hearing their chortling.

"WHAT'S WRONG WITH EVERYONE TODAY? SPEAK UP MAN!"

A cadet in the back of the line behind Genova, hid behind the cadet in front of him and screamed, "YOU'VE SHIT YOURSELF, SERGEANT-MAJOR. IT'S ALL OVER THE BACK OF YOUR SHIRT."

That's all it took. Genova's face started to turn the color of his swimsuit. He put his hand around and felt it. Something was there alright, so he slowly took off his shirt. When he saw it, he couldn't speak. He tried, but words just wouldn't come out.

The Musketeers were lying all over each other laughing like they'd never laughed before. Bergie could hardly catch his breath when he said, "Look at him. He actually thinks he's wiped his ass with his shirt."

Soon everyone on the beach was laughing as Genova made a mad dash to his pile of clothes and headed for the changing shack.

When he came out, he was still red. He probably wanted to die, but the worst was yet to come because while he was changing, the Officer Commanding Signals Company had arrived and asked for him. A cadet had told him that Genova was changing and would probably be out in a minute or two.

Genova came out in his bare feet. He was fully dressed other than he didn't have his boots on. When he saw his OC, he saluted and said, "We'll be wrapping this up in a few minutes, Sir."

Danyluk and Jackson had done their job well. As Genova bent down to pick up his boots, they saw the seat of his pants was covered with the same mixture. As luck would have it, he hadn't noticed it when he put them on.

The officer and the cadets discovered the stain as well; so did Genova's twitching nose.

"Sergeant-Major, I think you've had a problem?" the officer said. He could smell it, too.

Genova didn't know what to say. "Yes, Sir. I keep smelling shit, Sir."

"I have no doubt you do. It's all over the back of your pants."

The look on Genova's face was one of pure panic. He didn't know what to do or what to say as he backed into the changing shack carrying his boots. Within seconds the words, "WHAT THE HELL? OH, MY CHRIST!" could be heard everywhere.

Both companies were allowed to travel back to camp in their bathing suits. Genova's OC yelled that he would send a jeep back for him.

The ride back was one of pure jubilation for the Musketeers. Everyone was talking about Genova. Some cadet said, "Imagine a Sergeant-Major shitting himself?"

"They're a dirty bunch, those Signals," said another.

Bergie leaned over to Danyluk. "How could he smell it, they were only ground-up cookies?"

Danyluk was smiling. "We didn't end up putting the porridge in his boots. We saw a dog taking a dump by the fence, so we used the turds instead. He actually did smell shit."

Bergie was now on the floor of the truck rolling in laughter.

Wayne couldn't catch his breath, he was laughing so hard. "He's never going to live this down."

"Oh he's hard-nosed, he'll live it down, but I bet Signals will be doing extra drill," said Douglas.

As the trucks wheeled past the guardroom, only one truck wasn't singing Oh Provost, Oh Provost. The cadets in that truck had changed the words.

"Genova Genova, we know you're a twit;
but you'd better start taking good care of your kit;
cause like it or lump it, we'll give you a fit;
and the whole camp will know, that you're just full of shit!"

After Lights out, Danyluk said to Bergie, "You said earlier that you had some sort of a plan for tomorrow night. Is it still on?"

Bergie sat up in his bunk. "It sure is. Tomorrow night, we're going to look after your Irish 'friends.'"

Danyluk chuckled. "Bergie I, love ya. How do you come up with these ideas?"

There was silence for a few seconds before Bergie replied.

"Survival!"

CHAPTER IX

Lieutenant-General Douglas Brice didn't quite know what brought him out of his trance and back to reality. He thought he heard Colonel Forbes talking to him or he could have heard someone say, "Charlie Company." Whatever it was, it was powerful because he didn't want to come back to the present. His recollection of 1953 was so real. Although he was on the dais saluting, he was also in the back of an International three-ton truck singing about Genova.

It took only a fraction of a second for his mind to clear. His subconscious mind had raised and lowered his arm automatically as the Band, Alpha and Bravo Companies had passed the reviewing stand, but the combination of Peter Forbes saying, "Here they come," and the Cadet Company Commander screaming, "CHARLIE COMPANY EYES RIGHT!" made him want to return.

Although he was hot and his mind muddled, this was *his company* in front of him. He straightened his body and stood rigidly at attention as he raised his arm to return the salute.

The Cadet Company Commander had already called out the command, and every cadet in the company had snapped his head to the right, looking into the General's eyes as they marched by the dais.

"Each of them is aware of the significance of this moment, Sir," remarked Colonel Forbes.

Douglas didn't acknowledge the comment. It was obvious, because he was looking at them. They had their chests out and they were proud, possibly as proud as the original Charlie Company. But there was something different about them. He hadn't noticed it at first, but each of them wore a smile. It was not a normal smile, but more like one of defiance. He understood. In their own way, they were chastising him for not coming back sooner and for not standing up when Trades Training and the meaning of the word 'Army' was taken out of Army Cadets. That was it, they were saying, you had your chance and we've got to carry on the tradition, but with what?

As the last platoon in the company passed and they were given the eyes front, each cadet screamed, "CHARLIE!" It was totally unorthodox and it should never have happened, but it sent a jolt of guilt down Douglas' spine.

Colonel Forbes leaned forward. "I'm sorry about that, Sir. It didn't happen during the rehearsals."

Douglas turned around and smiled. "Charlie Company has just taught me a very valuable lesson, Peter. Something that everyone in Ottawa should relearn."

Delta Company was coming up next, but Charlie Company's actions a few seconds earlier had rekindled his memory. As he raised his right hand to return Delta Company's salute, his mind was magically recalling his experience in Vernon, in the year 1953.

'Istanbul, not Constantinople,' was blurting from Danyluk's radio. He had turned it up so that all cadets in Nine Platoon could hear it as they made their beds before going to breakfast.

It was Friday, which meant a weekend was coming up and finally they could get some well-deserved rest.

"Those Four Lads are mint," Danyluk said as he sang along with them.

Douglas was helping Wayne with his bed. "Diane and Debbie get back tomorrow. Why don't we go to the wharf at the Sutherland Arms Hotel?"

Wayne's face lit up. "Sounds good to me, but how do we get there?"

Douglas was fixing the last hospital corner on the blanket. "We could ask Tom and Ellen to take us, or we could hitchhike?"

Wayne shook his head. "It's confinement to camp for a week if we get caught hitchhiking."

Douglas thought for a minute then bounced a quarter on Wayne's bunk. "I'm sure her parents will take us. C'mon, let's get some breakfast; we've got a baseball game this morning."

While they were having breakfast, Bergie explained his plan to 'fix' the Irish Cadets. All the Musketeers were gathered around him and not a peep could be heard outside of the perimeter of their table.

Danyluk sat with a smug look on his face. "So it is going to take place after lights out? I knew it. I knew we'd do it then."

"Have you done this before?" asked Douglas.

"Many times," Bergie replied. "There may be trouble, but not to us, just their company."

Moose was sitting back rubbing his hands together. "Bergie, I'm so God-damned proud of you, I don't know what your plans are in the future, but you should consider politics."

Bergie stood up to leave. "Let's not count our chickens before they hatch. We've got a tough job ahead of us and the Military Police are wise to these things."

East stuffed a sausage in his mouth before he stood up. "Don't worry, Bergie, we'll pull it off. We'll do it, just wait and see."

Jackson pulled East back into his chair. "Jack, how many sausages have you had?"

East scratched his head while he continued chewing. "I don't know, why?"

"Well, you just sneaked the last one off my plate and I wanted it."

Playing baseball in temperatures exceeding ninety-five degrees fahrenheit can really build up a sweat, especially when there is no shade and the baseball diamond is a dust bowl.

This didn't seem to bother the cadets of Charlie Company because as far as they were concerned, the game was a reprieve from the parade square. That, plus the fact they were finally getting a chance to play the cadets from Driver-Mech, the same ones who had given them the finger, day after day, as they drove past the parade square.

When the teams were picked, Douglas found himself in the position of pitcher. He didn't really want the job, however, someone had told the sports staff that he was going to be a professional baseball player. He learned later that the 'someone' was Wayne.

Actually Douglas was as good as anyone else when it came to pitching. He had a good arm and he looked forward to "beating the bastards," as Danyluk had told everyone that's exactly what they would do.

Some civilians stopped their cars and walked over to join the 800 cheering cadets as the game progressed. In addition, the Commanding Officer of the camp, as well as at least forty Officers and Non-Commissioned Officers, stood on the sidelines to encourage their favourite team.

The game was tight and the score was tied after each inning. East was the back-catcher and between the two of them, they had worked out a set of signals that they used to 'handle' the sharp-looking players of Driver-Mech.

With only fifteen minutes left, Driver-Mech was up to bat and the bases were loaded with only one out. The noise was deafening.

Douglas had walked the players on the bases. For some reason, his throwing arm wasn't doing its job. The next batter wore a smug smile on his face as comments from both companies flew in Douglas' direction.

Douglas wound up and tossed a ball over the plate. It was perfect, but not that perfect because the D&M cadet hit it with all of his might and it came straight toward Douglas' head like a rocket. He could have ducked but for some reason he didn't and he caught it. The batter was out. He tossed it home, and the cadet running from third base was out, as well.

Charlie Company went wild. Although the game was not over, they had managed to hold the so-called 'best baseball team that Camp Vernon had ever produced,' to a tie.

To the sounds of "HE WAS TRIPPED, HE WAS TRIPPED," the umpire who looked like he used coke bottle bottoms for eyeglasses called "Time Out."

The Driver-Mech cadets were insisting that Douglas' toss to East was high and their runner would have reached home if East hadn't tripped him, two paces from the plate before the ball hit his glove.

"YOU'RE OUT!" The umpire had called.

"I WAS TRIPPED!" yelled the runner. The criticism from Driver-Mech was hot and heavy. Two hundred cadets were telling the umpire to get new glasses, while another two hundred IBT cadets were yelling, "GOOD CALL!"

East was standing there with his hands in the 'Pope' position with an innocent look on his face. The umpire asked him if he tripped the runner and East emphatically denied it.

"YOU SAW THE PLAY, UMP; THERE WAS NO POSSIBLE WAY I COULD HAVE TRIPPED HIM."

The umpire agreed with East. It had been a very fast play and if he had tripped the runner, other members of the sports staff would have seen it.

The runner pushed East and East pushed him back. The next second the umpire was in the middle of a fight and his glasses went flying into the crowd. It took five minutes to straighten out the mess and find the umpire's glasses.

Charlie Company was up to bat and now every member of the sports staff was watching the game closely along with other companies using the sports field. The last inning was about to begin and Driver-Mechanics at this point would have loved to settle for a tied game.

Four companies were on their feet with jubilation when Rothstein hit the ball out into centre field. It looked like a home run for a minute, but the fielder was fast, too fast, and Rothstein was out.

The next batter was 'the fat one' with the bandaged nose. He picked up some dirt and rubbed it into his hands before he stepped up to the plate. WWWhhizzz, the ball went over the plate. "STRIKE ONE!"

The pitcher smiled and received some sort of a signal from the catcher. WWWhhhizzz, the ball was tossed perfectly again. "STRIKE TWO!"

"YOUR NOSE IS BIG ENOUGH, HIT IT WITH THAT IF YOU HAVE TO. JUST HIT THE DAMNED THING," screamed Danyluk.

The third pitch was just as fast and 'the fat one' hit it with all of his might. Instead of going out of bounds, the ball just hung in the air and although the batter made first base, the catcher caught the ball. He was out.

Douglas was up to bat and the exact same thing that happened to the batter before him, occurred again. It was hot and the bat was searing in his hands. WWWHHHizzz, "STRIKE ONE!"

The Cadets from Driver-Mech roared their approval.

The pitcher threw the ball again. WWWHHHiizz, "STRIKE TWO!"

"GIVE UP! GIVE UP! GIVE UP!" The cadets from Driver-Mechanics shouted at the top of their lungs. "SCREW YOU! SCREW YOU! SCREW YOU!" was the response from Charlie Company.

Douglas looked at Wayne and shrugged. Things didn't look good and he knew it.

Wayne yelled, "Here, take this other bat, Doug," throwing a dry bat to him.

Douglas gripped it and focused on the pitcher. The pitcher wound up and threw a perfect pitch over the plate. CCRRAACK! Douglas hit it hard and the ball went flying 'way out past the player in centre field. As the crowd went wild, he took off like a horse out of the gate. He didn't realize he had hit a home run. He could have walked, but he ran like a cheetah. Charlie was with him. "C'MON, C'MON, C' MON."

When he was close to home, the catcher held out his leg. The exercise was futile because Douglas jumped over it and planted both feet on home base. The ball hadn't yet entered the diamond.

The next player was struck out, but with a half inning left, Charlie Company was ahead. There was pandemonium on the sidelines. Charlie's fans went wild.

With dirt stuck to his face, hair, legs and hands, Douglas struck out the first two batters. The next batter was none other than Don Lyons. He was standing there with a menacing grin on his face. "ALL'S FAIR IN LOVE AND WAR, DOUGIE."

"THIS AIN'T LOVE." He released the ball with all of his might. Lyons struck and missed. "STRIKE ONE!"

Douglas looked up at the sky. "Please Lord, let me get him," he murmured.

Danyluk cupped his hands to his mouth. "COME ON, DOUG, THINK OF FOSTER AND THE SALES TAX."

Douglas released the ball once again. WWWHIIZZZ! "STRIKE TWO!"

It was hard for anyone to hear themselves think. This was it and Lyons knew it because his 'smile' disappeared.

East gave the signal to throw one as fast as he could. When the ball was released, Douglas thought it would be a strike, but Lyons hit it. WWWHACK! The ball went flying out to the far right field. Lyons moved fast, but it was all for nought because Rothstein decided to play the role of Plasticman. His jump with an outstretched arm caught it.

Hundreds of cadets ran on the field. Rothstein and Douglas were lifted into the air and the cheering could probably be heard in Vancouver.

Charlie Company had won, and as the guys with the 'fingers' left the field, Douglas, Harvey and the rest of the team were given the treatment of heroes. Although their hands and backs were sore from all of the shaking and patting, they were on Cloud Nine and nothing else in the Universe mattered.

When they were washing up for lunch, Douglas felt a hand on his shoulder. Turning around, he saw 'the fat one' standing there with embarrassment on his face and his hand outstretched. "I er...I guess I deserved it."

"Did you apologize to the others?"

"Yes."

Douglas shook his hand. "Good, you'll get more kicks playing the game of baseball than blackball."

For obvious reasons, lunch tasted superb. The conversation was all about the game and although totally irregular and against camp rules, Lyons joined them again for lunch.

"East, did you trip him?" Lyons asked.

As usual, East's mouth was full, but he swallowed quickly. "Trip who? The guy tripped himself trying to get to the plate."

"He still says you tripped him."

"Listen, Don, the ump says I never tripped him. There was no possible way I could have."

Lyons leaned over the table and looked East squarely in the eyes. He had a smile on his face as he asked the question one last time. "I'm asking you if you tripped him?"

"Look," said East. "I never tripped him. I may have put my foot out a little further than I should have, actually a lot further, but I never tripped him." East was now laughing his head off.

"Then you should have tripped him, because he's the one who stole Doug's capbadge in church." Lyons handed a capbadge to Douglas.

Douglas was astonished. "My God, it is mine. Yes it is, I recognize it because the right side was slightly bent." He was now rubbing the badge on his P.T. shorts. "Thanks, Don. How did you get it?"

"I saw the guy polishing it along with about fifteen other badges he had. When I confronted him, he told me found it on the floor of B-3 after the church service had finished. He handed it over."

"Now I won't look like a 'gormph'," said Douglas.

"How do you guys eat this food?" Lyons asked. "Do you ever get turkey on weekends?"

"I think we've had turkey sandwiches once," said East. No one knew better than East when it came to food.

Lyons stuck his chest out. "Then you guys should come over and eat with us once in a while. They give us the good 'scoff' because we're driving all the time."

East's mouth was full again. "Yeah, we've seen your 'fingers.'"

"We're having turkey for supper on Sunday, why don't you guys all come over to the D&M mess hall?"

After a short discussion, it was decided that the Musketeers would eat over at Lyons' mess hall on Sunday afternoon. East was going to ask Lyons what they had for lunch on Sundays, but Lyons got hit in the face with a pea someone had flicked with his knife. The words, "NO D&M SLOBS IN HERE," followed.

It didn't take long for the Musketeers to load their knives with peas. The food fight was on.

During the next five minutes food flew in all directions. A blob of mashed potatoes hit Douglas on his forehead, and East got some Jello in his ear. The mess hall looked like the aftermath of a kindergarten hand-painting contest; walls, floors, and ceilings only.

"IF I'VE TOLD YOU PEOPLE ONCE, I'VE TOLD YOU A THOUSAND TIMES, WE ARE CHARLIE COMPANY! WE DON'T ACT LIKE THE OTHER COMPANIES, BECAUSE WE'RE NOT ANIMALS. WE ARE BETTER THAN THEM, DON'T YOU PEOPLE UNDERSTAND THAT?"

Called from the Sergeants' Mess by the Orderly Officer when the fracas began, Sergeant Beckford was furious. He had ordered Charlie Company to form three ranks outside of the building.

"IF THE COMPANY SERGEANT-MAJOR WAS HERE, ALL OF YOU WOULD BE CONFINED TO CAMP FOR A WEEK. I THINK YOU HAVE WORKED TOO HARD FOR THAT PUNISHMENT, BUT IT DOESN'T MEAN I'M LETTING YOU OFF LIGHTLY.

"NEVER AGAIN WILL FOOD BE WASTED BY THIS COMPANY. NEVER

AGAIN WILL I BE CALLED TO WITNESS WHAT THE MESSING-
SERGEANT HAS CALLED, 'THE WANTON STUPID INFANTILE ANTICS
OF TODAY'S MODERN YOUTH.'
"YOU PEOPLE ARE SUPPOSED TO BE THE PRIDE OF YOUR CADET
CORPS, THAT'S WHY YOU'RE HERE. THERE ARE CADETS THAT
NEVER HAVE THE OPPORTUNITY TO ATTEND VERNON. THEIR
NAMES ARE ON THE WAITING LISTS. WELL, LET ME TELL YOU, I'D
TRADE THEM FOR YOU IDIOTS RIGHT THIS MINUTE.
"NOW WHEN I FALL YOU OUT, THAT MESS HALL WILL BE
SCRUBBED SPOTLESS IN FIFTEEN MINUTES. I MEAN SPOTLESS. THE
FLOORS WILL BE WASHED, THE WALLS WASHED AND THE CEILINGS
WASHED. WHEN I INSPECT IT, IF I FIND A TRACE OF FOOD ANY-
WHERE OTHER THAN IN THE SERVING AREA, YOU PEOPLE WILL BE
CONFINED TO CAMP ALRIGHT...YOU'LL BE CONFINED FOR THE REST
OF CAMP. IS THAT CLEAR?"
"YES, SERGEANT!"
Lyons answered as well. He was praying that he wouldn't be recognized as 'a
foreign diner.'
As luck would have it, he wasn't. After Sergeant Beckford's 'dressing down,'
everyone hurried back into the mess hall. Although there was some complaining
as to who started the incident, the cadets completed the task within the time limit
and the mess hall passed inspection.
Lyons sneaked out the side door and headed back to his company's lines while
Charlie Company was being formed up again.
"YOU WILL BE ON THE PARADE SQUARE RIGHT UNTIL SUPPER
THIS EVENING, SO IF ANY OF YOU THOUGHT TRAINING WOULD END
AT SIXTEEN HUNDRED HOURS, YOU'RE OUT OF YOUR MINDS.
"NOW, YOU HAVE EXACTLY THIRTY MINUTES TO GET BACK TO B-
21 FOR A SHOWER, A CHANGE OF CLOTHES, SHEET EXCHANGE AND
MAIL-CALL. IS THAT CLEAR?"
"YES, SERGEANT!"

The showers were full when the Musketeers finally got their turn, and as usual
the water was cold. Nevertheless, cold water hastened their shower. They were out
in five minutes. The sheet exchange came off without a hitch and a Corporal came
into the hut.
"MAIL-CALL! DANYLUK...DANYLUK...DANYLUK...EAST...
JACKSON...HAGOPIAN...ROTHSTEIN...LESKA...DANYLUK...LEE...
BROOKS...RAE...BROWN...BAILEY...ALEXANDER...SMITH...
PATTERSON...LAIDLAW...MATSER...DANYLUK...BANKS...
DANYLUK...DANYLUK...DANYLUK...BRICKELL."
The Mail-Call was interrupted for a moment when the Corporal accused Dany-
luk of mailing letters to himself.
"Smell the perfume on these," Danyluk replied.

"COHEN...BRICE...FALCONER...DUNN..."

When Mail-Call ended, Danyluk sifted through his pile wondering which one he would open first.

"Ahhh," he said, smelling one of them. "It's from lovely, loosie Lucy."

"She's probably pregnant, as well," said Banks, but Danyluk didn't respond because he was lost in a dream world.

"CHARLIE COMPANY OUT ON THE ROAD...NOW!"

Sergeant Beckford stood at the entrance to the door. He made certain they all knew he was still upset with them.

For the next three hours, Charlie Company proved they owned the parade square. Every single drill movement was practised time and time again. The pop-truck did not appear and very few times did Beckford say, "O.K., relax and shake your heads."

When they finished, the lesson was understood. Food should stay on plates.

The temperature had been close to 100 and the soles of their boots were covered with tar and loose gravel.

At five o'clock, Douglas lay on his bed. "I am beat," he said to Wayne.

Wayne normally stuck his head over the side and responded. But not today, he was too tuckered.

Bergie asked, "Are you two going to dinner?"

Both Douglas and Wayne shook their heads. "I'm not too hungry," Douglas replied. "I think I'm going to take another shower."

Douglas and Wayne both stripped to their shorts and walked to the shower. Because everyone else had gone over to eat, they had the whole room to themselves.

Over the next fifteen minutes they talked small-talk, then turned up the cold water and held their heads under. It wasn't long before they started to feel 'human' again.

As they were walking back to their bunks, Sergeant Beckford came into the barracks. They were the only two in the hut, and they wondered why he came in.

"How's it going, guys?" he asked.

"Good, Sergeant," they replied, drying their hair with their towels.

The Sergeant sat on the bunk opposite them. "I just thought I'd come over and say we were all very proud of the job you guys did today at the baseball game. You didn't buckle under pressure and it made everyone happy when we beat those guys."

Wayne and Douglas continued drying their hair.

"Are you happy here?" he asked, looking at both boys.

"Yes, Sergeant," they replied.

Sergeant Beckford searched for words before he spoke again. "That's good. Y'know, this camp is filled with kids who come from every walk of life. Some are rich, poor, some are dirty, dumb...intelligent. It's a real melting pot. Our job is to try and get them working together as a team. To try and...well, to try and get rid of the bad habits of a few and replace them with the good habits of the majority.

Believe it or not, the system works pretty good. To make it work, though, we need cadets like yourselves...people who know how to survive. You guys seem to know how to keep your noses clean and, well, with no muss or fuss, get your jobs done. Do you know what I mean?"

Douglas and Wayne were sitting side by side on Douglas' bunk. "I think so, Sergeant," Douglas replied.

Sergeant Beckford smiled. "I guess I'm trying to say that you're setting a good example."

"We think YOU'RE setting pretty good standards," said Wayne.

"I bet you didn't think that on the parade square this afternoon? Nevertheless, I hope you understand what I'm saying. The system works well if good standards are set and if everyone works with it. You only get out of it what you put in. There will always be idiots and if you put yourselves above them, even they will see the light."

Both cadets sat there nodding.

Sergeant Beckford stood up. "Well, I'm going over to eat now, are you two coming?"

"You mean you're going over to our mess hall to eat?" asked Wayne.

"You bet I am. Everyone will think that I'm in there checking to make sure no food is thrown, but actually I'm going to have supper with a fine baseball team and some bloody good soldiers." He winked at them. "C'mon, get your clothes on."

Douglas and Wayne weren't hungry before, but now they were famished. On the way over to the mess hall, Douglas said, "May I ask you a question Sergeant?"

"Sure, go ahead."

"Er, how come you, er...?"

"Why did I have a talk with you today?"

"Yes."

"Well, whether or not you know it, Brice, you've impressed me."

"The baseball game was just luck," Douglas said bashfully.

"I'm not talking about the baseball game. I'm talking about the way you handled Hitchens and the way you put yourself on the line for Jackson. You too, Banks."

"Who's Hitchens?" Douglas asked.

"He's the guy you sent to the hospital with the broken nose."

Douglas was surprised. "You knew about that?"

"We all knew about it, except the CSM. In my opinion, Hitchens became a man the day that you slugged him. He's probably been a bully all of his life. He needed a lesson and you taught it to him. You handled it well."

"But I had to kick him in the nuts."

"He would have done the same or worse to you. I don't think he'll go around black-balling people anymore, do you?"

"No, as a matter of fact, he shook my hand today and told me he'd deserved it. I thought that was pretty good of him?"

"It was. You see what I mean? Also I hope you understand that as your Platoon Sergeant, my job is to know what everyone is up to?"

Wayne smiled. "If you know what everyone is up to, what do you think I brought back to camp the other night?" asked Wayne.

Beckford laughed. "I don't know everything that's going on, but I do my homework. You brought back a bra and Brice, you got your capbadge back today."

As they walked up the mess hall steps, Wayne looked at Douglas. "Jesus, he keeps track of his men," he whispered.

Sergeant Beckford held the screen door open for them. "You've got that right," he said, putting the palm of his big hand on top of Wayne's head.

It was a typical Friday night in Camp Vernon. In every hut, bunk beds were being pushed to one side while the floor was being scrubbed. Then they would be moved to the other side to allow the rest of the floor to be cleaned.

In B-21, the activity was in full swing. All the cadets were preparing for Saturday Morning Inspection to the sound of Dean Martin's, 'That's Amore,' blaring from the radio.

Jackson was reading Part One and Part Two Orders. "WE'VE GOT A PAY PARADE TOMORROW!"

East was eating a chocolate bar. "What time is it and how much do we get?"

"It's after lunch and we get the grand total of five dollars."

Danyluk was trying to pick up Kelowna on his radio. "I hear rumours that they're going to pay us in silver dollars so the merchants in Vernon will understand the importance of cadets," he said.

"Are we going to the Sutherland Arms?" asked Wayne.

Bergie stopped cleaning the windows by his bunk. "I think we should go on Sunday. More parents are probably free to take us then."

Over the next five minutes it was decided Sunday would be the best day to go.

Jackson was still reading Orders. "The movie on Sunday night is The Desert Rats, with Richard Burton and there's a dance at the Arena tomorrow night."

A Corporal passed by their bunks. "GET YOUR ASSES IN GEAR! WHAT AREA HAS THIS PLATOON GOT THIS WEEK?"

"We've got the grounds and windows, Corporal," replied East.

"WELL, GET TO IT!" The Corporal moved on, grunting.

"He probably wants to get over to the Junior Ranks Club for a beer," whispered East.

With the showers and taps going, the toilets flushing, the circuit breakers cutting off electricity because too many irons were being used, B-21 was the usual circus. So much activity was taking place that hardly anyone saw Foster running in, trying to catch his breath.

"Clarke has been put in the guardroom. Someone caught him whacking off a dog on Genova's bed."

Wayne had a look of pure disdain on his face. "He what?"

"A stray dog walked into our barracks and Clarke jacked him off on Genova's bed." Foster had settled down now and was waiting for a reaction.

"Who turned him in, Scheaffer?" Bergie asked.

"No, one of the Corporals caught him. At first we thought it was little goody two-shoes Scheaffer, but he's been staying away from Genova ever since the beach episode."

Smiles started appearing on the Musketeer's faces. East was rolling on the floor laughing his head off.

"Who's Clarke?" Jackson asked.

Danyluk's right hand was making 'masturbation-moves.' "He's a cadet in our home corps. I pity the dog. It's a wonder it didn't die from the smell of Genova's blankets."

Douglas grimaced. "Jeez, I can understand itching powder or dead fish, but jacking off a dog? That's pretty sick. I take it Clarke didn't like him either?"

The question started everyone howling again.

Every cadet on the Musketeer's side of the barracks was now gathered around Foster, trying to hear his story.

Danyluk stuck his chest out once again. "It's too bad a stray horse didn't walk into their quarters."

Wayne couldn't take Danyluk's remark, he had to go to the window to get some air.

"I went to the guardroom to see him," said Foster. "Have you guys seen the place?"

"What's it like?" Danyluk asked Foster. "Just in case I'm ever in that position."

"Well, there's eight cells with two cadets to a cell, and they're all full. They wear coveralls and have to shine their shoe-polish tins until they look like mirrors. The place is spotless and regardless of which meathead speaks to you, you have to answer *'Staff'*! Clarke wanted out anyway, he doesn't like the camp."

East was up now and still smiling. "That sounds rough."

"That's not all," Foster continued. "Clarke told me that his cell-mate said that tonight is shower night. Everyone gets marched into the shower room wearing their birthday suits and they're told to suds up. Then the water is cut off and they're marched back to their cells. Two hours later they get marched back to rinse off."

Danyluk jumped onto Douglas' bed and held onto the posts like he was behind bars. "Christ, they're not getting me in there."

It was decided none of them wanted the treatment Foster had described.

After Foster left and lights out was imminent, Douglas had a shower and went to bed with twenty minutes to spare. He took out the letter he'd received earlier and read it again.

Danyluk still had his radio on. "Here's a big new hit from Ferlin Husky," said the announcer. "It's called, Dear John."

It is totally impossible to get any peace in a barracks that has two hundred cadets running around, but somehow Douglas blocked out the noise. He felt homesick again and although no one noticed, the homesickness showed on his face as he stared at the lower part of Wayne's mattress, listening to the song.

When Crazy, man, Crazy, with Bill Haley and The Comets came on the radio, he was back to feeling normal.

"MY MOM SAYS SHE DOESN'T THINK SHE CAN MAKE IT UP HERE. THEY WON'T GIVE HER THE TIME OFF," he told Wayne.

Wayne was sitting 'up top' polishing his boots. "THAT'S TOO BAD."

Douglas stood up. "But she's going to send up a food parcel next week."

Wayne's face lit up. "Hey, goodies! It's about time someone in our group got one of those, everyone in B-21 has had one but us."

"She asks me to say hello to you and to tell you to quit collecting bras."

Wayne really looked concerned. "You didn't tell her, did you?"

"Naaah, I'm just joking. She sends her love and says to stay out of trouble."

"Whew, thank God for that."

When the Corporals came around to do bed check, all the Musketeers had 'hit the sack.' They didn't have to stand by their beds.

After lights out, Bergie came over to Douglas' bed and whispered in his ear. "We're up at 0200," he said, before he rushed away to tell the others.

Wayne leaned over again. "I hope we get away with it."

"Look at it this way," Douglas replied. "If we don't, we'll be replacing some of those guys in the guardroom."

Both of them chuckled when they heard Danyluk's response to Bergie. "THEY DESERVE ALL THEY GET, THOSE IRISH PONGOES."

It didn't take long before they were all asleep. The day had been a long one, and two A.M. was not far off.

Douglas felt an arm on his shoulder and he heard Bergie's voice. Bergie was shivering from the cold. "It's time Doug. Just wear your P.T. shorts, a sweater and socks. No running shoes."

Bergie finished his 'rounds.' In seconds, they were standing in the dark of the drying room going over last minute checks. Rothstein had brought a friend, which brought the total to eight.

Without making a sound, the eight of them quietly crept through the other wing of their hut and went out the centre doors. The night air was cold, but it didn't bother them, their hearts were pumping so fast.

Very slowly and about ten yards apart, they made their way around the back of the building behind B-21, then they ran up the road past the east wing of the kitchen and up the centre stairs of the next hut. By going in through the centre doors, they wouldn't wake the Corporals sleeping in the cubicles at each end of the barracks.

They followed Bergie as he stealthily moved to the other side through the washing area. A dripping shower sounded like a waterfall in the silence. The only other sounds were cadets snoring, or the squeak bunks make when their occupants turn over.

There was enough light coming from the shower room to see where they were going and before long they ended up at a bunk very close to the Corporal's cubicle.

Danyluk looked at the two sleeping 'saints.' "So there you are, you bastards," he said in a very low voice.

Bergie made a motion that Danyluk should shut up.

Banks started working. He walked silently to the inside end door and opened it. Then he picked up the fire extinguisher and used it to hold the outside door open. He had just crept back into the hut, when the headlights of a moving car lit up that area of the camp. Wayne moved quickly and brought the extinguisher in again, closing the door behind him. He could see the others looking at him but he couldn't help it. When the lights disappeared, he popped the door open again.

Not a word was spoken. Douglas' heart pounded like a hammer when Bergie pointed to the bunk. Four got on each end. The Irish cadets were sleeping soundly and the one on top had even started snoring.

Bergie was about to give the signal to lift when a cadet near them started talking in his sleep. "I WAS IN THE ARMY AND GRABBED THE PL.....!" His voice trailed off. Each of them nearly had a heart attack, but the cadet's voice didn't wake anyone up.

They bent down and slowly picked up the bunk. It was heavy and creaked loudly. Bergie shook his head and they put it down again, following him into the drying room.

Bergie whispered. "It's going to be tough on the hands because those two aren't light. I want each of you to grab a towel and use it under your hands. That way, we won't cut ourselves."

Creeping back into the wing, they each took a towel off someone's bunk and resumed their original positions. On the silent count of three, the bunk was lifted up and slowly moved toward the door.

The bunk was in the centre of the aisle and very close to the door when they took their first break. All of a sudden a cadet in an upper bunk threw off the covers and jumped down onto the floor. Everyone froze as he walked in the direction of the washroom. They now had to wait for his return and only an idiot wouldn't see the bunk that was out in the open. The cadet must have been automatically walking in his sleep, because he didn't bother with anything except climbing up to his bunk and going back to sleep.

Each breathed a sigh of relief and continued moving the bunk. Getting it outside wasn't too much of a problem, except it had to be carried on a slight angle because of the two steps to the ground. This didn't seem to bother the occupants one bit because the lower one rolled over to his other side and muttered some gibberish.

In about twenty minutes, they had positioned the bunk on the far side of the parade square, out of the lights, with the inhabitants still sound asleep.

East and Jackson went back to the hut with Rothstein and his friend and returned with the cadets' barrack-box, two pairs of boots, two pairs of running-shoes, two pith-helmets, two complete sets of serge, two wash basins and two towels.

The barrack-box was neatly deposited at the foot of the bunks. On it, they laid the two wash basins and on top of each wash basin they placed a pair of boots. Next, the running shoes were neatly lined up on the right side of the bunk, so the occupants could step into them when they awakened. The uniforms were hung at the ends of the bunks and then the towels reinstated in their proper positions. Lastly, the pith-helmets were fastened by their straps on each corner at the foot of the bunks.

When the 'job' was completed, they restored the fire extinguisher to its proper place, closed both doors, returned all towels and crept out.

Back at B-21, without making a sound, they shook hands and dispersed, ensuring their clothing was put away.

After a few whispers and chuckles, the group of them were in their nice warm beds again and only they knew of the ruckus that would take place in the morning.

CHAPTER X

For some reason, Danyluk was already up when the bugler sounded Reveille. As soon as he heard it, he turned up his radio. Doris Day was singing, Secret Love.

"STAND BY YOUR BEDS!" a Corporal shouted, as he walked the aisle, turning over mattresses. He didn't have to turn over many, the cadets of Charlie Company were going in all directions at once, trying to prepare for another Saturday Morning Inspection. This Saturday they were a little tired from all the recent drill periods, but they prepared their hut with vigor.

"No one could ever describe this place," Wayne said as he and Douglas washed the windows in the drying room.

"I know what you mean," Douglas replied. "I was going to try and explain it to my mother in a letter and I didn't know where to start."

Both of them were wearing coveralls, and while they cleaned the drying room and toilet windows, Danyluk and Bergie were on ladders outside the showers and furnace room.

The hut was like the inside of an anthill. Some cadets were trying to iron their clothes dry in the drying room, others were frantically looking around for articles of clothing which had been stolen off the line. While that was going on, cadets were coming in with brooms and mops trying to wash the floors.

The same kind of activity was taking place in the washing area and the shower room. While cadets washed their hands, faces and pith-helmets, other cadets were trying to clean the mirrors being used by those who were 'shaving.' Amidst all of this, cadets were wiping the sinks, polishing the brass on the urinal and cleaning the washing machine.

"WHAT ARE YOU, SOME SORT OF A VOYEUR?" A cadet screamed at Danyluk because he opened the shower room window from the outside and stuck his head in.

"There's so much steam in here, I can't see the dirt on the outside," Danyluk replied.

"OH SURE, I BET YOU SAY THAT EVERY TIME YOU'RE ON THE LADDER OUTSIDE OF THE SHOWER ROOM?"

Danyluk stopped being polite. "I CAN SEE WHY YOU'RE WORRIED. HEY BERGIE, COME AND GET A LOAD OF THIS ONE, HE'S GOT HIMSELF A RADISH FOR A PRICK."

Instantly the window was slammed shut. It's a wonder Danyluk didn't lose his fingers. He shook his head with a smile. "That got him."

Gossip was the main attraction in the lineup for breakfast that morning. The main topic was about two cadets who had been sleeping in their beds on the parade square. They were awakened by the camp Regimental Sergeant-Major at 0630, as he was passing. The other topic was someone had painted the cannon, pink.

"Christ, there was another 'hit squad' out there last night," Bergie said, under his breath.

"I saw everything," said a cadet from another company. "The RSM bellowed, "STAND BY YOUR BEDS" and waited. When they finally did stand up, they didn't know where they were for at least a minute."

The Musketeers were all smiles as they listened with interest.

"How come their company didn't notice they were missing?" someone asked.

"They knew the bunk was missing, but it was stuck way over on the other side of the parade square and nobody saw it. I guess they were busy preparing for Saturday Morning Inspection."

"Then what happened?"

"Well, they were shivering, standing at attention in front of the bunks. The RSM had his nose in their faces. "ARE YOU PEOPLE ON SOME SORT OF A CAMP-OUT? WHAT THE HELL ARE YOU DOING ON MY PARADE SQUARE?"

"Yeah, go on!"

"Anyway, the one without any gaunch on asked the RSM if he could cover himself up because some of the kitchen staff were whistling."

"You mean one of them was naked?"

"No, he had a T-shirt on, but no shorts and now the hoots and whistles were coming hot and heavy."

"Yeah, yeah, keep going."

"Well, the RSM ordered them not to move. He marched away and left them standing there at attention for about ten minutes. One of them wanted to take a leak so bad, he was almost bent over. By now their whole company was on the road, cheering them on."

"Anymore?"

"Yeah. When the RSM returned, he marched them, and I mean marched them, to their quarters. The cadets in the hut were yelling, IRISH FUZZYBALLS and IRISH FUZZYLEGS. They'll never live it down."

Bergie butted in. "Was the RSM mad?"

"I think he was at first, then he started grinning as he marched them in. The guy without the gaunch had someone's towel wrapped around himself when he and another cadet went out to bring the stuff back in. The other one was still in his shorts in some sort of a daze. That's them over there," he said, pointing.

The Musketeers joined everyone in looking at them. At the end of the line, two very red-faced cadets stood erect, looking straight ahead. Although their chins were up, they didn't seem as arrogant as they had been a few weeks back.

Inside the mess hall, the embarrassment continued. As the two 'campers' lowered their heads while passing the kitchen, one of the girls said, "Hey, you're the one with the nice-looking body." She leaned over to an older lady. "That's him, Gert, the one with no underpants on. That's the one you liked."

Gert was about sixty. Her face was full of humour. "Oh, go on Aggie, I liked the one with the shorts on. That one there, the one they called Fuzzylegs."

Although they were only hazing the boys, the two 'wonders of the world' took it seriously.

As Charlie Company was being sized by company rather than by platoons, Danyluk said, "Bergie, we did it. We pulled off the ultimate prank and got away with it."

Bergie nodded. "Let's keep it to ourselves. I think we taught them a lesson."

"Where did you learn how to do that?" asked Danyluk.

"It happened to me last year," he said. "But that's not all. I had a feeling those guys were planning on doing that to us." Bergie was pointing to himself and Danyluk. "We just got them first."

"GUARD! ATTEN...TION! FORM...TWO DEEP!"

When the guard marched away to pick up rifles, there was a certain spring in the steps of the Musketeers.

"Shit for brains, that's what they've got!" Danyluk complained, when he was told someone had convinced the Commanding Officer the parade square was too small and the parade should be held on the field on the other side of the highway.

Danyluk was right. The cadets were immaculate before they walked onto the field. But the morning sun, combined with the other elements, had changed all that the minute they had marched on. Now their boots, puttees and hose-tops were covered with dust, burrs and pieces of tumbleweed.

As a guard, they were formed up in two separate units of two ranks each. They were centred in the field approximately thirty yards from the reviewing stand they faced. For some reason, probably more bad planning, they also faced the morning sun.

Douglas whispered to Wayne out of the corner of his mouth. "Wouldn't you think the reviewing stand would be on the other side of the field?"

Wayne nodded slightly, "It would be too easy."

The Cadet Guard Commander was a tall cadet picked by Sergeant Beckford. He had a good voice everyone could hear.

"GUARD, ATTEN...TION! STANDAT...EASE! GUARD, ATTEN...TION! THE GUARD WILL FIX BAYONETS, FIX...BAYONETS! ATTENTION! GUARD, STANDAT...EASE! STAND EASY! O.K.! TAKE OUT YOUR BOOT-CLOTHS AND DUST OFF YOUR BOOTS. ALSO, TAKE AS MANY BURRS AS YOU CAN OFF YOUR HOSE-TOPS."

One by one, other companies marched onto the field and formed up behind the guard. The band this week was the cadet band and it formed up on the right side of the parade.

When all the companies were in place, the parade was given the Right Dress and everyone lined up on the markers, already on the field.

As soon as the Commanding Officer arrived, the parade took its normal course. The only difference between this week and last week's parade, was the addition of a guard with weapons. This meant the guard had to present arms when the order General Salute was given.

Colonel St. Laurent inspected the guard first. He stopped at Douglas. "Good turnout, Brice."

"Thank you, Sir."

"Did you notice I had the cannon moved back?"

Although Douglas was looking straight to his front, he had a small grin on his face. "Yes Sir, and I noticed it was painted as well."

The Colonel smiled. "I've been told that happens every week around here. Have you seen the birds who moved back into the barrel?"

"No, Sir."

"Well, they have and if they start another family, we can be distant relatives this time. Do you agree?"

"Yes, Sir."

"How's it going?"

"Good, Sir, but can I ask a question that's probably stupid, Sir?"

"Certainly, go ahead."

"Sir, we spent about three hours working on our kit for this parade and it was destroyed in the first minute. Also, they've got us facing the sun. Why, Sir?"

The Colonel thought for a minute. "Good question. MR. GARDINER!"

"SIR?" The RSM was in the reviewing party. When he heard the CO, he walked up and saluted.

"Mr. Gardiner, is there any reason why these cadets are facing the sun?"

"ONLY SO YOU DIDN'T HAVE TO WALK THE WHOLE WIDTH OF THE FIELD WHEN YOU ARRIVED, SIR!"

"Thank you, Mr. Gardiner. Also, why is the parade being held here?"

"I ASKED THE ADJUTANT THAT EXACT SAME QUESTION, SIR!"

"Thank you, Mr. Gardiner, retire the parade, please."

"SIR! GUARD COMMANDER, STAND THE GUARD AT EASE! PARADE COMMANDER, RETIRE THE PARADE PLEASE!"

Mr. Gardiner walked away and while the Cadet Parade Commander retired the parade and dressed it, the reviewing stand, microphone, chairs, guests, etc. were being moved to the other side of the field. The Adjutant would hear about it later.

With the changes made, the Regimental Sergeant-Major returned, saluted and informed the CO that his wishes had been fulfilled. It was probably the first and last time a parade at the camp was inspected in the retired position.

"How's that?" The Commanding Officer asked Douglas.

"Fine, Sir! Thank you very much, Sir."

"Thank you, Brice."

When the inspection was complete and the march-past was over, the parade was standing easy as Colonel St. Laurent spoke.

"ALTHOUGH I DIDN'T THINK IT WAS POSSIBLE, THERE HAS BEEN A GREAT DEAL OF IMPROVEMENT OVER LAST WEEK.

"MANY OF YOU ARE WONDERING WHY WE ARE PARADING IN THIS FIELD RATHER THAN ON THE PARADE SQUARE. WELL, I HAVE BEEN ASKING MYSELF THAT SAME QUESTION SINCE A CADET IN THE GUARD ASKED ME. I CAN ONLY ASSUME THAT THE ADJUTANT THOUGHT IT MAY BE BETTER TO PARADE HERE SINCE THERE WILL BE A NEW PARADE SQUARE BUILT IN THIS VERY SPOT VERY SHORTLY. DOES THAT MAKE SENSE TO YOU?"

"NO, SIR!" The response was thunderous.

"I AM EXTREMELY PLEASED WITH YOUR PROGRESS AT CAMP AND AT THE WAY IN WHICH YOU ARE HANDLING YOUR PERSONAL DEPORTMENT DOWNTOWN. EVEN THE MILITARY POLICE ARE HAPPY."

Grumbling could be heard everywhere and the CO smiled.

"BEFORE I PASS THE PARADE ALONG TO THE RSM, I WANT TO APOLOGIZE TO YOU FOR HAVING YOU FORMED UP WITH THE SUN IN YOUR EYES. IT SEEMS THAT THE RSM AND MYSELF HAVE TO READ THE BOOK AGAIN. THE ONE THAT SAYS TO KEEP THE SUN OUT OF SOLDIERS' EYES. THE ONE THAT SHOULDN'T BE FORGOTTEN! THANK YOU."

Following the address, the Advance In Review Order was given along with another General Salute. The Commanding Officer then left the Reviewing Stand and the RSM had the parade to himself.

The parade was standing easy when the RSM spoke. "NOT A BAD PARADE TODAY, BUT THERE'S ALWAYS ROOM FOR IMPROVEMENT. I EXPECT THAT IMPROVEMENT BY NEXT WEEK.

"RIGHT! THIS MORNING, MY EYES COULD NOT BELIEVE THE SURPRISING SIGHT THEY WERE IN FOR AS I PASSED THE PARADE SQUARE ON MY WAY TO THE SERGEANTS' MESS."

Laughter from all companies followed and a roar of approval from Fuzzyballs' and Fuzzylegs' company.

"I CAN SEE YOU'VE HEARD OF IT, ALREADY. MY TENDER YOUNG EYES HAD TO GAZE UPON A DOUBLE BUNK-BED ON MY PARADE SQUARE. IN THOSE BUNKS, ASSUMING THE HORIZONTAL POSITION, WERE TWO 'CHAMPIONS OF CAMP SOCIETY.' I DIDN'T ASK FOR THEIR NAMES AT THE TIME BECAUSE I DIDN'T NEED THEM. ALL OF THEIR 'FRIENDS' KEPT SCREAMING FUZZYBALLS AND FUZZYLEGS. RATHER ODD NAMES, I THOUGHT TO MYSELF.

"ANYWAY, AFTER I GENTLY WOKE THEM UP, MY INNOCENT AND DELICATE EYES HAD TO BE SUBJECTED TO VIEWING A MAGNIFICENTLY ERECT PENIS AND A SHINY HAIRLESS SET OF BUTTOCKS. I

SHOULD ADD THAT I USE THE TERM MAGNIFICENTLY ERECT PENIS RATHER LOOSELY."

All companies were now cheering, laughing and whistling.

"IF I'M GOING TO HAVE TO PUT UP WITH THESE DISCOVERIES, I WOULD MUCH PREFER TO BE SURPRISED BY A HAIRLESS SET OF FEMALE BUTTOCKS, BUT THEN AGAIN I'M NOT THAT FUSSY WHETHER THEY ARE HAIRLESS OR HAIRY. THE SURPRISE, HOWEVER, SHOULD NOT TAKE PLACE ON MY PARADE SQUARE.

"NOW, I THINK THAT FUZZYWUZZY AND FUZZYWILLY, OR WHATEVER THEIR NAMES ARE, HAVE LEARNED A LESSON THAT IS QUITE SIMPLE. FOR CHRIST'S SAKE, WAKE UP WHEN YOUR BUNK IS BEING MOVED!

"IT WILL NOT HAPPEN AGAIN, NOR WILL THE CANNON BE PAINTED! IS THAT CLEAR?"

"YES, SIR!"

"NOW, THE BEST COMPANY THIS WEEK IS...WAIT FOR IT...CHARLIE COMPANY, WHICH FROM THIS MOMENT ON SHALL BE REFERRED TO AS THE GUARD."

A resounding rumble of approval came from Charlie Company.

Danyluk slapped Bergie on his back."WE'VE DONE IT AGAIN!"

Bergie began pumping Danyluk's hand. He, like everyone else in Charlie Company, couldn't control his emotion."JUST KEEP EATIN' THE BARLEY, CHARLIE!"

"MY CONGRATULATIONS TO THE GUARD, BUT I DON'T WANT YOU TO WIN IT NEXT WEEK. IF YOU DO, THEN THERE IS SOMETHING SERIOUSLY WRONG WITH THE OTHER COMPANIES IN THIS CAMP." The RSM was staring at the Officers and NCOs standing on the sidelines. The only ones smiling were the ones from Charlie Company.

"CARRY ON AND HAVE A GOOD WEEKEND."

After the guard returned their rifles, bayonets, scabbards and frogs [bayonet containers and belt attachment] all their officers and NCOs gathered at B-21 to congratulate them. Afterward they were informed that Pay Parade had been moved up, and they marched to B-3 to receive five silver dollars each.

Two other companies were already lined up when they arrived, however, Sergeant Beckford ordered, "MOVE ASIDE YOU PEONS AND MAKE WAY FOR THE BEST COMPANY IN CAMP!"

The other companies actually did move aside and the cadets of Charlie Company were both shocked and proud to get paid first.

The smooth tones of Ebb Tide were playing over Danyluk's radio as Charlie Company made their beds after Pay Parade.

"That song is mint," Wayne said to Douglas.

Douglas was pushing his pillow into a pillowcase. "I know, Diane and I both call it 'our song.' "

Jackson came over. "What are we doing today, guys?"

Banks turned around. "Well, we're all going to the dance tonight, right? Why don't we pick up the girls and meet them in Polson Park after lunch?"

"I don't know if I should," said Danyluk. "I think Alma wants to get married."

Douglas laughed. "Jeez, you've only known her for a few days. Can't you wait until after you start shaving?"

East slapped Danyluk on the back. "He does shave. I saw him shaving the other day and the blood ran down both of his legs."

"Smart ass! I think she's after my money."

"Danyluk, you've go no money. How in the hell did she get that idea?"

"I told her I was rich."

"Well, you never really lied to her," Wayne said. "You are rich in one respect, but there's a problem."

"What problem?"

Banks stood there smiling. "It's all in your pants."

"At least it's in my pants, your fly is open," Danyluk said, pointing at Wayne's fly.

Wayne looked down to find his fly buttoned and Danyluk's finger being run up his chest to his chin.

"GOTCHA!" Danyluk shouted.

Douglas hit Jackson with his pillow. "What time do we write exams?"

"They've changed the time. It's at eleven-thirty."

"Then we've got time for a pop. Who's for going over to the canteen?"

It was unanimous and when they entered, cadets at every table were talking about the bunks on the parade square.

When the Musketeers sat down at their table, they talked about everything but that.

Saturdays and Sundays were always lazy days at Vernon. The camp staff planned it that way. After the parade, cadets could do whatever they wanted on the weekend, provided it was done in accordance with Daily, Routine, and Camp Standing Orders.

The seven cadets from Guard Company decided they would spend Saturday afternoon in Polson Park and go to the dance in the Arena that evening.

"Has everyone got their passes?" Bergie asked, as they passed Hop Sing's. All responses were affirmative.

"How'd you do on the exams?" asked Wayne.

"I think I 'aced' them," Douglas replied. "There were a few questions in Map and Compass I wasn't too sure of, but I really think I did well on everything else."

"Me, too."

Danyluk couldn't take his eyes off Hop Sing's. "Y'know, one day I'm just going to walk in there and say, "O.K., give me a dame.""

"And what would they say?" asked East.

"They would say,'Yesee, Sir, Mr. Danyruk, Sir, we gottee one here that have wet dleams since she saw you rooking in window.'"

"Hey, not a bad accent," said Bergie.

"You mean having wet creams," said East, smiling.

Danyluk moved next to East. "Since when are you the local expert, wet dreams, or wet creams, what the hell's the difference?"

East said, "Ah, then you don't know, do you? Go ahead and tell him Bergie."

Bergie was caught off guard, but he figured out pretty fast that East was just bugging Danyluk.

"Ah, yes. You see, Moose, it's the vernacular of the word. In most cases the word cream would be a noun, but in your case, it would be a verb. Right?"

"Err, yes, I er, I think so Bergie."

"Good, then you see the idiom, or method of the verb could be to cream or not to cream, that is the question?"

Danyluk's eyes lit up. "That's not the question as far as I'm concerned. I don't give a damn if it's dream or cream as long as I'm in the middle of it." He had put a finger into his mouth and pulled it out making a popping sound. "Screw the question, let's get on with the creaming."

Earl thought for a moment. "Do girls have wet dreams?"

Danyluk replied, "Why not, rabbits do."

"There's that song again," said Douglas as Ebb Tide started playing out of Danyluk's radio. "Turn it up please, will ya, Moose?"

"There are two versions of Ebb Tide. One is with Frank Chacksfield and His Orchestra, and there's another version with words. They're both great, I'm going to buy a copy of each record." Every time the song came on, he thought of Diane.

Earl grabbed Moose's arm. "What, er, what about the rabbits?"

Polson Park was cool compared to the walk down the hill. As they entered the gateway, Bergie said, "Did you guys know that this entrance is called Duke of Connaught Way?"

"Are you serious?" asked Douglas.

"I wouldn't shit ya, Dougie. Apparently the Duke of Connaught came here around the turn of the century and the citizens named this entrance after him."

Danyluk noticed the girls. "There they are, in living colour."

Diane walked up to Douglas and took hold of his hand. "Hi," she whispered softly, "did you miss me?"

Douglas was a bit embarrassed and looked a little shy. This was strange to him. "I missed you more than I thought I could," he said.

Diane somehow folded up in his arms. "I couldn't get you out of my mind while I was away. I was in a daze every day and when I tried to phone, they wouldn't take any messages."

He took hold of her hand. "I wouldn't have had the time to read them anyway. We've never worked so hard in our lives."

As they walked they stopped periodically to look into each other's eyes. Diane told him about Penticton and he told her about his experience in camp.

The sky was pale blue as it broke through the branches of the large tree Douglas and Diane lay down under. Douglas took off his beret and cocked his knees up, with one leg crossed over the other. He placed one hand behind his head, and one around Diane.

"That big white cumulus cloud looks so close I can almost touch it," he said, chewing on a piece of grass.

Diane nudged upward, took the piece of grass out of his mouth and threw it away. She was looking into his eyes as she placed her lips on his; they both closed their eyes as they kissed. Soon, she was lying on top of him and his arms were tightly closed around her. When their lips separated she looked into his eyes. They were both smiling and they could feel each other's body tingling. They kissed again and then she lay down next to him as before.

"My mom knows how I feel. She's a bit upset. She calls it puppy love, but I know what puppy love is and I know she's wrong?"

He sighed. "I've never had a girlfriend before. Not that I didn't want one, I did, but I never had any time what with cadets, my newspaper route and school. I met a girl up Grouse Mountain last winter, but it wasn't like this."

"Are you coming back next summer?" she asked.

Douglas laughed. "I've just started this summer, never mind next summer."

Diane was leaning on her elbow, looking into his eyes again. "I know silly, but...will you come back?"

He didn't answer right away and then she started to tickle him.

"I'll come back every year if you're here." He moved some of the hair on her forehead aside and kissed the tip of her nose.

"Oh, I forgot to tell you that I wrote to you every day. Have you got them yet?" she asked.

He laughed. "I haven't got one of them yet."

"Why are you laughing?"

"Because I'll get more letters than Danyluk does in Mail-Call."

"How many does he get?"

"Multiply all of the girls in Vancouver by ten and you've got the answer. Are we going to your house?"

Diane smiled. "I don't think we should, my parents aren't home."

They both had impish smiles on their faces. "That's why we should go."

"Well O.K., I......" Diane was going to say yes, but another decision was made for them. It was Banks trying to get their attention.

"HEY YOU GUYS, WE'RE ALL GOING BOWLING...COMING?"

"Saved by the bell...I mean the ball," she said.

Douglas wouldn't let her get up. "Blast, my big chance and Banks muffed it."

Diane looked hurt. "There'll be other chances," she said. "I'm sorry."

He squeezed her gently. "I was only kidding, I wasn't serious. Listen, as long as I'm even near you, I don't care if we go bowling or go to blazes."

As he took hold of her hand to help her up, nothing else needed to be said.

It was hot walking to the bowling alley. When they entered, the air-conditioning felt great. Answer Me, My Love, with Nat 'King' Cole was playing on the juke-box. Douglas went over to it, and within minutes, Ebb Tide started. Diane joined him. "That song was written for us," she said.

After five games of bowling, sitting around playing the juke-box and eating supper at the Capital Cafe, the seven couples, finally ended up at the Arena. The lineup was long and from a hundred yards away, they could hear Glen Miller's In The Mood, blaring out through the front doors.

When they finally got inside, the Arena was packed. It took them ten minutes to make it through the crowd to the dance floor.

"There are more cadets here than last week," said Banks, wiping perspiration from his forehead. "Good news must travel fast."

Douglas agreed. "What happens here when there are no cadets in town?" he asked Diane.

"Not too much. It's usually dead. There are more girls than boys because when the boys finish grade twelve, they usually end up going to the coast to get a job or to go to university."

"If I lived here, I'd never want to leave."

Diane placed her head on his shoulder. "If you lived here, I'd never want you to leave."

The disc-jockey had selected Vaya con Dios, with Les Paul and Mary Ford. They danced slowly as Diane held him tight.

Diane raised her head. Tears were running down her cheeks. "I love you, Douglas Brice. I never thought I could fall in love like this, but I have and it's killing me."

Douglas wiped her eyes with his thumb and gently kissed her. "Diane, I, er, I think I've fallen in love too, but I think we've got to remember, we're only fourteen."

"No one ever told me it was going to be like this," she said. "I want to spend my whole life with you. Do you think it's silly of me talking this way?"

Douglas didn't answer her right away. He knew how the other guys were talking about their girls. They weren't serious, they were just enjoying the summer. But with Diane, it was serious. His feelings were no different than hers, because he wanted to spend every spare minute with her as well. He loved everything about her. The way she opened up her heart, the way she smiled, everything.

"No it's not silly. I...I...guess, I mean...I feel the same way," he said, holding her tight. So tight in fact, he could feel her heartbeat. After a few seconds he relaxed and looked into her eyes.

"Diane, this is all new to both of us. We're just kids. It might sound funny, but when I...I hold your hand I don't know how hard to squeeze it before I'm hurting you and I don't want to hurt you. I guess what I'm trying to say is we don't know each other and well, Jesus, we've got our whole lives ahead of us. I won't be fifteen for another two weeks and we live over three hundred miles away from each other. I think we have to take everything in stride and play things as they come."

"I know what you mean, but I...I'm going to wait for you Douglas Brice. I don't care what happens and I won't let anyone get in the way. I'm going to write to you every day and come hell or high water, I'm going to travel to Vancouver to visit you."

Douglas thought for a few seconds. "I could take the bus up here in the winter and we could go skiing together."

The disc-jockey started playing, I'm Walking Behind You, with Eddie Fisher. They were dancing slowly and Diane said, "I'm going to walk beside you, Doug, do you feel the same?"

"You know I do," he replied.

It didn't concern them if the dance floor was full, they were in their own little world, all alone and nothing else mattered.

Periodically, throughout the evening, the girls got together and the guys got together. When the girls were with each other, they talked about their Musketeer. It was different with the guys; they talked about the others girls walking by.

Danyluk pointed at the two Irish cadets. "Just take a look at who managed to pick up some dames."

"Ah, I think they deserve them," Bergie replied. "I think they're down to earth now."

A fight started in the stands between some cadets and local boys, but it was over in a minute because there were just too many cadets. The locals thought better than to continue.

When it was time for the last dance, someone requested Ebb Tide and that made the evening perfect for all of them.

"Just hold me," Diane said. Although their feet were shuffling, they weren't moving very far and it didn't seem to matter. They were in love.

It was so hot inside the arena, when they got outside, the fresh air hit them like a full force gale.

"How are you getting home?"

"My parents will be here in a minute. Do you want a ride up the hill?"

"No, thanks. The other guys wouldn't forgive me if I had it that soft."

When Tom and Ellen's car arrived, they walked over to it and Diane's dad joked, "You must be Douglas Brice, the boy we've been hearing about every minute of every day in Penticton?"

"Oh, dad," Diane said, trying to look the other way.

"How's camp going, son?"

"Good, Sir. How was your trip?"

"Never better, except many times we thought we might have to come back for a wedding," he said, laughing. Diane was really blushing.

As the car pulled away, Douglas found himself saying, "THE THOUGHTS WERE MUTUAL, SIR," and he thought he heard Tom saying, "WHAT?"

About three-quarters of the way up the hill, Banks stopped to look at a bug on the sidewalk. "Jesus, look at the size of this thing." The bug was about one-and-a half inches long and two inches around and it was making a crackling noise.

"The poor thing must be injured," Douglas said as he picked up a rock. "Let's put it out of its misery. He slammed down the rock.

Bergie tried to stop him but it was too late. "Don't, it can't get off its back. Just turn it over. I think it's called a June Bug."

It was too late, the bug had been flattened.

Douglas was heartbroken. He slowly looked at Bergie. "Do you mean it was just trying to turn itself over? Oh Christ, what the hell have I done? What a beautiful creature."

He had his hands in his pockets and was walking away looking down at the sidewalk.

"It was just a bug," Banks said. "What are you feeling sorry for?"

"Did you hear the noise it was making? It just wanted to be turned over and I killed it. Jesus, I had to be the smart ass."

Bergie caught up with him. "Listen Doug, your intentions were good, that's all that counts."

They all thought it was a little funny at first, watching Douglas' reaction. But soon, everyone appeared a little sad.

When the lights were turned out, Wayne popped his head over the bunk. "Are you still feeling sorry for that bug?"

"Yeah, I thought it was injured and I......"

Wayne didn't bother to listen. He put his head back on his pillow. He knew when Douglas was in this state of mind, it would take time.

Douglas got out of bed and stared out the window for at least half an hour. It took him another hour to get to sleep. As far as he was concerned, he had killed a living creature that hadn't bothered a soul. It just couldn't communicate and that tortured him immensely. He'd learned a lesson about acting before thinking, and it would never happen again.

Douglas was silent over breakfast and everyone knew it would be no use talking to him. They had tried to cheer him up while they were making their beds, but to no avail.

Danyluk held the floor. "O.K., so we're being picked up at eleven o'clock, is that right, Earl?"

Earl was fumbling through some notes he had taken out of his pocket. "Yep. We're to meet Lyons and Foster at the guardroom."

East's plate was full when he asked, "Are we going on Church Parade, or are we going to hide in the furnace room?"

Bergie looked at him and chuckled. "We'd better go on Church Parade. They're wise to all of the tricks."

Finally Jackson found the notes he had been looking for. "Did you guys see our new timetable for next week?"

Wayne was stretching his neck trying to see the papers. "No, break the news to us gently."

Earl took a sip of his coffee. "Well, we can say good bye to the girls until next weekend."

Danyluk couldn't believe him. "ARE YOU SERIOUS? I DON'T KNOW IF I CAN GO FOR A WEEK WITHOUT WOMEN. MY BODY WON'T ALLOW ME TO."

Earl smiled. "Well, your body will have to adjust, because we're on the parade square Monday, Wednesday and Friday mornings. Then, we're up in Area Ten on Tuesday and Thursday mornings, taking Map and Compass and Section-Tactics. Guess where we are each afternoon during the week?"

"I know where I'd like to be," Rothstein said. "On the beach playing baseball."

Everyone agreed that would be the place to be, however, Jackson knew otherwise. "Nope. We're on the ranges. Then in the evenings, from Monday to Friday, we're back on the parade square."

Jackson's words had jolted Douglas' mind away from the bug incident. "Jeez, don't we even have one swim or sports parade?"

Earl was shaking his head. "Not one. Between doing our kit, the range, Map and Compass, Platoon-and-Section-Tactics, and the parade square, they've got us nailed."

Now Bergie was upset. "THIS IS SLAVE LABOUR!"

Jackson nearly broke up. "But that still isn't the last of it."

Danyluk just about spit out his coffee. "C'MON EARL, WHAT ARE YOU TRYING TO DO TO US? YOU MEAN THERE'S MORE?"

"Yep, I'm afraid so. The following week, we're going to a place called Glenemma. It's a large training area about thirty or forty miles north of here. We're bivouacking there from Monday until the next Monday."

Wayne stood up to get another glass of milk. "Jesus, if you're correct Earl, then we all better make the most out of our Church Parade today."

The group of them howled as Bergie's fist lightly came down on the top of Wayne's head.

"I'm going to have to cancel my appointment with Hop Sing," Danyluk said, holding open the screen door for the rest of the Musketeers when they were leaving.

Everyone looked at him, not knowing if he was joking. In Danyluk's case anything was possible.

"Do rabbits really have wet dreams?" Earl asked. Danyluk ignored him.

During Church Parade, Danyluk as usual, hid in the jon.

Although Douglas was 'mouthing' the hymns, he only had one thing on his mind. How was going to break the news to Diane that he wouldn't be able to see her for two whole weeks?

When the 'congregation' stood up to sing Jacob's Ladder, Douglas put his beret down next to himself on the bench. Instantly realizing his mistake, he reached for it nearly knocking over a Regular Force Sergeant who was standing next to him.

He smiled sheepishly at the Sergeant and looked at his cap. His badge was there. Then he looked behind. Sure enough, the same two grinning Irish Cadets were looking at him. Continually singing, he sneered back, giving them the 'finger.' Not this time, you bastards, he thought.

When the Musketeers arrived at the guardroom in full walking-out dress, four civilian cars were waiting for them. All the windows were open and girls were hanging out, yelling their names and waving.

Douglas and Wayne headed over to Diane's car, but just before they reached it, Douglas saw Cunningham the cardshark coming out of the guardroom.

"Who were you visiting?"

Cunningham looked a little upset. "I wasn't visiting anyone. I was just trying to get downtown with my black puttees on and the meatheads here say I can't."

Douglas gave him an inquiring look. "But you've got your black beret and web-belt on. Black puttees are part of our regimental dress."

"Tell that S.O.B.," said Cunningham.

Douglas asked Diane's dad if he could wait for a minute. "I'm going to find out who this Corporal is."

Within minutes he was facing him. He took a deep breath. "Corporal, this is our regimental dress. We wear black puttees and a black web-belt because we were once a rifle regiment."

"And just who the hell are you?" asked the Corporal.

"My name is Brice. If I can use your telephone I'll call up the Commanding Officer. Do you know my uncle?"

"Er, YOUR UNCLE? So that's you're regimental dress, is it?"

"Yes it is, may I use your phone?"

"No, you won't have to, er..that's alright, he can go."

"Thank you, Corporal."

Outside, Cunningham said. "I didn't know the Commanding Officer is your uncle?"

Brice gave him a weird look. "Who said he was? I simply asked the Corporal if he knew my uncle. How in the hell did you get the impression the Commanding Officer is my uncle?" He slapped Cunningham on the back and got into the car. They both gave each other the 'thumbs up.'

Douglas couldn't believe just how grand the old hotel looked, as he stood staring at it. It needed a coat of paint, but its character made up for any surface damage that showed.

The Sutherland Arms was surrounded by very large, tall old trees that must have been planted at the turn of the century. They provided a great amount of shade for the few holiday-makers who were there.

Although the building and grounds were run down, it was a natural setting for campers. People with families rented trailer sites fifty yards on either side of the hotel, and the pub doors were always open. It was full of patrons having a 'cool one' out of the hot sun.

An old wharf ran out into the water with high and low diving boards; logs were used for breakwaters around the diving areas. The water was crystal clear. It didn't matter how deep it was, the bottom could always be seen.

Douglas noticed people had built houses on both sides of the arm of the lake and each house had its own wharf. Lawns were manicured, stretching from the houses right down to the lakeshore.

Across the lake, rolling brown hills rose up from behind the houses to touch the blue sky. Although difficult to see, cattle roamed the hills and looked like small brown and black dots from where Douglas was standing.

As he scanned the scene from right to left, he could see Kin Beach at the extreme northern end of the arm. Looking south, the lake gently curved allowing the western arm to join up.

Diane stood next to him. "It's really beautiful, isn't it?" she said.

"If I were a painter I'd want to spend my whole life right here. Words can't describe this, only a picture or a painting could." He was gazing at the summer cottages on the far side. Their lawns were so green and they had their own little wharves as well. A few houses even had flag poles with Red Ensigns (the previous Canadian flag) flying.

"Dad's launching his boat so that everyone can go water-skiing later. He's also brought along the barbecue."

Douglas looked around. "Where is everyone?" he asked.

"They're changing in that shack over there." Diane pointed to a small white shack near the water. One side said 'IRLS' and the other side 'OYS' because someone had stolen the first letter from each sign.

"Make sure you go in the 'OYS' " she said, laughing.

When Douglas went in to change, all the boys had their swimsuits on and Danyluk had his eye glued to a knothole looking into the girls' side.

"Pssst, take a look at the tits on this one. I can't quite see her face, it looks like Lyons' dish. Yes, that's who she is."

Wayne took a look. "That's Diane, stupid."

Douglas pushed him aside. "You guys are perverts."

Wayne laughed. "At least take a look."

Douglas looked mad. He had taken his army shorts and his underwear off, and was getting ready to pull up his swim suit. "I'm not going to look."

Wayne had never seen Douglas move so fast as when he said, "Well, someone's looking at you."

Douglas' face turned a shade red. "You mean someone was looking at me?" he said, putting his eye to the knothole, and seeing another eye. "Jeez...you're right." He kept looking, but the other eye quickly disappeared. Then he heard giggling. All of a sudden Alma was standing there with nothing on, doing some sort of a dance. It was almost as if she knew someone was looking at her and she didn't care. As he continued to look around he noticed that Diane had changed into her bathing suit, but Debbie hadn't put on her top. "I think it was Alma who was looking at me," he said.

Wayne said, "Now who's the pervert? Who are you peeping at?"

Douglas chuckled. "Oh just Alma and Debbie. Nice bodies." He was pushed aside by Wayne, Danyluk, Jackson and East, all trying to get to the hole at the same time. The sounds of giggles could now be heard on the other side of the building.

Shortly everyone came out. Alma looked at Wayne. "I really like your appendix scar."

Wayne started laughing and pointing at East who appeared embarrassed. "Oh, it was you?" she said. "Well, it's a nice appendix scar."

Not to be outdone, East replied. "When did you start shaving it, Alma?"

That question broke everyone up except Danyluk and Alma. "AT LEAST SHE'S GOT SOMETHING TO SHAVE," said Danyluk coming to her aid.

East laughed. "I WAS TALKING ABOUT HER CHEST!"

No sooner had he said it, Danyluk went chasing after him.

Douglas smiled at Alma. "You two are made for each other, you know that don't you?"

Alma giggled bashfully. "Yes, I think you're right. As a matter of fact, after I finished staring through the wall, I said the same thing to myself."

That statement did it. The girls were laughing and the boys were blushing. Wayne came to the rescue. "Alma, can I ask you a question? Are big nipples caused by the owner sucking them, or other people? You know, like yours?"

Wayne didn't wait for her answer, he didn't have time. Alma and Debbie started chasing him all over the beach. They didn't give up and Wayne eventually had to dive into the water to survive.

Eventually, the group of them lounged at the end of the wharf and just had fun. All the boys dived, jumped, and cannonballed from both boards and belly-flopped from nearly every place else.

Although the sun was red hot, the cool water of the lake helped them from getting sunburned.

At first, the girls didn't want to get their hair wet, but that didn't last long. They were pushed in, pulled in, and thrown in. A few had bathing caps, but in a matter of minutes, the caps disappeared.

After a while, the couples found their own special space on the wharf. It was time to relax and just listen to the sounds coming from the lake. Diane's dad made hamburgers and some of the other parents brought pop and chips. These were all distributed evenly.

Diane put lotion on Douglas' back. "When the paddle-wheelers used to chug up and down this lake, this place really used to be busy," she said. "It was a landing stage, that's why they call it Okanagan Landing.

"It's unbelievable," he replied.

When Douglas turned over to lie on his back, Diane slipped a pair of sunglasses on him.

"Hey, these are great, where'd they come from?"

Diane ran her hand through his hair. "I bought them for you when I was in Penticton."

He smiled and shook his head. "You're really something else. I'm glad nobody's nabbed ya before now."

"I'm the one who's lucky," she replied, tickling him a little, before curling up next to him, her head nestled on his arm.

Douglas was looking at the sky. "It must be really beautiful here at night."

Diane sighed. "It is. The lake becomes a mirror for the moon and the sky is lit up with a billion stars."

"Jesus, I'd love to live here," he said. "I don't know how those travellers could have left this paradise when they got off the paddle-wheelers."

Diane stretched across his chest and looked into his eyes. "When you're gone, I don't think I'll ever be able to come back here."

"Why?"

"Because you won't be here."

He smiled. "Oh, sure you will. We had fun here and the memories will be great. Just make sure you don't meet anyone else."

"There will never be anyone else, Doug, and this place won't be the same without you."

Douglas cleared his throat. "I, er..have to tell you something. I won't be able to see you until next weekend and then we won't see each other for another whole week."

"What?"

"It's our timetable. We've got a busy week on the ranges and out at Area Ten, then we're going to Glenemma for a week."

Diane was still looking into his eyes. A lost smile came to her face as she shook her head. "I think someone in that big sky up there is trying to keep us apart."

Douglas rolled her over and looked into her eyes. "No one will ever keep us apart. As far as I'm conc...."

He never had the chance to continue because a wall of water hit them. Wayne and Debbie were running away carrying large empty buckets. That was it. Watertag was the order of the day and they tossed each other into the water again.

Danyluk managed to get hold of Alma's top while she was in the water. He wouldn't give it back and she wouldn't come out.

Finally, someone pushed him back in and for the next fifteen minutes, Alma tried to get his trunks off him. She didn't have much luck until the guys helped out and the trunks flew in her direction. Now he had her top and she had his swimsuit. Neither would give an inch. Eventually, when Tom yelled, "The hamburgers are ready," they had to grab towels to cover themselves as they emerged from the water.

Two or three times while they were eating, they tried to get their respective clothing back, but it was a Mexican stand-off. That is until Danyluk passed East trying to get another burger and East grabbed the towel. It happened so fast, Danyluk didn't know what to do. He was standing there in his birthday-suit trying to cover his front with one hand and his seat with Alma's top.

"EXHIBITIONIST," Rothstein screamed, as Danyluk made a bare-assed bee-line-run for the changing shack, to grab his clothes. No such luck, the girls had already taken them and hidden them all.

After much pleading, Alma threw his trunks in to him, and he threw out her top.

When they finally arrived back at the beach holding hands, a red-faced Danyluk stuck out his chest and said, "You didn't see me panic, did ya?"

Ellen laughed. "Oh, so that's what you call it? No, I think we saw a little bit more than your panic."

The look on Danyluk's face started the group of them laughing.

For the next two hours, the Musketeers and the girls tried their best at water-skiing. East was the best skier of the boys. He had skied before and his advice from the stern of the boat came in handy to the novices at the end of the rope. The girls were experienced water-skiers and they bugged any boy who went tumbling into the water. Eventually though, all of them managed to keep themselves up, and they didn't want the day to end.

At five o'clock the cadets were dropped off at the guardroom. While they were saying good-bye and thank you, Tom walked over to Douglas.

"We've still got to show you fellows Cosens Bay."

Douglas beamed. "That would be swell if it could be arranged. We'll promise to make sure Danyluk keeps his pants on. Today was a blast, thanks very much."

"Don't thank us, we enjoyed it just as much as you guys did."

Douglas and Diane waved at each other until the car was out of sight.

As they were walking towards B-21, Bergie put his arm around Douglas' neck and clenched it. "That was undoubtedly the best time I've ever had here at camp. I never thought anyone could have that much fun here at Vernon."

Danyluk, who was in front, turned around and started walking backwards. "Maybe it was fun for you, but you weren't standing naked in front of the wives and other onlookers. I owe you guys one, boy, do I ever."

Banks said, "Quick, here comes an officer. Moose, you're the closest, salute, hurry up."

Danyluk swiftly turned around and saluted the person who was passing.

"YOU, YOU HORRIBLE LITTLE MAN! HOW MANY TIMES HAVE I TOLD YOU PEOPLE THAT I AM NOT AN OFFICER. I AM THE REGIMEN-TAL SERGEANT-MAJOR. YOU DO NOT SALUTE ME. COME OVER HERE!"

As the rest of them marched on, Douglas kept looking back. "Shouldn't we have stayed with him?"

They all looked at each other. "Naaaaah!"

"That was cruel," said Bergie. "I nailed him the same way last week."

East looked astonished. "And I got him the same way a few days ago."

Wayne had the sneakiest smile on his face. "That's the second time I've got him. The RSM knows him so well, he must think of him as a son."

"There you are. I told you we have turkey for Sunday dinner."

Lyons was boasting and holding his plate out so that food could be heaped onto it. He had the habit of holding his plate out a little longer so that the kitchen staff knew he wanted more than usual.

East caught on quickly and did the same. "You guys in Driver-Mechanics have all the luck. Can you imagine this, guys? Beautiful roast turkey every Sunday."

Danyluk smacked Lyons on the back. "We won't say it's who you blow. From now on, it's who you know. And we just happen to know Don Lyons."

Lyons shook his head lightly from side to side and closed his eyes with boastful confidence. "Ah, think nothing of it, fellas. I know that deep down inside, you would all love to be in D&M."

Rothstein leaned over and whispered in Douglas' ear.

"Does he know we're only being nice because of the turkey?"

Douglas replied out of the corner of his mouth. "I don't think it matters. He's pretty naive at times."

Wayne stood there with a lost expression on his face. "There's only one problem. We can't all sit together."

Lyons' looked as proud as a peacock. "Not to fret, Banks old chum, we'll have to separate and meet after dinner. There's a table with three seats, I'll join you and Doug."

No sooner had they sat down, Lyons dug right in and his plate was cleaned almost instantly. Douglas had taken a small bite, as had Wayne, but something was wrong.

"This stuff smells. Something's wrong. Wayne, I think it's bad."

Wayne gave Douglas a disgusted look. "Oh come off it, Doug. You're just too bloody fussy."

"Wayne, just get your nose down there and smell the stuff."

Wayne sniffed. "Jesus, I think you're right. Don, I wouldn't eat any more of that if I were you. It smells bad."

One of the other D&M cadets at the table looked at Wayne. "WHAT'S THE MATTER, DON'T YOU LIKE OUR GRUB?"

Wayne thought fast. He didn't want to be in another food throwing circus. "Er, sure, but we can't eat turkey on Sundays, we're Henways."

After saying good-bye to Lyons, they headed for the door.

"HEY, WHAT'S A HENWAY?" the cadet asked.

"ABOUT TWO-AND-A-HALF POUNDS," Wayne said, letting the screen door close behind him.

"Have we got time to make it to our own mess hall, Doug?"

Douglas looked at his watch. "Yup, we've got twenty minutes. Jesus, I'm burping that stuffing already and I only had a forkful."

"Me, too. Oh, I forgot to ask you Doug, how come you helped out Cunningham at the guardroom?"

Douglas gave him a knowing look. "Who's the best stuke player we know?"

Wayne thought for a second. "Cunningham."

"And who wants to make some money playing stuke on the way home?"

"We do." He had caught on.

"Right, we do. Cunningham is going to help us win."

"But I hear he's ruthless when it comes to money. He doesn't help anyone out."

"Ah, but I helped him, that means he owes me a favour. Since you happen to be my best friend, his gratitude will rub off on you too. Now we'll both make some money on the way home. Right?"

Wayne nodded with a smile. "RIGHT!"

After supper, B-21 looked like the usual tornado had hit it. Every cadet in the building was inside preparing his kit for the following day. It was catch-up time, because no one had bothered to perform their tasks on the weekend.

Danyluk was bitching at Bergie. "I tried to wash my pith-helmet but the sinks were full. Then I tried to scrub my clothes and the sinks were still full. Finally, I decided to have a shower and found that it also was full. Having a shit was next on my list, but the 'crappers' were full. What the hell is happening around here?"

Bergie was in the same boat and was sympathetic. "Look at it this way Moose, you're not alone. Anyway, what did the RSM say to you?"

Danyluk looked straight into Bergie's eyes. "You've got a nerve to ask me that?"

"It wasn't me, Moose."

"No, but you've nailed me before. How can you do that to your pal, your buddy, your one-and-only bunk-mate?"

When Douglas passed them on the way to scrub his clothes, they were still 'talking.' If Danyluk had been paying attention, he would have found a scrub-brush and a place at the sink.

Douglas and Wayne took turns outside, guarding their washed clothes, which were dry in ten minutes. Afterwards, they spent an hour ironing them. They then had to gently fold the clothing and lock it in their barrack-box. If clothes were left out, they would disappear in two minutes. It was better to put them away fast and touch them up with an iron, just before they were to be worn.

Some cadets never learned. They still hung their wet clothes in the drying room, only to find them replaced with dirty clothes, or nothing left at all.

Danyluk ironed while listening to his radio. "Hey, have you guys heard this?"

The Musketeers gathered around him. Stan Freberg was doing an absolutely hilarious spoof on Dragnet. It was called St. George and The Dragonet.

Moose turned up the radio and looked at the group. "I betcha I'd make a great detective. I'd say, 'Just give me the facts and your panties, Ma'am.' "

East belly-laughed. "Wouldn't you ask her for her bra?"

"Nah, Alma doesn't wear one, she says they're a thing of the past."

"Yeah, I know what you mean," East replied, walking back to his table. "She doesn't need to wear one; they're positively perfect the way they are."

Danyluk stopped ironing and walked over to East's table. "What the hell do you mean by that? Did I hear you correctly? Did you say they're positively perfect the way they are? Is that what you said?"

East was smiling and was about to reply, when Douglas said, "I smell something burning."

"SON OF A BITCH!" Danyluk rushed back to his iron. He had left the hot iron on his pants, making one giant burn mark in the seat.

"Now see what you've made me do," he said, picking up the khaki shorts and heading for the drying room. In seconds, he was back with a replacement pair. Not long after, some cadet at the other end of the hut was swearing about the 'ROTTEN BASTARD' who had left him with a pair of pants with a burn-hole on the seat. The cadet, in turn, took the pants to the drying room in the next hut and came back smiling with a 'traditional' pair.

Wayne slapped Danyluk on the back. "Those pants of yours will end up across the camp tonight."

"I hope they end up in Signals or Driver-Mech," said Jackson, reading a National Geographic Magazine on his bunk.

"Hey, isn't that the book you always read in the jon?" Wayne asked.

Jackson didn't miss a beat. "Only when you're looking over the shitter partition," he shot back.

"IT'S MUG-UP TIME FELLAS!" East was rooting in his barrack-box trying to find his mug. "Get your mugs and your knives and let's get into the line before it builds up."

"My mug is finished," said Jackson. He was referring to the fact that while waiting for mug-up, all the cadets used the handle of their knives to try and hit other cadets' enamel mugs. The result was a chipped hole.

Bergie was too busy to go over to the kitchen. "YOU CAN BORROW MINE IF YOU BRING ME BACK A PEANUT BUTTER AND JAM SANDWICH."

Jackson accepted and headed out the door. Actually, East was so hungry, he was pulling him.

The hangar B-3 was packed that night. Every cadet in camp went to see The Desert Rats. When the Musketeers walked in, a wall of cigarette smoke, combined with darkness, made it difficult for them to find a seat.

Bergie and East left the movie between reels, each complaining of an upset stomach.

"You got too much sun today," Wayne told them. Douglas agreed, then Wayne said he would be right back. When he returned, he said all of the toilets in B-3 were full so he had to run up to B-21.

"What did I miss?" he asked.

Douglas' stomach was starting to act up. "Not much, the projector kept breaking down," he said with a loud belch.

After the movie ended, Douglas and Wayne returned to B-21 to find Bergie, Jackson, Rothstein and Danyluk in bed. Danyluk was snoring.

Wayne couldn't believe it. "Maybe that sun was pretty strong today?"

Jackson and East were still awake and Wayne sat on Earl's bunk.

"What's wrong with you guys?"

Jackson was pale, so was East. Earl belched. "There must have been something wrong with those hamburgers today. We've been throwing up and visiting the jon every ten minutes."

"But Doug and I are alright and we ate the same burgers. Is it poss......?"

Wayne didn't finish because Douglas butted in. "Did you guys eat a full turkey dinner in the D&M mess hall?"

Jackson burped heavily. "Yeah, East even went back for seconds."

Douglas walked over to Wayne. "I think these guys have got food poisoning. It might be wise if we took them up to the camp hospital."

East and Jackson felt so bad that they didn't argue. They got out of bed and walked up to the Medical Inspection Room. When they arrived, at least forty cadets were there complaining about the same thing: stomach pains and cramps.

On the way back to B-21, Douglas put his arm around Wayne's shoulder. "Aren't you glad you listened to me at lunch? These guys are really suffering from food poisoning."

Both Wayne and Douglas never really appreciated how lucky they were until twelve o'clock that night. Wayne got Douglas up and told him to put his P.T. shorts on and a sweater. Screams of agony were originating from the D&M hut and every available ambulance in Vernon was taking cadets to the Vernon Jubilee Hospital.

When they arrived outside the D&M hut, there was total disorder. Cadets were everywhere holding their stomachs after being plagued by diarrhea. The mayhem wasn't limited just to the one hut. Two other huts were affected as well. It was so bad in the D&M hut, cadets were sticking their bottoms out the windows defecating on the ground below.

Douglas looked inside the building. The occupants were using anything they could, including wash basins. In addition, toilets were overflowing, showers were pressed into service as toilets and some cadets even used pith-helmets as their last resort.

"Christ! Wayne, this looks like a battle scene from the picture we saw tonight."

Police cars were now assisting military vehicles in transporting the worst cases to the Vernon hospital.

"YOU, YES YOU! WHAT HUT ARE YOU IN?" a Sergeant yelled.

"B-21 SERGEANT!"

"ANY SICK CADETS IN THERE?"

"NO, SERGEANT!"

"WELL, DON'T JUST STAND THERE, PITCH IN AND HELP SOME-ONE!"

For the next hour, Wayne and Douglas did their best to assist the dazed cadets out of the barracks. Most of them were in pain, looking for a place to throw up or relieve themselves. It was coming out of both ends and no sooner had they finished, it started all again.

At one point, the smell got so bad that both of them started to retch. But this wasn't the time to slack off on the job. These kids were really ill.

When they went in the jon to get some people out, they found all of the cubicles full, and one cadet had stuck his bottom over the rim of the washing machine.

"At least his ass will be clean," quipped Wayne. "I hope nobody plugs it in on him, he'll get a ream job." They were both laughing but wondering how they could find any humour in the midst of this crisis. Sergeant Beckford had instructed them to keep smiling at the worst of times, but this was tough.

After breakfast the following morning, the two were the centre of attraction. Most cadets in the guard had slept through the ordeal and wanted to know what had happened.

Although it wasn't exactly breakfast conversation, they related their experience with explicit detail. Initially, the cadets who listened said they would have loved to have helped out. After hearing the full story, however, most said they wouldn't have gone within a hundred feet of the place.

By the time Douglas and Wayne went back to B-21, Driver-Mech jokes were being told throughout the hut.

"Does this mean that D&M really have their shit together?" asked one cadet.

Another said, "Leave it to D&M. They always get to the bottom of their work."

Rothstein laughed. "I guess when D&M says they're in deep shit, they mean it."

Someone screamed. "I HEAR THAT THEIR HUT IS IN SHITSHAPE CONDITION."

"That's probably true because when they're out driving, they really give it shit," another remarked.

When Charlie formed up on the road, a Corporal got into the act. "COME ON YOU PEOPLE, LET'S GET YOUR SHIT TOGETHER LIKE DRIVER-MECH!"

An anonymous voice in the back row responded by saying, "AWW, CORPORAL, QUIT GIVING US SHIT."

"THE CORPORAL'S A GOOD SHIT, LEAVE HIM ALONE," said another.

Before long, Driver-Mechanics slogans were heard throughout the camp. Everyone was in the act now.

Sergeant Beckford had informed the cadets of Charlie Company many times that when he was through with them, they would look better than Regular Force troops on the parade square. To accomplish this, he never stopped telling them, who they were and what was expected of them There were no let-ups because there could be no let-ups. He wanted pure perfection and he would accept nothing less. If he didn't get it, heads would roll.

He was true to his word. Sergeant Beckford was a perfectionist himself on the parade square and nothing whatsoever was left to chance. As far as he was concerned, age was not a barrier. They all had to work together as a team. That meant when they were on the parade square, two hundred of them had to think and act as one. If an arm was out of place, Beckford noticed it. If someone slacked off, Beckford noticed it. If their feet didn't rise 'six inches off the ground and slam down twelve inches,' they heard about it.

Guard Company worked on the parade square each morning and evening from Monday to Friday and they improved minute by minute. They realized that one bad apple could make them all look horrible, so they assessed themselves carefully. If a cadet wasn't in the mood, he heard about it, and then he made damn certain he got in the mood, instantly.

In addition to the parade square, physical training was increased and higher standards were set in the lecture rooms and in field training. That meant their examination marks had to be above average or they would be moved to another company. The cadets themselves ensured no one was transferred. By continually assisting each other and working in teams, the cadets in Guard company remained there.

The morning after the D&M crisis, Guard Company was on the parade square when Douglas sensed the small amount of food he had eaten the night before was having a belated effect on him. It was an extremely hot day and they had only been on the square for an hour when he felt it happening. Fortunately they were at-ease and they had grounded arms.

"Jeez, Wayne, I can't stay here. I'm going to make a dash for the hut. I can't explain; cover for me when Beckford starts up."

He started running slowly at first so he wouldn't attract any attention, but then he had to run as fast as he could.

"BRICE, GET BACK HERE!"

He turned around but that was agony and it was impossible for him to do or say anything. His bowels had already started to move and now he found himself running stiff-legged, holding his buttocks so tightly that he was afraid to breathe. To make matters worse, the rest of the company caught on and he could hear bellows of laughter, including those of Sergeant Beckford.

Although B-21 is a relatively short distance from the parade square, Douglas didn't make it. He just couldn't hold on any longer and by the time he arrived at the bottom of the steps, it had started to ooze into his shorts. The toilets were just another twenty yards away and when he got there, his legs were covered.

The next fifteen minutes was the worst time in his entire life. Fluid ran out of him like water from a tap. When he stood up, it started again and again and again. Eventually, when it stopped, he didn't know what to do because his undershorts, pants, hose-tops, puttees, and boots were covered.

Douglas sat there feeling rotten. He couldn't believe he was in such a predicament. Although the hut was quiet, it was impossible for him to walk over to his wing, in case someone came in. He didn't want anyone seeing him looking like this.

Minutes seemed like hours, but he had to make a decision. If he could make it to the shower room, he might be alright. Slowly and awkwardly he undressed and cleaned up the mess as best as he could. He was naked now as he bundled all of his clothing into his shirt and gradually opened up the cubicle door and looked out. No one was there and the barracks were still silent as he slowly walked over to the doorway and looked both ways. There wasn't a sound. Thank God, he thought as he ran through the washing area into the shower room.

God was not on his side. When he entered, the cadets from Nine Platoon were waiting for him. The laughter was deafening. A welcoming committee of the Vernon Girls Drum and Bugle Band would have been less embarrassing.

Apparently Sergeant Beckford had fallen out Nine Platoon and they had crept into the barracks while Douglas performed the earlier process of flushing the toilet.

Douglas just stood there. He couldn't speak. As it turned out, he need not have worried. This was Nine Platoon, and when something went wrong, everyone pitched in. Instantly, Wayne took the bundle and flung it under a shower. Douglas was thrown beneath the next nozzle, and when he came out, his clothing had been washed and his boots had been shined.

As he sheepishly walked to his bunk, his embarrassment disappeared as each member of Nine Platoon patted him on the back and he was made an Honorary Member of Driver-Mechanics, along with Banks, Danyluk, Rothstein, East, Bergie, and Jackson.

A Corporal came up to Douglas. "You've been in there half an hour. Are you clean enough, now?"

"I think so, er..Corporal. I'm sorry that..."

"SORRY? IF THIS WAS DRIVER-MECH, I'D BE ABLE TO CALL YOU A SHITHEAD. BUT IT'S NOT AND IT NEVER WILL BE SUCH! RIGHT?"

"RIGHT, CORPORAL!"

During lunch, a rumour spread that the cooks in the D&M mess hall had cooked the turkeys without first cleaning them. The error was apparently caught by the head cook, who decided to serve them anyway.

A cadet at the next table said, "They've fired the whole lot of them and good riddance."

East looked up from his plate. "It was good of you guys to take us to the hospital. I spent a year in that place overnight. If I get my hands on the bastards that cooked the turkey, I'd shove it down their throats.

Douglas smiled. "I know what you went through. Look what I went through and I only had a forkful before I noticed it was bad."

He may have said the wrong thing because East stopped eating.

"You mean, you mean you knew the food was bad and you didn't tell us?"

Wayne shrugged. "We couldn't. We didn't know where you guys were sitting."

Bergie leaned over the table. "Oh, so now the truth comes out. You left and didn't warn us. You walked out on your buddies, your pals, your compatriots in Nine Platoon. You couldn't care less if we had to endure what I call the results of the jet-assisted hundred yard dash."

Danyluk got into the act. "Bergie, I think this calls for the gauntlet?"

Bergie had a deceitful smile on his face. "It calls for more than the gauntlet, Moose. Our time will come."

Wayne leaned over and whispered in Douglas' ear. "I hate it when he talks this way. I wonder what he's got planned for us now?"

Bergie sat back. "Whispering won't help you. You just wait, Wayne."

CHAPTER XI

In 1953, the rifle range at Camp Vernon was south of Area Ten adjacent to the upper camp. A long, winding, dusty road with two locked gates kept out anyone who wasn't supposed to be there. At least the gates were supposed to keep people out. After hours, or on weekends, cadets used to jump over the gates and collect lead from the back-stop of the butts. They would eventually take it home and melt it down to make better weights for their battledress pants. If they found undamaged bullets, they would thread them in large sports shoelaces to form weights.

The range was about 800 yards long. At the 600 and 800 yard firing points, small mud ponds contained tortoises. They were big, about nine inches long, six inches wide and two-and-a-half inches thick.

As the trucks transporting Guard Company passed the ponds, Danyluk noticed them first.

"Christ, look at the giant turtles."

Bergie laughed. "They're not turtles, you dummy. They're land tortoises and Sergeant Beckford has told us that they'll soon be on the endangered species list because they're disappearing so fast."

Danyluk wiped the dust from his eyes to get a better look. "Do they bite?"

"No, they're quite gentle," Bergie replied. "I think it's a shame how cadets take them down to camp and try to keep them as pets. They eventually die. Last year we rescued a whole lot of them and brought them back."

When the cadets unloaded, they smacked their pants and shirts to get rid of the dust from the ride. Dust clouds hung in every direction.

Wayne looked around. "This place is a desert. I'd sure hate to be left up here without any water. Hey Bergie, what's the temperature up here?"

"It's always over a hundred. Sometimes it can go as high as a hundred and twenty." Bergie started coughing from the dust stirred up by the trucks leaving to take a company to Kin Beach. The only truck left at the range was a safety vehicle.

Douglas picked up a handful of dust and let it sift slowly through his fingers. "This isn't too bad, but it's not exactly like Blair Range, is it?"

Wayne snickered. "Give me Blair Range anytime."

They were both referring to the fact that all cadets from the 2290 British Columbia Regiment (Duke of Connaught's Own) were very proficient in rifle shooting. The Commanding Officer of the Cadet Corps, Captain Arthur Lungley, along with the Regimental Sergeant-Major, RSM Pat Patterson, made certain that all cadets accompanied the regiment when it went to Blair Range in North Vancouver for .303 rifle practice, as well as Bren and Sten Gun shooting. Both indoor and outdoor range-work was an integral part of the cadet training program, particularly with the cadets of the British Columbia Regiment (Duke of Connaught's Own).

There were approximately fifteen firing positions at each firing point. After they were formed up in three ranks, a Range Officer appeared.

"RIGHT, PAY ATTENTION HERE. ELEVEN AND TWELVE PLATOONS WILL BE MARCHED DOWN TO THE BUTTS. NINE AND TEN PLATOONS WILL BE DIVIDED INTO RELAYS OF FIFTEEN. SERGEANT BECKFORD, YOU'LL HANDLE THE BUTT PARTY. YOU WILL FIND THE TELEPHONES AND FLAGS HAVE ALREADY BEEN SET UP. PLEASE CARRY ON."

Sergeant Beckford marched the other two platoons down to the butts.

Douglas' name was taken for the first relay, along with the rest of the Musketeers. Being on this relay allowed them to get out of the work-detail, loading magazines behind the firing point. Cadets from other relays were also appointed Flagmen and Telephone men.

Over the next half-hour while the butt party was moving targets and learning how to indicate, ponchos and ground sheets were spread at each firing position and all relays received instructions on safety precautions, firing the weapon and immediate actions.

When they were nearly ready to begin firing, the butt party demonstrated how a hit on their target would be indicated.

"YOU WILL NOTICE THAT THE WHITE PART OF THE INDICATOR WILL BE POINTED TO THE BULL'S EYE IF YOU HIT IT," the Range Officer screamed.

"IF YOU GET AN INNER, THE INDICATOR WILL WAVE ACROSS THE TARGET AND POINT TO THE HIT WITH THE BLACK SIDE SHOWING. THE CENTRE RING IS CALLED A MAGPIE, THE INDICATOR WILL BE TWIRLED AND POINTED TO THE HIT WITH THE BLACK SIDE SHOWING. WHEN YOU GET AN OUTER, THE INDICATOR WILL BE MOVED UP AND DOWN THE TARGET AND WILL POINT TO THE HIT WITH THE BLACK SIDE SHOWING. IF YOU MISS THE TARGET, EITHER A SMALL RED FLAG WILL BE WAVED ACROSS THE TARGET, OR THE STICK-END OF THE INDICATOR. IT WILL SHOW YOU TO WHICH SIDE OF THE TARGET YOUR ROUND WENT AND IF IT WAS HIGH OR LOW. SO YOU SEE, THE ONLY TIME YOU WILL SEE THE WHITE SIDE OF THE INDICATOR IS WHEN YOU GET A BULL'S EYE. ARE THERE ANY QUESTIONS?"

A cadet held up his hand. "Sir, is it safe down there in the butts?"

The Range Officer gave him a glowering look. "WE'VE NEVER HAD AN ACCIDENT HERE BECAUSE WE DON'T LIKE HAVING TO CLEAN UP THE MESS. ALSO, THE PAPERWORK IS TIME CONSUMING. DOES THAT ANSWER YOUR QUESTION?"

The cadet sheepishly smiled and nodded.

"GOOD! RIGHT! THIS FIRST RELAY, STAND UP BEHIND YOUR WEAPONS. WHEN YOU HEAR THE COMMAND LOAD, YOU WILL ASSUME THE HORIZONTAL POSITION, PLACE THE MAGAZINE ON THE RIFLE, CLOSE THE BOLT AND APPLY THE SAFETY-CATCH. YOU WILL NOT AIM THE RIFLE, ALL YOU WILL DO IS HOLD IT AND REST. YOUR TRIGGER FINGER WILL NOT BE ON THE TRIGGER."

"THIS RELAY...LOAD!"

When the command was given, the first relay dropped to the ground and completed the first movement. The Range Officer then continued giving his instructions.

"YOU HAVE SEVEN ROUNDS IN YOUR MAGAZINE. YOU WILL NOTICE THAT YOUR TARGET IS NOT UP YET. WE ARE GOING TO FIRE TWO ROUNDS WARMING INTO THE BANK BELOW YOUR TARGET. AFTER YOU HAVE DONE THAT, YOU WILL REST AGAIN WITH YOUR TRIGGER FINGER OFF THE TRIGGER. WHEN WE ARE ALL FINISHED, THE TARGETS WILL APPEAR AND I WILL TELL YOU WHEN TO SHOOT AGAIN.

"THE NEXT FIVE ROUNDS WILL BE FIVE ROUNDS GROUPING. I AM NOT INTERESTED IN WHERE YOU ARE SHOOTING, I JUST WANT TO SEE HOW CLOSE YOUR ROUNDS ARE TO EACH OTHER. IF ALL OF YOUR HITS ARE TOGETHER, BUT NOT IN THE BULL'S EYE, THEN WE'LL ADJUST YOUR SIGHTS. I WANT YOU TO AIM THE SAME WAY, BREATHE THE SAME WAY AND SQUEEZE THE TRIGGER EXACTLY THE SAME WAY WITH EACH SHOT YOUR FIRE."

The Musketeers of the B.C. Regiment were used to this. They had planned ahead and each brought some sort of padding which they slipped into their shirts to protect their shoulders from the pounding of the steel plate of the butt coming back at them when the rifle was fired. They knew that these rifles 'kicked.'

"IF YOU HAVE ANY PROBLEMS WHATSOEVER, SIMPLY REST AND HOLD UP YOUR HAND. ONE OF THE CORPORALS WILL COME TO YOU. ARE THERE ANY QUESTIONS? NO? O.K., CHANGE THE FLAGS!

"NUMBER ONE RELAY, RANGE TWO HUNDRED. TWO ROUNDS WARMING INTO THE BANK...IN YOUR OWN TIME, FIRE!"

Each cadet flipped up his rear-sight and made certain it was set at two hundred yards, the lowest it could go. They could have used their battle-sight, but it wasn't as accurate and was used only then there wasn't time to adjust the rear-sight. The battle-sight was good up to three hundred yards.

When their sights were up and set at two hundred, they took off their safety-catches, took aim and fired.

Danyluk was on the left side of Douglas. "SON OF A BITCH, THIS BABY REALLY KICKS!"

When the Range Officer noticed that everyone had fired their two rounds, he asked the Telephone Cadet to tell the butts to put up the targets.

"NUMBER ONE RELAY, FIVE ROUNDS GROUPING. THERE WILL BE NO INDICATIONS. REMEMBER NOW, DO EVERYTHING THE SAME WAY. THIS RELAY, FIVE ROUNDS GROUPING, AT YOUR TARGET IN FRONT, IN YOUR OWN TIME FIRE!"

Within minutes they had all finished and were in the 'rest' position. The targets in the butts remained up.

When the command 'unload' was given, each cadet closed and opened his bolt two or three times, finally dry-firing the rifle, leaving his bolt open and the magazine off the weapon, on the ground. At this point, the Corporals checked each rifle to make certain it was 'clear.'

"CHANGE THE FLAGS! WE ARE NOW GOING TO WALK DOWN TO THE BUTTS TO LOOK AT THE GROUPS AND TO HAVE YOUR SIGHTS ADJUSTED. WE WILL WALK IN EXTENDED LINE SO MAKE SURE THAT YOU DON'T GET AHEAD OF ONE ANOTHER. BRING YOUR RIFLE WITH YOU AND KEEP IT POINTING DOWN AT THE GROUND."

While the number one relay was walking the distance of 200 yards to the butts, the other relays were sitting in groups halfway between the 200 and 300 yard firing points. Some just chewed the fat, while other groups took lectures on the weapon.

Rothstein's firing position was close to Wayne's. "Hey, Wayne, your idea of taking off my helmet really made a great difference. I think I did pretty good."

Wayne nodded knowingly. "Attaboy, Rothie. I don't know how these other guys can shoot with their helmets on."

After arriving at the butts, they looked down. Sergeant Beckford was going from target to target with a gauge, marking the size of each group. The cadets in the butts looked hot as hell and asked if there was drinking water on the firing point.

Danyluk laughed. "What do you think this is, the Capital Cafe? Next you'll be asking us for nice, ice-cold banana-splits. We've got lots of water back there, as a matter of fact, all the rest of the guys are having a swim with the turtles and drinking Kik-Kola."

Many 'comments' from the butts were 'thrown' in Danyluk's direction, only to fall upon deaf ears.

The Range Officer and his assistants adjusted as many sights as they thought necessary and the relay returned to the firing point. As they walked back, every cadet was talking about his group. Some of them had missed their targets altogether, but the Musketeers all had good groups and were now looking forward to the rest of the practices.

When they arrived back at the firing point, the ammo party had collected the empty magazines along with the brass casings and had distributed loaded magazines.

"CHANGE THE FLAGS! NOW PAY ATTENTION HERE! THIS NEXT PRACTICE IS TEN ROUNDS APPLICATION. ALL HITS WILL BE SCORED. THE BULL'S EYE COUNTS AS FOUR, AN INNER AS THREE, A MAGPIE

AS TWO, AND AN OUTER AS ONE. YOUR TOTAL POSSIBLE SCORE IS FORTY, SO MAKE EVERY SHOT COUNT!

"NUMBER ONE RELAY, LOAD! TEN ROUNDS APPLICATION. EACH SHOT WILL BE INDICATED. DO NOT FIRE AT THE INDICATOR. IF YOU DO NOT RECEIVE AN INDICATION, RAISE YOUR RIGHT ARM AND WE'LL ASK FOR ONE. THIS RELAY, AT YOUR TARGETS IN FRONT, IN YOUR OWN TIME, FIRE!"

Douglas took aim and squeezed the trigger. Although his sights were adjusted, he had a knack of aiming off if his rounds were not hitting the target where he was aiming.

WHAM, his rifle kicked and the butts indicated an inner close to the bull but to the right. He aimed slightly left for the next nine shots and all of them were bulls, basically located in the same spot. After he was finished, he rested.

Shortly, the application practice was completed. The Range Officer then carried on with his instructions.

"THIS RELAY UNLOAD! CHANGE THE FLAGS! TELEPHONE, TELL THE BUTTS TO PULL, SCORE AND PATCH!"

Wayne looked over at Douglas. "How do you think you did?"

"Nine bulls and an inner," he replied. "How about you?"

Wayne smiled. "You lucky creep. I got eight bulls and two inners."

Danyluk was complaining. "THERE'S SOMETHING WRONG WITH THIS RIFLE. I'M A BETTER SHOT THAN THIS. CHRIST, FIVE BULLS AND FIVE INNERS."

"Maybe it's the same rifle you used at Blair Range," said Wayne. "I've told you, you've got to use your head."

Danyluk was flustered. "What do you mean it's the same rifle? I always use my head, you creep."

Wayne wouldn't let up. "If I've told you once, Moose, I've told you a hundred times…you've got two heads and you think with the wrong one."

"Up yours, smart ass," replied Danyluk.

Bergie started breaking up. "And his other head is larger than the one attached to his shoulders. The mouth spits, too."

East had one hand in his pocket and was eating a cookie with the other. "And you should see the neck on that sucker."

East's remark eventually got Danyluk laughing after he'd called all of them 'pongoes, creeps, and grunts.'

"O.K., settle down!" Even the Range Officer was smiling at the banter coming from the Musketeers.

That afternoon both platoons fired grouping, application, snap-shooting and rapid-fire practices from 200 yards.

When the trucks came to take them back to the camp, they had to clean rifles for an hour before handing them in.

Danyluk went over his weapon from top to bottom. "No wonder I wasn't shooting well, just look at my foresight, it's turned sideways."

"HEY, YOU'VE JUST DONE THAT," screamed Jackson. "You would have noticed it on the range if it had been that way. COME ON, MOOSE, YOU CAN'T SHIT US!"

Danyluk had a sly smile on his face. "Damn it, I can't put anything over on you guys. O.K., who won the pot?"

Each had put 25 cents into a pot. The winner would take all.

Wayne replied. "We won't know until the end of the week. It's not just the scores on the .303; it includes Bren and Sten as well."

"Then I've still got a chance," Danyluk said. "I know I'm better than you guys on the Bren Gun. SHIT, I've got my pull-through stuck in the barrel. Someone give me a hand."

Bergie held the rifle while Danyluk wrapped the pull-through two times around his hand and pulled it out.

"No wonder it was stuck, you folded your four-by-two wrong. I thought you guys in the B.C.R.s were supposed to know how to clean rifles?" said Bergie, looking at the small four-inch-by-two-inch piece of white flannelette with a bit of oil on it.

Rothstein found that he had the same problem. "What happens if we can't pull it out?"

"I've seen them blow it out with a blank round," said Bergie. "It's dangerous, but it works."

Ten minutes later, they had Rothstein's pull-through out and he also received Bergie's lecture on folding the four-by-two.

After a good supper and two more hours on the parade square, B-21 was the usual madhouse. Cadets were stepping over each other, having showers, washing pith-helmets, K.D. Longs, and shirts and taking the burrs out of their puttees.

With their boots shined and their ironing done, Nine Platoon got together and studied in sections. Everything that had happened on the range was noted. They all knew there would be questions on the next Saturday Examination, so they shot questions back and forth to each other.

"How big are the targets?"

"Four feet by four feet."

What's the indication for a bull?

"Point with white only."

"How are the targets scored during the application practice?"

"Four, three, two, and one."

They finished studying after an hour and a Corporal entered the hut.

"MAIL-CALL!"

This time all cadets from both sides of the hut gathered in the area of Nine Platoon.

"DANYLUK, DANYLUK, DANYLUK, DANYLUK! Jesus, Danyluk, what the hell are you...a God-damned member of a lonely hearts club?"

"Eat your heart out, Corporal. They all love me. Those are lip-prints you see on the envelopes."

"BRICE, BRICE, BRICE! Don't tell me you're doing the same as Danyluk. Christ, the female assistant in the Post Office wants to meet him. Now she'll want to meet you as well."

Douglas went red in the face and smiled.

"PROUSE, QUERIN, GLOVER, SAWASY, JACKSON, EAST, FRANCOIS, KONISHI, STEWART, DALLAS, GEDDES, BACON, PEMBROKE, ROTH-STEIN, BHAMJI, LOCHAN....!"

Mail-Call continued for at least twenty minutes and the Corporal saved the best until last.

"AND PARCELS FOR COHEN, BRADSHAW, DANGERFIELD AND BRICE."

As Douglas walked to his bunk with his parcel, he was trailed by the Musketeers. East was first in line, licking his lips.

"C'mon Doug, open it, open it."

The parcel was from his mother and it was loaded with a cake, cookies, potato chips, chocolate bars and six packages of some sort of a cold-drink mix.

Douglas started handing everything out. "I told my mom there were six of us and since we're now seven, we've got to split these up. Let's cut the cake later."

Within seconds, the box was empty and seven tired cadets were sitting on their bunks enjoying the blessings from home. Even a few cadets on the other side of the aisle had the chance to participate. It was nice to have contacts in the outside world.

Douglas lay on his bunk and read his letters. He opened up the one from home first. It was great hearing from his mother because she made everything happening in Vancouver seem so very simple. The weather was hot and the house was quiet because he wasn't there. Both the cat and his dog were moping for him. She had gone to a bingo game with some friends and won and she had given some thought to papering the front room. She enjoyed putting the parcel together because she had read a newspaper article about the food in the army being horrible and that more and more soldiers were requesting parcels from home.

After he read his mother's letter twice, he opened up Diane's letters. They were entirely different and yet in many ways, the wording was similar. Diane missed him and was counting the days until she returned to Vernon. Many of her friends in Penticton had invited her to various functions but when she went, she didn't feel like she could contribute anything without him, so she left early. Her mother and father recognized the problem and tried to rekindle her interest in other things, but she found it totally impossible to enjoy anything because he wasn't with her. She was in love, but she didn't know what love was or what to do about it. Her life had changed since he arrived and although she wanted to return to the way it had been, she couldn't.

Every letter from Diane explained her feelings and her frailties. She knew it was silly because of their age, but she considered herself mature and knew this wasn't just an affair that would end the minute he was gone.

Douglas read and reread Diane's letters. He totally ignored the bombardment of noise going on around him, but when he stopped reading, the barrage returned and his mind couldn't sort out the peacefulness of Vancouver, or his involvement with Diane.

After he had finished reading, he went over to the window and stuck the upper portion of his body out. The Cadet Canteen and Sergeants' Mess were busy, and there was nearly as much noise outside the barracks as inside.

Douglas stayed at the window for ten minutes. Finally, he brought his head back in and got his beret. Cadets were running up and down the aisles; activities of every kind were going on. He needed time to think, so he headed toward the door.

Wayne saw him. "Where are you going?"

"Just out for a walk."

"Can I come along?"

"Sure."

Neither of them said anything until they reached the fence overlooking the golf course. The distant hills looked beautiful and serene as the sun went down. Some golfers were wrapping it up for the night and a few crickets had started to announce the coming of darkness.

Wayne could read Douglas' mind and he knew something was wrong.

"How's your mom?"

Douglas paused for a moment as they sat on the grass.

"She's fine and sends her love."

Wayne picked up a blade of grass and put it in his mouth. "You're tired of it here, aren't you?"

Douglas took a deep breath and let it out slowly as he shook his head.

"I don't know. I think it's a combination of things. I don't mind admitting that I miss home and at the same time I can't get Diane off my mind. It's as if I've known her all of my life, yet we scarcely know each other. Those things, plus the fact that we aren't given too much time to think and when we do get a few minutes, there's so God-damned much noise, it's impossible to sort things out. Don't you wish you had some peace and quiet once in a while?"

Wayne sighed. "Yeah, I guess I do. Life's a little different when you're being raised by a father. We've got a lot in common, but...we don't show any emotion. I don't think I've ever hugged him in my life. My sister Valerie does, but that's different. Why do you think I spend so much time at your house? Your mother adds something to my life."

Douglas looked at him. Wayne had received a letter from his dad and although he hadn't said anything, it was obvious memories were racing through his mind as well.

"Isn't that funny. I enjoy going over to your place and talking to your dad. Anyway, I don't know where my brain is. I think a lot of Diane but I live three hundred miles away and my mom doesn't earn very much money, so how can I get involved? I really don't even know if I want to get involved, yet if she walked away, I wouldn't know what to do."

There was silence for a few minutes until Wayne picked up a rock and threw it over the fence. Unlike Douglas, he did things with his hands when he had some deep thinking to do.

"Doug, there are times when you leave the barracks to get away from the noise. Where do you go?"

Douglas smiled. "My secret place is the Lookout on the highway. Just looking at the lake helps me with my problems. I don't have too many, but Jesus, they sure seem real now."

Wayne chuckled. "I've listened to you for I don't know how long. How many times have you told me that you would be the last of the two of us to ever get hooked? Don't tell me…at least hundreds of times. Christ, Doug, you're just turning fifteen and you've never had a piece of tail yet."

"How do you know?"

"How do I know? Because I'm your best friend, that's how I know. You've only told me a million times. Don't you remember, we had a bet who was going to get screwed first?"

"Wayne, we got screwed out of some money by the cashier at the bowling alley when we were setting pins."

"I don't mean that kind of screwing, you pongo. You know what I mean?"

They both laughed.

Douglas picked up a rock and threw it. "I know, I know. You won the bet, you lucky stiff."

Wayne put his hand on Douglas' shoulder. "Well, actually, I..er, I lied. But I did get some tit. That's close isn't it?"

"Close, where's my two bucks?"

Wayne held his hand out for a shake. "Can I buy you a pop instead?"

They shook each other's hand and stood up. "Yeah, I guess that'll do. We've got about fifteen minutes left," said Douglas, as they walked away.

Nearing the canteen, Wayne stopped in his tracks. "Dukes don't let anything get them down. RIGHT?"

"RIGHT!" Douglas replied.

"Want to make another bet for two dollars? I think I'm getting close. Debbie's quite the gal."

Douglas rolled his eyes and looked up at the sky. "You heard Sergeant Beckford's lecture. One mistake is alright, but two……forget it."

"But who am I going to take to the cleaners if you pay attention to all of this leadership stuff?"

"How about Danyluk?"

Wayne nodded and smiled. "Great idea and he's good for more money, too."

Guard Company got a break from P.T. the next morning. For some reason, Sergeant Simpson gave them a respite.

"ONLY ONE MORNING OFF, MIND YOU," he had said the night before. "YOU'LL NOT BE GETTING USED TO THIS. A LAZY BODY LEADS TO A LAZY MIND AND A LAZY MIND IS THE SAME AS SITTING ON A CROWDED BEACH WITH YOUR PRICK IN YOUR HAND AND YOUR HEAD IN THE SAND."

"I don't know what you mean by that Sergeant, but it sounds like a fine idea," Danyluk had replied.

With Eddie Fisher singing, Oh! My Papa, the cadets in B-21 prepared for another day. Everyone was up except Wayne.

Douglas was mopping the floor around and under their bunk space. "C'mon Wayne, what the hell are you still in bed for? We've got to get over to breakfast shortly and you haven't even had a shower yet."

Wayne sat up in bed and yawned. "You guys go ahead and I'll follow you shortly."

The rest of the Musketeers gathered around him as he lay there. Bergie was getting ready to pull the blankets off him. "We're not going without you, now get your ass out of bed."

Wayne looked annoyed. "Listen, I'm not having breakfast this morning. If I want to stay in bed a while longer, I bloody well will. Now bug off!"

His message got through because he looked upset.

Bergie released his hold on Wayne's blankets and the group headed for the door. "O.K., don't get your nuts in a knot. Are you coming, Doug?"

"Yeah, I'll be right there. Save a seat for me."

Douglas walked over to Wayne. "What's wrong, how come you're not up?"

Wayne didn't say anything, then he grimaced. "I've pissed the bed. I don't know what the hell happened because I only had two pops last night."

Douglas had a quizzical look on his face. "I don't believe it, you've what?"

Wayne wouldn't tell anyone except Douglas. "I actually pissed the bed last night. I'm soaked. Christ, the last time I did this, I think I was four. I don't even think I..."

Wayne didn't finish because the rest of the Musketeers walked in the barracks again. All of them were smiling and once again Bergie was the spokesman.

"We've decided we're not eating without you."

Everyone gathered around Wayne's bunk and now Douglas knew they had been up to something.

"O.K., you guys win. What have you done?"

East laughed. "We didn't do anything, we just want to go and have breakfast." Then he looked at his watch. "Oh, what the hell, we'd better tell ya, otherwise it will be too late to eat. We held your hands in warm water last night and brought on a deluge."

Wayne menaced his fist in their faces. "YOU CREEPS!" His look softened into a smile with the realization he hadn't reverted to taking up the habit of a four-year-old.

Douglas grabbed the front of Bergie's T-shirt. "You didn't get me though, did ya?"

"We tried, but it didn't work on you. Now that Wayne's out of the way, you're next."

Wayne threw off the covers and jumped down. The whole front of his under-shorts was sticking to him.

Amidst the sound of laughter, Wayne casually strolled to the showers with his towel wrapped around his neck. As he walked, the rear end of his shorts stuck to his buttocks.

At breakfast that morning, the conversation focused around how the other Mus-keteers managed to get Wayne to wet the bed. It had taken them an hour to pull it off. Bergie, Rothstein, and East had worked on Wayne, while Jackson and Dany-luk held Douglas' hand in a basin of warm water.

Wayne joined in the laughter, knowing he had paid the price for not tipping them off about the D&M 'turkey delight.' His best friend laughed as well, but throughout, Douglas wondered what they would do next, considering it hadn't worked on him.

That whole week, the cadets in Guard Company worked hard on the range and the parade square. They fired the rifle and Bren Gun from as far back as 500 yards, and the Sten Gun from 100 yards in the standing and lying positions.

The Musketeers were in the butts on the last two days.

The butts, as they are called, is a cement enclosed area dug about nine feet into the ground at the front of a range. For every firing point position, the butts has a steel framework designed to hold a large, cardboard target fitted to a wooden cas-ing. Weights are used to counter the weight of the target so it can be raised and lowered with 'relative ease.' When a target is fired upon, it is lowered, scored and patched with small one-inch-squared stickers.

After a target has been raised, the person manning each apparatus can look up and see where the hit occurred. He or she then uses an indicator which is usually a flat steel arrow sign about ten inches at the base, painted black on one side, white on the other, and is attached to a wooden ten-foot stick handle. This is used to point at the hole in the target, indicating where it was hit.

Although the butts are dug in below the ground, a mound of dirt is also built up in front of the butts. Down below, each 'marker' has a small cement enclave with a wooden bench inside so he or she can observe the target. When the target is hit, the marker stands and uses the indicator which is then observed back at the firing point.

On the days the Musketeers were in the butts, there were fifteen markers, one Telephone Cadet, one Flag Cadet, the Butts Officer, which was Sergeant Beck-ford, and his assistants, two Corporals from Nine Platoon.

"CHANGE THE FLAG, STAND BY YOUR TARGETS...TARGETS UP!" ordered Sergeant Beckford, after he was informed by the Telephone Cadet that the Range Officer wanted the targets up.

All the markers bent down together and grabbed the lower part of the apparatus and lifted it up. The counterweights made it easier but it was hard on the back and hard on the arms.

"I feel like I've spent my whole life in here," Wayne said to Douglas, as he picked up his indicator. They were both looking up at their targets waiting for the first shot in an application practice.

CRACK! The dirt on the mound behind Douglas' target splattered, but there was no hole on the target. From where the dirt splattered, Douglas knew the bullet had missed the right side of the target, so he turned his indicator upside down and waved the butt end of the stick across the target. Then he hit the right side of the target with the stick. The cadet who was firing would then know he missed on the right side.

"WAKE UP ON TARGET FOUR! AN INDICATION ON TARGET FOUR!"

Douglas looked up at the target again. There wasn't a hole.

"MISS ON FOUR AND I'VE INDICATED IT AS A MISS."

CRACK! The dirt splattered on the mound again, only this time it was on the left side. He indicated the miss.

CRACK! This time the miss was above the target, so Douglas indicated a miss and hit the centre of the target with the butt end of the stick.

"INDICATION ON TARGET FOUR. THEY SAY YOU'VE MISSED THREE INDICATIONS!"

"I'VE INDICATED THEM. THEY WERE ALL MISSES. I THINK THE GUY NEEDS GLASSES. IF IT'S THE SAME GUY WHO SHOT THE GROUPING PRACTICE, HE'S A REGULAR FORCE CORPORAL AND HE REALLY DOES NEED GLASSES."

"ARE YOU SAYING THE REGULAR FORCE CAN'T SHOOT, BRICE?"

"NO, SERGEANT, I'M SAYING THIS CORPORAL CAN'T SHOOT!"

Sergeant Beckford picked up the telephone. "Who's firing on target number four? Oh, so it is a Regular Force Corporal? Well, tell him he's missed the target three times and he's the laughing stock of the butts."

The phone rang and it was answered by the Telephone Cadet. "It's for you, Sergeant Beckford."

Beckford picked up the receiver and a smile came to his face. "Brice, after we've finished today, the Corporal wants to bet you twenty dollars he can beat you in application."

"TAKE IT, DOUG," Danyluk yelled. "WE CAN HAVE DINNER DOWNTOWN FOR A CHANGE."

"I CAN'T, MOOSE, I HAVEN'T GOT TWENTY DOLLARS!"

Within seconds, the Musketeers had raised the twenty.

"TELL HIM HE'S ON, SERGEANT!"

CRACK! Douglas looked up. It was a bull's eye, dead centre. He indicated it.

"I've got a feeling we were set up?"

Beckford was called to the phone again. "HE WANTS TO SHOOT FROM 300 YARDS. IS THAT ALRIGHT WITH YOU?"

CRACK! Another bull's eye.

Douglas looked down the platform at Beckford. "WHERE'S HE SHOOTING FROM NOW?"

Beckford smiled. "FROM 500."

Douglas looked at Wayne. Although he was busy indicating his own target, he said, "Go for it at five hundred."

CRACK! An inner.

Rothstein laughed. "At least he's human. I agree with Wayne, take him on at 500."

"SERGEANT BECKFORD...I THINK THREE HUNDRED WOULD BE TOO EASY. I'LL TAKE HIM ON AT 600 YARDS, IF HE CAN HANDLE IT."

CRACK! Bulls eye.

The next three shots were two bulls and an inner.

When the targets were pulled to score and patch, Sergeant Beckford indicated that the Range Officer had approved the competition from 600 yards. "You know you've been set up, don't you?"

Douglas smiled. "Is that what the Corporal thinks?"

Beckford looked around. All of the Musketeers had a grin from ear to ear. "Oh! Oh! Now I don't know who to put my money on." He paused for a minute. "O.K., Brice, I'm with you."

The afternoon in the butts was long and hot. After all practices were finished, the equipment was put away except for the rifles Douglas and the Corporal were to use. The telephones were moved back to 600 yards along with two ponchos and two loaded magazines with ten rounds in each of them.

Douglas had met the Corporal before. He was with Eleven Platoon and rumour had it he was the best shot in the Patricia's.

The Corporal took off his beret and held it out. "MONEY IN THE HAT!" He threw in his twenty, and a handful of mixed bills and coins were thrown in by the Musketeers.

"I love taking candy from babies."

East spoke up. "THIS BABY HATES GIVING IT AWAY. HE'LL THROW THE WRAPPER AT YOU, THOUGH."

Now the Corporal was psyched a little. "So you think you're good, eh, Brice?"

"No, Corporal."

"Then why are you doing this?"

"Because I know I'm good."

Although Douglas had said it to psyche out the Corporal, he didn't have a clue how good the Corporal was at 600 yards, nor himself for that matter. He would have loved to back out, but Nine Platoon was counting on him.

With the whole company watching from behind the 600 yard firing point, the shoot commenced. Sergeant Beckford passed on his job as Butts Officer to another Corporal so that he could watch as well.

Douglas learned later that his opponent loved setting people up and he had never lost. Even Beckford had paid twenty dollars a few years earlier.

CRACK! CRACK! The Corporal shot a bull's eye and Douglas got an inner. His heart was pounding and everything he had heard or read about shooting was going through his head. He took a deep breath and relaxed. After all, this guy wasn't that good. If he were great, he would have had a possible (highest possible score) at 500.

CRACK! CRACK! Two bull's eyes were indicated and the exuberant Company was asked to keep the noise down.

CRACK! CRACK! The Corporal shot a bull's eye and Douglas got an inner again.

Douglas rested without moving his left arm. He wiped his brow with his right hand. Now he was a little bit worried. How the hell did he get involved in this in the first place, he asked himself.

The Corporal didn't rest. CRACK! The Corporal shot an inner. That was all Douglas needed. CRACK! Douglas shot a bull.

CRACK! CRACK! A magpie for the Corporal; an inner for Douglas, relaxed now because he knew the Corporal would be disheartened.

The Corporal was resting as Douglas shot his next round, a bull and the Corporal saw it. Now Douglas knew the warm breeze. He was reading the range flags and was familiar with the heat-waves coming up from the ground.

CRACK! The Corporal shot another magpie. CRACK! Douglas, another inner.

The Corporal wiped his brow. He had kept his beret on, but now flung it aside.

CRACK! CRACK! They both got bulls and glanced at each other.

The Corporal smiled. "Want to go for thirty dollars?"

Douglas returned an unyielding smile. "What have I got to lose?"

He rested as the Corporal's rifle fired. A bull's eye.

CRACK! CRACK! They both got bulls.

Now the pressure was on. They each had one round left and could hear the rumbling behind them. Every cadet was keeping score, but some were wrong. Many different scores were being discussed.

Both rested. When Douglas took aim first, he held too long and had to rest again.

The Corporal aimed. CRACK! A bull.

Douglas saw the indication. His heart pounded again and he had to rest to slow it down.

Finally, he was ready but out of the corner of his eye, he could see the Corporal's white face looking at him. There wasn't a sound. If a pin dropped, it could have been heard. All he'd been taught raced through his mind. He aimed twice more and held too long again. Decisively, Douglas told himself he had to do it, and raised his rifle. He totally closed his mind to the peripheral image of the Corporal's face, and concentrated on his target. What only took seconds, seemed like minutes.

CRACK! For some reason the indication was slow. The tension in the air mounted and the rumbling of voices got louder.

The Corporal wasn't staring at Douglas anymore. He and over two hundred cadets and staff were looking at the target.

The silence disappeared when the indicator popped up. Douglas had shot a bull and won the match by one point. Charlie company went wild.

As the winner was being lifted on shoulders, the Corporal shook his hand. "You're a lucky little bugger."

"YEAH, BUT HE'S A RICH LUCKY LITTLE BUGGER NOW," East said, as he helped carry Douglas away.

At supper that night, Douglas had the honor of being the topic of the mess hall. Even cadets from other companies came over to the Musketeers' table to congratulate the one who "beat the shit" out of the pride of the Princess Patricia's Canadian Light Infantry.

With full stomachs, they all went back to their hut to prepare for tomorrow's Saturday Morning Inspection. It was here the 'culprits' caught up with Douglas Brice. Usually, they had never had to form up in three ranks outside the hut on a Friday night, however, this night was different.

Sergeant Beckford entered the barracks. "FORM UP IN THREE RANKS ON THE ROAD! QUICKLY NOW, QUICKLY!"

Wayne was next to Douglas. "Something's up. We've only just started working on the hut and...oh oh, here comes the Company Commander."

"COMPANY ATTEN...TION! STANDAT...EASE! STAND EASY!"

The Company Commander put his hand in his pocket and pulled out an extended condom. When everyone saw it, laughter rang out throughout the ranks.

"SETTLE DOWN. I AM HOLDING AN OBJECT IN MY HAND. BRICE, WHAT IS IT I AM HOLDING?"

Douglas had been laughing like everyone else, but when he heard his name mentioned he didn't know what was going on. "Er..er, it's a rubber, Sir."

The Company commander was looking straight at him. "AND WHAT DO WE DO WITH THESE, BRICE?"

"We, er, well... you know, we..." Everyone in the company was grinning and listening with intense interest to his every word. His cheeks were turning red and he could feel the perspiration building on his forehead.

"SPIT IT OUT MAN! WHAT DO WE USE THESE THINGS FOR?"

Danyluk whispered. "Tell him it's used for a good fuck."

Those within earshot laughed at Danyluk's remark. Everyone that is, except Douglas. He still didn't know why he was being singled out.

"WE USE THEM WHEN, WHEN, ER...WE HAVE SEXUAL INTERCOURSE, SIR." Douglas was smiling now because the whole company was howling. Even the Company Commander was grinning.

"AND WHAT DOES IT DO, BRICE?"

"IT, ER..IT...ER...."

"Tell him it holds the load," Danyluk whispered, roaring his head off.

The Company Commander heard him. "I DIDN'T ASK YOU, MR. SEX ENCYCLOPEDIA."

"IT STOPS THE, ER..THE DEPOSIT OF SPERM FROM GOING INSIDE THE FEMALE PARTNER, SIR."

Banks leaned over. "Did you say that? Very well done, Douglas my boy."

"AND WHAT ELSE DOES IT DO, BRICE?"

He looked at Bergie and whispered, "Why is he picking on me?" Bergie didn't answer. He couldn't, he was laughing so hard looking at Douglas' face."

"IT STOPS THE PASSAGE OF DISEASES, SIR!"

"RIGHT! IT STOPS THE PASSAGE OF DISEASES. HAVE YOU EVER USED ONE OF THESE, BRICE?"

The smile had disappeared now. He could feel a million eyes burning their stares into his body.

"ONLY WHEN NECESSARY, SIR."

"AND WHEN IS THAT, BRICE?"

"THAT'S A PERSONAL QUESTION, SIR."

"YOU BET IT IS, BRICE." The Company Commander sensed he couldn't go any further.

"DID YOU USE ONE OF THESE WHEN YOU VISITED HOP SING'S?"

"I DON'T GET MY LAUNDRY DONE AT HOP SING'S, SIR."

"YOU DON'T? WE'VE BEEN TOLD THAT YOU DO, AND YOU BRING BACK A LITTLE MORE THAN YOUR LAUNDRY."

"Sir, I've never been to Hop......"

The Company Commander cut him off. "NOW ALL OF YOU PAY ATTEN-TION HERE. I WANT THE WHOLE COMPANY TO KNOW THAT THESE ARE AVAILABLE FROM THE MEDICAL INSPECTION ROOM. ALL YOU HAVE TO DO IS ASK FOR THEM. DO YOU HEAR ME BRICE, THEY'RE AVAILABLE FREE?"

"How many can we get?" asked Danyluk.

He was ignored. "NOW BRICE, DO YOU KNOW WHAT CRABS ARE?"

"YES, SIR. CRABS ARE THOSE LITTLE CREATURES THAT CRAWL UNDER ROCKS AT THE BEACH."

"THEY CRAWL UNDER MORE THAN ROCKS, DON'T THEY BRICE?"

"THEY PROBABLY DO SIR, BUT I'M NOT THAT FAM....."

"YOU MEAN YOU DIDN'T KNOW THAT THEY CRAWL AROUND THE GENITAL AREAS OF WAYWARD MALES AND FEMALES?"

Douglas thought it was funny now. "THEY DO?"

"YES THEY DO AND RIGHT NOW WE HAVE INFORMATION THAT THESE LITTLE CREATURES, AS YOU CALL THEM, ARE CRAWLING ALL OVER YOUR CROTCH."

Douglas' jaw hit the asphalt. A look of pure innocence came over his face. He didn't have a clue as to what was going on.

"IT'S THE BLUE OINTMENT PARADE FOR YOU CADET BRICE!"

Bergie slapped Douglas on his back. "WE GOT YA! WE GOT ALMA TO CALL THE CAMP HOSPITAL AND TOLD THEM THAT YOU PICKED UP A DOSE AND CRABS AT HOP SING'S!"

Bergie didn't laugh too long. "FURTHERMORE, ALL CADETS WITHIN THIRTY FEET OF BRICE'S BUNK SPACE WILL REPORT WITH HIM TO THE HOSPITAL IMMEDIATELY."

Now it was Douglas' turn to laugh and point at the ones who were going with him. That included six of them, plus some other 'close friends.'

In the shower that night, the Musketeers got used to the odd looks they were getting from cadets joining them. One cadet even suggested they should form a musical group and call themselves the "Blue Balls."

At lights out, Banks leaned over his bunk. "This blue stuff won't come off for weeks."

"Good," replied Douglas. "And I hope everyone's ass is still sore from the needles."

Danyluk got out of bed and walked over. "Hey, you guys should look on the bright side of things. Those nurses that did the job were kind of nice. Isn't that right, Bergie?"

"Don't talk to me. You were the one who set this whole thing up and now my balls are itchy as hell. How come every time you come up with an idea, it originates between your legs?"

"It was your idea," Danyluk shot back.

"It was OUR idea. Anyway, it worked didn't it?"

"It worked alright," said Danyluk. "If I was in Vancouver right now, my girls wouldn't go near me."

Bergie was now chuckling. "Your balls look no more different now than they usually do."

Douglas smiled and rolled over on his side. What a group, he thought as he went to sleep.

"Up yours, Bergie."

"You'd probably say, 'Hey Girls look at my blue balls.'"

East walked over to Danyluk's bed. "Did I tell ya the joke about the guy in the bar who said to the guy next to him, 'Stick with me and we can make some money. Hey everyone, I'll bet fifty dollars that between me and my friend here we've got five balls between us.'"

"What happened?" asked Jackson.

"Well, the guy sitting with him said, 'Jesus, friend, I hope you've got four?'"

It took a while for everyone in Nine Platoon to catch on. When they did, the jokes continued from bunk to bunk. Half-an-hour later, all of them were asleep. It had been another good day.

CHAPTER XII

Although the cadets in B-21 were completely organized when it came to preparing for a Saturday Morning Parade, a visitor would undoubtedly compare it to bees in a hive.

Cadets were stepping on each other as they made their beds Saturday Morning Style and cleaned the hut for the inspection that would follow. Although a lot of work had been done the night before, the 'touch-up' jobs required planning.

The washing area, toilets, drying room, and shower room were cleaned last, before everyone went to breakfast.

All cadets wore their P.T. strip over to the mess hall. When they returned, they changed into their uniforms and formed up on the road. After they had been given a preliminary inspection, the company marched to the weapons room, picked up rifles and marched onto the parade square.

That morning, the cadets in Guard Company did not win the best company award. As Sergeant Beckford put it, "Although you were the best, it wouldn't be wise to keep giving it to the same company. It would lower the moral in the other companies."

Following the parade, the cadets of Guard Company wrote their exams, attended a sheet exchange and were paid. They had just returned to the barracks when a Corporal walked in. "MAIL-CALL."

This time Bergie received five letters and Danyluk was a bit jealous. "You're just writing to yourself," he said to Bergie.

"Oh, sure, and I suppose I change my handwriting five times?" was Bergie's response.

Douglas lay on his bunk and read the letter from his mother. Half way through it, he sat up and continued reading. When he was finished, his face was white as he stuffed the letter in his pocket, took his beret out of his barrack-box, and left the hut.

Wayne rushed to the door and called after him, but he didn't answer.

"DOUG, WHERE ARE YOU GOING? HEY DOUG, WHERE THE HELL ARE YOU GOING?"

At lunch that afternoon, Sergeant Beckford sat at the Musketeers table in Douglas' chair.

"Where's Brice?" he asked.

Everyone shrugged and Wayne told him that Douglas had just left the barracks and walked away. They had searched the camp and no one could find him.

"Do you think you might know where is?"

At first Wayne shook his head and then his face indicated that he might know. He nodded. "I have an idea."

"I've got my car outside. Come on with me."

As the car pulled into the Lookout parking lot, Sergeant Beckford stayed inside while Wayne went over and looked down the hill. He saw Douglas sitting about five feet down, resting his head on his knees. He had his beret off and wasn't moving.

Wayne walked down and stood behind him. "What's wrong Doug?"

Douglas didn't move. He just kept staring at the ground between his knees.

Wayne sat next to him and put a hand on his shoulder.

"Can I help in some way?" What's the matter?"

Douglas slowly turned and shook his head. He'd been crying and his eyes were red. "Thanks anyway. I just want to be left alone."

Wayne didn't know what to say. His best friend always told him when there was a problem. This time was different and he thought better of it than to enquire any further.

"Well, I..I'm always here if you need any help. I'll see you later."

Wayne stood there for about ten seconds before he walked back to the car and explained matters to Sergeant Beckford.

Sergeant Beckford thought for a moment, then leaving Wayne in the car, he walked over to the embankment. Douglas looked the other way when Sergeant Beckford sat down next to him. He didn't want the Sergeant to know he'd been crying.

Sergeant Beckford cleared his throat before he spoke. He took off his beret and although he was a little tense, he started speaking softly.

"Brice, as we get a little older in life, we learn to understand and solve our problems a tiny bit easier. Everyone has them and until this old planet packs it in, they'll always be there. Nobody ever said that life was easy. It would only be easy if we lived in a perfect world, and you and I both know we don't."

Douglas turned his head and tried to smile. He wanted to say something but he couldn't. Tears were slowly rolling down his cheeks.

The Sergeant took a deep breath before speaking again.

"A few days ago we got a message to call your mother and I was the one who talked to her. She told me that your dog Major was killed. You were pretty close to him, weren't you?"

Douglas just nodded his head.

"Anyway, I told your mother that I would prefer to talk to you after you received her letter. For some reason it didn't seem right for me to break the news to you."

"We rescued him from the pound," Douglas said, trying to wipe his eyes with his right hand.

"I know, your mom told me. You got Major when your first dog Laddie died of distemper."

Douglas accepted Sergeant Beckford's handkerchief and wiped his eyes. "Why did those kids have to open the gate?"

"Some people don't think," replied the Sergeant. "They had no right to open the gate and throw a ball for your dog to chase. But they did it and the driver couldn't stop in time. As it was, he carried your dog home. If it's any consolation, Major didn't suffer and the boys who opened the gate cried their eyes out when they realized what they had done."

"It wouldn't have happened if I'd been there."

Sergeant Beckford extended a sympathetic smile. "Listen son, yes, it would have. It might not have happened at that moment, but for some reason the good Lord wanted him. What you have to realize is that nothing can bring him back. You've got some wonderful memories of the two of you together and time will heal the pain you're going through now. Major wouldn't want to see you in this condition. He's probably looking at us right now wondering how come you're not over at Hop Sing's place getting some crabs."

Douglas managed a small grin. "I've never been in Hop Sing's in my life."

"I knew that and I think the OC knew it as well. But there have been a few problems with other companies, so this was his way of making certain. He probably made a mistake in setting you up as an example and he may apologize to you for that, but I don't think our company will have those sort of problems now."

"Did the other cadets pick up what whatever they got from Hop Sing's?"

"We don't know. As far as the Commanding Officer of the camp is concerned, Hop Sing just runs a laundry. Some cadets a few years ago started the rumour it's a whorehouse. "Listen, do you want to drive back to camp with us?"

"No, thanks, Sergeant. I just want to stay here for a while longer."

Sergeant Beckford looked down at the lake. "It looks kind of peaceful, doesn't it?"

Douglas stood up. "I think this is one of the most beautiful sights I've ever seen in my life."

Beckford nodded and replaced his beret. He understood why Douglas wanted to be left alone. As he ran his hand over the top of Douglas' head, he smiled. "It's easy for me to try to tell you to get it out of your mind, but I know what you're going through. Watch the traffic when you walk back to camp and give your mother a phone call. Alright?"

"Alright. Thanks for coming up here, Sergeant."

As Beckford's car pulled away, Douglas broke down. His pal was dead and every memory of him hastened through his mind from the time they picked Major up at the dog pound until the time he left the house to attend camp. Where Douglas went, Major went. Even when he rode his bike to the Drill Hall for shooting on Saturday mornings and band practice on Sunday mornings, Major sat outside and waited patiently until he came out. Now he was gone.

Traffic was slow on Highway 97 that day. People in the few cars that did pull off the road didn't see a boy sitting down below the crest, crying. Most of the cars didn't wait too long anyway because of the intolerable heat.

At five o'clock in the afternoon, a car did stop for a while at the Lookout. Four people came out of the car and one walked down to Douglas. Initially he didn't turn around although he knew someone was there. Diane's voice was very soft.

"I'm really sorry about what happened. I..I think I know it's like losing a member of the family. Wayne told us how close you were to him."

Douglas wiped his eyes and turned around and smiled.

Diane sat down next to him and he put his arm around her. "He was a great dog and I'm really going to miss him."

Nothing else was said after that. Douglas stood up and the two of them walked to the car where Diane's dad and Wayne and Debbie were waiting.

Diane's dad waved and got back into the car with Debbie, while Wayne put both hands on Douglas' shoulders and pulled him in for a second. "C'mon, buddy. I knew Major and he wouldn't want you to be sad for a second. He was the best and in his own way, he's still with us."

After they left the Lookout, they drove directly to Diane's house. Supper was already prepared.

Douglas gracefully declined the offer, when Ellen asked him if he wanted another piece of chicken.

"O.K. then," said Ellen. "Why don't you men go and have a talk downstairs while we girls do the dishes."

In the basement, Wayne noticed some rifles in a glass-enclosed case on one of the walls.

"This is a Chinese rifle and this is Russian," Diane's father said, opening the case and taking out the Chinese rifle to hand to Douglas. "If the army knew I had these, there would be hell to pay. No weapons were to be brought back from Korea."

The two rifles were kept in immaculate condition along with other various rifles and shotguns.

Just looking at them brought Douglas back to life.

"Are you a hunter, Sir?"

"Not really. I used to do some hunting, but after Korea, well...I sort of lost interest in the sport. I just collect rifles now, for the fun of it," he said, handing the Russian rifle to Wayne. Automatically, without thinking, they proved them, (made certain they weren't loaded).

Wayne kept his bolt open and aimed the rifle at a bowl of ceramic fruit which lay on the table in front of them. "Wow, you sure have an impressive collection."

Tom smiled. "Thank you. I can see by the way you're handling them that the range-work you've just been through has really paid off. Do you two do much shooting?"

Douglas and Wayne exchanged rifles. Wayne replied, "We're both on the .22 rifle team at home and once every two months we go to Blair Range and shoot .303s."

Tom lit up his pipe and nodded. "How did you make out at the Vernon Rifle Range?"

Wayne laughed. "Well, Doug was the best rifle shot in the company and I topped the rest on the Bren and Sten guns."

"Very impressive," Tom said, as he returned the rifles to the case, locked it and sat down facing them. "Have you won any trophies?"

"We've won a few, Sir." replied Douglas. "During the past year, we've entered quite a few competitions and won."

Ellen walked down the stairs. "Tom, have you forgotten the time? We're due in the Sergeants' Mess in a half hour."

Tom looked at his watch and jumped up. "What plans do you kids have? Are you going to the dance?"

"I'm in the mood, but I don't think Doug wants to go," Wayne said, as Diane and Debbie came down the stairs.

Ellen lifted up her leg behind her and looked to see if her stocking seams were straight. "There's cake and pop in the icebox. We'll leave you four in charge of the house. Remember now, no hanky-panky and leave the house in one piece. We won't be late," she said, smiling and pointing at Diane. Tom just winked at both of the boys and followed Ellen up the stairs.

Diane put some records on and about ten minutes later, the screen door slammed and they heard the car start and drive away.

After a few dances, Wayne and Debbie headed upstairs. No sooner had they disappeared, the sounds of Ebb Tide filled the room.

"You bought it?" he whispered, as the two shuffled in the middle of the floor.

Diane took her head off his shoulder for a moment. "I bought two, one for each of us. "It'll remind you of me when you're gone."

Douglas gently kissed her ear. "I don't need Ebb Tide to remind me of you. I don't need anything to remind me of you. You're on my mind day and night."

Diane's voice quivered. "Hold me, just hold me."

Their feet stopped moving and the few minutes Ebb Tide played seemed like an eternity to both of them.

When the song stopped, magically, without any words, they walked over to the couch. Douglas lay down and Diane lay beside him, resting her head on his chest. He reached up and turned out the table lamp. It was dark, pitch black in the basement. As they held each other tightly they could feel their hearts beating faster and faster.

Diane moved so that she was on top of him. He kissed her forehead, the tip of her nose and then her lips. This wasn't like the last time. He was relaxed and felt like he was in a warm cocoon, totally oblivious to anything except this moment with Diane. She was pressing against him moving her body slowly up and down. The feeling he had was wonderful as he moved his hands down to her bottom and pushed her tighter toward him.

They could both feel the pleasure through their clothes as he slowly moved her skirt up and slid his hands down inside her panties. Her skin was smooth, like silk, and his mind was going wild as he kissed her harder and harder and started pushing her panties down.

Diane moved her hands behind her back and stopped him. "Doug,...I...I don't think we should. I want to...but..."

Douglas stopped, but his head was exploding and he wondered what was the matter. He could never in a million years believe it would be like this.

"What's wrong? I'm sorry, I couldn't help it...I, I want to......"

Her soft voice trembled. "Me, too. It's not you. It's just that we can't. I...love you too much to...I want..."

Diane sat up and straightened out her clothing before turning on the light. She was blushing and she had a sad look in her eyes as he drew her toward him and kissed her.

"I'm sorry," he said. "I guess there are times when a guy can't help himself."

He held her in his arms for about five minutes before Diane broke the silence. "I wanted you to do that and more, but maybe there's a time and a place. I've dreamt about this since I met you, but...maybe we're too young, or...?"

Douglas didn't let her finish. "Listen, I understand. I'm sorry, I...I didn't mean to rush and well, maybe you're right. But I've got to tell ya, I've never felt like that in my life."

Diane kissed him again. "I didn't want you to stop, but....."

"But, let's dance," he said.

After dancing slowly to Ebb Tide, they both made a lot of noise going up the stairs, so that Wayne and Debbie would hear them coming.

The cake and pop disappeared over ten games of charades until Tom and Ellen arrived home.

"Did you guys have a good time?" Tom asked as he dropped the boys off at the guardroom.

Both Wayne and Douglas looked at each other. "Yes, Sir," they replied in unison.

"Since you're going to bivouac for the next week, how would like to go to Cosens Bay tomorrow? Just the six of us?"

"Mint," Wayne replied.

The 'shack' was a shambles when they returned, but it was always like that on weekends.

The other Musketeers were still at the dance, so Douglas and Wayne prepared their kit listening to Danyluk's radio, and watched the normal nightime antics take place.

Wayne headed to the showers. "C'mon Doug, this is the only time we're going to have all the hot water to ourselves."

The water felt like Heaven, and Wayne had shampoo all over his head and face when he said, "I was going to go all the way tonight, but Debbie stopped me."

Douglas laughed at the sight of Wayne's head and at the statement. "You mean you didn't bring a new bra back?"

Wayne rinsed off. Although he couldn't see too well without his glasses, he opened the window, leaned his upper body out, looked around, took a deep breath of air and released it slowly. "Naah, not tonight," he said, as he closed the window, shaking his head. "God, I came close. How'd you make out? We noticed it was kind of quiet down below."

"We just danced," Douglas replied, smiling.

"Sure ya did. How did you manage to dance without any music? You must have been whistling very low so we couldn't hear you, right?"

"Exactly. You know I'm a good whistler."

The shower room started to fill as most of the cadets returned from the dance.

"Are we going to have a wedding at camp this year?" asked Wayne, flicking his towel at Douglas' rear end. It connected. "AGGHHH!"

Douglas did the same and caught Wayne square in the middle of the right buttock. "YEEEOW!" The scream was loud and the red mark would probably remain on Wayne's bottom for quite some time. "No, Wayne, no wedding this year."

When they walked back to their bunks, Sergeant Beckford was there. "Everything fine guys?"

Both of them nodded and Douglas said, "Thanks for everything today, Sergeant."

Beckford smiled. "All in a day's work, AND DON'T LET ME SEE YOU FLICKING THOSE TOWELS AGAIN! RIGHT?" He winked.

"RIGHT, SERGEANT!"

Good night guys?" he said as they were getting into bed.

"G'night, Sergeant."

As Beckford left the barracks, the other Musketeers were returning and Bergie was arguing with Moose.

"Danyluk, for God's sake, don't be a pongo. It's called pubic hair, not public hair. Doug, tell this poor misinformed creep what it's called."

Douglas gave both of them an odd look. "I don't even know what you're talking about?"

Danyluk came over and sat on Douglas' bunk. "The hair on a woman's thing, that's what we're talking about. It's called public hair, isn't it, Doug?"

Wayne sat up in his bunk and started laughing. "Moose, if it was called public hair then you wouldn't have to beg every time you wanted to stroke it, isn't that right?"

"HEY, WHO BEGS? IT'S ALWAYS OFFERED TO ME!"

East came over. "I told 'em on the hill, just call it crotch hair and that's that."

"It's called pubic hair," Wayne said. He was still chuckling thinking about the work 'public.'

"What started all this?" Douglas asked.

Everyone wanted to talk, but East was the loudest. "THAT'S WHAT WAS LOADED INTO MY HOT DOG AT THE DANCE TONIGHT."

Now Douglas sat up, grimacing. "What? You mean you had crotch hair all over your wiener?"

Although East was smiling, it was obvious he had been put off by the whole affair.

"Everywhere," he replied.

Danyluk put his arm around East's shoulder. "Well, you should have your wiener wrapped in crotch hair."

"There he goes again," said Bergie. "The sexual exploits of 'Danyfuck.' Tell them what you did with it East. Go on, tell them."

East didn't really want to talk about it, so Bergie continued. "He was picking them off and he was going to eat it anyway. I grabbed it off him and took it back to the girl who served him. D'ya know what she said? D'ya? She said, had she known they were in there, she would have charged extra." Bergie was roaring with laughter now and so was everyone else.

Jackson had a real look of pride on his face. "Did you see the one who asked me to dance tonight?"

Rothstein started limping around in a circle. "You mean the one with her leg in a cast?"

Jackson licked his lips. "NOT HER! The blond with the big bazookas sticking out. She was really nice."

Danyluk was trying to get between his sheets. "Nice, my ass. I danced with her when she came out of the jon. I kept wondering why everyone kept laughing at us, until Alma came over and whispered that the bottom of the dame's dress was sticking inside her girdle. Not only that, her breath would knock out a hippo at forty paces."

Bergie belly-laughed. "I suppose you pulled her dress out and told her?"

"No, Jackson did when he danced with her. It'll be the closest he'll ever get to a girdle."

Jackson glared at Bergie. "SCREW YOU, MOOSE! SHE TOLD ME ABOUT YOUR HANDS AND YOUR QUESTION. 'CAN I CHECK AND SEE IF THOSE ARE RUBBER?'"

When the lights were turned out, Danyluk was still trying to get into bed.

"SON OF A BITCH! SOMEONE'S USED JIFFY-SEW AND GLUED MY SHEETS TOGETHER. O.K., WHO'S THE WISE ASSHOLE?"

A voice was heard from across the aisle. "Your Irish friends visited tonight."

"WHAT? ARE THOSE BASTARDS AT IT AGAIN? THIS IS WAR!"

Wayne leaned over his bunk and whispered. "You asked me if I brought a bra back tonight. I brought these back instead." He was waving a pair of pink panties at Douglas.

"Not bad, eh?"

Douglas grinned. "Jeez, Wayne, Debbie always goes home half dressed when she's been out with you."

"Yeah, she loves it. G'night, Doug."

"G'night, Wayne."

As Douglas rolled over onto his side, Bergie said, "Doug, I'm sorry about your dog."

Other voices then joined in expressing their sympathy.

"Thanks," he replied. It took him an hour to get to sleep.

The following day was absolutely fantastic for the cadets of Charlie Company. They were allowed to sleep in and there was no P.T.

After Church Parade, Douglas phoned home and his mother explained what happened to Major. It made him feel a lot better, and he was in a good mood when Diane arrived with Tom, Ellen, and Debbie and the six of them went to Cosens Bay.

Kalamalka Lake, as usual, offered all it had. The coolness of the water was accompanied by a light breeze and a pale blue sky.

They spent the whole day water-skiing and exploring the countryside. Tom brought a barbecue, so between water-skiing, swimming, exploring, getting a sunburn and eating, there wasn't much time for what Wayne wanted; 'another souvenir.'

Once again, Douglas was taken in with the beauty of this countryside. When Tom offered them the boat to relax and roam the north end of the lake, Douglas was perfectly happy to sit in the back with Diane and let Wayne do the steering.

He put his arm around Diane. "You've lived here all of your life; when you come here, do you find it boring?"

Diane held his hand. "No. I think everyone who lives here cherishes every day that they can adore this country. The unfortunate thing is that it's changing. More and more people are moving up here and although the transformation is slow, it's happening. With each passing year, I notice this country losing more and more of its inherent charm."

Douglas smiled and brought her closer to him. "Wow, you sure have a way with words."

She laughed. "I read that in a newspaper."

He sighed and looked around. "I know I've probably told you this before, but this country seems to speak to me. I could spend hours here or at Okanagan Landing, just wanting to be allowed to be a part of it. If I didn't know any better and I don't, I'd say that God created this for Himself and decided to share it with a chosen few. You saw me at Okanagan Landing when the sudden wind whipped up the lake. I stared at the other side for half an hour, just trying to find words to describe the total feeling of freedom it gave me."

The boat was going very slowly through the crystal-clear, jade-coloured water. "I know your feelings for this region, Doug. Why can't you move up here?"

"We don't have any money and if I want to get any sort of an education, I'll have to stay on the coast."

Diane squeezed his hand tighter. "When you told my dad you're planning on going into the army, were you serious?"

He nodded. "My mother wants me to be a doctor but I don't think I've got the stomach for it. Maybe I should though, if you're going to take up nursing, we'd probably make a great team?"

Diane didn't say anything for a minute or so. She was lost in thought and time didn't seem to matter. "Don't you think we'd make a great pair regardless of what we end up doing?"

He lowered his arm from around her shoulder and held both of her hands. "You know I do," he replied gently with a lost smile. "Don't think I'm ever going to let you get away from me."

On the way back to camp, Tom stopped the car and bought a tube of sunburn lotion for the boys to take back to camp. "You probably don't realize it now, but you're both going to need this."

Tom was right. Shortly after the semi-burned duo had supper and watched, *Shane,* with Alan Ladd, they spent half an hour under a cold shower, and smeared themselves with the soothing balm.

Cadets in B-21 made it an early night. Tomorrow was the start of a week in the great outdoors.

When the lights went out, East was still up ironing dry his pair of K.D. longs.

"I hear there's wolves in them thar hills," he said, trying to talk like Alan Ladd.

"FOR CHRIST'S SAKE, HIT THE SACK AND LET US GET SOME SLEEP," Bergie yelled. "THE ONLY WOLF WE'LL HAVE WITH US TOMORROW NIGHT IS DANYPRONG HERE."

Laughter rang out from their end of the barracks.

"HEY, DANYLUK," said Jackson. "HOW ARE YOU GOING TO MANAGE WITHOUT WOMEN FOR A WHOLE WEEK?"

Moose put on his best sexy voice. "I've always got you, Early Pearly."

East was putting his pants away. "OH, NO YOU DON'T! HE'S MINE!"

After Jackson's cussing ended, the laughter died down and there was silence in B-21.

CHAPTER XIII

Simpson moved briskly down the aisle, pulling off blankets and turning over mattresses, "STAND BY YOUR BEDS!"

"Aww, not today as well, Sergeant?" Danyluk had joined the others in expressing their 'restrained exuberance' of having to take P.T. on the day they were leaving for the 'great outdoors.'

The Sergeant's face lit up when the whining started. "Oh, so we've got some nambi-pambie's in the ranks, have we? That means an extra twenty pushups for all of you gentlemen and I use the term gentlemen loosely. If you're not up by the time I get to you, you'll wish you were still in your mother's womb."

It was cold and the sun had just started to show itself above the horizon as the cadets of Guard Company started jogging across the highway to the upper camp.

"What time is it anyway?" East asked. He looked like he'd been up all night.

Douglas looked at his watch. "It's just turned five-fifteen. Jesus, we've only had five hours sleep."

Wayne was huffing and puffing. "They don't mention these jogs in the brochures. The information bulletin I read, made this camp look like a holiday resort."

Although Danyluk was still half asleep and didn't really know if he was running or not, he had enough life in him to continue complaining.

"This sort of thing is definitely ruining my sex life. My balls told me the other day that they were fed up with being hammered against my legs every morning."

Sergeant Simpson was jogging next to him. "This is the best thing for your sex life, my boy. By the time you do the extra pushups, your fist will be stronger."

Everyone laughed, except Danyluk. Then a voice in the crowd said, "Speak for yourself, Sergeant."

It was the wrong thing to say.

"Ah ah, we have a smart-ass with us. That will mean another twenty pushups. Danyluk, if this keeps up, your sex organs will fall in love with your hand."

Another voice in the crowd said, "He needs two hands to do it, Sergeant."

Sergeant Simpson laughed with them. "Ya see what you get for pulling it, Danyluk. If you keep this up, you'll have to hold the end of it with your feet."

Bergie tried to change his voice. "He can't Sergeant, he needs his feet to hold up his balls."

When they arrived back, the Musketeers made sure they were the first in the showers. The hot water felt great and they couldn't have cared less if the cadets lining up for showers got cold water.

Jackson dried himself off. He had been first in and first out. "I bet he got us up this early to make up for the day off he gave us last week."

Bergie snickered. "Simpson's got a memory like an elephant."

Jackson was now leaning out of the open window. "Hey, look outside guys. The other companies are just getting up to do their morning P.T."

Danyluk rushed over. "GOOD MORNING, YOU CREEPS. WE'VE GOT OUR P.T. OVER WITH. YOU'VE GOT TO GET UP P R E T T Y EARLY IN THE MORNING TO PUT ONE OVER ON GUARD COMPANY."

He barely got the words out when five or six huge bars of 'sergeant's soap' went flying through the air, heading in his direction.

Being first up meant that Guard Company was first in the mess hall.

As Banks held his plate forward, more than the regular portions were being heaped onto it.

"Look at the food we're getting? Now that we're going away, they're starting to feed us in the manner to which we'd love to become accustomed."

Bergie smiled. "Maybe this is a sign that the food ain't going to be that good in the field."

As they sat down to eat, one of the kitchen staff girls came over to Danyluk. "I made certain you got lots, just so that you won't lose your strength while you're gone." She was blinking her eyes at him and gently rubbing his shoulder. Danyluk in the meantime, was looking the other way.

Bergie put two and two together. "Ah haaa, now I know why your plate is always piled up while the rest of us starve. You've been diddling her, haven't you?"

Danyluk's face turned beet red and guilty looking. He tried to search for words. "I...I...don't even know..."

"How in the hell do you find time to 'service' all of your women?" asked Douglas.

The question made Danyluk feel proud. He stuck out his chest. "It's only a matter of organization. Eat your hearts out."

Rothstein pointed his fork at him. "She wants you to be big and strong when you return. Hey, guys, don't you think Alma should hear about this?"

Danyluk dropped his utensils. "You wouldn't? Aw, c'mon guys, give me a break? Alma's got arms like a logger, she'd kill me if she found out."

For the next fifteen minutes Danyluk begged for compassion. He was still begging when they left the mess hall heading for B-21.

"RIGHT! PAY ATTENTION HERE!" Sergeant Beckford said, addressing the company which was formed up on the road outside of the hut.

"OUR COMPANY SERGEANT-MAJOR, CSM WALSH, IS NO LONGER WITH US. IT WAS NECESSARY FOR HIM TO RETURN TO HIS REGIMENT. I HAVE BEEN APPOINTED ACTING COMPANY SERGEANT-MAJOR FOR THE BALANCE OF CAMP AND I WILL STILL RETAIN MY

POSITION OF PLATOON SERGEANT OF NUMBER NINE PLATOON." The company responded with resounding approval.

Bergie leaned over toward Douglas. "I wonder what happened?"

Douglas snickered. "Nothing. They finally figured it out that the guy just couldn't get along with cadets."

"You got that right," said Wayne. "The guy couldn't even get along with his own race, which, by the way, isn't human."

The laughter of the Musketeers and of those around them indicated complete general agreement throughout.

"ALRIGHT, SETTLE DOWN. YOUR PLATOON CORPORALS ARE GOING TO SHOW YOU HOW TO PACK YOUR LARGE AND SMALL PACKS. WHEN I FALL YOU OUT, I WANT YOU TO REPORT TO THAT TRUCK OVER THERE AND SIGN FOR ONE ADDITIONAL BLANKET AND TWO EXTRA GROUND SHEETS. WE HAVE BEEN INFORMED THAT A STORM FROM THE COAST IS ON THE WAY UP HERE. IT'LL PROBABLY REACH US THE DAY AFTER TOMORROW. THAT MEANS RAIN! ARE THERE ANY QUESTIONS?"

All cadets signed for their extra gear, and as Bergie put it, the barracks looked like 'Danyluk's bedroom at home.'

The bulletin board was the centre of attention as the cadets gathered around to read what they should take with them. Once again Nine Platoon had the edge because Sergeant Beckford had issued a list to each member. Earl, of course was at the bulletin board anyway. "HEY, YOU GUYS, IT SAYS HERE THAT SIGNALS COMPANY IS GOING TO JOIN US FOR THE WEEK."

"GREAT, THAT MEANS FOSTER WILL BE WITH US," yelled Banks.

Douglas stopped packing for a moment. "Yeah, but unfortunately, it also means Genova."

"AND SCHEAFFER THE WAFER!" bellowed East, his mouth half full with a cookie.

"Has Scheaffer still got his cold?" Bergie asked.

Banks started to laugh. "Probably, but Doctor Genova doesn't smear the Vicks anymore. Foster told me that everyone stays away from him after the beach incident. When he turns around to hand over the company to the Officer Commanding, everyone looks at his pants to see if the shit stain is still there."

Banks could hardly get it out, he was laughing so much.

"He'll never live that down, even when he returns to the regiment."

Rothstein was now howling as hard as Wayne. He had to jump down from his bunk, otherwise he would have rolled off.

"I betcha no one goes near his boots, either."

Danyluk put his arm around Rothstein. "That's not true, Rothie. The other day I heard that when Genova was on the parade square, he got chased by four dogs that wanted to screw his leg."

Wayne couldn't take it anymore. He was holding his stomach. "STOP IT, STOP IT!"

"C'MON YOU PEOPLE, LET'S GET PACKED UP," one of the Corporals 'suggested.'

The Corporal's stance made it perfectly clear that this was no time for talk. They were packed within the hour. In addition, the barracks was cleaned, barrack-boxes locked, mattresses rolled with their pillows inside and all the windows shut.

When they were formed up on the road, trucks arrived to take them to Glenemma. No one had to stand this time. Enough vehicles had been ordered so that everyone had a seat.

Douglas and Wayne had the opportunity to sit in the front of one of the trucks. With two companies going, the convoy was long. Each truck's 'choir' could be heard before the first vehicle left the camp.

Glenemma Range, as it is called, has been used periodically by the military during and since the War. It is land owned by the Okanagan Indian Band and leased to the government for training purposes.

The military has a good relationship with the Okanagan Indian Band. Any land used is looked after. Only once has the Chief complained. When he did, training areas were cancelled for a year and future applications to use the lands, were thoroughly reviewed by the Band Council.

Although the Glenemma area had been used for mortar, tank and anti-tank training, its rolling hills, high ground, low ground and open areas were ideal for company, platoon, and section-tactics.

The perimeter of the range is approximately three miles by two miles. Most of this is open area, however, there are enough stands of trees and bush areas to accommodate the bivouacking of large groups of people.

Even though there is a fresh water lake at the south end of Glenemma, all water is trucked in. Apparently there have been times when the water in the lake was 'suspect.'

Civilians driving their cars on Highway 97 that day must have been astounded at the size of the convoy taking the Guard and Signals Companies to Glenemma. Although room is left between vehicles so that civilian cars can pass, it was totally impossible because the Driver-Mechanics Company was coming the other way, heading back to camp. Their convoy consisted of another forty or so jeeps, three-quarter ton and three-ton trucks. These vehicles were being driven by cadets, some of whom were so small they could barely see over the steering wheels.

East got upset at a short co-driver who gave Charlie the 'Driver-Mech finger.' "SAME TO YOU!"

"I hear they have to put special wooden stilts on the pedals for some of those guys," he told Bergie.

Bergie smiled. "I can believe it. They're all shorter from the amount of shit they lost. It's a wonder they can sit at all."

Danyluk stood up quickly. "Hey, there's Lyons. "GIVE HER SHIT, DON!"

As Lyons' vehicle passed, all Danyluk could see was Lyons' finger.

"Did you guys see that? One of our own giving us the finger. UP YOUR NOSE

LYONS! AND SCREW YOUR SALES TAX AS WELL!"

Jackson had an excited look on his face. "That's the course I'm going to take next year. Just imagine what it must be like driving one of those things."

"Listen, Earl, it's all bull shit," said Bergie. "You're only seeing the good part of the course. Most of the time, those creeps are up to their necks in grease and oil."

Jackson nodded. "I know that, but they also get a trades badge out of it and that means trades pay. You know, lolly, dolly, moolah?" He rubbed his forefinger and thumb together in front of Bergie's face.

"Earl's right," said Rothstein. The Regular Force is holding an exercise in Wainwright, Alberta, shortly. It's called Buffalo Four and they've asked for fifty D&M cadets and fifty Signals cadets to attend. Those guys are going to be driving and the Signals people are going to look after communications.

Bergie wasn't listening. He was staring at the last D&M jeep. "I HOPE YA GET TURKEY FOR LUNCH, YA SHITHEADS!"

The jeep driver and co-driver both responded by waving back, then giving him the finger.

East was tightening the straps of his large pack. One of his blankets was coming loose. "We should be given the opportunity of going, as well."

Bergie gave him an inquisitive look. "You've got to be out of your cotton-pickin' mind. You spend six weeks here and then you want to spend another two weeks in 'Rainright'?" He pronounced Wainwright that way because it was the start of the long summer rain period in that part of Alberta.

"Not only would you be soaked to the skin all day, but you'd be eaten alive by the mosquitoes."

East winced. "There's mosquitoes there?"

"Are there mosquitoes there? Is that what you're asking?" Bergie had a grin from ear to ear. "Is that what you're asking?"

"Yeah, that's what I'm asking?"

"Let me tell you, Jackie, old boy. There's mosquitoes here in Glenemma, but these bastards don't pick you up and fly home with you like they do in Rainright. It's the hellhole of the world for mosquitoes. They're not happy with just taking a few drops; they all work for the Red Cross and want the whole thing. Why I knew a guy who..."

East was convinced. "O.K., YOU WIN. CHRIST, I'M STARTING TO ITCH ALREADY!"

As the trucks pulled off the highway and started climbing a very dry and dusty hill, the cadets in the back of Douglas' truck were singing.

"There once was a man from Nantucket,
whose cock was so long, he could suck it.
He said with a grin, as he wiped off his chin,
if my ear was a cunt, I would fuck it!"

Douglas and Wayne found it hard to see the vehicle in front of them because of the dust.

"Can you imagine what the guys in the back are going to look like when we unload?" Wayne said, trying to close his window which was only open a quarter of an inch and dust was everywhere inside the cab.

The truck was swaying from side to side as it climbed over a road that hadn't been graded in years.

Douglas was sitting in the middle and he had nothing to hold on to. He had to put his arm around Wayne to stop from bouncing around. At one point, his head nearly went through the roof.

"If we make it, and do unload, you mean?"

Although the driver had his hands full trying to see the road and the truck ahead, he was smiling. "This is mild. Just wait until you see the road up ahead."

Wayne and Douglas took their eyes off the 'road' for a second to look at each other. Although they were sitting in the cab, their faces were covered in dust.

The driver laughed. "This section of the road always stops the singing," he said. "I wonder why?"

At the top of the hill, the trucks came out into a large clearing and continued north for ten minutes along another very bumpy and dusty 'road.'

When they finally stopped at the north-end of the open area, Genova was already out of his truck. "ALL SIGNALS CADETS FORM UP IN THREE RANKS WITH YOUR GEAR!" He was pointing to a section of ground about four hundred yards away.

Sergeant Beckford spoke next. "GUARD COMPANY OVER HERE. I WANT YOU TO GATHER AROUND ME."

It was hard to see because of the dust, so cadets just followed each other hoping they were heading in the proper direction.

Banks was digging the dust out of his eyes. "Gather around him? I can't even see him."

When the two did see Sergeant Beckford, they also saw what it was like to ride in the back of the trucks. It looked like a scene from the movie 'The Desert Rats.' Cadets were literally covered all over in dust. Their pith-helmets were brown and the only pink spaces on their faces were around their eyes and lips. Their arms, hands, and the portion of their legs that weren't covered by hose-tops and short khaki pants were topped with dust and dirt.

Rothstein smacked his pants. With every slap of his hand, a haze appeared and stayed. It just hung in what little air there was. He looked at Bergie, "If this is army life, they can keep it."

When Bergie laughed, even his teeth were brown. "I feel hot, dirty and clammy," he said.

"You look it," replied Rothstein.

Bergie spotted Douglas and Wayne. "You lucky grunts. Compared to the rest of us, you look like you just stepped out of the showers."

As the company gathered around Sergeant Beckford, Danyluk and East were once again engaged in an earnest discussion about sex.

"For God sakes, Jack, it's impossible to get it stuck in there. People aren't built the same as dogs. HEY, GUYS, EAST HERE BELIEVES THAT EVERY TIME YOU SCREW A DAME, SOMEONE HAS TO THROW A BUCKET OF WATER OVER THE TWO OF YOU TO GET YOU UNSTUCK!"

East held his left thumb and forefinger together and was poking them with the forefinger and middle finger of his right hand.

"Well, I read that it tightens up like this." His left fingers clamped down on his right fingers.

Bergie went at them. "Jesus, will you guys give us a break. Here we are in the middle of the most God-forsaken place on earth, where we can't even breathe without filling our lungs with dust and you two are talking about getting stuck when you do it."

East wouldn't give an inch. "You're not going to convince me otherwise. I've seen my dog get in that predicament and I know that it happens to us, too."

Danyluk grimaced. "You mean to tell me you actually watched your dog get it on? That's sick, Jack."

"Well, how the hell am I supposed to learn? You can't talk, because I've seen you sneak Bergie's National Geographic and head to the jon."

Danyluk threw down his packs and held his arms in the air. "O.K., you win. If you can ever talk a chick into joining you in bed, I'll stand at the end with a bucket of cold water."

"O.K. GUYS, SETTLE DOWN. THE CORPORALS ARE AWARE OF WHERE THE PLATOON AND SECTION AREAS ARE LOCATED. EACH BIVOUAC AREA HAS BEEN DIVIDED INTO FOUR SECTIONS. YOU ALREADY KNOW WHAT SECTION YOU'RE IN. THE FOOD TRUCK WILL BE ARRIVING SHORTLY, SO WE'LL BE HAVING LUNCH IN AN HOUR. WHAT I WANT YOU TO DO IS SET UP YOUR INDIVIDUAL BIVOUAC AS YOU'VE BEEN TAUGHT.

"REMEMBER, I WANT TWO MEN TO A HOOTCHIE. YOU WILL BUILD IN-ROUTES AND OUT-ROUTES AND I DON'T WANT ANY TREES CUT DOWN.

"EACH PLATOON WILL HAVE ONE CENTRAL LATRINE. THE LATRINE WILL BE AWAY FROM ANY OF THE MAIN ROUTES WITHIN YOUR AREA.

"NOW PAY ATTENTION HERE. I MENTIONED TO YOU THIS MORN-ING THAT RAIN IS ON THE WAY. I WANT YOUR HOOTCHIES BUILT PROPERLY AND I WANT YOUR BLANKETS FOLDED IN SUCH A WAY THAT THEY WILL BECOME A SLEEPING BAG."

He stopped for a moment. "Corporal, did you show them how to make a sleeping bag out of their blankets?"

Everyone nodded as the Corporal replied, "YES, SERGEANT."

"GOOD. IT'S UNFORTUNATE THAT WE COULDN'T GET SLEEPING BAGS, BUT AS I TOLD YOU, THEY'RE ALL BEING USED FOR A REGU-LAR FORCE EXERCISE IN WAINWRIGHT. IF YOU FOLD YOUR BLAN-KETS PROPERLY, YOU SHOULD BE WARM AT NIGHT.

"NOW I WANT YOU TO REMEMBER THAT THIS IS A VIRGIN AREA. THERE IS NO FOULED GROUND HERE......"

Bergie whispered to Danyluk. "Did you hear that? This is a virgin area, do you think you can handle it?"

Sergeant Beckford heard him. "YOU HAVE A QUESTION?"

"Er, no Sergeant, but I don't think Danyluk will like it here because it's a virgin area."

All smiling faces were now on Danyluk.

"COME ON NOW, DANYLUK. MOST OF THE GIRLS IN VERNON WERE VIRGINS BEFORE YOU YOU ARRIVED. SURELY YOU CAN MAKE THE MOST OF THIS?"

Danyluk was grinning, even though he had turned red under his cover of dust. "I'LL DO MY BEST, SERGEANT."

He then leaned over to Bergie. "I'll get you for that one, you creep."

"RIGHT! NOW FOLLOW YOUR PLATOON CORPORALS IN LITTLE GOBS AND BUNCHES AND PAIR YOURSELVES OFF WITHIN YOUR SECTION. CARRY ON."

After the Corporals had shown them their area, Wayne and Douglas paired up. Because the rest of the Musketeers were in the same section, they were close to them. Bergie and Danyluk teamed up and Rothstein, Jackson and East built a hootchie for three.

Within an hour they had their hootchies built with boughs of evergreens for mattresses and fallen trees for the A-frames. Ground-sheets were joined together before they were wrapped and tied around the A-frames. The extra ground-sheets issued were used under their blankets. Each pair of cadets had six ground-sheets, so their hootchies were actually quite comfortable.

Wayne showed Douglas his hands as they dug the latrine. "Can you believe it, I've got blisters already?"

They had to dig down three feet and then using small logs, build six seats along the ten-foot trench.

Bergie and Danyluk had 'volunteered' to build what they called 'The Pisser,' nearby.

Other cadets were setting up a washing-up stand and nailing mirrors to trees above counters that had been build so wash basins could be set on them.

A water truck arrived and backed into a small area behind the washing-up counters. It resembled a large fuel truck with taps along the sides and at the back.

Two cadets from Signals Company joined each platoon of Charlie Company. They installed a Nineteen Set radio in their hootchie. Next to the set were spare batteries that looked like regular automobile batteries.

In addition to the Nineteen Set, the signals cadets also had a Fifty-Eight Set with them, a radio set of the type that could be strapped to a person's chest. The front opened up like a door, showing all of the various dials. A large six-foot aerial was attached to the top of it.

Other Signals cadets were everywhere, erecting poles from which wire would be strung. The poles only carried a single wire, because it wasn't necessary to have two. They hammered spikes into the ground thereby making the ground itself another wire. This was called a ground return.

With all the main work done, Wayne and Douglas lay back on their blankets in their hootchie.

Wayne had taken off his boots and his hands were behind his head. "The Vancouver Hotel was never this comfortable," he said, looking at their 'work of art.'

Douglas snickered. "So true. But we don't have the hot and cold running chambermaids running in and out."

"If we did, we'd never get rid of Danyluk," Wayne replied.

A Signals Cadet stepped out of his hootchie after he had picked up a message on his radio set. "LUNCH IS IN FIFTEEN MINUTES!"

Wayne and Douglas grabbed their towels and wash basins and joined the other throngs heading to the washing-up area. Refreshed, they returned to their hootchie, picked up their combination knife, fork and spoon, their mess-tins, and walked over to the large tent set up for serving food.

Although Glenemma is hot and dusty, the trees around the mess tent gave considerable shade cover. The officers and NCOs had selected a favourable piece of ground.

When the Musketeers arrived, the lineup for lunch had already started. Large stainless steel containers were lined in a row with smiling 'volunteer' cadets standing behind them with ladles in their hands.

Wayne asked, "What's for lunch?"

"Vegetable soup, pork chops, mashed potatoes, peas, corn, carrots, gravy, and for dessert, it's apple pie."

For those cadets who didn't drink coffee, milk, water or tea were also available.

When Douglas and Wayne were served, their mess tins were heaped up in a hurry. Afterward, they sat against trees and ate the meals fit for a king. Everyone was starved.

Danyluk was sucking the bone of a pork chop. "This food is better than the slop they serve in camp."

Bergie swallowed some mashed potatoes and nodded. "Yeah, but you don't have your little darling to give you extra helpings, do you?"

"I keep telling you guys, I've only been out with her once. She nearly ripped my shirt off when we were alone."

Hearing Danyluk say that was more than Bergie could stand. "Oh, come on, do you expect us to believe that?" You probably had her blouse off before she told you her name."

Danyluk laughed loudly. "That, Bergie my boy, is not quite true. I had her blouse off after she told me her name, which by the way is, Aggie."

Bergie didn't let up. "Aggie? Haaa, give me a faggie Aggie, I want to sing 'Smoke Gets in Your Eyes.'"

"Hey, does anyone want my pork chops?" asked Rothstein.

East stood up in a hurry. "I'LL TAKE 'EM!"

"Jesus, I've never seen you move so fast in your life," said Bergie.

"I'm a growing boy. What's the matter Rothie, don't you like pork chops?"

"I don't eat pork, it's against my religion." He picked them out of his mess tin and shoved them into East's.

Douglas looked over to the mess tent that was now empty. "Isn't there any other kind of meat over there?"

"Yeah, there was turkey, but it was gone before we reached the front of the line."

"Jeez, don't mention turkey. If I see another piece of turkey twenty years from now, it'll be too soon for me."

Banks looked at East. "How's your hootch? Did you find a flat piece of ground?"

East's mouth was full, so he waited until he swallowed before answering. "Not bad. It would take a full force gale to tear it apart."

"All we have to do now is build a sump," said Rothstein.

The word sump perked up Wayne's ears. "What the hell's a sump?"

"It's a small ditch you dig around the hootchie to drain off the rain," Rothstein. Replied. "Did you miss those lectures?"

Both Douglas and Wayne gave each other a quizzed look. "We must have," said Wayne.

Bergie smiled. "I dug our sump because you know who," he was pointing at Danyluk, "wanted to be the first to use the 'Pisser.' "

"That's right. I figure if this is virgin land, I was going to be the first to un-virgin it."

Jackson stood up because his shirt was sticking to him. "Christ, it's hot. What I wouldn't give to be in the Capital Cafe right now."

"Yeah, eating a nice, large banana-split," said East.

After eating, they washed their mess tins and utensils in a soap-and-water-filled container and rinsed them off in another one full of fresh water.

Back at the hootchie, Douglas and Wayne took off their boots and lay back.

Wayne let out a big sigh. "This is the life. No drill for a week and no Saturday Morning Inspections."

"Yeah, but no Diane and no Debbie, either. I wonder what they're doing right now?"

Wayne rolled over on his side. "They're probably saying exactly the same thing."

Jackson came up to their hootchie. "Hey, you guys, come and look at this."

Wayne and Douglas followed him to the latrine. Danyluk was there carving out a special seat. When he saw them, he put on his proud look. "Anyone can be uncomfortable, but not me. When I use the shitter, it'll be like the Throne Room at Buckingham Palace."

Bergie inspected it. "We're only here for a week, not a year. Now, I suppose you're going to go and kill some poor animal to put fur around it?"

Danyluk laughed. "I like things with fur, or hair around them, but this will have to do."

"Then it's for you and me?" asked Bergie.

"Not on your life. If I find people using this seat, I'll have their balls for book-ends."

"LECTURES IN TEN MINUTES," screamed a Signals cadet. "MAP AND COMPASS IN THE MESSING AREA."

Wayne gave Douglas a sneaky look. "We'll have to do something about his seat." Douglas nodded. "You bet we will."

Blackboards had been set up in the shade of the messing area. There wasn't too much grass, however, considering the rest of Glenemma, it was pleasant even though there wasn't a breeze.

Individual Platoon Officers and NCOs then proceeded to refresh the memories of cadets who had sat in those dark and dingy, stifling-hot huts, watching old British World War Two films on the subject.

Although a considerable amount of 'hands-on training' had taken place at Area Ten in the upper camp, the size of Glenemma allowed everyone the opportunity to travel a fair distance and understand the importance of being able to read a map in relation to the ground.

After an hour of lectures, each section was on its own, roving the ground and doing simple exercises. Each cadet was issued with a prismatic compass, a map, and a protractor. An orienteering exercise had already been set up and cadets worked in teams of two or three, going around various check points, which were manned by Regular Force staff. They had to check in on time and then give an eight-figure grid reference of their location.

The exercise was planned so that each section, after walking about four miles in total, would follow their last bearing right to their platoon bivouac area. The exercise ended at four o'clock.

Wayne was sitting with the rest of the Musketeers in a small common shady area, close to their hootchies. "My feet are killing me," he said. "I've got dust in my crotch, dust up my ass and when I brush my teeth, my toothbrush is never going to forgive me. It'll come out black."

Danyluk took off his boots. His feet were black and he was laughing. "Looking at these reminds me of an old joke. Did you guys hear the one about the drunk who comes home and his wife is in bed with a negro."

No one said anything, so he continued. "Anyway, this guy crawls into bed and pulls up the covers. When he sees the feet he counts them. One, two, three, four, five, six. He shakes his head, jumps out and walks around to the end of the bed, where he counts them again. One, two, three, four."

"What did he do then?" Jackson asked.

"Well, he gets back into bed and shakes his wife. 'Hey Mabel,' he says. 'Remind me to wash my feet in the morning.'"

As tired and as dirty as the Musketeers were, laughter filled the bivouac site of their section of Nine Platoon.

More jokes followed and they forgot about the dirt and dust of Glenemma. Then a call from a Signals cadet indicating that supper would be ready in half an hour, helped matters even more.

That afternoon, Rothstein was first in line for dinner. The rest of the Musketeers stood behind him.

"I made sure I was first in line this time, guys. Guess what we're having for dinner? Beef Stew."

"Hey, good scoff," Bergie said, rubbing his stomach. "It sticks to your bones, but in Danyluk's case, his bone."

Danyluk shook his head. "Bergie, how can you be so crude?"

"I'm crude, you say that I'm crude? I'm the guy that has to share a bunk space with you and listen to your stories, your snorting, snoring, farting, and most of all, your boasting and sexual advice. You say that I'm crude? The other night you were talking in your sleep. Do you know what you said?"

Danyluk had that smile on his face. "No, what did I say?"

"You said, 'Sweetheart, I'm going to cover you all over with whipped cream, then I'm going to put the cherry right there and lick it all off.' "

"So what's wrong with that?" asked Danyluk.

"Ahhh, but I'm not finished. Then you said, 'Now you do the same to me and put the cherry right here.' You paused for a minute then said, 'WAIT A MINUTE, HOLD IT, STOP! IT LOOKS SO GOOD I'M GOING TO LICK IT OFF MYSELF.' You see how selfish you are?"

Everyone within earshot enjoyed the conversation. East had a laughing fit every time these two went at it. He knew that Bergie was the only one who could verbally handle Danyluk, and when he did, it was usually a riot.

A crowd started to gather, which included Sergeant Beckford and some of the Corporals.

Danyluk countered. "Well, I also have to share a bunk space with you and put up with you, Bergie, and believe me, it's not exactly Heaven. You snort and fart in your sleep, as well. Also, you talk. The other night you were talking in your sleep. You said, 'Danyluk, old boy, my girlfriend really likes to get it in the ear. It's really odd, but every time I try to put it in her mouth, she turns her head.' "

Fits of laughter came from the crowd.

"Are you guys always at each other like this?" asked Sergeant Beckford.

Bergie answered first. "Yes, Sergeant. I never, ever said a word until I had to bunk with this guy."

"Me, too," replied Danyluk. "I was an altar boy before I came to Vernon. Now, after bunking with this guy for a few weeks, the church probably wouldn't accept me to wash the floors."

Bergie laughed."Yeah, tell Sergeant Beckford what you put in the Holy water. Go on, tell him."

"I'd rather not."

"Well, I'll tell him then. Fish juice."

Sergeant Beckford cringed. "What?"

"That's what I said, when he told me," replied Bergie. "The whole church and everyone in it smelled like rotten fish." Danyluk went around saying it was just another miracle. You know, like the time Jesus divided up two fish or something like that."

"I thought you were a Protestant?" asked Douglas.

"Naah, but B-3's got a jon I can hide in."

"Hey, Sergeant, are we doing anything tonight?" Wayne asked, hoping nothing was planned.

"Yes, we intend to have a parade."

There was a loud sigh of disappointment from the crowd.

"A SWIM PARADE," said Beckford. "WE'VE MADE ARRANGEMENTS TO USE THE LOCAL LAKE."

Sergeant Beckford knew the news would travel quickly and wake everyone up.

"But Sergeant, we ain't got no swimmin' trunks."

Danyluk grabbed the front of East's shirt with both hands. "We don't need them, you dummy. We go in bare balls; there's no dames around."

As they washed their mess-tins and utensils, Banks heard Jackson say to East. "You know, this place ain't so bad after all."

When the company walked to Round Lake that night, Douglas never took his eyes off the surrounding countryside. A couple of old tank turrets were stuck in the middle of the flatland, and to the east and west of them, were large mountains. The one to the west was green and lush with beautiful evergreens. What grass there was, was coarse and yellow. He could see where vehicles had left the dusty roads at one time or another, leaving a visible trail of tire imprints that would remain there forevermore. As tough as this land was, it was also fragile.

After walking for thirty minutes, they saw the lake. It was small, about two hundred yards square. The water looked calm, clear, blue, and so inviting that they wouldn't have bothered taking off their clothes, they would have just jumped in.

Curious cattle on the shore moved closer to get a better look at these weird two-legged creatures, but moved away fast, leaving more clouds of dust as the cadets approached.

For ten minutes, everyone attended a lecture on water safety. They were told to use the buddy system, which meant every cadet had to have a partner. In case of an odd man out, there had to be a threesome.

When the lecture finished, the Company Commander asked if there were any questions. "No?" he asked. "Alright, GET IN THERE!"

It doesn't take long to take off your clothes when you're so hot they stick to every inch of your body. No sooner had the last word left the OC's mouth, clothes went flying and 180 sweaty, bare bodies jumped into the lake, frigid water or not.

In seconds, the normally quiet oasis of Round Lake was transformed to a scene that rivaled the frenzy of revelers on New Year's Eve at Coney Island.

The shock of the cold water didn't dampen the enthusiasm one bit. Excited cadets splashed, spit, kicked, punched, beat, and churned the water of the small lake. With hands and feet flailing, the cadets of Charlie Company loudly voiced their gratitude of Glenemma's offering, and their exuberance echoed in the nearby hills.

"THIS IS WHAT THE DOCTOR ORDERED!" Danyluk could hardly hear himself amidst the noise around him. He and Bergie cupped their hands to make a step-up for East and Jackson who dove in over their lifters' shoulders.

Wayne was mounted on Douglas' shoulders in a horseback fight with Rothstein carrying a cadet called Adams. At first, Wayne was dumped, but they got Adams the second time. Switching around, Rothstein got on Wayne's shoulders, and as a team, they were unbeatable.

When somebody threw in a basketball, the next half hour was taken up with a game of waterball, played with imaginary nets.

Round Lake proved it was the perfect remedy for curing the ills of a long hot day in Glenemma. When waterball ended, other new games were instantly devised, and the exhilaration continued.

At first it was hard to hear East's voice, so he turned up the volume. "HEY, THERE'S A DEAD COW IN THIS LAKE!"

Apparently East had swum out and spotted a dead cow on the bottom. He was now standing next to Sergeant Beckford. "I saw it Sergeant, honest I did."

The activity slowed down fast and within seconds, everyone was out of the water.

"SETTLE DOWN, SETTLE DOWN. East the beast, here, wasn't supposed to swim that far out. There is a dead cow in the lake but we've had the water tested by the City of Vernon officials and our own staff and they report that it's fine for swimming. We wouldn't let you go swimming if the lake was contaminated. THE WATER'S FINE."

That's all that they wanted to hear. Within seconds, the cadets were back in the water.

Over the next hour, no one gave any thought to the poor cow who probably got stuck having a drink and drowned. The water was just too great to miss.

On the way back to the bivouac area, Charlie Company could have won the 'World's Top Choir Contest.' They sang most of the well-known 'army' songs, but one song was louder than ever.

"Oh Provost, oh Provost, your eyes are so blue,
But, good people are dying for bastards like you.
The army may think that you're physically fit,
But you know, and I know, you're just full of shit."

Cadets' spirits were up, but if someone had taken a picture, it would have looked like Mao's Long March. Some cadets were wearing their undershorts; others who had worn their clothes into the lake were wearing them wet; and others just wore their khaki shorts, or just their shirts.

The main thing was they were happy, and when they passed Signals Company on its way to the lake, everyone made certain Signals knew about the dead cow. The news didn't depress the tired-looking cadets. They just wanted a swim.

"WHAT COMPANY ARE WE?" asked Sergeant Beckford.

"GUARD COMPANY, THE BEST!" came the response.

A few seconds later, Genova tried to match the exhilaration of Charlie Company, with his 'men,' but they hadn't been in the lake yet and couldn't really give a damn which company they were.

When they arrived back, Wayne lay in the hootchie wearing a T-shirt and a fresh pair of khaki shorts. "I feel like I've just been born again."

Douglas smiled. "Me, too. We needed that."

For a few minutes, both just stared at the top of the hootchie, neither one talking. Wayne broke the silence first.

"Doug, I'm having second thoughts. I really don't want this to end. I don't think I understood at first, what was required of......"

Douglas lay on his side to face Wayne. "Yeah, I know what you're saying. We've been kind of lucky to get into this company. Did you think camp was going to be like this?"

Wayne slowly shook his head. "If I did, I probably wouldn't have come. I...I think you have to be a part of it to understand what's...I mean, if you don't do it yourself, then you really never know if......"

Douglas interrupted him. "I know. No one could ever write about what we've been through. We work our butts off until we don't have anything left to give, then they pile on more and we handle that as well. It's like they slapped us with a gauntlet and then threw it down. We were hesitant to pick it up, but when we did, it wasn't so bad after all."

"Exactly," said Wayne. "Now I think I now know what Sergeant Beckford means, when he says, 'It's not necessary to trip over your own shadow.' "

A pair of running shoes appeared in front of the hootchie's opening. Socks flopped around the owner's ankles. "What are you guys doing?"

"Who is it?" asked Wayne.

"It's me, Rothstein."

"Well, don't just stand there, Rothie, crawl in. What's up?"

Rothstein was smiling as he ducked in. "My memory must be going. I just remembered it's my birthday today and the cake I got from home is back at Vernon in the freezer. I was going to bring it, but I forgot."

Douglas saw the look on the cadet's face. Rothstein was going through a bit of homesickness, similar to what he himself had gone through recently.

"Well, look at it this way, Rothie, it'll be there when we get back and we can all have a piece of it." Douglas then crawled toward the exit. "Many happy returns," he said, shaking Rothstein's hand as he left.

Wayne watched Rothstein sit on top of Douglas' blankets and tie his shoelace. "How old are you today, Rothie?"

"Fifteen."

"The BIG ONE-FIVE, eh? Douglas and I make the BIG ONE-FIVE in the next two weeks. Our birthdays fall close to each other's."

As Wayne talked, he didn't notice five pairs of running shoes and knobby knees lined up outside of the hootchie.

"HAPPY BIRTHDAY TO YOU, HAPPY BIRTHDAY TO YOU. HAPPY BIRTHDAY DEAR ROTHIE, HAPPY BIRTHDAY TO YOU."

Rothstein and Wayne rushed out to find Douglas holding a cupcake with one lit match in the middle of it. The rest of the Musketeers formed the choral group.

Rothstein beamed as he blew out the match. The next minute, he was in the middle of a blanket, getting fifteen royal bumps and a pat on the back by all of his friends.

"This'll taste better than the big cake," he said.

East was licking his lips. "Don't forget Rothie, we all get a piece."

It wasn't easy for Rothstein to split the cupcake seven ways, but he had fun doing it.

That night during mug-up, a small fire was lit in a large clearing and the company carried on singing army songs with limericks.

"There once was a man from Bengal,
who had a hexadronical ball.
The cube of its weight,
plus his pecker, times eight.
Was four fifths, of five eighths,
of fuck all. "

The chorus sang, *"Oh, that was a cute little song. Sing us another one, just like the other one, sing us another one do-oo. "*

East got up.

"There once was a girl from Dundee,
who was raped by an ape up a tree.
The result was most horrid,
all ass and no forehead.
Three balls and a purple goatee. "

After the chorus chimed in, Jackson began.

"There was an old fag from Khartoum,
who took a lesbian up to his room.
They argued all night,
over who had the right,
to do what, and with which,
and to whom. "

Bergie arose when the chorus finished.

"There once was a hermit named Dave,
who said, 'think of the money I've saved,
by avoiding vacations and sexy relations,
and taking a shit while I shave.' "

When they got tired of singing, cadets took turns getting up and telling a joke, or relating weird stories that had happened to them.

Danyluk was the star of the show. He told a story about how he ended up going around with a girl who had a twin sister he didn't know about. They would trade places to fool him and while one of them liked his advances, the other one smacked or punched him every time he made a move. He said he gave up going around with her because he couldn't get used to her 'split' personality.

After that, he told a joke. "What's the difference between a Salvation Army girl and a girl taking a bath?"

"WHAT?"

"The Salvation Army girl has her soul full of hope."

He received a big hand, so he didn't stop.

"Did you hear the one about a woman who went to the doctor for an examination?

"NO!"

"Anyway, when she stripped off, she had one normal tit and the other one hit the floor.

"The doctor said, 'My God, madam, what happened?'

"'Nothing doctor,' she replied. 'It's just that we have twin beds.'"

Bergie, East, and Jackson had to hold their stomachs, they were laughing so hard as Danyluk gave his 'smile of pride,' when he took his bow.

It gets pitch black at night in Glenemma. Each cadet had been issued with a flashlight, and beams were seen everywhere.

Wayne and Douglas were lucky because they were close to the Signals hootchie that had a Coleman lantern. Signals exercises continued throughout the night and the cadets took turns sleeping and listening to the radio sets.

At times, the two Musketeers could hear despair in the voices coming from the Signals hootchie. "Christ, not another netting call. That's the tenth one in the last hour. How about another tuning call just to break up the monotony?"

Then the Signals cadets would have a 'discussion' about the proper way to use the 'flick mechanisms' of the Nineteen Set. Shortly, even they settled down.

"This is pretty comfortable," Wayne said. They had just crawled into their blankets and were warm.

"You know, Doug, it's true what Beckford said about not tripping on your own shadow. If a person gets organized and works within a team, nothing can stand in his way."

Douglas as usual, had his hands behind his head. "I know. I think a person can still be an individual, but he has to work with others and he has to take their perspective and suggestions into account."

"You mean no one can be an island?"

"That's right, not in the military. Do you remember what Sergeant Beckford told us in those leadership periods? He said a leader wouldn't ask anyone to do something that he hasn't done himself."

"But what if it had to be done and he hadn't done it?" Wayne asked.

"Then he'd do it with them. Respect has to be earned. It can't be bought and it can't be obtained by bullying. We're lucky to have Sergeant Beckford. He has that uncanny knack of making everyone want to work for him and with him."

Wayne switched off his flashlight. "You're right. Every cadet in this platoon knows that Beckford is concerned about him. Even when he's pissed off with someone and goes up one side of him and down the other, when he's finished, he winks before he sends the guy on his way. The cadet knows he's done something wrong, but he also knows the Sergeant's still with him and he'd better not let it happen again."

Although he couldn't see him, Douglas was nodding as Wayne spoke. "Have you noticed he spends time with each of us? Not just the guys in our platoon; the whole company? He's always there and because of that, so are we."

Their voices began to trail off and their eyes started to close, when all of a sudden there was a loud CRACK, followed by a piercing scream and the words, "SON OF A BITCH! I'M COVERED IN SHIT! BERGIE, PASS ME A TOWEL. WHERE THE HELL IS THE WATER TRUCK?"

Wayne laughed. "It sounds like Danyluk's chair fell into the shitter. Doug, you did it. How did you do it?"

Douglas didn't hear him, he was asleep.

"OH, MY GOD, I'M COVERED IN IT. SON OF A BITCH! I'LL GET YOU, JACKSON. I CAN HEAR YOU LAUGHING."

Storm clouds can move fast and sometimes even the weather office can be fooled. The coastal storm that wasn't supposed to appear in the Vernon area for a day or two decided to trick the weatherman once again. It arrived with the potency of a flash flood.

The clouds opened up during the night, and at seven o'clock in the morning, when Sergeant Beckford's voice bellowed through the bivouac area, it was still pouring.

The sound of rain hitting the ground-sheets was comforting and most cadets of Charlie Company had great difficulty getting out of their warm, dry blankets.

The bickering of the Signals cadets 'discussing' who should have built a sump around their hootchie was loud enough to wake Wayne up.

"I CAN'T DO EVERYTHING, YA KNOW. I'VE BEEN UP HALF THE NIGHT ANSWERING THOSE STUPID NETTING CALLS."

"WHATDOYA MEAN? I'VE BEEN UP JUST AS MUCH AS YOU. YOU KNEW WE HAD TO DIG THE TRENCH. JESUS, I'M SOAKED TO THE SKIN."

Wayne lay back and listened with a sadistic smile. He thought to himself that if Genova was on the ball like Sergeant Beckford, he would have made certain all of his relay stations were built properly.

He shook Douglas. "Doug, wake up, it's raining cats and dogs out there."

Douglas opened his eyes, stretched and yawned. "I'm awake." He loved the sound of the rain hitting the hootchie and didn't make any attempt to get out of bed.

"After you went to sleep last night, Danyluk's chair fell into the shitter with him in it."

Douglas sat up, his face filled with delight. "You mean he used it?"

Wayne laughed. "Used it? He was covered in it. He thinks Jackson did it, instead of you."

Douglas grinned. "I didn't do it. When I got there, Bergie had already cut the log. He just left an inch to hold Moose's weight for a few seconds."

"Bergie did it? God, I pity Jackson," said Wayne as he pushed down his blankets and pulled on his K.D. longs.

Within minutes both of them were wearing khaki shirts, their military sweaters, K.D. Longs, boots, puttees, and weights.

With towels over their shoulders, they picked up their wash basins and headed to the water truck.

Douglas was brushing his teeth and although his words were mostly unintelligible, Wayne could understand him when he talked.

"Did he make much of a fuss when he went in?"

Wayne was also brushing his teeth. "Did he make a fuss?! I thought it was the start of the Third World War."

Because of the heavy rain, other cadets were having a quick wash and leaving, going back to their shelter. They couldn't understand why Wayne and Douglas were out there laughing and getting soaked to the skin.

After combing their hair, they were patting each other on the back, mentally and verbally imagining what Danyluk must have gone through in the black chill of the night.

Arriving at the messing tent, boxes that had been piled the day before were being issued to cadets.

"These are Five-In-One-Rations," a Corporal told them. "They last one man for five days, or five men for one day. They've got to last two of you for two days."

Back at their hootchie, Wayne opened the box. "Hey, these are mint. We've got canned bacon, powdered eggs, canned Christmas cake, canned stew, packets of powdered mashed potatoes, cans of every kind of vegetable, crackers, gum, chocolate bars, cigarettes, tea, coffee and everything. If this is what the Regular Force uses in the field, those guys have got it made."

Douglas took out the small stove and placed a tin of jelly-like substance called Sterno underneath it and lit it. Then they cooked bacon, sausages and eggs over the flame, in their mess tins. Although the rain was pelting down, the nice smell of breakfast wafted through the cold morning air.

Danyluk's voice rang out. "WHO WANTS TO TRADE THEIR CIGARETTES FOR CHRISTMAS CAKE?"

"OVER HERE," replied Douglas. He passed over all the packets of cigarettes holding five each. Danyluk, gave him two tins of cake.

"Come on in out of rain. I hear you fell in the shitter last night?"

Danyluk squeezed in. "Fell in the shitter? I had to strip off in the cold and wash my whole body down at the water truck. Then I had to wash my clothes. I'll get that God-damned Jackson, you just wait and see if I don't."

Wayne was smiling. "How do you know it was him?"

Danyluk's face changed. He looked at both of them. "It wasn't you two, was it?" His face was firm with a trace of suspicious grimace.

"You know we wouldn't do anything like that. What happened anyway?" asked Wayne.

Danyluk was eating a piece of bacon, one piece of three he held in his hand.

"Well, last night when I went to bed, I had to take a crap. I put my long pants on, grabbed my flashlight and headed for the shitter. Nothing happened until I reached for the toilet roll, then all hell broke loose. My chair gave way and I ended up lying face up in the ditch. It was a nightmare."

Douglas and Wayne both roared laughing.

"Go ahead and laugh, but I wouldn't wish that on my worst enemy, not even those two Irish creeps."

"Thank God it was face up," said Douglas.

"Yeah, you can laugh. Sergeant Beckford laughed when I told him, as well. If I catch the bastard that put me through that, I'll have his nuts," he said as he left the hootchie.

Douglas smiled. "Jeez, I pity old Jackson."

Wayne was still snickering. "Oh, he'll calm down until the next time."

"The next time? Wayne, you wouldn't?"

"Good things always happen in threes," he said, slapping Douglas on the back.

"You're cruel, Wayne. When do we do it?"

Wayne replied with a sly look on his face. "Let's give him a few days to recuperate, then we'll surprise him."

The cadets of Charlie Company loved the rain. Not only did the air smell so fresh, they got a reprieve from the blazing sun.

It was raining so hard that all training was cancelled that day. Cadets just visited each other in their hootchies, told stories, played cards, or sang songs. At lunch time, they delved into their Five-In-One Rations and made lunch.

At about three in the afternoon, the rain eased off a bit and the company agreed that rain or no rain, it would be great if they went for another swim.

This time, the dead cow wasn't even considered. When they arrived back, their bodies were clean, but their pants and running shoes were covered in mud.

The rain increased and Glenemma was quiet that night. Most cadets stayed in their hootchies trying to keep warm.

At mug-up, a large fire was lit and both companies gathered around singing songs or telling stories. There were a lot of laughs about Danyluk's affair with the shitter.

Someone passed the word around that his knife, fork and spoon combination tools were lost in the trench and that he had gone in to retrieve them. The stories didn't seem to bother Danyluk. He and several others were quiet because they had received the wrath of Sergeant Beckford for not making their hootchies properly. Loads of blankets and clothes were spread out by the fire.

When it rains in the Vernon area, the clouds normally don't stay around long. It's almost as if they didn't want to dampen God's country. This particular storm was different and wouldn't cooperate; it decided not to move on.

It was raining hard the next morning as Douglas and Wayne cooked breakfast. Both were dressed in Khaki longs and shirts, sweaters, boots, puttees, weights, and web-belts. They each took a ground-sheet from under the blankets to protect them from the rain.

Although they had had a good night's sleep, their hootchie was damp and along with the dampness came a musty smell.

Wayne's bacon was crackling in his mess tin as he held it above the stove. "Can you imagine doing tactics in this stuff?"

Douglas also had his little stove going. "We're going to look like Danyluk did when we finish today."

After breakfast, they walked over to the water truck and washed their utensils.

"At least we're wearing our berets today," said Wayne.

"Christ, we look like men from Mars with these ground sheets on."

Wayne gave him a shove. "Let's get a move on, spaceman, or we'll wish we were on Mars if we're late for Beckford's parade."

For the next two days, with only breaks for lunch, the cadets of Charlie Company went through section and platoon tactics in the open area of Glenemma. They were shown arrowhead, diamond, extended line, and single file formations. There was a Bren Gun section to every rifle section and they were issued with blank rounds to create more realism in 'advance to contact' tactics.

Throughout, Sergeant Beckford kept giving them little tips. "NOW REMEMBER, YOU NEVER SALUTE IN THE FIELD. THE ENEMY MIGHT HAVE A SNIPER OUT THERE AND NATURALLY HE WANTS TO KNOCK OFF THE OFFICERS AND THE NCOs!"

The officer or section commander never took up a lead position in any of the formations. He was always back with the men and his commands were whispered from man to man until they reached the person in the front. The person in front would then give the appropriate signal for whatever formation the section commander wanted.

Danyluk made a point of telling Sergeant Beckford that the poor guy up front would get 'knocked off' quickly.

"YOU'VE GOT THAT RIGHT," Beckford replied.

In addition to section tactics, they learned how to judge distance on the ground, including 'dead ground,' how to space themselves and how to scan ground from right to left.

"ALWAYS REMEMBER THE FIVE Ss. SHAPE, SILHOUETTE, SIZE, SHADOW AND........."

Some cadet yelled out, "SHIT, RIGHT DANYLUK?"

As Danyluk looked around. The company and all of the NCOs were laughing.

"LISTEN, DON'T BE SO ROUGH ON DANYLUK. HE'S HAPPY IN HIS WORK. THE WORD IS SPACING!"

When they were back in Camp Vernon, every cadet wrote 'shit' as the fifth word on the exam.

Had the rain continued, it would have ruined what the boys considered was a perfect week. The rain stopped on Wednesday afternoon and when the sun appeared, it soon was back to the normal arid heat for which Glenemma is famous.

On Friday morning, mess trucks began to reappear. The Five-In-One Rations had been excellent, however, when they asked for more, they were informed that those rations were too expensive and they should just be thankful they had had them in the first place.

After breakfast, the company started climbing the mountain to the west, on the other side of the highway that runs parallel to Glenemma. The going was tough all day because there were no trails and the various routes took them through very heavy bush.

Each cadet carried a rifle, but the ones who really hated the climb were the Bren Gun Sections. Every rifle section had a Bren Gun and the three cadets who had to carry it were cursing all of the way up.

Blisters on their feet slowed them down and even cooling their feet off in mountain streams didn't help that much. First aid kits emptied quickly.

Late that afternoon, Bergie had his feet propped against a tree. He had taken off his boots and socks and was trying to count the number of blisters he had on each foot.

"If this is what the infantry does, I'm definitely going armoured."

The other Musketeers around him agreed. They were limping and putting plasters and bandaids on their feet.

East picked up his boots in one hand. "These are ruined. They'll never look the same, regardless of how much polish I put on them."

Everyone knew he was unhappy because he had had the best boots in the company. If East wasn't eating, he was working on his boots. They were truly a work of art.

"Look at it this way," said Douglas, as he sat down, grabbed his right foot and blew air on his toes. "I know it was a hell of a climb, but have you ever seen a view like this in your life?"

Danyluk spread ointment on his feet. "Jesus, Doug, give us a break from all of that artsie-fartsie stuff."

Douglas just smiled and hobbled away from the rest, gazing at "the view that God must get, looking out over his domain," as he later recalled to Wayne.

The climb down was also rough. They were tired, dirty, cut, limping, bleeding and bitchy when they returned to Glenemma. The water truck was attacked instantly.

Over supper that night, Sergeant Beckford reminded them, "If the men are not bitching, something must be wrong."

Douglas made a note of that in his notebook. He actually made quite a few notes of what he called 'Beckford's Concepts.'

"How come the officers weren't with us?" asked Jackson. I thought this was supposed to be leadership by example?"

Banks spoke up. "Maybe they did the recce?"

Jackson shook his head. "No, Sergeant Beckford told me that he and Sergeant Simpson did the reconnaissance."

Danyluk was starting to come back to life. All eyes were on him as he interjected. "I know where they were. They were in the Officers' Mess having a tall, cool one."

"Either that or they went for a shit and the crows got them," said Bergie.

Jackson wouldn't let it rest. "No they were in the mess all right. Hey guys, why don't we get edjumicated and become officers?"

East laughed. "It's educated, you dummy."

Jackson stood up in pain. "No, it's not, if they were educated, they would have been with us. Those guys were edjumicated."

Everyone agreed with Jackson. Little did they know, their bitching took their minds off the pain.

A light breeze and a full moon came up that night. The big kind of a moon that you can almost reach up and touch.

Wayne and Douglas had taken down their hootchie and were stretched out on their blankets, looking up at a sky full of stars.

They could hear the voices of other cadets talking and the radio set's whine seemed louder than usual when the microphone switch was pressed.

"Do you think we'll ever land a man on the moon?" Wayne asked.

Douglas put his hands behind his head. "I don't think there's any doubt about it, but I don't know if it's the right thing to do. In Liverpool, when I was around six or seven, I remember leaving the house of a friend on a cold crisp night in December. Every star in the universe seemed to be hanging over our heads, like a chandelier was being held just for us. The moon was full and bright, but not as close as it is tonight. My mom wrapped a scarf around my neck and placed a sixpence in my hand. She told me to look at the moon and make a wish, but that I wasn't to tell anyone what I wished for."

"Although I was young, as I looked up, I thought I was looking at a wise old man that had seen everything that had ever been done on the surface of this planet."

"I don't think that old guy up there should ever be touched or bruised. He's watched the earth from the beginning until now. He saw the first cavemen, the birth of Christ, and all of the atrocities, all those that man has made, and he has watched them in his helplessness. If he could talk, he'd be too ashamed to tell. He would make even the most ardent believers in God, hide their heads in shame. We should leave him alone."

They didn't say anything for a few minutes; they just stared at the wise man above.

Wayne stared at the moon's face. It was so clear. The way Douglas had told his story made him appreciate the moon more than ever. He could see the craters and they looked like the lines on the face of a wise old person who says nothing. A person you could tell your troubles to and he would listen with a warm look of understanding. Wayne slowly shook his head.

"That old friend had seen and heard it all before, billions of times. Everyone was usually too busy to give him a second thought. They took him for granted," Douglas continued.

Wayne leaned over on his side facing Douglas. "What happened to your old man, Doug?"

The question took Douglas by surprise. He thought he'd explained it to Wayne many times before, but maybe he hadn't.

"During the War, he met someone else. I don't think it happened overnight, it probably took time. He also had a drinking problem."

"Do you write to him?"

"Sure, once in a while. He always writes to me and at Christmas time, there's always a present in the mail. You know, I've always had the feeling that he's still in love with my mom."

"What about your mom? Do you think she's still in love with him?"

"Yeah, I do. She hasn't told me, but I believe she's still in love with him. But what happened, happened. Crazy isn't it?"

Wayne didn't answer; he had lost his mother the same way. She had met someone else and left him and his sister Valerie with their dad.

Douglas knew Wayne's situation and he liked Wayne's dad. When the three of them wrestled, usually after Mr. Banks had a few drinks under his belt at Christmas time, the two of them would pin Mr. Banks' arms down until he surrendered.

"Are you coming back here next year?" Wayne asked.

Douglas gave the question some thought. "Probably. I wouldn't have said that a few weeks ago, but there's something I like about this place that I don't have at home. I also really love the country and now I've met Diane. You must think I'm some sort of a mental midget rambling on like this? I'm not even fifteen yet."

"No, I know what you mean Doug. But maybe it's the combination of Diane and her parents and grandparents. You've never had a family. Is it possible you like the combination?"

Douglas chuckled. "Could be. But what do you mean I've never had a family? I'm never away from your house, nor you from mine. Christ, if I had a brother living here, I'd never see him, I'm always with you."

Wayne snickered. "You didn't come with me when that creep, Mr. Fanning chased me out of the classroom at school. If he had caught me that day, he would have killed me. I can still feel the heat of his hand near my neck when I was running with my bicycle. I only escaped by a fraction of a second."

Douglas laughed. He remembered the scene vividly. Mr. Fanning had been Vice-Principal of their school this past year. Fanning, an ex-logger was a big man. He taught math as well, and one day picked on Wayne for not doing his homework.

"Where's your homework, Banks?"

"I never had time to do it, Sir."

"Why?"

"I had a school baseball game, Sir."

"What about after the baseball game?"

"I had to do my paper route, Sir."

"What about after your paper route, Banks?"

"I had a date, Sir."

"A WHAT?"

"I had a date."

"When I was your age, we didn't have dates; we did our homework."

"I don't think you were ever my age, Sir."

"WHAT? REPORT TO THE PRINCIPAL'S OFFICE."

"NO!"

"DO YOU WANT ME TO GIVE YOU THE STRAP RIGHT HERE?"

"I'VE HAD ENOUGH OF THIS, GO FUCK YOURSELF, SIR!"

Fanning made a mad grab for Wayne. They chased each other around the classroom until Wayne finally made it out the door. With Fanning after him, he ran down two flights of stairs and headed for his bike. Every kid in the room squeezed in and cheered out the windows watching Fanning run after Wayne who was trying to get on his bike.

When Fanning came back into the room, he was breathless and fuming.

Wayne stayed away from school for two days. When he did return, he was given the strap, but Fanning showed a little more respect for him after that.

"You're right, I didn't join you that day. But I did join you when you talked me into playing baseball and I was supposed to be attending a detention. "I got the strap for that."

Wayne lay on his back again. "It hurts, doesn't it?"

"Damn right it hurts. It's bull shit when someone says to put a hair over your palm, or rub orange peel into it before the strap. None of that works, I've tried it all."

They were both getting tired now and their eyes were beginning to close.

"G'night, Doug."

"G'night, buddy."

"RIFLE SECTION SUPPLY COVERING FIRE, BREN SECTION MOVE NOW! COME ON, GET A MOVE ON, BREN SECTION. THERE'S TWO OF YOU TO CARRY THE WEAPON, THE THIRD MAN CARRIES THE AMMO AND THE EXTRA BARREL. YOU, GET YOUR ASS DOWN IF YOU DON'T WANT IT BLOWN OFF." Sergeant Beckford's voice was loud and clear as Nine Platoon continued platoon and section tactics the next day.

All cadets were up early that morning. "We'll start early when it's cool and finish early when it's hot," Beckford had said earlier.

As the Bren Section was running, every man in the rifle section was supposed to be supplying covering fire, but they had just run for 100 yards and most of them were lying on their backs, breathless. Danyluk looked like he was having a heart attack.

"It must be the smoking. This running is killing me."

"IT'S NOT THE SMOKING, IT'S THE LADIES!"

"SCREW YOU EAST! WHAT WOULD I DO FOR PLEASURE, IF I DIDN'T HAVE THE DAMES? YOU DON'T WANT ME TO BECOME A MONK LIKE YOU, DO YOU?"

Bergie pushed Moose away. "DON'T POINT THAT RIFLE AT ME, YOU CREEP!" Danyluk had turned over onto his stomach and nearly knocked Bergie in the head with his rifle.

"What are you doing this close to me, you're supposed to be ten yards away."

Jackson shouted. "DANYLUK THINKS A CIGARETTE IS LIKE A DAME. IT'S COOL, SMOOTH AND GOES DOWN EASY."

Danyluk laughed. "That's a cigar advertisement, you pongo."

"I don't care what it is," said Bergie getting up and running again, "If you start smoking cigars, you can get yourself another bunk mate."

Sergeant Beckford was watching. "COME ON, DANYLUK. GET THE LEAD OUT OF YOUR ASS. YOU'RE NOT IN THE BUSHES AT POLSON PARK NOW."

As Danyluk ran harder, he turned to East. "HOW IN THE HELL DOES HE KNOW THOSE THINGS?"

Lunch was held at one o'clock that afternoon. Charlie Company had been at it since seven and they were beat. After they filled their mess tins, they sat against the trees bantering a little. Jackson tried to straighten Danyluk out on the cigarette slogan.

"My slogan is correct. You're getting mixed up with the other one. They're smooth, firm, and fully packed."

Danyluk laughed. "In my case, I like 'em fully stacked."

While Bergie was chastising Danyluk for having a one-track mind, MAIL-CALL!" rang out.

"MALCZYNSKI...GEDDES...DALLAS...DANGERFIELD...DANYLUK... DANYLUK...BRICE...BERGIE...BHAMJI...ABEL...BRADFORD...BRICE

"...ADAMS...FRANCOIS...CLARKE...LAIDLAW...MCLACHLAN...PARR ...LAMMIE...BANNI...JACKSON...ROTHSTEIN...EAST...TRAINOR... AITKEN...COOPER...YOUNG...PAYNE...LIDDELL...POTTS...DANY-LUK...DANYLUK...DANYLUK...BURGESS...BANKS."

Mail-Call continued for at least fifteen minutes. Douglas had received one letter from home and one from Diane. He and Wayne returned to their hootchie and began reading.

"My mom says that it's really quiet in the house now that Major's gone and Diane says to say hello to you."

Wayne was reading his letter. "My sister has enrolled in some sort of drama class and my dad has received a raise in pay. Hey, maybe I can get a raise in my allowance? Nahh, it would take a million years for that to happen. I...."

He was going to say something else, but a Signals Cadet came over. "SERGEANT BECKFORD WANTS ALL OF NINE PLATOON IN THE MESS-ING AREA!"

"Is everyone here?" Sergeant Beckford asked, counting heads. "Good. We've just received word from camp that the Guard has been invited to participate in the Kelowna Regatta and Penticton Peach Festival parades."

There was general approval throughout the platoon.

"I haven't finished yet. In addition, a couple of Irish cadets have challenged Charlie Company to a boxing match next week in camp."

As Sergeant Beckford spoke, he looked everyone in the eye, one by one.

"I think it would be fitting if the boxers came from this platoon, considering a certain bunk stunt that was pulled off by some of our members not too long ago. Don't you?"

"How in the hell did he know?" Danyluk whispered in Douglas' ear.

Beckford's smile was contagious. The cadets started smiling, even those in Nine Platoon who didn't know anything about the nighttime caper.

Sergeant Beckford was still smiling when he said, "I need volunteers. Has anyone got any boxing experience?"

All heads were looking at each other. It was quiet until Danyluk held up his hand.

"I've taken boxing lessons, so put me down."

Nine Platoon clapped. The words, "ATTABOY, MOOSE," could be heard everywhere.

Bergie was next to volunteer. "I think I know who challenged us, so count me in."

This time Nine Platoon sang their approval. "HERE'S TO BERGIE, HE'S GOT CLASS. HERE'S TO BERGIE, HE'S A HORSE'S ASS. ATTABOY, BERGIE!"

"How do you know who challenged us?" asked the Sergeant.

Bergie got flustered. "Well, I don't, er...I don't really know, but I er, I have an idea."

Beckford sat down. He had let Bergie off the hook. "We're not getting off that easily; they've challenged us to four matches. That means four Irish cadets want to box."

"Jesus, I would never have guessed that those two had any friends," said Danyluk.

Rothstein held up his hand. "I box. I'm not the greatest, but I box."

"ATTABOY, ROTHIE!"

"So do I," said Jackson.

"HERE'S TO ROTHIE AND JACKSON, THEY'VE GOT CLASS. HERE'S TO ROTHIE AND JACKSON, THEY'RE A HORSE'S ASS."

Sergeant Beckford stood up again. "Good. When we get back, we've only got two weeks left. We want you guys to train hard. We'll inform the sexual intellectuals that we'll take them on during the last week of camp. Is that all right?"

Everyone agreed.

Danyluk put on his loud voice. "EXCUSE ME, SERGEANT, COULD YOU TELL ME WHAT A SEXUAL INTELLECTUAL IS, PLEASE?"

"Certainly, my boy. A sexual intellectual is an 'effing' know-it-all. Do you know any of them?"

Danyluk smiled. "Yes, Sergeant and they're all Irish."

Douglas made a note of the expression in the 'Beckford' section of his notebook.

The rest of that afternoon was hot and lazy. After a swim parade, the cadets of Charlie Company just lounged around or watched the cadets in Signals Company go through their training. Foster was usually stationed two miles away so they didn't see him very often. Today, however, he was with Wayne and Douglas and they went exploring.

"Here's the cabin I told you about," said Foster, pointing to the old log house close to the highway.

The front door was open. Although they had no right to enter, they did anyway. The place was a mess and the table had four plates set, loaded with mouldy food.

Foster swallowed nervously. "Christ, this place looks like someone just got up and left. They didn't even finish whatever they were eating."

There were only two rooms in the cabin. The bedroom was just as messy as the main room. It looked like someone had just cast the bedclothes aside and walked out.

On the kitchen table, Douglas saw an old family photo album and loose pictures laying around. He picked one up.

"Christ, natives live here. If we get caught, they'll cut our nuts off."

They didn't rummage further; they just ran out the door.

On the way out, Wayne picked up a Coleman lantern, full of fuel, with the mantle in one piece.

"We'll return this when we leave Glenemma. I don't think whoever owns the place will be back for a while."

Douglas stopped them in their tracks. "But what if they do come back and find it missing? We're on their land you know!"

Wayne held up the lantern and looked at the glass. "O.K. then, I'll leave them a note, does that please you?"

Douglas nodded. They walked back into the cabin, found a piece of paper and a a pencil and left a note saying that they had borrowed the lantern for a few days. Then the two of them signed it. Foster refused.

After supper that night, another sing-song was organized, but most cadets were too tired to attend. Douglas and Wayne went to their hootchie area and shortly afterward, the other Musketeers arrived. Once again Danyluk was discussing sex.

"Jack, why don't you listen to me. First of all you tell me that if you screw some dame, you're going to get your thing stuck. Now, you tell me that if you french kiss a girl, you're going to get your tongue stuck. What the hell kind of girl are you kissing? Someone with shark's teeth?"

East wouldn't listen. "I had a friend who did that once and he told me he couldn't get his tongue out of her mouth."

"Are you sure he had it in her mouth?" asked Danyluk.

East laughed. "Where the hell else would he have it?"

Wayne interrupted. "Jesus, are you two at it again?"

"Where'd you get the lantern?" Bergie asked Douglas.

"We found it in a cabin not too far from here."

"Talk about luck," said Jackson. Then he thought for a moment. "Hey, we're on native land, you didn't steal it from them, did you?"

Wayne said, "No, we left a note that we were only borrowing it."

"Do you know the native people who live here?" asked Bergie.

Earl shook his head. "No, but we're all related." He normally changed the subject when someone asked him questions about his background. Tonight for some reason, he was willing to discuss it.

"I lived in a small village near Smithers, up north in British Columbia. Although I was young when I left, my mother told me about white people coming on our land and stealing things. Nobody ever locks their doors up there; they trust people."

"Have you been back to Smithers?" asked Douglas.

"A couple of times, but I don't really enjoy it. I've lived on the coast too long. Sometimes I think I'm stuck in the middle of the white man's world and the native world. I don't really feel native and yet I'm not white."

Wayne was listening attentively. "But that's kind of neat isn't it? Haven't you got the best of both worlds?"

Earl forced a smile. "Not really. You guys know as well as I do that my marks on some subjects have been the highest and I've been picked as the best dressed in the company a few times. Well, not once has anyone ever placed me in a position of authority. I've got the best drill voice in the company and when they pick cadets to fill supernumerary positions, either in the company or the battalion, I'm always left out."

Bergie stood up. "Oh bull shit, Earl, you're just feeling sorry for yourself. None of us have been picked for those positions either. To get a battalion position, you've got to be noticed by RSM Gardiner, like Danyluk here."

Danyluk snickered. "If Gardiner had his way, I'd be in charge of blank files and right wheels. Either that, or standing on the sidelines repairing spiffies. After you got me to salute him, I........."

A strange voice entered the conversation. "Are you the people who took my lamp?"

An elderly man stood about ten feet away. It was a bit hard to see him in the darkness; he was hunched over and he looked native.

"Yes, Sir," Douglas replied. "I know we shouldn't have been in your cabin but we thought it was abandoned."

"May I sit down with you?" As he spoke, he spread tobacco on a piece of cigarette paper.

The cadets had been sitting down, but when they had heard his voice, they stood up. Wayne pointed to his set of blankets, "Sure, sit right here. I'm the one who borrowed your lantern."

The visitor didn't accept Wayne's offer. Instead, he sat at the end of the semi-circle the rest of the Musketeers had formed. Although he was grizzled, he was quite agile, and had no problem sitting and drawing his legs into him, and crossing his feet.

"I have lived in that cabin all of my life. I raised my family there. Many people have stolen things from it but you are the first to leave a note." He handed the note to Jackson. "What does it say, son?"

Jackson looked at him. He realized then that the gentleman couldn't read.

"It says, 'We are cadets training at Glenemma. I hope you don't mind if we borrow your lantern. We'll return it shortly. Thank you, Brice and Banks.'"

The old man smiled and everyone noticed he had a few teeth missing. "How's your training going?" He was looking at Earl.

"Good," said Jackson.

"Are you native?"

"Yes."

"What's your name?"

"Earl Jackson, Sir."

"Where are you from?"

"I live in Victoria now, but originally I'm from Babine Lake."

"I've been there. You've left the reserve?"

"Yes, my mom is in a wheelchair. She gets better treatment down there."

The caller was really looking Jackson over. "Are these your friends?"

"Yes, Sir."

"Are they good friends?"

"The best, Sir."

"Do you have many good friends in Victoria?"

Earl thought for a moment. "Not a lot, but some."

The old man sighed and nodded. He seemed to be looking right through Earl and tracing memories of bygone days.

"When do you guys leave here?"

"In a couple of days," Earl replied.

He stood up as quickly as he had sat down, then clasped both his hands around one of Earl's and shook it. "I lost two sons in the war," he said as he quietly walked away. After ten feet, he stopped and waved.

"Good bye, boys."

"GOOD BYE, SIR."

When he was gone, they all sat down again. East said, "What a nice fella."

"I though he'd be furious," Douglas remarked.

"He's not the kind of person who gets upset," said Earl. "He's had to earn his patience."

When the other Musketeers left, Douglas and Wayne went to bed, and Wayne leaned over on his side. "I'm trying to figure out what Earl meant when he said the old man had to earn his patience?"

Douglas didn't answer right away. "So am I. G'night, Wayne."

"G'night, Doug."

When the weather is splendid, it's always enjoyable waking up in Glenemma. The air is fresh before the sun warms it up.

The morning after the visitor, Douglas and Wayne were awakened early by the sound of a truck trying to park a water trailer that didn't wish to fit into its customary space.

The driver who obviously had to get up in the middle of the night to deliver the water to Glenemma, was hurling obscenities in the trailer's direction. He wasn't the only one yelling because cadets in the immediate area of the truck were 'informing' the driver he was too close to their lines. By the time the trailer was parked, many cadets had gotten up earlier than usual.

Douglas held his head under the water tap. It felt great, even though cold water was running down his back into his pants. "I had a wonderful sleep last night. I must have been beat."

Wayne was brushing his teeth. He had a towel wrapped around his waist to ensure that he didn't get any toothpaste-froth on the front of his pants. "Same here. If it weren't for that damned water truck, I'd still be in the sack."

"Good morning, boys," said a voice. "How's it going?"

They both looked. Standing next to them was the Commanding Officer of the camp, Colonel St. Laurent.

Douglas and Wayne quickly stood to attention, arms placed stiffly by their sides. "Good morning, Sir," they replied in unison.

"Please, just relax. There are no formalities in the field."

"We're doing fine, Sir," said Douglas.

The Commanding Officer was dressed in a bush uniform and he carried his leather-covered swaggerstick under his armpit. "The two of you seem to be up before the others."

Wayne smiled. "We woke up early, Sir."

"Good, I'm glad to see that you're so keen. I intended to make it up yesterday, but the night before, a car crashed into the power generators just off the highway by the camp."

"Was anyone hurt, Sir?" Wayne asked.

The Commanding Officer bent over and drank some water from a tap. "Yes unfortunately, a young man and his lady friend were hurt and had to be rushed to the Vernon hospital. We're still going through the paperwork with the police. It's happened at the very same spot before, so they might have to do something about that curve. What time do they serve breakfast?"

Douglas was running a comb through his hair. "In about a half hour, Sir."

"Well, in that case, I hope you don't mind if I stay with you gentlemen until that time? Where's your bivouac area?"

The CO walked back with them and sat back against a tree while the two of them made their beds and straightened out their space.

"I guess it was pretty wet here a few days ago? Did you carry on with training?"

"We took some time off," Douglas replied. "But we were out most of the time, Sir."

Colonel St. Laurent was drawing pictures on the ground with the end of his swaggerstick. "We had to do the same thing in camp, but I'm proud of the way the cadets handled themselves in the deluge."

"By the way, I received a phone call last night from a fellow by the name of 'Brewer.' Apparently he has a cabin here in Glenemma."

The cadets glanced at each other. They knew who he was talking about. The CO must know about the lantern.

Wayne straightened up. "Yes, Sir. We didn't know his name, but he joined us last night and spent a few minutes with us."

"I know, he told me. He said that he met a group of boys close to the water trailer. Is a cadet named Jackson in your platoon?"

"Yes, Sir, he's a friend of ours," Douglas replied.

"Well, Mr. Brewer said it's been a long time since he met such a polite group of teenagers. He phoned me to ask if Jackson and his friends could go horseback riding with him and some teenagers on the reserve at the north end of Okanagan Lake. Do you think you would like that?"

"YES, SIR!"

"Good. I'll speak with the Officer Commanding your company and see if he approves. If he does, I'll take the group of you back with me. Now where's that breakfast?"

When things go wrong, they always go wrong at the wrong time. On the way to breakfast, the CO asked the boys if they would take him through the platoon areas on the way to the messing tent.

Although Douglas and Wayne were familiar with Nine Platoon's area, they hadn't really been through the lines of the other platoons.

Finally they found the pathway of Ten Platoon and the CO paused a few times to talk with cadets as he proceeded. Then it happened. Just as they turned a bend, six bare bottoms appeared. Ten Platoon had built In and Out routes next to the latrines. Cadets were sitting on the log over the 'trench' relieving themselves. Amidst a few, 'Good Mornings,' from the 'buttocks brigade' as they later came to be called, some cadets stood to attention with their pants down around their ankles. Others wiped their derrieres and waved at the same time, with smiles on their faces. The Commanding Officer also smiled as he returned their waves.

When they arrived at the serving area, a Corporal who had lost a few teeth playing hockey in his youth, discovered his partial upper plate was missing. He had accompanied the food truck from camp to Glenemma and couldn't recall if he had left his teeth at camp, or if they had fallen into the scrambled eggs, which he was serving.

As it turned out, he didn't leave them in camp. They were discovered in the OC's mess-tin, but only after the officer had half-finished his meal.

The Company Commander had a 'good talk' with the Corporal and it was reported later by Sergeant Beckford that Colonel St. Laurent had a good sense of humour. The Colonel told the Company Commander he liked seeing people getting their teeth into things.

The journey to the Okanagan Lake Reserve was a great treat for the Musketeers because they rode in the Commanding Officer's three-quarter-ton truck. Jackson was asked to sit in the front with East. The rest of them, Bergie, Rothstein, Danyluk, Banks and Brice, sat in the back breathing the fresh air and enjoying the countryside.

They arrived on the west side of the range of hills separating the split tongue of the north end of Okanagan Lake. Mr. Brewer was there, looking younger than he had on the previous night. Wayne said later the darkness must have made him look older.

After introductions, which included the Commanding Officer meeting everyone, cadets were paired off with their native hosts and given saddle-horses. The Commanding Officer said he hoped they would have fun and would send a truck to retrieve them at three o'clock that afternoon. He spent ten minutes alone with Mr. Brewer and they warmly shook hands before he headed back to camp.

Wayne and Douglas were in the company of two girls and two boys as they climbed on their horses. Neither had ridden before and they made a point of mentioning it to their hosts.

The four teenagers just smiled. "These animals are pretty gentle," said a boy, called Tommy.

He was right and the rest of the afternoon went exceedingly well. They rode through the small village and along the lake, before riding up into the hills where there were other lakes and trails. At the very top, they unlocked a fence-gate and descended slightly on the other side of the ridge. Douglas was astounded. He could see the Sutherland Arms Hotel on the other side of the lake and Kin Beach to the north. A swim parade was taking place and two hundred cadets were frolicking in the water. To them, he would be just a speck on the hillside.

At two o'clock, they tied up their horses and went swimming with their clothes on at the Indian side of the lake. It was much different from a swim parade because they had the whole beach to themselves.

"Do you come here often?" Douglas asked Tommy.

Tommy was trying to drag an old log into the water. He nodded. "As much as we can, but sometimes it gets a little lonely so we go to Kal or Kin beach."

"You guys are lucky to have all this land," said Wayne.

"We had a lot more but it was stolen from us," Tommy replied.

Douglas liked him. Tommy was a clean cut kid about fifteen, with long jet-black hair.

Although the cadets' horses had saddles, Tommy and his sister rode bareback. Never at any time had they tried to impress, or embarrass their new cadet friends with their riding experience. Instead, they explained how to ride and how to look after horses.

Douglas mentioned there was a dead cow in the lake at Glenemma. Tommy knew about it and seemed concerned. He told them that they try their best to keep track of the animals but they range free and once in a while, a few do get trapped in the water at the various lakes on the reserve.

Before leaving at three o'clock, they had sandwiches in a small house in the village. Mr. Brewer shook hands with the cadets and invited them back at anytime. Both the cadets and their hosts had really enjoyed the day and the Musketeers didn't want to leave.

Boarding the truck, each cadet was given a feather by his respective teenage host. Mr. Brewer gave Earl a woven headband with a feather in it. Jackson's face beamed with pride when Mr. Brewer slipped it on his head.

"Earl, never forget you're one of us," Mr. Brewer said, with his arm around Earl's shoulders. "And the rest of you are honourary members of this band."

The cadets promised to invite their hosts to camp and to get them a military souvenir.

After shaking hands, the truck pulled away. Both groups waved until they were out of each other's sight.

On the way back, Rothstein said the whole trip was fantastic. "These people really went out of their way for us. Did you notice how we all ended up at the lake at the same time? They were organized, because we came from every direction."

Danyluk agreed. "Those guys are really nice. When my horse started to take off on me, William was there in a flash, slowing it down." William was one of the boys with Bergie and Danyluk.

"And tell 'em the rest," said Bergie. "C'mon, tell them."

Danyluk grinned embarrassingly. "Tell them what? There's nothing more to tell."

Bergie insisted until finally Danyluk blurted it out. "O.K., I fell in love again."

"That's telling it mildly," said Bergie. "Didn't you guys notice anything at the lake? When the rest of us were lifting guys over our shoulders and diving through each others legs, he was fooling around in the water with Brenda all of the time. If he had ink on his hands, Brenda would be covered in it, especially her ass."

Earl frowned. "Christ, Moose, can't you give your balls a rest once in a while?" Although he was frowning, the rest of the Musketeers knew Earl wasn't serious, but he was concerned.

Danyluk went a little red in the face. "Guys, if her hands were covered with ink, I'd have it all over me as well. It was just one of those things. Love at first bite."

"Just wait until I tell Alma," said Earl. "She'll straighten you out in a hurry."

Douglas asked East and Jackson where they went with Mr. Brewer.

"We split up for a while," said East. "Earl, where did you go?"

Jackson shrugged. "We just rode around and he told me that when he was young, he was taken away from his family for a year. He was in Kamloops, living with a white family. They were really nice to him, but he had a hell of a time with the white kids in school. Although he was only in grade one or two, he still has bad memories about it today."

Wayne looked through the window into the cab of the truck. "Have you guys noticed something?"

Everyone glanced around puzzled.

"There's no one sitting up front with the driver. That means we actually like each others' company more than comfort."

There was a moment's silence, then Bergie spoke. "UP THE MUSKETEERS!"

"UP THE MUSKETEERS!" the rest responded.

East put his arm around Rothstein and pulled him in. "You were number seven. That's a lucky number, so don't forget the cake."

Rothstein laughed. "Trust you to remember the cake."

As the truck turned off the highway onto the dusty roads of Glenemma, the Musketeers were singing the last verse of, NELLY, PUT YOUR BELLY CLOSE TO MINE.

When they unloaded, Danyluk came up to Earl. "You wouldn't would you?"

Earl didn't know what he was talking about. "I wouldn't what?"

Danyluk swallowed. "You wouldn't tell Alma about Brenda, would you?"

Jackson laughed. "Have you been worrying about that since we left?"

A few sounds came out of Danyluk's mouth. "Well, er, I..."

"No, you dummy. I wouldn't say a word to her. What do you think I am?"

Danyluk looked relieved. "Whew, thanks pal."

Jackson slapped him on the back. "I might write her a letter, though."

They sang on the way back to their bivouacs:

" *There once was a man from Boston,*
 who drove a baby Austin.
 There was room for his ass,
 and a gallon of gas.
 And his balls hung out and he lost 'em. "

At supper that night, the Corporal serving the food was smiling and showing a full set of front teeth. The cadets knew they weren't in for any surprises on their plates, and so they ate their meal with great vigor.

Before mug-up, all cadets and staff gathered around the Musketeers to hear the story of what happened during their excursion,

Each member told his account of the day's happenings, but allowed Danyluk to expound on his relationship with Brenda.

"YOU LUCKY CREEP," some cadet bellowed.

"IT'S NOT LUCK, IT'S SKILL," Danyluk replied, scanning the crowd to find out who called him a creep.

There were questions about horses, the countryside, and the hosts. Nearly every cadet in the company wished that he had taken that lantern and left the note.

"We're going back on Sunday afternoon rather than Monday," said Sergeant Beckford. "We've got to practise for a few fights and prepare for the Kelowna and Penticton parades."

When Wayne turned out the lantern that night, they were covered by an blanket of a billion stars.

"Y'know Doug, I wouldn't trade this summer for a million dollars."

"A million?" Douglas asked.

"Well, make it a few thousand dollars. Naah, it would have to be a million. G'night, Doug."

"G'night, Wayne."

They were just dozing off when, CRRRAAACK!

"SON OF A BITCH! OH, MY GOD! BERGIE, I CAN'T SEE, PASS ME A TOWEL. CHRIST, I'M COVERED IN SHIT!"

"YOU'RE NOT GETTING MY TOWEL, DANYLUK!"

"PASS ME SOMETHING BERGIE, I LANDED FACE DOWN."

"WELL, DON'T COME NEAR ME, I CAN SMELL YOU FROM HERE!"

"I CAN HEAR YOU LAUGHING JACKSON, YOU ROTTEN CREEP. JESUS, I CAN'T GET OUT. NOW, IF I CAN GRAB THAT TREE. AH, THAT'S BETTER. CHRIST, I'M COVERED! I'LL GET YOU FOR THIS!"

A shot of the lower camp and some of the upper camp. The new parade square is up top, centre left.

Two shots of lower camp. The white area up top, centre right is the old parade square.

Cadets of the Vernon Army Cadet Camp on the new parade square. Nine companies, including the band.

General George Kitching returning their salute. Shortly afterward, it was "Gather around me!"

"How do you like the food here, son?"
"I really like it Sir. Especially the powdered eggs."
"Yes, I know what you mean. You don't get them like that at home, do you?"
"No, Sir, but I'm going to request them."

The guard and band at Kalamalka lake.(F.N. rifles.)

A spiked-pith-helmeted guard of honour on parade with the then new F.N. rifle.

The guard on parade. Note the bush-uniforms.

Bren-Guns on the range. That night, a Corporal living in one of the huts heard many cadets talking in their sleep. "Piston, barrel, butt, body, bipod."

Two Alberta cadets with Bren guns. "This is the way we'd like to approach rustlers down on the farm."

Driver-Mechanics cadets with their three-ton vehicles. By the time they finished the course, they knew the trucks and jeeps inside and out. To this very day, they're still getting the grease out from under their fingernails.

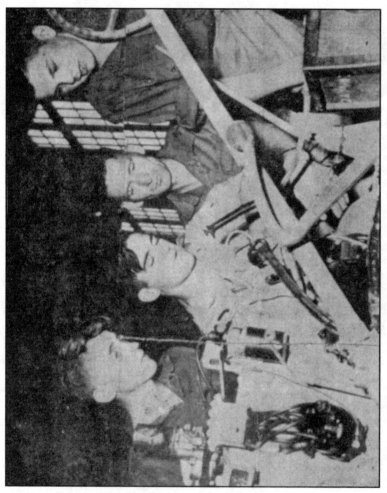

Driver-Mechanics cadets receiving instructions on how the emergency brake works...amongst other things. Later, these 'innocent' individuals would drive their convoys past the parade square and give 'the finger' to the cadets of Guard Company who were picking their feet up six inches and driving them down twelve.

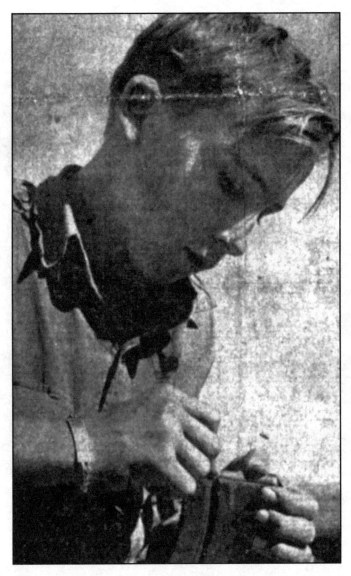

"The Sergeant said if I load twenty-nine rounds instead of twenty-eight rounds in this Bren-Gun magazine, it's twenty nine push-ups - even in this heat."

Signals cadets operating Nineteen-sets. "Hear netting call, net now!"

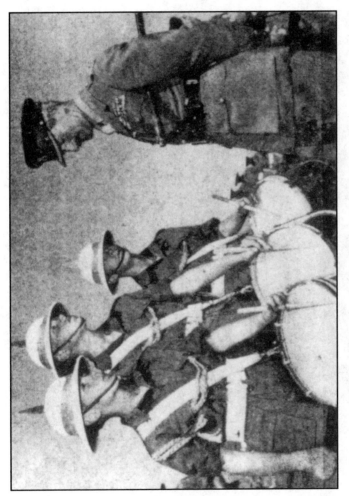

General George Kitching talking with three members of the cadet band. This particular year, the guard and band wore bush-uniforms.

Lectures on the rocket-launder and mortar.

The band of the Irish Fusilier cadets, marching with the guard.

Signals cadets laying line.

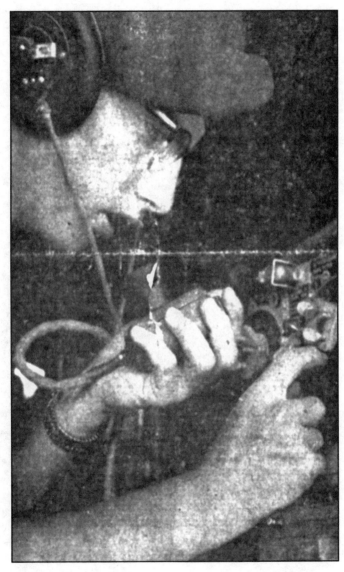

"O.K., if I undo this little screw, I can have the flick mechanism working on this Nineteen set."

An Irish Fusilier cadet taking Signals Training. "O.K., guys, now that we can talk, who put the itching-powder in my bed last night?"

CHAPTER XIV

The experience of Glenemma ended too soon for the cadets of Charlie Company. When Sunday finally rolled around, each cadet was packed by ten A.M. and the area was left as clean as it had been before they arrived.

Douglas and Wayne returned the lantern and left another note for Mr. Brewer, expressing their thanks.

As the trucks entered the clearing, there was a slight delay with Danyluk and Jackson. Apparently, Jackson had been given the job of assisting to fill in the 'shitter' and posting 'foul ground' signs. He had only thrown his first shovel of dirt when he was nudged from behind and went flying, face down. Danyluk stood there laughing, so Jackson grabbed his ankle and Danyluk went in for the third time.

The filthy pair's jobs had to be assigned to other cadets while the two went down to the lake to wash themselves and their stinking clothes.

The company went wild at the sight of them walking away. It must have been highly embarrassing for both of them.

Only safely on the trucks, did Bergie admit it was he who cut the crossbar on Danyluk's 'seat,' twice.

"WHAT? YOU CREEP! MY BUNKMATE? O.K. BERGIE, YOU'RE FIRST ON MY LIST! I'm sorry Earl, I thought it was you."

"I'LL GET YOU," Danyluk said a few times on the way back to camp.

Even though they were now both spotlessly clean, few cadets would sit next to them, not even the other Musketeers, who were thoroughly enjoying the 'comedy.'

As the trucks passed the guardroom entering the camp, the voices of Nine Platoon were singing *O'Provost, O'Provost.* A Sergeant came to the door smiling.

"HEY, THE MEATHEADS DO SMILE!" Rothstein said.

Douglas bumped him with his arm. "No, they don't. It's only a gas pain and ya gotta watch 'em closely when ya see gas pains."

When two hundred cadets come out of the field and enter their barracks, nothing can describe the disorder that ensues. B-21 looked like Piccadilly Circus at the end of the war. Cadets were tripping over themselves getting prepared for normal camp routine. The showers were fully occupied, the washing machine was going full tilt, and there were dirty clothes, ground-sheets, and blankets everywhere.

"HOME, SWEET HOME," Wayne yelled, rushing to the showers with the rest of the Musketeers. The hot water felt good, and this time they shut the window to keep in the steam.

Brushing his teeth in the showers, Bergie said, "Genova certainly kept a low profile at Glenemma."

Wayne agreed. "So did Foster. Apparently, someone told Genova that cadets from our company got him at Kin Beach, and he thought Foster might lead him to us."

Douglas thought it over. "Does that mean that he suspects us?"

"Yeah, but he doesn't know for sure," Bergie snickered.

Danyluk, like Jackson, had shampoo all over his body and both of them were scrubbing like hell. "Why didn't someone cut Genova's shitter-chair instead of mine?"

"I thought of it, but you were a much safer choice," Bergie replied. He had to duck from a bar of Sergeant's soap thrown in his direction.

Douglas called over to Wayne. "ARE YOU GOING TO CONTACT THE GIRLS TONIGHT?"

"YEAH, BUT DON'T FORGET WE'RE CONFINED TO CAMP."

East was drying himself off and had opened the window. "What's the movie tonight?"

"It's *House of Wax*, with Vincent Price and I hear it's pretty gory," replied Rothstein.

Bergie was laughing once again. "Nothing could scare me, because I saw the ultimate monster today crawling out of the shitter."

"GO AHEAD AND LAUGH, BUT I'VE GOT PLANS FOR YOU, BERGIE."

After lunch, the cadets of Charlie Company handed in the equipment they drew for Glenemma. Every square inch of the barracks was covered with blankets, clothing, bits of rations the cadets had brought back as souvenirs, and dirt, dust and grime. Some cadets had to wash their blankets because they too, had collected every type of stain available at Glenemma. Danyluk tried to exchange his blankets but he was told to wash them and stop complaining about his landing in the 'shitter.'

The Musketeers spent the afternoon polishing their boots and working on their uniforms. Douglas was lying on his back with a boot in one hand and a brush in the other. "It's great to be back. This was a dump before we left, now it looks and feels like a palace. Although I really enjoyed Glenemma, just give me civilization."

Wayne indicated he agreed. He was shining his capbadge and trying to tune Danyluk's radio into the Kelowna radio station playing Secret Love, by Doris Day. "I'm really starting to like this song but I can't remember what movie it's from."

Jackson rushed into the barracks. "Hey, guys, come on with me and get a load of what's happening on the highway."

The Musketeers jumped off their bunks, grabbed their berets, and headed out the door. They ran past the Chapel, past the main street of the camp, two rows of huts and arrived at the highway.

"What's the big deal?" Wayne said breathlessly. "It sounds like it's just the pipes and drums band. It's a parade?"

"It's a parade, all right," Jackson replied, "But not the kind you usually see on a Sunday."

Danyluk took off his beret as he ran, and started combing his hair. Bergie was laughing, telling everyone, "Moose believes it's the Vernon Girls Drum and Bugle Band. He's got his eye on the base drummer because someone told him she doesn't wear any panties."

As they got closer, East was amazed to see so many cars. "Christ, whatever it is must be big; the cars are nearly backed up to the Lookout up on the highway."

When they stopped, Wayne couldn't believe it. "Oh my God, if I had a camera I'd film this."

The whole pipes and drums section of the cadet band was marching on the highway. Their music and drill were perfect, but all they had on were shoes, spats, regimental hose-tops, glengarries, belts, and sporrans.

East cheered them on, yelling to the other Musketeers at the same time. "THEY CALL US BAD, JUST LOOK AT THESE GUYS, THEY'RE BARE-ASSED TO THE BREEZE. THEY HAVEN'T EVEN GOT SHIRTS ON!"

It was obvious how hot the summer was, because each cadet had a white bottom swaying to and fro to the music. The rest of their bodies were tanned.

Bergie grabbed the back of Jackson's neck. "Did you drag us all the way here just to see this. It's only a sporran parade. They do it three or four times every year."

"Well, I've never seen it," Jackson replied. "How come the Military Police don't don't stop 'em."

Bergie started walking back to the hut. "Because it's a camp tradition. They do it for ten or fifteen minutes and nobody bothers them. Even the Provost leave them alone."

"HEY, YOU'RE CUTE," some girl screamed from a car trying to pass.

The pipers and drummers seemed oblivious to the remarks and just continued marching with ordinary everyday looks on their faces.

When they finished and put on their kilts, their laughter was louder than the hand of approval they received from the military and civilian audiences.

"Jeez, that takes guts," East said as they sauntered back to the barracks.

Danyluk stopped. "What guts? Bergie told me that last year, the Guard gave their drill sergeant an ulcer by dropping their pants on the parade square and bare-assing the Driver-Mech convoys. Driver-Mech stopped giving the finger after that."

"God, if we did that, Beckfora would have a bird," said Douglas. "I don't think we'd ever recover."

Danyluk wasn't finished. "Bergie also told me about the cannon always being painted with polka dots on the last day of camp just prior to the final parade. Well, last year the Commanding Officer put a nighttime guard on it to make sure it didn't happen. That didn't stop the painters, because when the CO arrived at the reviewing stand the next morning, someone had written, 'SCREW THE CANNON, WE WERE AFTER THE PARADE SQUARE ANYWAY.' They also put a size forty-six bra up the flagpole and cut the hoisting rope. There was no time to get it down, so the parade continued with a massive bra flying in front of the Headquarters building."

Danyluk's story got the Musketeers laughing. Now there was spring in their step as they went back to B-21.

Supper that night was turkey and the cooks were smiling as they dished it out. Although there was some apprehension on the faces of the recipients, they didn't take long to go back for seconds.

Danyluk sat in Rothstein's chair at the end of the table and was playing 'dad.' "No one is getting up from this table until he finishes every pea on his plate," he said, hammering the salt shaker against the top of the table like a judge demanding quiet in the courtroom.

A guy at the next table asked them if they heard about the cadet caught stealing in Baker Company. They had tried to catch the guy for weeks but he had outsmarted them all. "A blanket was put over his head, and they made him walk the gauntlet. After that, they shaved and black-balled him. He won't steal again, I betcha."

Douglas looked up from his plate. "They should've just sent him home."

"They are going to send him home," said Bergie. "But he's learned a lesson he won't forget."

The cadet continued. "He told the Military Police he fell down a flight of stairs."

"Surely the Military Police are wise to that?" Wayne asked. "They must know what's happening?"

Bergie nodded. "They do, but what are they going to do about it, send the whole company home? If the company staff catches cadets giving a thief the treatment, they make it rough on everyone in the barracks. I've seen it and 'shorts-wrestling' many times."

"But what if they've made a mistake and haven't caught the real thief?" asked Rothstein.

"Them's the breaks. It's usually black and white. They wouldn't do it if they weren't certain."

Douglas shook his head. "It sounds a little barbaric."

Bergie got louder. "OH COME OFF IT DOUG, THERE'S NOTHING WORSE THAN A BARRACK-ROOM THIEF. THEY GO EVEN TOUGHER ON THEM IN THE REGULAR FORCE. LISTEN, SERGEANT BECKFORD HAS MADE IT CLEAR TO ALL OF US THAT WE'RE A FAMILY AND NOBODY STEALS FROM HIS OWN FAMILY, OR FROM ANYONE ELSE, FOR THAT MATTER!"

"But what about clothes?" asked Rothstein. "You know as well as we do,

Bergie, that clothes move through this camp like water buckets at a fire."

"That's different. I noticed today that I've got three pairs of khaki shorts. I don't know how I got the extra pair? I must have picked them up in the drying room by mistake, so I put them back."

Danyluk had a mouthful of food. He couldn't swallow it quick enough. "THOSE WERE MINE YOU CREEP. NOW I'M GOING TO HAVE TO GO ON THE PROWL. I BET YOU'VE GOT SOME OF MY UNDERWEAR, TOO?"

Bergie had calmed down. "Moose, let me tell you. Never in a million years would you find me wearing your underwear. I'd wear Hog Sing's underwear before I'd wear yours!"

Danyluk grinned. "Oh, yeah? Hop Sing probably doesn't wear any underwear. It would take him too long to get them off when he's with his dames."

"Come on," said Bergie. "How long does it take you to get them off when you're with a dame. Let me tell you. It takes about one thousandth-of-a-second. Right?"

Danyluk looked him in the eye. "Wrong......! It takes a millionth-of-a-second."

East slapped Danyluk on the back. He couldn't talk; he was laughing and his mouth was full.

"You mentioned shorts-wrestling. What's that?" Banks asked.

Bergie started eating again because he'd talked so much his food was getting cold.

"I haven't seen it this year, but it's a riot. It's a tradition in this camp that if the staff catches cadets black-balling other cadets, a space is cleared in the drying room and it is used for a competition.

The guys who were doing the 'job' have to strip to their shorts and enter the area. Each of them is then handed an open tin of shoe polish and they face each other in the enclosed area. Then the wrestling starts. The first one to black-ball the other, wins. Believe me, when you see something like that, you realize how lucky you are not to be a part of it."

"Who referees the match?" Wayne asked.

Bergie couldn't contain his smile. "The victim. By the time it's finished, they've ripped the shorts off each other trying to win. Both of them are always covered from head to toe with shoe polish. It's a good lesson."

All eyes and ears were on Bergie as he told the story. At one point Danyluk's crotch got itchy just listening to him.

Wayne agreed with everything Bergie was saying. "I think that's fair. If they both deserve it, they gotta pay the price."

When they left the mess hall, the seven of them were in deep conversation, 'discussing' the trial of 'shorts-wrestling.'

"Remember, it's only done when the staff catches them," Bergie reiterated. "If cadets catch them, anything goes."

With the movie under their belts, the Musketeers conversed back in their barracks while getting prepared for the following day.

Danyluk put a towel over his head and sneaked up on Bergie. "I am the phantom and I'm going to slit your throat. I'm after your blood."

Bergie yanked off the towel. "That's was a good movie, don't ruin my memory of it. I hear it's in 3-D in Vancouver."

Danyluk went back to cleaning out his side of the barrack-box. "Bergie, are these your dirty undershorts on my side?"

Bergie looked at them. "Not on your life."

Danyluk walked into the centre of the aisle holding out the dirty garment. "O.K. WHO'S THE WISE ASSHOLE WHO PUT THESE IN MY BAR-RACK-BOX?"

A cadet across the aisle said, "Hey, let me see those. They're mine. I left them washed in the drying room, inside a pair of khaki shorts. AH HA!"

Danyluk smiled and pointed at Bergie. "He helps himself in the drying room too, ya know."

The cadet didn't argue, he just grabbed his shorts and walked back to his bunk.

Bergie was trying to move the piece of cardboard in the middle of the box so that both sides were even.

"Danyluk, how come I always end up with a quarter of the box and you get the rest? Don't answer that, let me tell you why. Because you've got more food rotting in here than the Vernon garbage dump, that's why." He was holding up a rotten apple.

Danyluk took a close look. "So that's what the smell was? I thought it was your shorts."

For the next five minutes Bergie chased Danyluk, bashing his head with a pillow.

Just before the lights were out, Danyluk stepped on one of the folding tables. "PAY ATTENTION HERE! WHY DON'T WE SURPRISE SERGEANT SIMPSON TOMORROW BY BEING UP BEFORE HE GETS HERE? LET'S PLAY HIS GAME FOR A CHANGE."

Their side of the hut agreed. For once Danyluk had come up with a good suggestion.

The next morning at five-thirty, all cadets were dressed in their P.T. strip. They waited and waited, but the Sergeant didn't turn up. Not only couldn't they find Sergeant Simpson, shortly thereafter, Danyluk was nowhere to be found either. He knew he had inspired his whole side of the hut, and the cadets wanted to 'express' their thanks.

Charlie Company got back into camp routine quickly. They participated in the Kelowna Regatta and the Penticton Peach Festival parades and made Sergeant Beckford proud of them.

The opportunity to attend both events was a real dividend for the cadets of the guard. None had visited those two cities before, so after each parade they were allowed to tour the town and observe the various festivities.

The Musketeers explored each city vigorously. They walked the beaches and the main streets, looking in shop windows without buying anything.

When Danyluk found out the Vernon Girls Drum and Bugle Band was there, he spent hours looking for the base drummer, to no avail. When told she was sick from stomach flu, he said, "She'd better start wearing panties. That way, she won't get it again." Dr. Danyluk must have been really concerned, if he wanted her panties, on.

The ride to both the parades took place in the morning when the weather was hot. Unfortunately the trucks returned to camp quite late at night and it was dark and cold. Cadets huddled against each other to stay warm. But that didn't dampen their enthusiasm, because each truck's chorus, inspired to song on the way to the parades, was just as loud on the return trip.

"These box-lunches aren't too bad," said Douglas, biting into a roast beef sandwich he had taken out of a box lunch issued to him prior to the ride back from Penticton. Each box lunch had two full sandwiches, a handful of fresh vegetables packed in a small cellophane bag and an apple or an orange.

He was huddled against Wayne in the back of a three-ton truck with no canopy on it. They were travelling about fifty miles an hour along the winding highway and the wind was cold.

Rothstein opened up his box lunch and checked out the sandwiches. "WHO WANTS TO TRADE ME SOMETHING FOR TWO HAM SANDWICHES?" He had to yell to be heard above the sound of the wind and the motor.

"PASS 'EM OVER HERE," Jackson replied, as he threw two chicken sandwiches in Rothstein's direction.

Danyluk and Bergie were the only two who had brought sweaters. They had hidden them under the driver's seat of the truck. Their fervor for the trip was more intense than the others, because they were warm.

"Did any of you guys check out the chicks on the beach?" Danyluk asked, biting into an apple.

Bergie was also eating an apple. "Sure did. Them's the kind you want to take home to mother."

Danyluk laughed. "You've got it all wrong, Bergie. Them's the kind you want to make mothers."

East, collecting anything out of the box lunches that people didn't want, replied to Danyluk's remark. "There he goes again. Y'know Moose, if there was such a thing as a human stud farm, you would be a one man show."

"Ya got that right," said Moose, "I could be father to the world. But you can't talk, Jack. With thousands of people sitting on the sidewalk watching us march by, you had to take a Tootsie Roll off that little girl."

"How could I help it, she came out and offered it?"

Danyluk chuckled. "You were supposed to be swinging your right arm, not holding it out to grab some candy. I wonder what her mother thought?"

"Not only that, he put it in his mouth," said Bergie.

Wayne leaned forward so that Bergie would hear him. "What was that meeting about that you had with Beckford and Simpson earlier today?"

"Sergeant Simpson is going to start training us boxers tomorrow," Bergie said. "There's no more P.T. for the company, he's just going to work with the four of us. He's also setting up a secret gym with boxing bags."

Wayne nodded "Then you're taking this thing pretty seriously?"

Bergie replied with a full mouth. "Ya got that right. We have to, these Irish guys box at their armories on Gilford Street in Vancouver."

The words 'Gilford Street' jolted Wayne's memory. "You know what those guys call us in Vancouver? They call us the 'Black bastards from Beatty Street.'"

"That's O.K., we call them the 'Green fuckers from Gilford Street,'" Danyluk interjected. "Every St. Patrick's Day and Armistice Day, they come in the middle of the night and paint green shamrocks all over the tank in front of our armories. Last year we cut out a stencil and painted black tanks all over their main doors."

Rothstein laughed. "That's ppprettty funnny." His teeth were chattering, so Bergie took off his sweater and passed it to him. "I don't want ya coming down with a cold Rothie; we've got to beat these Irish creeps."

"When's the match?" asked East.

"Sunday, Bergie replied. "There's no movie that night. They're setting up a boxing ring for us. Simpson told me that other companies are going to participate as well."

"Are guests invited?"

Everyone knew what Wayne was getting at. They knew he wanted to invite the girls.

"Yep, the girls can come, anyone can come," said Rothstein.

Wayne looked at Bergie. "But do you want them to come? What if you get the shit knocked out of you?"

Danyluk gave his usual sneaky smile. "We've got just as good a chance as they have. I think the girls should come and see us knocking the shit out of the Irish."

Wayne saw the look on Danyluk's face. "You've got something up your sleeve, haven't you?"

Moose shook his head, but not convincingly enough. As he looked at the other three 'boxers,' he said, "Well, let's just say it's not going to be a cakewalk for them."

The four 'boxers' now had smiles on their faces as Bergie became their spokesman. "We'll play it straight if it's evenly matched, but we just want to get it over with."

Danyluk gave Bergie a mock punch. "Bergie, I love ya!"

They all broke up when Bergie responded, "Yeah, that's what worries me."

Jackson cupped his ears and stood on a box so he could look over the cab of the truck. "HEY, THE GUYS IN THE OTHER TRUCKS ARE SINGING!"

"They're warm, they've got tarps on their trucks," East remarked.

Bergie stood up. "A little cold never stopped the Musketeers from singing, did it?"

He was right. When the trucks entered camp, 'Old King Cole' blurting out from the Musketeer's truck woke up quite a few cadets sleeping in the rows of darkened huts. A few middle fingers appeared out the windows, but that 'gesture' didn't dampen the 'songbirds' enthusiasm.

Danyluk answered, "THE SAME TO YOU!"

Although they were asked to keep the noise down, when two hundred cadets unload from trucks, turn in their rifles and bayonets and enter their barracks, it's totally impossible for them to be quiet.

Within minutes the showers were jammed, the washing machine was humming, toilets were flushing, boots were being shined and uniforms pressed for the following day.

Rothstein came over to Bergie and gave him his sweater back. "Thanks, Bergie, I've cut you an extra big piece for your generosity." With that said, he handed Bergie a piece of birthday cake on a cardboard plate.

Bergie's eyes exploded. "Wow, thanks Rothie, when did you get this out of the mess hall?"

Rothstein was piling cake on six other plates. "This morning. I hid it in my barrack-box until we got back."

East was there in a flash. "Rothie, you're the breath of life to a starving cadet. Which one is mine?"

In seconds all of the Musketeers were eating cake and then Rothstein handed them each a Kik-Kola. "My mom sent me up seven of them; they're a little warm, but what the heck."

Bergie stood up to lead the chorus of Musketeers.

"Altogether now, one, two three......"

"Here's to Rothie, he's got class.

Here's to Rothie, he's a horse's ass."

Everyone gave Rothstein a big hand of approval and he bowed with a very proud grin.

Danyluk undressed, threw his clothes in Bergie's side of their barrack-box and jumped up on his bed. Immediately, he was lying on Bergie's bunk. Actually, Bergie's mattress was touching the floor. He was lucky Bergie wasn't in it.

"SON OF A BITCH!" It took him a second to realize what had happened, then he stood up rubbing his rear end.

"WOULD YOU LOOK AT THIS? SOMEONE HAS UNHOOKED ALL OF THE SPRINGS HOLDING MY BUNK TO THE FRAME!"

Bergie came out of the shower and laughed the hardest, only to find that when he hit the sack, the same thing happened. Well, nearly the same thing, because whoever did it to him left a few springs attached. That's what saved Danyluk from going all the way to the floor. Bergie's body was like a half opened jackknife. He was holding onto the frame, but his rear end was in the "sagging position," as East described it.

Bergie was furious. "Don't those Irish 'fuzzyliars' ever give up?"

"Does this change our ring plans?" Danyluk asked.

"You bet it does," replied Bergie, reattaching his springs.

For the rest of the week, the boxers trained hard. On Friday morning when they arrived back in the barracks after their workout, no one was up. They had run about three miles and pounded the bags for an hour.

Danyluk stood at the door. "COME ON YOU LAZY BUGGERS, LET GO OF YOUR WANGS, AND START BRUSHING YOUR FANGS!"

Wayne sat up wiping his eyes. Then he put his glasses on and looked at his watch. "God, you're starting to sound like Sergeant Simpson already. How'd it go today?"

Danyluk was running on the spot. "It went absolutely fantastic. We ran for three miles, did about a hundred-and-fifty pushups and we've just finished doing a hundred setups, and punching the bags."

Douglas finally woke up. "I'm glad I didn't volunteer," he said.

"GUESS WHO WE SAW TODAY?" Bergie was also running on the spot and speaking loudly so everyone would hear him.

East was out of bed eating a banana which he'd sneaked out of the mess hall the previous night. "Who?"

"WE PASSED OUR IRISH 'FRIENDS' AND DO YOU KNOW WHO WAS RIDING IN A JEEP BEHIND THEM, SAYING HUP, HUP, HUP?"

No one answered him. "WAIT FOR IT......IT WAS NONE OTHER THAN GENOVA."

Now everyone was gathered around Bergie and Danyluk's bunks. Douglas had a towel wrapped around himself, about to head for the shower when he heard Genova's name.

"The turncoat. He's a Duke! Why would he assist Irish Cadets?"

Danyluk had stripped off and he was wrapping a towel around his waist.

"He must have heard that I'm fighting. You know how he hates my guts. I gave him the finger when he passed today."

"If you gave him the finger, he didn't see it," said Bergie.

"Bull-shit, he didn't see it. I know the guy, he's got eyes in the back of his head."

"You mean in the back of his nose," quipped Wayne.

All seven were heading to the showers, with Danyluk walking backwards, facing the other six. "Jesus, I'd love to face him in the ring. I'd have a reach advantage of three feet just because of his nose."

Banks was obviously upset. "What a creep he must really be! He wears a BCR capbadge, yet he trains Irish cadets. If Patterson found out about this, he'd ship him off to the Irish."

Wayne was referring to Pat Patterson, the Regimental Sergeant-Major of the British Columbia Regiment.

"I'm going to pass this along to Captain Lungley when we get back," he said.

For some reason there was plenty of hot water left when they reached the shower room.

"Who's got shampoo?" asked Wayne.

Rothstein threw him a bottle and added, "You guys are Dukes. Like anyone, you love your regiment. That guy may wear the same badge, but he doesn't love his regiment. If I had to leave my regiment for some reason or another, that would be it for me, no more badges."

No sooner had Rothstein finished talking, Danyluk rushed into the shower room with a bucket of cold water and got Bergie square in the back.

"AGGGH! YOU ROTTEN...YOU ROTTEN......"

Bergie couldn't speak; it's a wonder the shock didn't give him a heart attack.

Danyluk stayed back, his head sticking around the doorway. "THAT'S THE ONE I OWE YA FOR THE SHITTER, AND HERE'S ANOTHER ONE FOR THE HELL OF IT."

The second one got Bergie right in the middle of his chest. Although he couldn't talk, he could run, and he was after Danyluk.

The two wore nothing but looks of comical determination as they ran down one side of the hut and outside. Danyluk had intended on coming in through the centre doors, but they were locked. He made it down the stairs and around the corner again, but Bergie caught him just outside the shower room, so did the Camp RSM.

"YOU TWO! STOP IN YOUR TRACKS!"

Both of them stood at attention with water dripping off their bare bodies.

RSM Gardiner slowly walked over and stood in front of them. "IS THIS THE DRESS OF THE DAY IN YOUR COMPANY?"

"NO, SIR!"

The other Musketeers were looking out the shower room windows at the two nudes standing to attention on the road. In fact, the whole of Charlie Company was either hanging out the windows or standing at the top of the stairs staring at what East dubbed, "THE BALLS BRIGADE!"

"DO YOU THINK THIS IS A GOD-DAMNED NUDIST COLONY? DO YOU THINK YOU'RE A GUEST AT SUNNY FARMS?"

"NO, SIR!"

"THEN WHAT ARE YOU DOING?"

At that point, some of the kitchen girls walked by on the other road. "Hi, stud," one of them sung. Both Bergie and Danyluk tried to cover their 'front.'

"STAND TO ATTENTION! I'LL TELL YOU WHEN TO BE BASHFUL. WELL, I'M WAITING?"

Bergie tried to speak. "Well, Sir, er, well, we......"

"YOU TWO ARE EXHIBITIONISTS, AREN'T YOU? IS THAT WHAT YOU'RE TRYING TO TELL ME?"

"No, Sir, we..."

"WHAT?"

"YES, SIR, WE'RE EXHIBITIONISTS, SIR!"

"THAT'S WHAT I THOUGHT."

The RSM stood there in silence for a moment with the duo.

"THE ONLY PROBLEM I CAN SEE IS THAT ONLY ONE OF YOU CAN QUALIFY FOR THAT POSITION. WHAT ARE YOU TRYING TO DO, LEARN THE ROPES?" He was looking at Bergie.

"I'm his assistant, Sir."

A small smile came over the RSM's face. At least it looked like a small smile. East called it the start of another gas attack.

"WELL, LET ME TELL YOU MR. STUD AND YOU, HIS ASSISTANT, IF I FIND YOU PEOPLE RUNNING OUTSIDE AGAIN WITH NO CLOTHES ON, YOU'LL STAND THAT WAY ON THE PARADE SQUARE FROM MORNING UNTIL NIGHT. IS THAT CLEAR?"

"YES, SIR!"

He looked at Danyluk. Aren't you the one who keeps saluting me?"

"Sir, yes Sir."

"GET OUT OF MY SIGHT!"

The two of them started running.

"MARCH, DON'T RUN!"

"YES, SIR."

Both stopped instantly in their tracks and started marching. With their arms shoulder high, their chins up and their chest out, Stud and his assistant marched around the building, up the stairs, through the wing and into the shower room. When they arrived they were both in stitches. So was everyone else in the Company.

"YOU IDIOT, DANYLUK, HOW COME EVERY TIME I'M WITH YOU I'M IN SHIT?" Bergie was now back in the shower trying to get his feet clean.

"IT'S 'MISTER STUD' TO YOU. YOU SAY THAT I GET YOU INTO SHIT? IS THAT WHAT YOU SAID?"

As the rest of the Musketeers left the shower room, Wayne was holding his stomach and shaking his head. "What the hell would we do without them?"

"I think it would be a boring summer," replied Douglas.

On the way back to his bed, Douglas read the bulletin board. "Final tests are tomorrow, we'd better study like hell tonight."

Wayne nodded and turned up Danyluk's radio. The vocal version of Ebb Tide was playing. "I'm going to call Debbie at lunch and tell her we've got Saturday afternoon and all day Sunday off. Is there anything you want her to pass on to Diane?"

"Yeah, tell Diane I'll call her tomorrow and that we're going to the final dance. Also, don't forget to mention the boxing matches this Sunday."

"Ditto, Roger out," Wayne replied as he made his bed.

The conversation at breakfast that morning concentrated on the two nudists who had a run in with Mr. Gardiner. Even cadets from other companies that used the mess hall were talking about it.

"Apparently, one of them was either hung like a horse, or he had a hard-on," a cadet said from the table across from them.

Danyluk stuck out his chest. "That was me, you dummy, and I didn't have a hard-on."

"Oh, sorry, you could have fooled me," the cadet replied.

Danyluk sat back in his chair with a puzzled look on his face. He couldn't quite figure out what the cadet's last statement meant.

Bergie was discussing the Camp Regimental Sergeant-Major. He had a piece of bacon in his hand and he was waving it.

"That guy is everywhere and I mean everywhere. He found our Irish 'friends' on the parade square and now he finds us. Christ, he MUST think this is a nudist colony.

Douglas snickered. "He's probably seen all this before. I think he's a good guy."

East stood up to go back for seconds. "He is a good guy and I hear it's a hell of a lot worse than this on Regular Force bases. Those guys are animals."

A young girl filling up the salt and pepper shakers came by the table. "Hi, Moose. You looked good in your birthday suit this morning."

She was smiling bashfully and had a gleam in her eye. The Musketeers waited for his reply. They didn't have to wait long.

"You've seen the body beautiful before."

"Yes, but not like that, it was too dark before. I really like your birth mark." She now had her elbow on the table and was resting her head in her hand, looking into his eyes.

Danyluk sat back in his chair. "I like yours, too."

"I don't have one, darling." When she said darling, wolf whistles were heard in the immediate area.

"Oh, yes you do. It's on the end of your right......"

"Nooooo darling you're getting mixed up. That was a hickey you gave me."

She was still smiling and looking at Danyluk as she moved on with her tray. When she was about five feet away, she stopped and smacked her right buttock.

"That's telling him," said Bergie. He then looked at Danyluk. "Did I hear you say the body beautiful? My bird's cage has got better ribs than you."

Danyluk was halfway out the door when he turned around. "You can't talk, shorty." He then walked down the stairs roaring out loud.

Bergie yelled, "IT'S NOT THE SIZE OF THE CANNON, IT'S HOW GOOD THE 'CANNONEER' IS, YOU IDIOT!"

Danyluk paid no attention to Bergie.

"IT'S NOT THE SIZE OF THE CANNON, IT'S THE CANNONEER THAT COUNTS!"

Danyluk was about twenty-five yards away and didn't turn around when he gave Bergie the finger.

For the rest of the morning, Charlie Company received refresher lectures on subjects they had studied since they arrived in camp.

"Always remember the code-word APUMSHIT," said Sergeant Beckford, referring to the Principles of Instruction in Technique of Instruction.

"Banks, what does the A stand for?

"Aim, Sergeant."

"Good. Brice, the P?
"Planning and Preparation, Sergeant."
"Good. East, the U?"
"Use of the proper senses, Sergeant."
"Good. Rothstein, the M?"
"Maximum activity, Sergeant."
"My God, I think you people have actually learned something. Danyluk, the S?"
"Simplicity, Sergeant."
"Is that what you told the RSM?"
"What?"
"That you guys were simple?"
"No, Sergeant, I didn't want to embarrass Bergie."
"Bergie, the H?"
"Human factor, Sergeant."
"Good. Jackson, the I?"
"Interest, Sergeant."
"Good. Romer, the T?"
"Testing by stages, Sergeant."
"Barker, what's the whole code-word?"
"Apumshit, Sergeant."

When they went for lunch, Nine Platoon was more than prepared for Saturday's tests in Technique of Instruction, Leadership, Map Using, Military Writing, the rifle, Bren and Sten guns.

Although that afternoon was one of the hottest days of the summer, Charlie Company was back on the parade square. By four o'clock they had covered every drill movement in CAMT 2-2, time and time again.

As he dismissed them, Sergeant Beckford said they had a tough job ahead of them that night. Not only did they have to study, but the barracks had to be the best in camp for Saturday morning's inspection.

As they marched away from the square to hand in their rifles and bayonets, Sergeant Beckford's face revealed his pride. He was really proud of them and they knew it. That's why they worked so hard for him.

After supper, B-21 was once again ripped apart for cleaning.

As Wayne and Douglas lifted up their set of bunks to move them to the other side, Wayne said, "Just think, we won't have to be going through this next Friday."

He had barely finished speaking when he saw Danyluk at the other end of the hut holding a wash basin against the ceiling with the stick-handle of a broom. Although Danyluk was tall, both of his arms were raised and his face showed some concern.

Wayne walked over. "What are you doing?"

Danyluk didn't take his eyes off the wash basin. "There's a mouse in it and I'm holding it until some cadet gets back with a sack."

Wayne laughed. "Moose, you've just been caught with the oldest trick in Vernon. That wash basin is full of water and if you move, you're going to be drenched."

"SON OF A BITCH! ALRIGHT, WHERE'S THAT PRICK THAT SET ME UP?"

Wayne pulled over a folding table, stood on it and grabbed the wash basin. "He probably lives on the other side or for that matter, in the next hut over. How long have you been standing there like this?"

"Twenty God-damned minutes. It got to the point where I thought the guy was weaving a sack. Nobody around here would help me either."

"Moose, where have you been? That trick has been going on all summer."

As Wayne handed the full wash basin to Danyluk, East and Jackson were going at each other with two of the hut's fire extinguishers. It didn't matter where they squirted because all of the bunks from one side had been moved to the other, and cadets who were on their knees scrubbing, needed the water. They got water alright, they were drenched from head to toe.

While that was going on, Rothstein and Douglas were outside the hut on ladders, cleaning windows.

At one point, Douglas was cleaning the outside of a window and a cadet inside was cleaning the same window. They were facing each other through the glass, each absorbed in his work.

When the window got stuck, Douglas asked the cadet inside to give him a hand moving it. The cadet assisted, but while Douglas was doing the upper half of the window, he didn't realize his shoe laces were being tied together by the guy on the inside. Two seconds later he landed on the ground; the water bucket on the head of the guy whitewashing the rocks. It looked like a scene from the Keystone Cops.

Douglas and Rothstein gave the 'whitewasher' a hand, which kept his cussing down to a minimum.

At nine o'clock that night, East looked around. "This place is so clean I could eat off the floor."

"You might get a few slivers in your food," Douglas remarked as he grabbed his beret. He was going to the Cadet Canteen for a pop.

Rothstein was in the drying room. He saw and heard Douglas through the inside window.

"Hey Doug, wait for me." Rothie was getting his hair cut by a cadet who had brought clippers to camp to make money. The lineup at the camp barbershop made it nearly impossible to get a haircut, so some cadets made money on the side by cutting hair.

Rothstein had to get a haircut, because Sergeant Beckford had stood behind him on the parade square and said, "Am I hurting you, Rothstein?"

"No, Sergeant."

"Well, I should be, I'm standing on your hair. Get it cut by tomorrow. Right?"

"Right, Sergeant."

Rothstein caught up with Douglas at the door. He was rubbing the back of his head.

"Christ, that guy's clippers pull."

Douglas looked at the back of Rothstein's head. "You must have had your hair cut by Baldy Boomer, did you?"

Rothstein nodded.

"Rothie, you took your life in your hands. I'm not going to tell you what kind of a job he did because I don't want you to have a bird. If you appear like that on the parade square, Beckford is going to be all over you."

Rothstein grimaced. "What the heck should I do?"

"How much did Baldy Boomer charge you?"

"Fifty cents."

"What Baldy did to you isn't worth one cent. C'mon, I'll take you to Smoothy Stevens."

Smoothy was a BCR cadet in another hut. When they got there he had a lineup but he owed Douglas a favour and took Rothstein next.

Smoothy chuckled when he saw the back of Rothstein's hair. "You've been to Baldy Boomer haven't you?"

"Yeah."

"Baldy has no experience at all. Also did you know that Baldy's clippers were used to shave Jones before he was black-balled?"

Douglas laughed at the frown on Rothstein's face.

The lights were left on until midnight to allow all cadets to study. When they were finally turned off, most of the hut and all but two of the Musketeers were asleep.

"Say, Moose, who's cadet Jones?" Rothstein asked.

"He's the guy who had the crabs. I think they also black-balled him."

It wasn't long before a shower could be heard running full blast in the dark shower room. Rothstein's bed was empty.

CHAPTER XV

"STAND BY YOUR BEDS!" Sergeant Simpson made his usual trek down the aisle, turning over mattresses and pulling off blankets. It was six o'clock Saturday morning and the sun was just barely up.

"IF OUR BOXERS HAVE TO GET UP AT THIS TIME, I WANT THE REST OF YOU UP AS WELL. LET'S GET THIS BARRACKS IN SHAPE. I WANT US TO WIN TODAY AND, BY GOD, WE SHALL."

It didn't take long. Everyone on the Musketeers side of the hut was standing by their beds and most of them were shivering.

"CARRY ON."

Danyluk turned on his radio before he pulled his P.T. shorts over his normal morning erection. The radio announcer sounded alive.

"Good Morning Okanagan. John Deere Tractor and Equipment bring you 'Country Morning Hoedown.'

"JESUS, DANYLUK, GET KELOWNA, I CAN'T STAND THAT FIDDLE SHIT," screamed Bergie. He was still in a daze and didn't know if he should make his bed or have a shower. As it turned out, he could do neither because he was due on the road in twenty seconds.

Danyluk was tieing up his running shoes. "Bergie, we must have been out of our cotton-picking minds to volunteer for this."

"I agree, Moose, but you're one of Genova's boys. Don't you want to show that asshole up?"

Bergie must have said the right words, because as soon as Danyluk heard the word Genova, he started shadow boxing and sniffing as he put the side of this thumb against his nose as boxers do. A few seconds later, the four of them were on their way to the upper camp.

Although B-21 was the normal madhouse, Douglas was sitting on the side of his bunk reading his notes.

"Did you get much studying done last night?" he asked Wayne.

"A bit, but I must have fallen asleep pretty early. When I woke up this morning I was still in my coveralls. Who covered me over?"

"I did."

"Thanks, pal. How do you think you'll make out today?"

Douglas nodded. "Good. Let's grab a shower and we can study over breakfast."

When it was time to head over to the mess hall, their hut looked really good. All the bedding was arranged in Saturday Morning Inspection style. In addition, all windows in the hut had been opened at the top and bottom showing the same amount of space; towels were clean and hanging properly; barrack-boxes had been lined up; bunks lined up; everything taken off the shelves and wash basins shined and placed on the bedding. The centre of the hut also gleamed because the toilets, showers, and washing and drying rooms looked like they had been gone over with a magnifying glass.

Breakfast was quiet that morning. The boxers returned and were studying like everyone else when Danyluk's kitchen girl came over to say hello and run her hand through his hair. He was so wrapped up in his Map-Using notebook, he hardly noticed her.

Bergie tapped Danyluk on the shoulder. "Moose, something must be going right in this camp if you've got your mind on training and not girls.

Danyluk looked up for a moment. "It's a matter of Planning and Preparation. If I play hard-to-get now, just think of the Maximum Activity treatment I'll get around noon."

Bergie laughed. "Well, at least you've got two of the Principles of Instruction in motion."

"Was Genova with his boys today?" Wayne asked.

The question was enough to stop Danyluk reading again. "Was he there? I'll say he was there. He was madder than hell when all four of us gave him the finger. Sergeant Simpson had to smile and say, "Sorry, Sir."

"Did Simpson give you a blast?"

"Naah, Simpson's pretty good. I don't think he likes him either."

Wayne was still asking questions. "Have you guys got anything planned for tomorrow night?"

All four boxers smiled and looked at each other. Rothstein who was studying in the corner chair started chuckling but didn't say anything.

Wayne knew something was planned, but it was obviously being kept a secret.

Jackson popped his head up from his notebook. "Did you guys read orders this morning?"

The other Musketeers indicated they hadn't.

"We've got a pretty easy week ahead of us. We've got sports on Monday morning and a swim parade in the afternoon. Then on Tuesday morning, we have a swim meet practice at Kal beach. In the afternoon, we've got a sports meet practice at Polson Park.

"Fantastic," said Wayne.

"I'm not finished yet. All day Wednesday, there's a swim meet at Kal beach and all day Thursday, there's a sports meet at Polson Park.

"What about Friday?" Wayne asked.

"Oh, I almost forgot. Each night next week we're practising from 1900 until 2000 on the parade square for the Graduation Parade. The Graduation Parade is on Thursday night at Polson Park. After lunch on Friday we hand in our gear and we've got the rest of the day off."

Grinning, Danyluk put his book down. "And just think Bergie, as of tomorrow night, we won't be boxers anymore."

Bergie smiled and looked at his watch. "Jesus we've got to get going. If we're late, Simpson will kill us."

The boxers got up from the table in a hurry.

"What about this morning's parade?" asked Douglas

Rothstein was the only one left. "We're not on parade this morning," he said pulling his beret out from the elastic waist band of his P.T. shorts. "We're hitting the bags, or I should say the bags are hitting us."

The screen door slammed behind him.

For some reason, a lot of tourist cars watched the Saturday Morning Inspection from start to finish. The parade went very well and only a few cadets passed out.

After the parade, Sergeant Beckford told them that the Guard looked better than Regular Force troops who had been doing it for years. "It must have been the Penticton Peach Festival and the Kelowna Regatta that pulled everyone together."

When Charlie Company was 'informed' they were the best company in camp that week, their cheers could be heard all the way to the golf course.

As they marched off the parade square it was evident that every cadet in the Guard was proud. There were no errors. Their quarters, dress and drill were letter perfect and they knew it.

After they had handed in their weapons, the company was marched over to the upper camp. Lecture rooms had been set up for the tests.

"Each of you has a map, a protractor, and a compass in front of you. I'm going to pass out your test papers, one by one. You have forty minutes for this test. Afterwards you have a full hour for a combined test dealing with all of the subjects you have taken at camp."

"Some of the questions may have appeared on other tests you have had before. This is your opportunity to answer them correctly if you hadn't done so previously."

Sergeant Beckford handed out the papers. "When I say carry on, you may turn them over and start. Make sure that you put your name on them. CARRY ON."

They had been informed that when they were finished, they could make their own way back to the lower camp.

Douglas waited outside for Wayne. In ten minutes, they were walking back.

"How do you think you made out?" Douglas asked.

"I think I aced them, but I had a problem with Magnetic Declination. I keep screwing up on the Annual Change, but other than that, I thought they were easy," Wayne replied.

"How'd you do, Doug?"

"I think I got all of them. They seemed easy."

When they arrived back in B-21, they were making their beds as the other cadets straggled in, one by one. Everyone was discussing the test they had just finished. Danyluk was in a philosophical interchange of words with Bergie.

"I'm not asking you, I'm telling you Bergie. On the attention from the unfix bayonets, the right hand grabs the rifle below the upper sling swivel, thumb touching it." He had a broom in his hand and he was demonstrating the movement.

"We're both saying the same thing," Bergie replied. "If I've got a shorter arm than you, my fingers could be wrapped around the upper sling swivel."

Danyluk nodded. "Well, I'm glad we sorted that out. For some reason you must think I'm just another pretty face. I've got kidneys, you know?" he said, pointing to his head.

Bergie sat down on his barrack-box. "Danyluk, let me tell you one thing. Never in a million years would I think that you're just another pretty face. I bet when you were born, your mom asked the nurse what she was holding in her arms. At that point, the nurse probably said something like, 'Madam, if you would take the time to peel the foreskin off your baby's face, you'd know what it is."

Banks, doubled over in laughter, begged, "Please guys, not again!"

Danyluk now had a silly grin on his face as he made his bed. He wasn't intimidated by Bergie's statement, he just couldn't think of anything to counter it at the moment.

"I think you've got it all wrong, Bergie," said Earl. "When his mother asked the nurse what it was, the nurse said, 'Madam you've given birth to a giant foreskin. In other words Mrs. Danyluk, you're holding a prick in your hands."

Danyluk was up like a shot after Jackson, but Jackson was fast and he was out the open door before Danyluk was even close to it. Danyluk stopped at the door. "I'LL GET YOU FOR THAT ONE, JACKSON!"

Douglas was lying on his bunk laughing and pushing his feet against Wayne's springs. Wayne was bouncing up and down and had to hold on from being kicked off the bed.

After lunch, Mail-Call, a sheet exchange, and Pay Parade, the Musketeers headed toward town. They were in pairs and gave their usual eyes left to Hog Sing's as they passed on the other side of the street.

A Chinese guy sweeping off the sidewalk looked at them.

"Is that Hop Sing?" asked Douglas.

"It can't be, he's got his pants on," Bergie replied.

East handed out the midnight passes. "I hope you boxers know you can't go to the dance tonight." He didn't have passes for Jackson, Danyluk, Bergie, or Rothstein.

Danyluk nodded. "We know. We've got to hit the bags at eighteen hundred. Being a boxer is like living in a police state; it can ruin a guy's sex life."

"What are you talking about?" Wayne replied. "I thought Alma was your instructor?"

"She could be, her arms are big enough," said Danyluk.

Polson Park was green and cool when they walked in. It was like ten degrees had been knocked off the thermometer.

The girls were sitting at a picnic table under a giant tree and each had packed a lunch. When they saw the boys they ran up and wrapped their arms around them, as if they hadn't seen them in years, instead of only two weeks.

Diane flung herself into Douglas' arms. He picked her up and swung her around.

"Did you miss me?" she asked.

"More than you'll ever know," he replied as he kissed her.

Douglas took hold of her hand and they walked away from the others. They stopped by the small stream and lay down side by side.

"It's your birthday next Wednesday, isn't it?"

Douglas looked puzzled. "You're right. We've been so busy, I almost forgot about it. How's your mom and dad and grandparents?"

Diane took hold of his hand. "They're great and they all said to say hello to you. Dad was asking when you're going to come over to the house for supper? Can you come tonight before the dance?"

"Sure, I'd like that. Are Wayne and Debbie invited?"

"Yes, Debbie's staying with us. Her parents are in Vancouver. Tell me about Glenemma, was it fun?"

Douglas spent the next hour going over the exploits of the Musketeers in Glenemma. Among other things, he mentioned the lantern episode, the dead cow and Danyluk ending up thrice in the 'trench.'

"It was great receiving all your letters."

Diane was still laughing at his story. "I wrote a lot more but I didn't mail them."

Douglas sat up and looked at her. "Why?"

"I probably said things that I'd be embarrassed about. It's funny how people say things in a letter that they'd think twice about saying in person, isn't it?"

"I guess you're right." He didn't push her to find out what she said.

Diane had adopted her favorite position of lying at a 90 degree angle and resting her head on his chest. Both of them were looking up at the blue sky.

"God, I'd love my mother to see this but she can't make it. Oh, well, maybe sometime in the future."

"Did you say she had never been up here?"

"She's never been out of Vancouver, but I've explained this country to her. I've also got a whole bunch of pictures to take back."

"Are you going to take back the one of me in my bathing suit?"

He laughed. "I'm having that one enlarged. It'll sit in my room forever."

For the next few hours they talked about everything. Finally Diane said, "I've got some sandwiches and pop, should we join the others?"

At dinner that night, Douglas invited Diane and her parents to visit the camp to see the boxing matches on Sunday night. He also mentioned the swim and sports meets at Kal Beach and Polson Park.

"We won't be able to make the beach or Polson Park, but we'll be at the boxing tomorrow night," Tom said.

Diane smiled. "You know I'll be at all of them."

Over dinner, Ellen said, "You know, Douglas, you're welcome up here at any time. If you like skiing, why don't you come up in the winter?"

Douglas liked the way she asked. "Thanks, Ellen, I'll take you up on that."
The two couples tossed to see who would do the dishes to give Tom and Ellen a break. Douglas and Diane lost. When Diane and he were washing dishes, he said, "You know, I really like your folks. They're super people."

"What about their daughter?" she asked.

"I don't like their daughter, I love her." He gave her a kiss on her forehead. They both had big grins on their faces.

On the way to the dance, Debbie heard from Diane that Douglas was coming up during the skiing season. She nudged Wayne until he agreed he'd come with him.

The Arena was packed. It seemed all the girls in town knew this was the last dance the cadets would be attending.

East had had dinner at his girlfriend's house and met them there. "Jeez, this must be a farewell dance. The whole town is here."

Douglas and Diane fought their way to the dance floor and before long, Ebb Tide was played. There was no space between them or around them.

Diane wasn't looking at him when she said, "I'm sorry about the other night."

"That's what you put in the letter, didn't you?"

"Yes."

He moved his head back so that Diane could take her head off his shoulder. They were both looking into each other's eyes. "Why are you sorry? I think there's a time for everything and I'm sorry I pushed you to the point where......"

"You didn't push me," she said softly. "I think I acted a little immature."

Douglas shook his head. "No, you didn't. You know as well as I do that there are limitations. We would have gone all the way and there's loads of time. Jesus Diane, we're both new to this whole thing. It's different with guys, but girls should......"

"I know what you're saying. Thank you," she said kissing him and resting her head on his shoulder.

"What made you think of that?" he asked. "Not that I couldn't get it out of my mind, either."

"When I talk to other girls, they tell me that they let their boyfriends......"

Once again he looked into her eyes. "Hey, we shouldn't care what others do...they're not us. We've got our own lives to live and a long way to go. Everyone's brought up differently. What we do is our business."

Although they were already as tight at sardines in a tin, Diane squeezed him tighter. "I hope I'm not sounding like some sort of a creep?" he said.

Diane relaxed and looked at him as if she was looking right through him. "No, you're not."

"That's good. I want you to know if I didn't feel this way about you, I'd be at ya like a dirty shirt. But they say it's better if it don't come easy."

He tickled her and they both laughed.

Diane rested her head again. "Before I met you, I didn't have an inkling of what love was like. Now I know."

Douglas chuckled. "I'm glad you do, because if you didn't, I'd have a real problem, wouldn't I?"

It was obvious that someone liked Ebb Tide because over the next two hours, it came on six times. Douglas and Diane left the floor only once, because when they danced, they were in their own little world and nothing else mattered. Nothing at all.

When two people are in love, they want time to stand still. Unfortunately, it doesn't, and in Diane and Douglas' case, the evening disappeared quickly. Time had flown and Tom and Ellen arrived to drive the boys back to camp.

When they were dropped off, both cadets mentioned they were going to help the boxers train all day Sunday, and that they should meet at the fights on Sunday night.

As the car pulled away, Tom yelled, "MAKE SURE YOU DON'T GET A BLACK EYE!" Diane and Debbie waved until the boys were out of sight.

Strolling back to the 'shack,' Douglas was in some sort of a dream world. "I'm in love, I AM IN LOVE!"

Wayne stopped in his tracks. "How in hell can a fourteen-year-old-going-on-fifteen fall in love?"

Douglas shook his head. "I don't now? A few weeks ago I would have said the same thing."

"Jesus, Doug, not too long ago you were sitting on your mother's knee eating pablum and now you want to tie the knot."

After a long sigh, Douglas put his hand on Wayne's shoulder. "Well, I've heard that us Brice's don't let grass grow under our feet. I'm telling ya, I've really fallen for Diane."

Wayne smiled. "Sure, sure, and the next thing you'll be telling me is that you're going to run for Prime Minister."

"No, I think I'll have to be at least sixteen before I try for that. Besides, I'm too honest for the job and the Commanding Officer might have a problem with my booting out his brother Louis."

The lights were on when they entered 'Grand Central Station.' Most of the cadets in the company had been at the dance and they were letting off more steam as they returned.

In addition to the deafening song spewing out of Danyluk's radio, cadets were racing up and down the aisle, jumping on and off bunks, squirting each other with fire extinguishers, playing stuke, throwing pillows, turning over mattresses, practising their drill, frenching the beds in the cubicles, washing and ironing their clothes, writing letters home, taking showers and tossing Sergeant's soap around, scrubbing their belts, shining their boots, and generally having a good time.

In the midst of the racket, Danyluk slept like a baby, but the other boxers were up eating cake.

"Grab yourself a plate and have some," East said with his mouth full.

"Whose is it?" Wayne asked.

East smiled. "It's mine. My mom sent me two of them."

Bergie was just finishing his piece, "Yeah, and he finished off one of them all by himself, can you believe that?"

Douglas smiled and stared at East. "He wouldn't be our good old Jack if he didn't."

Danyluk was out of bed in a shot. "Did I hear the magic word, cake? Where's my piece?" he said grabbing a cardboard plate.

Bergie pointed at him. "Ya see what you've gone and done, Jack? You've done what the Japanese said after Pearl Harbour. You've awakened a sleazy giant."

Danyluk had that sneaky smile on his face. "Come off it, Bergie, even I know they said a 'sleeping' giant."

"How'd the boxing practice go tonight?" Douglas asked.

"Good," replied Rothstein. "We really worked our butts off. We stand a pretty good chance of beating them tomorrow night."

Jackson came over to Douglas' bunk. "Yeah, we were working our fingers to the bone while you guys were out with dames. What was the dance like?"

"Quiet," said Wayne. "All the women stayed at home because Danyluk wasn't there."

"I'll bet that's the truth," quipped Danyluk. "But I didn't need them anyway because Alma came here. We went up to the outdoor chapel."

Wayne laughed. "What the hell were you praying for on a Saturday night?"

"He wasn't praying, he was playing," remarked Bergie.

A Corporal appeared. "LIGHTS OUT IN TEN MINUTES!"

After the lights were out, Wayne leaned over his bunk. "We might get our marks tomorrow."

Douglas lay with his hands behind his head. "This time next Saturday, we'll be on the train. God, the time dragged at first, now it seems to be flying."

It was quiet in the hut, but not for long. A light appeared in the Corporal's cubicle.

"FOR CHRIST'S SAKE! OH! OH! OH! OH! SO SOMEONE HAS FRENCHED MY BED, HAVE THEY? DANYLUK, GET YOUR ASS IN HERE."

"Corporal, it wasn't me, honest."

"I SAID GET YOUR ASS IN HERE, NOW!"

Danyluk threw back his covers and walked into the cubicle cursing.

"I had nothing to do with it!"

"IF YOU DIDN'T DO IT, WHO DID?"

"WELL, IT...IT COULD HAVE BEEN, ERR...I KNOW I DIDN'T DO IT. HOW THE HELL COULD I FIND A DEAD FISH, I'VE BEEN IN CAMP ALL NIGHT?"

There was silence for a few seconds. "A FISH? WHERE THE FUCK IS THAT? I WAS ONLY TALKING ABOUT THE FRENCHED BED. AHH, SO WE ALSO HAVE A FISH. JESUS THAT STINKS. SO YOU PUT A DEAD FISH IN MY BED, DID YOU?"

"I...er...ah...I think...um..."

There was muffled laughter throughout the barracks. Cadets couldn't control themselves, laughing at Danyluk's response and predicament.

Within minutes, Moose was getting dressed in full uniform. For the next hour he was doing drill on the parade square, with a dead fish in this pants.

The lineup was long and winding for breakfast the next day. All cadets decided to eat at the same time.

A shout came from the front. "ALL BOXERS UP AT THE HEAD OF THE LINE!"

Danyluk was once again in his element. "Make way, me hearties, it's us, the boxers, the people who put their lives on the line for you bums."

He had grabbed Bergie by the arm and was shepherding Jackson and Rothstein in between the two of them, walking to the front. "WE'LL SAVE SEATS AT OUR TABLE FOR YOU THREE," he yelled pointing at Wayne, Douglas and Jack East.

"Maybe we should have volunteered and then we'd get treatment like that?" Wayne remarked.

East grabbed him by the arm. "Are you out of your mind? I've seen those Irish, they're mean."

Wayne was finally starting to wake up. "What do you mean , they're no tougher than our guys?"

"I think they're going to be. They know who did the job on them and Genova's wise to the fact that we did the job on him, as well."

"That's impossible, Douglas said. "They're only guessing. Who would tell them?"

East was adamant. "I bumped into Gord Cunningham and you know as well as I do that nobody has an ear closer to the ground than him. How do you think he wins all those stuke games?"

Finally, they were inside the mess hall. "So what did Cunningham say?" Douglas asked.

"It's not only what he told me, it's also what he's going to do."

"Jack, get it out. What did he tell you?"

Jack's face turned serious. "He told me that someone finked on us and that he's going to work in their corner."

Both Douglas and Wayne were stunned at Jack's statement. Instead of putting his tray down to receive his breakfast, the girl serving Douglas took the tray from his hands and slammed it down to wake him up.

"Cunningham would never work on their behalf. He just wouldn't do it...he's a Duke."

East had a smile on his face. "He has to do it because he owes Genova money. Genova's really rubbing it in."

"Jeez, said Wayne, "If he's not rubbing in one thing, he's rubbing in another."

When they arrived at the table, the other Musketeers had saved them seats and they were eating steak.

Wayne looked at his two pieces of bacon and looked at their plates.

"I don't believe this, you guys got steaks?"

Danyluk had a big chunk on the end of his fork. "Yeah and we get it for lunch too."

Douglas asked East to tell the rest of them the story. When he finished, Bergie said, "We know that, but things might not turn out exactly as Genova expects they will."

Wayne looked bewildered. "Cunningham's a Duke, he wouldn't help out the Irish?"

Bergie's face lit up. "Quit worrying. He's going to help them out all right, but it will be on our terms."

As Bergie held court at the table, smiles started appearing on the Musketeers faces and only the words, 'brilliant,' 'great' and 'fantastic,' could be heard above his voice.

"C'MON, HIT IT HARDER!" Wayne was holding the boxing bag for Bergie. "Hit it! Hit it!"

Douglas and East were holding the bags for Danyluk and Rothstein. They had been holding them all day, except for Church Parade.

Bergie put his arms down by his sides. "If I hit it any harder, I'll dislocate my arms." He was puffing like he was in the ring already.

"O.K., let's start skipping again," Sergeant Simpson demanded. "I know you guys want to rest, but if you want to win, you've got to put in the time."

For the next two hours, the four boxers lifted weights and skipped. Shortly, the minor complaints stopped and before long, each one of them was getting his second wind.

"Is Cunningham clued in?" East asked.

"You bet he is," Bergie replied. "He's looking forward to it."

"O.K., HIT THE SHOWERS! IF WE'RE GOING TO DO THIS THING, I GUESS WE'RE BETTER PREPARED NOW THAN WE'VE EVER BEEN."

"How's our chances, Sergeant?" Douglas asked Simpson when the boxers were in the showers.

Sergeant Simpson smiled. "To tell you the truth, I really don't know. I've tried to take a look at what our opponents are doing, but Al Genova's really got the cloak of secrecy wrapped around them. We've got a good chance, I think."

"Is anyone taking bets?"

"Brice, if you're planning on betting, you've got to put your money on our guys just out of pure loyalty. I teach this stuff at Military College and these four have worked harder than anyone I've worked with. They really deserve to win."

When fight time finally came, the hangar, B-3, was packed with cadets, officers, non-commissioned officers and guests.

Every chair in the camp was assembled to accommodate the crowd and at least five hundred people were standing, as well.

The boxing ring and lighting were set up professionally, with the referee and judges brought in from Vernon, Kelowna, and Penticton.

Douglas sat with Diane and her parents, and Wayne sat next to them with Debbie. Sergeant Simpson had arranged for seats near the front so they all had an excellent view.

At exactly seven o'clock, a cadet entered the ring and stood in the centre with a microphone in his hand. "LADIES AND GENTLEMEN...AND I USE THE TERM GENTLEMEN LOOSELY."

The crowd roared appropriately.

"TONIGHT, WE HAVE A FULL CARD OF ACTION FOR YOUR ENTERTAINMENT. DRIVER-MECH AND SIGNALS ARE HERE TO TAKE ON THE INSTRUCTOR'S BASIC TRAINING WING."

Another thunder of approval was heard.

"WE'VE GOT TWENTY FABULOUS FIGHTS FOR YOU TONIGHT."

The cadet was doing a good job acting like a real professional ring announcer and the resounding applause he received from the audience made him work harder.

"EACH FIGHT WILL BE OF THREE ROUNDS DURATION AND EACH ROUND WILL BE THREE MINUTES. THE FIGHTERS HAVE BEEN WEIGHED AND I THINK YOU'LL AGREE THAT THEY'RE EVENLY MATCHED."

Yells of "Get on with it," and "Get the lead out," rumbled from the eager supporters.

Diane took hold of Douglas' hand and squeezed it tightly. "This is fun."

Banks was sitting on the other side of Douglas. He pushed the program under his best friend's nose. "Have you read this?"

Douglas took it from him. "No, why?"

"Just look at the names they've given themselves."

A grin dawned on Douglas' face as he read it. Morgan Brown versus Daunting Danyluk, Sean O'Shaughnessy versus Ripper Rothstein, Michael Griffin versus Jugular Jackson and Edwin Shanks versus Barracuda Bergie.

"Jesus, they must think this is world-class wrestling," he said to Wayne as he passed it back.

East grabbed the program and started belly-laughing. "Daunting Danyluk sounds like a homo out on his first date."

The first ten fights went fairly smoothly with IBT winning five of them against Signals and Driver-Mech, however, the ring announcer was certainly wrong about their being evenly matched.

The last fight ended before intermission; Wayne was furious.

"This has been fixed. The guy that matched these fights must have been out in the sun without his helmet on. Our guy was five foot two and the Driver-Mech cadet was five foot eleven. It's no wonder we lost."

Jack grabbed Wayne's arm. "Cunningham told me that Bergie and Danyluk's opponents are about the same, but Rothstein and Jackson are fighting two giants."

During the fights, comments like, "He's killing him," and "Throw in the towel," came from the girls clinging to the arms of the 'men.' At one point, Ellen said, "I can't take any more of this," but she stayed anyway and appeared to enjoy it even though there was a little blood.

If a cadet got too rough and was too much of a match for his opponent, the fight was stopped immediately, usually to the roar of, "FIX, FIX, FIX, FIX!"

"How did you enjoy the first half?" Tom asked Douglas.

"I thought it was great. Those guys are really hitting."

Wayne was nodding his head. "I should hope so, this isn't tiddlywinks, you know."

"Doesn't it hurt them?" Diane asked. Every time a cadet had connected with a punch, Diane acted like she had felt it as well.

"A bit, but those are extra big gloves," Wayne replied.

Tom took his pipe out of his mouth and started clearing the ashes out by hitting it on his shoe. "Well, let's see what the last half has to offer," he said, winking at Douglas.

The group had barely returned to their seats after intermission when the ring announcer picked up his microphone.

"THE ELEVENTH FIGHT OF THE EVENING FEATURES TWO OF VERNON ARMY CADET CAMP'S TOP FIGHTERS. IN THE BLUE CORNER, WEARING BLUE TRUNKS, FROM GUARD COMPANY, DAUNTING DANYLUK."

All three IBT companies were on their feet cheering, while boos and hisses came from Signals and D&M.

Banks leaned over and whispered in Douglas' ear.

"Christ, look at his shorts, they're too small and too tight. Any second now, his balls and his dong are going to be hanging out his pant leg. What's be trying to prove?"

East leaned over. "He's got a jockstrap on."

"He's going to need two of them," Banks said, shaking his head.

All of the girls giggled at Bank's comments.

Before East sat back, he whispered to Wayne and Douglas.

"If he coughs, he balls will end up in his throat. Apparently, he wanted to be cool for Alma."

"AND IN THE RED CORNER, WEARING GREEN SHORTS, FROM SIG-NALS COMPANY, MORGAN BROWN ."

When the fighters were called to the middle of the ring by the referee, Danyluk was dancing around. He never once took his eyes off his opponent, even when they touched gloves.

At the sound of the bell, they went at it. Danyluk, being thin, was very wiry. He moved fast and his left jabs connected. The Irish cadet couldn't seem to catch him. When he tried to get inside, Danyluk let him have it with a right. It took the whole round for the Irish cadet to finally get inside and give Danyluk a left uppercut. It didn't land that well and Danyluk's right caught him square on the nose.

At the end of he first round, the Irish cadet's cheekbones were red. Genova jumped into the ring and Cunningham, handed him the stool. Cunningham also made a slight motion to Douglas that no one saw. Nothing was going to happen in this fight.

As Genova pulled out Brown's shorts to give him air, he also washed his fighter's face and chest with a wet towel. Cunningham, in the meantime, was flapping a towel in front of Brown's face.

Wayne got mad. "WHY DON'T YOU PUT YOUR HEAD IN THERE AND TAKE A GOOD LOOK?" He was referring to the fact that Genova had pulled Brown's shorts out a mile. "God. That guy's weird. I can't stand him."

In the other corner, Simpson was telling Danyluk what to do and what to look out for. Smoothy Stevens was helping out by flapping a towel and holding the spittoon.

East tapped Wayne on the shoulder. "I sure don't like the look of Genova. He looks sick."

All three of them smiled.

At the sound of the bell, Danyluk was out like a shot. His first right knocked Brown back about five feet. Danyluk was on him before he stopped against the ropes and gave him another right. Brown was now on the ropes and wide open to all of Danyluk's punches. They clenched and the referee separated them. Brown connected with a right uppercut that shook Danyluk a bit, but he kept jabbing and jabbing.

Blood started to appear out of Brown's nose at the same time Danyluk gave him a right cross that everyone could hear. That was it, Brown was down. He wasn't out, but the referee counted to ten and grabbed Danyluk's raised arm.

The crowd went wild. Danyluk was jumping up and down along with Sergeant Simpson and Smoothy Stevens. Genova was holding his stomach, he wasn't happy at all.

After Danyluk was announced the winner, Wayne whispered in Douglas' ear. "One down and three to go."

Diane's dad said that Danyluk should become a boxer and that he and Ellen had both enjoyed the fight. Tom's upper arm was red from all of Ellen's punching.

"IN THE BLUE CORNER, WEARING WHITE TRUNKS AND WEIGHING IN AT ONE-HUNDRED-AND-FIFTY POUNDS...FROM GUARD COMPANY, BARRACUDA BERGIE."

The audience responded tumultuously. It was obvious the spectators weren't happy with the Irish.

"AND IN THE RED CORNER, WEARING GREEN TRUNKS AND WEIGHING IN AT ONE-HUNDRED-AND-SIXTY-ONE POUNDS...FROM SIGNALS COMPANY, EDWIN SHANKS."

This time every cadet in Signals tried to drown out the boos coming from Charlie Company, but they weren't quite loud enough.

Bergie was cool and slow. He walked slowly to the centre of the ring and like Danyluk before him, never took his eyes off his opponent's eyes.

Shanks was good. He was a southpaw and the jabs from his right hand kept Bergie off guard, because he couldn't get used to jabs coming from that direction. Bergie was also too slow.

"DANCE A LITTLE," yelled Simpson. "DON'T LET HIM GET YOU ON THE ROPES. GET AWAY FROM HIM, BERGIE."

All of a sudden, WHAM, Bergie was down. The referee started counting but Bergie was up by the count of two and no sooner had the referee wiped off his gloves, the bell sounded.

Genova climbed into the ring slowly. He looked pale as if he wanted to throw up.

Cunningham glanced at Douglas and moved his head slowly so no one would notice. Nothing was going to happen in this fight either.

In the meantime, Danyluk had changed and was assisting Sergeant Simpson and Stevens in the Musketeer's corner.

"SECONDS OUT!"

Sergeant Simpson had done a good job between rounds. Bergie came out moving a lot faster this time. Also, he was staying away from Shank's right hand. Simpson had figured out the problem and Bergie was now dancing to his right, sort of in a circle.

Shanks was missing his jabs and Bergie was getting in some good shots with his right hand and moving swiftly.

Tom leaned over to Douglas. "I think Bergie was just feeling him out in that first round, he looks serious now."

"THAT'S THE OLD BERGIE," screamed Douglas. He had one arm around Diane and his other arm around Wayne. Both friends were getting squeezed in his excitement.

Shanks couldn't jab now and his left hand was stopped by Bergie's right. WHAM, Bergie connected with a right to the middle of Shanks' face. Shanks backed off and then started coming at him again. WHAM, Shanks had left himself wide open again and Bergie got him with the same punch.

Now Bergie was in the swing of things. He knew his opponent's style and as far as he was concerned, he was going to finish off the match quickly.

Bergie was wrong. Shanks was not the kind of person who backed off. He kept coming and landed a left hook on Bergie's chin, followed by a right uppercut. Bergie went flying onto the ropes and Shank was on him.

"GET OFF THE GOD D......!" Sergeant Simpson covered his mouth. "GET OFF THE ROPES, BERGIE!"

Danyluk jumped up and down. "DID YOU HEAR THE SERGEANT? HE KNOWS YOUR NAME."

Bergie must have heard Danyluk, because he connected with a full-force right on Shanks' nose again and followed through with two hard jabs to Shanks' stomach. When Shanks tried to stop the stomach blows with his jabbing hand, Bergie gave him a hard jab to the face. Blood was running from Shanks' hose as the bell rang.

Danyluk got into the ring with Simpson. While the Sergeant was coaching, Moose washed off his friend and Stevens held the spittoon.

In the other corner, Genova was nowhere in sight. Cunningham was just washing his fighter's face and smiling.

"It must be working on Genova," Wayne said.

In the final round, Shanks tried to get close in. He kept clenching Bergie, but the referee separated them each time. The crowd had difficulty containing their enthusiasm. They could smell blood and the finish of the match. All of Charlie's Cadets were on their feet, including Tom, Ellen, the girls, and the Musketeers.

Bergie didn't have to move to his right anymore, his method of ducking allowed him to start a continuous stream of jabs with his left hand and they were all on the 'nose.'

Just as Tom said they should end the fight, Bergie gave his opponent a right uppercut and Shanks went down. He got up slowly on wobbly knees. The referee looked at Shanks' right eye and moved the fighters to neutral corners.

Three quarters of the spectators were on their feet cheering as Bergie jumped around with his right hand in the air. When the referee announced him as the winner, the sounds of "GUARD, GUARD, GUARD, GUARD," filled the place to the rafters.

"That was almost, no, not almost, that WAS the real thing," Tom said. "You have to pay damned good money to see matches like that."

Douglas smiled. "I don't know if you'll say the same about the next two."

"IN THE BLUE CORNER, WEARING WHITE TRUNKS AND WEIGHING IN AT ONE HUNDRED AND NINETEEN POUNDS. FROM GUARD COMPANY, RIPPER ROTHSTEIN."

All the people in the hangar except Signals Company were cheering and waving their arms.

"AND IN THE RED CORNER, WEARING GREEN TRUNKS AND WEIGHING IN AT ONE-HUNDRED-AND-FIFTY-THREE POUNDS. FROM SIGNALS COMPANY, SEAN O'SHAUGHNESSY."

The boos were loud, and they drowned out the cheers from Genova's company.

Diane noticed Douglas fidgeting. "What's wrong?"

He smiled and put his arm around her. "I'm not too certain what's going to happen in these next two fights."

When the bell rang, O'Shaughnessy was definitely out for Rothstein's blood. Now Genova was having fun. He was yelling and screaming, "HIT HIM, HIT HIM."

O'Shaughnessy didn't need any coaching, he was hitting him and Rothstein was being knocked all over the ring.

O'Shaughnessy wasn't a dancer, he took large paces and always made certain he had his feet firmly planted on the mat.

Rothstein was now trying to stay away from him, but his opponent, who was both heavier and taller, didn't allow him to get away, and was on him every second.

In the whole first round, Rothstein only managed to get one good punch in. But to do that, he had to get close and take four punches because O'Shaughnessy had a much longer reach.

At the bell, Rothstein's face was a bit of a mess. Douglas saw Simpson asking him if he wanted the towel thrown in, but Rothstein shook his head. He was in for the duration.

Then the fun started. Cunningham passed the bottle of water to Genova who held it to his fighter's mouth. O'Shaughnessy took a big swig and nearly fell off his stool. He was standing up yelling and the bottle dropped. Genova was trying to find out what the problem was. He asked Cunningham for the bottle and took a swig himself. There was nothing wrong with it and he made it perfectly clear to O'Shaughnessy that everything was fine.

O'Shaughnessy was still yelling at both of them when "SECONDS OUT," was announced.

On the way out of the ring, Cunningham nodded slightly to Douglas at the same time as Genova let out a vociferous fart. He then turned around and gave Cunningham an accusing look trying to convince the people in the immediate area that the cadet had passed gas.

Cunningham acted as if nothing had happened and just carried on doing his job.

Wayne was out of control. "I gotta tell ya, that Cunningham is smooth."

Douglas couldn't answer, he was nearly in Diane's lap, he was laughing so hard.

The second round started out in O'Shaughnessy's favour, but halfway through, Rothstein got in some really good punches. The bleeding had stopped and he was much more serious in his intent to win.

Rothstein danced around O'Shaughnessy like a pro and although O'Shaughnessy was getting in a few jabs now and then, he wasn't landing the major punches he had in the first round.

Before the bell rang, Rothstein hit O'Shaughnessy with a straight right hand and sent him flying against the ropes.

Danyluk went wild. "ATTA BOY, ROTHIE!" In his excitement, he had his arm around Simpson.

O'Shaughnessy was still alluding something was wrong when Genova entered the ring and Cunningham passed up the chair.

"THERE'S NOTHING WRONG WITH THE WATER, YOU STUPID IDIOT. I DRANK SOME MYSELF, YOU SAW ME."

O'Shaughnessy started to get out of the ring, but the referee went over to his corner and talked to him. Then the referee took a swig from the bottle.

"It's all in your mind. That happens sometime when you take a hit."

"SECONDS OUT!"

Genova slipped the bottle to O'Shaughnessy again and this time the fighter spit it all over Genova and threw the bottle at Cunningham.

Cunningham picked up a towel and wiped off Genova. That O'Shaughnessy's got a screw loose," he told him.

"LET ME TASTE THAT GOD-DAMNED STUFF AGAIN," Genova said, reaching for the bottle in Cunningham's hand.

"THERE'S NOTHING WRONG WITH IT! I'LL HAVE HIS BALLS WHEN WE GET BACK TO THE BARRACKS."

Genova didn't make it back to the barracks that night. In fact, he scarcely made it out of the ring before it happened. He was putting his leg over the first rope when he let out another resounding fart and held his rear end. He stood there, in the half-in, half-out position, not knowing quite what to do.

The referee went over. "You're holding up the fight."

Genova was mortified. He gently climbed down holding his rear end and walked away stiff-legged.

"YA DIRTY THING YA," someone bellowed as he passed them on the way to the jon.

The fight was momentarily delayed until Cunningham got an assistant.

Wayne jumped up and threw his program into the air. "WE'VE DONE IT, GENOVA HAS SHIT HIMSELF!"

Although Tom and the girls were all smiling, they didn't have an inkling as to what was happening and no one told them.

Rothstein didn't fool around in the third round either. When he came out, he was all over O'Shaughnessy.

"Jesus, this kid can fight," Douglas remarked to Wayne.

Within the next three minutes, Rothstein pounded O'Shaughnessy all over the ring. He was getting even for the licking he had taken in the first round.

At the sound of the bell, both boxers went to their corners to await the decision.

Douglas could hear Cunningham. "I TOLD YA, THERE'S NOTHING WRONG WITH THE WATER."

The referee came back from the judges and asked both boxers to join him in the centre of the ring.

"THE WINNER BY A UNANIMOUS DECISION...THE RIPPER!"

Rothstein made the usual gesture of walking to his opponent's corner and tapping him on the head. Then he walked around the ring with a grin that would stop a bear, and both hands in the air. He had won and boy was he proud when the cheering started.

Cunningham was chewing gum and calmly looking at the referee with his thumbs up when Jackson came into the ring. The first part of the plan had been executed perfectly, now for second part.

"IN THE BLUE CORNER, WEARING THE BLUE TRUNKS AND WEIGHING IN AT ONE-HUNDRED-AND-TWENTY POUNDS. FROM GUARD COMPANY, JUGULAR JACKSON."

Earl raised both hands up into the air and smiled at the wild and enthusiastic crowd. So far it had been Charlie's night and he intended to keep it that way.

"AND IN THE RED CORNER, WEARING GREEN TRUNKS AND WEIGH-

ING IN AT ONE-HUNDRED-AND-FIFTY-FIVE POUNDS. FROM SIGNALS COMPANY...MICHAEL GRIFFIN."

Griffin's Company never had a chance in the cheering department, they were drowned out.

East tapped both Douglas and Wayne on their shoulders. "Look who's over at Jackson's corner."

"Hey, he came," replied Douglas.

Standing behind Earl's corner was Mr. Brewer, the man who had 'volunteered' the loan of the lantern.

"I feel sorry for Griffin," Wayne said, leaning over to Douglas and Tom.

Tom smiled, and Ellen asked why. When she didn't get a reply, she said, "What are you up to now, you little devils?"

Both Jackson and Griffin were fast. Although it was an even match at the start, Griffin had both a weight and reach advantage.

Simpson had taught his boys well. Jackson was landing punches with his right hand and he seemed to be having a field day jabbing Griffin's middle section with his left hand.

One of his jabs went a little low and he received a warning from the referee. This gave the cadets from Signals Company an opportunity to boo the dirty fighter who was roughing up their man.

Both fighters were about even on the judges' scoring cards when the bell rang to end the first round.

Cunningham did a good up-top and indicted to Douglas that nothing needed to be done, 'yet.'

The second round was tougher for Jackson. Right at the start, Griffin landed some heavy right-hand crosses and the last one sent Earl flying across the ring. As he bounced off the ropes, he fell into a barrage of more right-hand shots. Griffin wasn't fooling around, he knew he had to make up for the other Irish boxers and as far as he was concerned, he was going to hammer this guy Jackson into the ground.

When the bell rang, Earl had a bloody nose and a cut on his cheek. The referee looked at it and didn't seem worried.

In between rounds, Sergeant Simpson worked on Earl's face and instructed him on tactics.

"Let the guy think you're going one way and then with a jerk, reverse your movement and hammer him."

Douglas noticed Cunningham nodding to Danyluk who was in the ring helping Simpson. As Jackson headed back into the 'lions den' he heard Danyluk yelling, "HIT HIS GUT, HIT HIS GUT."

It took Jackson ten seconds to get his chance. When he finally did hit his opponent's midsection, Griffin's shorts fell down to his ankles and he tripped over them.

Griffin was helpless. He tried to get up but he couldn't. As he lay there wearing nothing but an athletic supporter, he kept trying to pull up his shorts, but he couldn't do that either because he had boxing gloves on.

The roar of the crowd was deafening, "FLASHER, FLASHER, FLASHER, FLASHER."

The referee helped him up, yanked up his shorts and helped him to his corner. Griffin's face was scarlet, not from the punches Jackson had delivered, but from the embarrassment of lying there in front of the crowd wearing only a jockstrap.

Earl had gone over to a neutral corner and was yelling at Simpson and Danyluk. They, in turn, were looking at where Douglas and Wayne were sitting, but only Douglas was waving back. Wayne was outside getting some air. His stomach was sore from laughing and had this been in B-21, he would probably have fallen out the window by now and Nine Platoon would have gone with him.

A few minutes later, round three began. Griffin wasn't as confident this time, he seemed to be favouring his waist. The referee had secured his trunks with a safety pin, but Griffin didn't trust it and sure as hell didn't want to end up on the canvas again.

WHAM, Jackson got him square on the chin and he went into the ropes. Once again Griffin's shorts started to slip, so they called another halt to the fight while a second safety pin was installed.

When the fight was over, the judges called it a draw. Both boxers held their hands high in the air and hugged each other as the crowd applauded and cheered.

When Earl left the ring, he received an embrace from Mr. Brewer and a slap on the back from all of his friends. When he walked to the back of the stage to change, his chest was out and his chin was up. He had upheld his part of the bargain like his three predecessors; this was the proudest moment of his life.

The next six bouts were just as exciting, and the group of them stayed to watch. When they were over, Diane's parents went for a drink in the Sergeants' Mess and the Musketeers took the girls into the Cadet Canteen for a pop.

There were quite a few civilians in the Cadet Canteen that night, so the wolf whistles weren't limited to just the Musketeers' girls.

Lyons rushed in with Foster and congratulated the boxers. Foster said that Genova was nowhere to be found after the 'accident.' That was confirmed later, when Diane's parents returned from the Sergeants' Mess and told the couples that the 'welcoming committee' was disappointed he didn't turn up. Tom laughed when he described how the Camp Regimental Sergeant-Major, Mr. Gardiner, had asked for Genova when he entered the Mess.

"WHERE'S SHITTY? OH, HE'S NOT HERE? SEND OUT A SEARCH PARTY, THERE MUST BE FEW HUNDRED TOILETS IN THIS CAMP?"

The commotion in the barracks that night was like a busy Hollywood set. All the cadets were taking pictures of their 'heroes' and Danyluk looked and felt like a movie star when he was asked to sign autographs.

Amid the brooms, buckets, mops, garbage, clothes, towels, and whatever else was lying around the barracks, the cadets of Charlie Company lifted up their four idols, one by one, and carried them into the showers. The water was ice-cold but it didn't seem to dampen the enthusiasm and exhilaration on the faces of Bergie, Danyluk, Rothstein and Jackson. An atomic bomb exploding couldn't have taken the smiles off their faces either.

When a Corporal came into the barracks to announce lights would be out in ten minutes, the looks he received, combined with the threat of a sudden shower, changed his mind promptly. He knew unless he relented, he'd have to change before going to the Junior Ranks Club.

"ALRIGHT, ALRIGHT! LIGHTS OUT IN HALF AN HOUR."

Both sides of the barracks were gathered around the boxers' end of the hut after the Corporal left. Shortly, Sergeants Beckford and Simpson came in with the other NCOs and Officers to have their pictures taken with the celebrities. Danyluk was amazed to hear Sergeant Beckford say 'yes' when he asked the Sergeant if he wanted his autograph.

When the lights finally did go out, Cunningham snuck in and said, "O.K., I've paid you back for the assistance you gave me at the guardroom. We're even now. That means no special favours in the stuke games on the way home." He then shook their hands and left.

"How did we do it?" a cadet asked.

Bergie became the spokesman because he was the mastermind of the plan.

"Well, we knew we were going to have a problem with their last two fighters. Genova wasn't playing fair with the weight advantage they had, so we had to cut the pie a little more even."

"But how did you do it?"

"If we were going to win or draw the last two fights, we realized we had to distract and throw O'Shaughnessy and Griffin off guard. To do that, we needed Cunningham's cooperation. He had three bottles, not one. One bottle was filled with plain water, another was filled with water and lemon juice and the third bottle was filled with a diarrhea-causing liquid in water. The bottles looked identical and only Cunningham knew which was which. As it turned out, Rothstein might have beaten O'Shaughnessy without the 'prop,' however, after taking two swigs of lemon juice, O'Shaughnessy lost his cool and that's all Rothie needed.

"So when the referee took a sip, all he got was plain water?"

That's right. But when Genova took a sip, he got the bottle with the diarrhea liquid in water. It tasted like water and he didn't have a clue."

"So that's what made Genova shit himself?"

Bergie chuckled. "No, that only assisted. Danyluk talked his favorite kitchen girl into getting Ex-Lax, or something similar, put into Genova's food in the Sergeants' Mess. He probably had the shits before he went to the fights. Did you see him, he looked pale as hell?"

"Incredible," the cadet said, wringing his hands with glee.

"So taking a few swigs of the mixture was the final straw in getting him to shit himself?"

"Exactly," Bergie replied.

"But how did you get Griffin's shorts to fall down?"

"Ah, that's where Cunningham really excelled. When he pulled out Griffin's shorts to let him breathe a little easier, he snipped the elastic band just to the point where it would break. That's why Danyluk kept yelling at Jackson to hit him in the gut. Not below the waist, at the waist. For a moment we didn't think it would work, but it did. If something went wrong, we had a backup plan. Smoothy Stevens had given us some sneezing powder to put on Jackson's gloves. As it turned out, we didn't need it."

"Wouldn't you call that cheating?"

"Bergie gave the cadet a look of disgust. "No, you dummy, not in this case. The Irish thought they could beat the shit out of our guys because of their weight, height, and reach advantage. Don't think for a moment Genova didn't know what he was doing. He was the one who paired them together in the first place. If anyone was trying to cheat, it was him."

"You mean he waited until he found out the size and weight of our guys?"

"You've got that right. He knew we could beat the guys whose bunk we moved, that's why he asked for four fighters. When he found out the size of our guys, he made his move."

Bergie had been sitting up in his bed. Now he lay down and rolled over on his side.

"My dad always tells me that old age and treachery will overcome youth and skill. In this case, youth and skill overcame Genova's old age and treachery. Right?"

"RIGHT!"

When the cadets had returned to their bunks, Wayne leaned over.

"You know, Doug, Bergie really is a genius. It's too bad he's not a Duke?"

Douglas snickered. "We've made him an honorary Duke. I wonder where Genova is now?"

"He's probably face down in some shitter were he belongs. G'night, Doug."

"G'night, Wayne."

CHAPTER XVI

The last week in camp was like Heaven for its twelve hundred inhabitants. There was only a bit of training and for some reason, even the meals tasted better.

Guard Company did not have to get up early in the morning to run and do pushups with Sergeant Simpson. As a matter of fact, drill practices were limited to only an hour a day on the parade square.

The timetable was confirmed and all cadets were notified that the final Graduation Parade would be held Thursday night at Polson Park. In addition to displays by Driver-Mech and Signals, Charlie Company would show the townspeople of Vernon what a Guard of Honour looked like and they would fire the 'feu de joie' (fire of joy). They looked forward to this demonstration because they had practised it all summer.

After breakfast, every cadet in camp was on the sports field playing soccer, volleyball and baseball. The four best baseball teams in camp played off to see which company won the trophy. It was a tough fight between the Guard and Signals, but Genova's company won. If the Guard had won, plans were made so that Sergeant Beckford would be carried around on the shoulders of the winning team. It could never be said that the same thing would happen with Signals. They carried their Officer Commanding around. Signals Company worried if they carried Genova, he'd shit on them. Not that he didn't do that all of the time anyway, but this time, it would be literally.

In the afternoon, all cadets in the camp went swimming either at Kin Beach or Kalamalka Beach. During the trip it was proven once again that some people never learn. When the trucks rolled through town, the townsfolk had to 'bare' witness to the antics of the 'chosen' few who insisted in performing the 'bare-bottom parade.'

This time, hundreds of cadets had their P.T. shorts pulled down and they couldn't get them up because the usual running shoe belonging to a seated comrade was stomping on the crotch.

When the guard arrived at Kin Beach, Moose was caught up a tree above the girls' changing shack. He had taken his camera with him to get some 'good' pictures and he knew if the company staff caught him, there wouldn't be a problem.

No such luck. No sooner had he snapped a few when the Camp RSM, who had decided to visit the beach, caught him.

As things turned out, no girls were in the changing shack, just a group of elderly ladies who decided it would be nice to have a day at the beach. Their screams attracted Mr. Gardiner.

"GET DOWN HERE!"

"ARE YOU SOME KIND OF PERVERT?"

"No, Sergeant-Major."

"ARE YOU A SEX MANIAC?"

"No, Sergeant-Major."

"AREN'T YOU ONE OF THOSE NUDISTS I FOUND OUTSIDE OF B-21 AND THE ONE WHO KEEPS SALUTING ME?"

"Yes, Sergeant-Major."

"MY GOD MAN, IF YOU'RE LIKE THIS NOW, WHAT WILL YOU BE LIKE WHEN YOU'RE OLDER?"

"Probably become a doctor, Sir."

"A DOCTOR! WHAT KIND OF A DOCTOR, A HORSE DOCTOR?"

"No, Sir, a gynaecologist."

"CHRIST, I PITY YOUR PATIENTS. WHAT IS THE ATTRACTION OF TAKING PICTURES OF ELDERLY LADIES?"

"Er, I was only taking pictures of the trees, Sir."

"WHAT?"

"The study of human anatomy, Sir. Beauty has no barrier."

"GET OUT OF MY SIGHT, YOU MISCHIEVOUS SCOUNDREL AND MAKE SURE YOU APOLOGIZE TO THE LADIES."

Danyluk marched over to the ladies. "I'm very sorry ladies."

The RSM walked over, as well. "I must apologize for the inconvenience he's caused. He was taking pictures of birds' nests."

Bergie got a kick out of that. "HEY DANYLUK, THAT'S WHAT YOU SHOULD HAVE TOLD THE RSM IN THE FIRST PLACE. THEY'RE THE SAME THING AREN'T THEY?"

By the end of the day, Moose couldn't live it down.

"There's that pervert Danyfuk," some cadet said. "He takes pictures of old women and gets his jollies off."

It seemed no one wanted to know Danyluk. No one, that is, except every cadet in Charlie Company. That night he was mobbed by cadets asking him for copies of any pictures he had taken.

"That'll be fifty cents a print and if you want to place your order, the line forms in front of my bunk. The first lady was only in her sixties, I should charge seventy five cents for her."

Moose was back to normal.

On Tuesday, the whole camp participated in sports and swim eliminations at Kalamalka Beach and Polson Park. This was every cadet's chance to prove he could be a winner.

After breakfast, all companies in camp marched down to Polson Park, with the band leading. The line was so long that cadets were still leaving the camp at the same time as companies were turning into the park. It looked like a scene from the Second World War, with soldiers marching to their embarkation point. The only difference was, these 'soldiers' were wearing white T-shirts, blue P.T. shorts, white running shoes with heavy wool socks, and pith-helmets.

By noon, it had been decided which cadets would participate in the various meets the following day.

When the trials ended, the line going up the hill blocked traffic for five miles. The band kept up a fairly brisk pace, so more perspiration was shed during the walk up than on the playing field.

In the afternoon, all cadets in camp were trucked to Kal Beach where the swim eliminations were held. The City of Vernon had been kind enough to block off the wharf for the cadets to use. The civilians, unhappy about it at first, seemed to get a better understanding when twelve hundred cadets arrived with staff.

At five o'clock that night, the camp was trucked back for supper. It had been a long, hot day for the cadets of the Vernon Army Cadet Camp, and the normal banter heard at suppertime was almost nonexistent as the tired cadets picked up their trays and walked listlessly, like robots, past the food servers.

On Wednesday morning, the trucks arrived after breakfast to take all cadets to Kalamalka Beach for the swim meet.

Every girl in town going out with a cadet turned up and many brought parents along. The beach was jam-packed from end to end. It was nearly impossible to find one square metre of sand that didn't have a blanket covering it.

One by one, the events took place. The sound of the starter's gun and the voice coming over the loudspeakers kept participating cadets on their toes.

All the Musketeers were entered in the competitions and by noon, Douglas had won a medal for the back- stroke and Wayne had won one for the breast-stroke.

Between events, the Musketeers had the opportunity to get together with their girls. Ellen brought a huge lunch basket crammed with everything from sandwiches to pies. She knew seven teenaged boys could deplete the beach store, so she had planned appropriately. What she never counted on was Jack East's appetite. Jack ensured he received more than his fair share from the basket, and he and his girl made regular trips to the concession stand for hotdogs.

Earl felt really proud that day because Mr. Brewer turned up and brought along all the kids from the reserve who had taken the Musketeers riding. When Earl was in an event, Mr. Brewer's voice cheering him on was one of the loudest. It wasn't long before it became a little raspy, but he didn't let such a minor ailment dampen his enthusiasm for Earl's efforts, or for that matter, the Musketeers' efforts, as well. Earl had made some fine new friends for life and he was really grateful they had attended just to see him.

The civilians who had grumbled the day before now understood the importance of the affair and joined in, cheering along with the invading army.

As the Musketeers and their friends ate lunch together during the lunch break, Diane whispered in Douglas' ear.

"Have you forgotten something?"

Douglas looked puzzled. He knew he had a sunburn because he hadn't put enough lotion on, but other than that, he didn't know to what she was referring.

"No, I don't think so."

Diane laughed. "OH, YES YOU HAVE, DOUGLAS BRICE." She really had to scream to be heard over the noise.

"Happy Birthday, Doug," she said, handing him a beautifully wrapped present and kissing him on the forehead.

Douglas collapsed. "Jeez, how could I...I..." He was lost for words because he had totally forgotten it was his birthday. Ever since he'd been in Canada, only his mom and Wayne ever celebrated it. The fact that Diane cared, really hit him emotionally. A sentimental look came over his face. "You bought a present...for me? I...what?"

"Don't say anything, Doug, just open it."

Smiling, he opened the present in a hurry and held out a sterling silver chain bracelet. The engraving read, 'Happy 15th Birthday, from Diane. August 1953. I love you very much.'

Tears rose in his eyes. He was dumbfounded, so he just shook his head and smiled at her. Finally he said, "Thank you. I...I don't know what to say."

The look on Douglas' face revealed his feelings to his gathered friends, and there was silence as he held her in his arms and hugged her for a moment.

The quiet didn't last long. Although they couldn't drown out the crowd with their cheering, the Musketeers, Tom and the girls placed Douglas on one of the blankets and gave him fifteen royal bumps. Because of the soft sand, they were relatively gentle compared to those Rothstein received in Glenemma, however Douglas had doubts at times whether he'd be caught, or sent flying.

Rothstein was one of the lifters. With a smile, he said, "Now you know what it feels like."

As Douglas was flung into the air, he blew kisses to Diane and kept saying, "Thank you, I love you."

At the end of the day, Guard Company had won the most medals and Colonel St. Laurent congratulated them in front of thousands of cheering cadets and civilians.

When it was time to return to camp, they said their farewells and informed the girls they were confined to barracks that night but would see them at the sports meet the following day at Polson Park.

Once again, Diane and the other girls waved hard until the trucks were out of sight.

The conversation at supper that night centred around the number of medals Charlie Company had won compared to the other companies.

"We're not only the best company in camp, we're the best company in swimming as well," stated Danyluk.

He had won two diving medals and another for a relay swim with his partner, Bergie.

"Why the hell are we confined to camp tonight?" asked Wayne.

"Because we've got to put in an hour on the parade square practising the feu de joie and our kit has to be perfect for Thursday's parade," Bergie replied.

"There's something else," said Earl. "Have you guys forgotten we're having a company picnic tonight at Kin Beach from eight to eleven?"

East grinned. "Yeah, there's hotdogs, watermelon, pop, hot chocolate, cookies and chocolate bars."

Earl glared at him. "Trust you to think of your stomach while you're having dinner."

The company picnic had slipped their minds. Now, they were looking forward to it.

"Are you going to take your camera?" Rothstein asked Moose.

Danyluk put on his sneaky grin.

"I was just thinking about it, but with my luck, Gardiner would be there again."

After supper, the company practised on the parade square from 1800 until 1900 and then the members worked on their personal kit until 2000 hours. At 2030, the trucks arrived and a singing Charlie Company headed to Kin Beach. This was their night.

There was a jovial overthrow of authority at the beach. All the company officers, non-commissioned officers and half the cadets in the company got tossed into the water. In addition, the company staff members served all the food.

"Jesus, they are human," Moose told Bergie.

At midnight, the trucks returned with Charlie's chorus distributed evenly in the trucks.

It was cold in the backs of the trucks, but stories and song warmed up the revellers. When they passed the guardroom, the canvas on that side of the trucks was rolled up, and each truck sported ten 'smiling' bare-faced bottoms, facing the shack.

When four Provost Corporals came out to see what all the commotion was about, it almost looked like the rear-ends were singing "Oh Provost, Oh Provost."

The sports meet on Thursday was just as successful for Charlie Company as the swim meet the day before. Charlie won the majority of the events and Colonel St. Laurent commended them on the high spirit in the company.

"It would appear that this company never gives up," he said.

Although only certain cadets were entered in the various events, everyone in camp had attended. When they were fallen out, the spectator stands at Polson Park were full of cheering cadets and civilians.

Danyluk won the mile run, and Bergie won all of the jumping events. Although the tug-of-war was close, Charlie won it in the end, and Genova, who didn't shit himself this time, was really upset.

Douglas, Wayne, Rothstein, East and Jackson won medals for the relay races and East and Jackson also won medals for the javelin throw, and the long jump. Rothstein also won a medal for the 100 yard dash, and established a new camp record.

Although jubilation was in the air throughout the meet, all the cadets knew camp was coming to a close and in their hearts, they were a little sad.

While the events were taking place, hundreds of cadets sat with their girls or walked hand-in-hand, talking about the previous six weeks of fun.

Douglas and Diane were no exception. Between events, he never left her side. Diane was very quiet. She just wanted to be near him and nothing else mattered.

Douglas felt the same way, but he had been trained to snap out of a daze when his name was called and his company's honour was on the line.

When the meet ended, Sergeant Beckford, who rarely ever got hoarse on the parade square, couldn't talk. He had cheered so much his throat had finally worn out.

"The Graduation Parade is at seven o'clock tonight. It would be wise if you got here early to get a good seat," Douglas advised Diane.

"Your mom still couldn't make it?"

Douglas shook his head. "No, she can't get off work, but I'm going to make sure she sees this country soon."

When the camp RSM screamed for everyone to fall in, Douglas kissed her and ran for the ranks, yelling, "DID I TELL YA I LOVE YA?"

"YEAH AND YOU KNOW YOU DON'T NEED ANY ANSWER!"

As they marched away behind the band, Charlie Company was singing and the girls were wiping their eyes and waving.

It was an early supper that night and Danyluk couldn't believe his eyes.

"Can you believe this, they're giving us steak again? The first two weeks, all we got was spaghetti and meatballs and now we're getting steak nearly every night. Is it possible they want us back next year?"

Actually Danyluk's steak was bigger than the rest because he got special treatment from his girl who was serving.

Bergie looked at his own plate and then at Danyluk's.

"Christ, your steak is three times the size of ours. I think I'm going to complain to the management of this fine establishment." He snapped his fingers to an imaginary person and yelled, "GARÇON! GARÇON!"

Rothstein stood up with a glass of water. "Well, guys, we did it. I think we deserve a toast. TO US!"

The other six stood up. "TO US!" Then they touched glasses and sipped their water before sitting down again.

Danyluk ripped into his steak because he saw East eyeing it, as he said, "THE C IN CHARLIE STANDS FOR CREAM OF THE CROP!"

"After we've finished with the parade tonight, there's a movie in B-3," Earl said, as he stood up to go back for seconds.

"What is it?" asked Wayne. He knew how Jackson devoured Routine Orders, so if anyone knew, it would be Earl.

"It's *Road to Bali*, with Bob Hope, Bing Crosby and Dorothy Lamour."

Moose wiped his mouth. "WHAT? DOROTHY LAMOUR? I'D WALK OVER A THOUSAND MILES OF RED HOT COALS JUST TO HOLD HER HAND."

"With your boots on, of course?" quipped Bergie.

"Of course. You don't think I'd want to burn my feet, do you? There's a limit to what this man does for dames."

Douglas tapped Wayne on his head with a fork. "We'll just have time to hand in our rifles before the movie starts."

Jackson shook his head. "I never thought I'd want to see the inside of that building again."

"Ya tied, didn't ya?" Bergie said, pointing his fork with a large piece of steak on the end. "It could have been slaughtersville, you know?"

"Bergie, you've already had your kiss," Earl replied.

"What? If there's any kissing to be done around here, I'll be doing it with my little kitchen darling. She says I owe her one for arranging the Ex-Lax in Genova's food."

When he heard that, Bergie almost spit his coffee out over the table.

"You mean she does the dirty work and you get the benefits? Danyluk, you lucky creep."

Danyluk leaned back on the back two legs of his chair with his chest out.

"Luck isn't involved. Someone has to do it for Queen, Country and Charlie Company. That someone will be me. I know it's going to be tough, but my skin is thick enough."

"You can say that again," said Bergie. Especially the skin on the end of your knob."

"When are you going to do it?" asked East.

"Hey, that's a very personal question. Do I ask you anything when you sneak the National Geographic into the jon?"

"No, that's because I never get to see it. You've usually got it."

"I'll get around to her as soon as my strength returns."

Rothstein's interest was aroused. "What's she like?"

Danyluk's face turned serious. "She's not bad, but it's murder because I'm sore for days afterwards."

Now Rothstein had a puzzled look on his face. "What do you mean sore? What's sore?"

Danyluk paused for a moment. "My leg of course. She likes to leg-wrestle."

Bergie laughed. "That's a weird looking leg. I wouldn't mind seeing hers."

Danyluk still had his chest out as he picked up his glass of milk. The glass stuck to the table for some reason, and when he pulled, the milk went all over him.

"SON OF A BITCH! WHAT THE HELL......?"

Jackson had put a rubber suction cup under the glass. It was stuck, all right. Stuck to the point that Danyluk was covered from hair to boots.

Jackson was already running toward the door.

"GOTCHA! THAT'S WHAT I OWED YA FOR THE SHITTER."

Danyluk went after him like a flash, but it wasn't a contest because Earl was the faster runner.

It was good to see Ellen and Tom at the sports and swim meets," Wayne said. "I thought they couldn't make them?"

"I didn't expect them either," Douglas replied. "I have a feeling they're getting attached to us. I know I'm certainly getting attached to them."

Wayne nodded. "They're really great folks."

After supper, Sergeant Beckford marched into the quarters and posted notices on the bulletin boards of both sides of the hut.

"I WANT EVERYONE READY BY 1815 TONIGHT. WE'LL DRAW WEAPONS THEN AND WE'LL BE READY TO MARCH TO POLSON PARK AT 1845. BE SHARP!" Then he marched out.

Jackson was the only one on his side of the hut that seemed interested. He sauntered over.

"HEY, HE'S POSTED THE RESULTS OF THE FINAL EXAMS AND EACH OF OUR STANDINGS IN THE COMPANY!"

The rush was on then, on both sides, as cadets shuffled together like the standup crowd behind the goal posts in a British soccer game. Each wanted to know his standing.

Douglas and Wayne were in the crowd, but Wayne was closer. "DOUG, DOUG, YOU'VE DONE IT! YOU'VE ACTUALLY DONE IT!"

Wayne didn't get excited very often but now he was jumping up and down like a Mexican jumping bean. "YOU'VE DONE IT!"

Douglas still couldn't get close. "What have I done?"

"YOU'VE GOT THE TOP MARKS IN THE COMPANY!" He grabbed Douglas' arm and pulled him in.

Douglas' heart was pounding as he read the results. His grin increased as his eyes moved down the paper. He had received 96 percent. The highest in the company.

"I CAN'T BELIEVE IT. WHERE DID YOU COME IN?"

"TAKE A LOOK, I GOT 86 PERCENT."

Everyone was patting Douglas on the back and congratulating him.

"We've all done pretty well," said Bergie. "Even Moose."

Danyluk was grinning and running his finger down the results. "What do you mean, even me? You only beat me by six percent."

Wayne was still reading. "JESUS, LOOK AT THIS AT THE BOTTOM, DOUG. THEY'VE MADE YOU THE GUARD COMMANDER FOR THE GRADUATION PARADE. YOU'VE MADE IT! YAHHOOOO!"

Douglas was speechless. He never dreamed for a minute that he'd done that well. Now he'd been appointed Guard Commander for the Graduation Parade.

He shook Wayne's hand, took his beret out of his pocket, and started running for the door.

"WHERE ARE YOU GOING?" Wayne yelled.

"I'M GOING TO PHONE MY MOM AND DIANE."

Wayne ran to grab his beret. "HOLD ON, I''M COMING WITH YOU."

Bergie yelled after them. "MAKE IT QUICK. WE'VE GOT A GRADUATION PARADE TONIGHT AND WE'RE SIGNING COURSE-REPORTS IN TEN MINUTES. YOU WANT TO SEE YOUR COURSE-REPORTS, DON'T YOU?"

Although the Guard looked perfect when 1815 rolled around, the barracks looked like a shambles. This didn't seem to bother the cadets, they were more concerned about their dress. Any one of them could have been selected to be the best dressed cadet at camp. Their shirts were starched, their pants were starched and soaped, their belts shone, and their boots gleamed like mirrors.

By 1845 all companies were formed up on the Parade Square and ready to march down to Polson Park.

Douglas faced the guard. "GUARD, STANDAT...EASE! GUARD ATTEN...TION! THE GUARD WILL FIX BAYONETS! FIX...BAYONETS! GUARD, ATTEN...TION! GUARD, STANDAT...EASE! STAND EASY!"

The Parade Commander was a cadet from the other side of B-21. He was a sharp cadet, "Even though he does belong to the Irish," Wayne had remarked earlier.

Any cadet in the guard could have been Guard Commander that night. They had practised for all those weeks; the words of command drilled into them daily. For this night, however, Douglas was the Guard Commander and he had carried out the preparatory procedures of taking over the guard from the Cadet Company Sergeant-Major, with precision.

Bergie was Second in Command, Wayne the Guard Sergeant-Major, Jackson and Rothstein were Guard Officers and East and Danyluk were Guard Sergeants. All the Musketeers were in leadership positions, with the rest of the positions of the Guard filled by cadets from other platoons.

The positions at the battalion level were filled by cadets from Signals, Driver-Mechanics, Charlie Company and other Instructor's Basic Training Companies.

With the preliminary battalion drill completed, the young Parade Commander faced everyone.

"PARADE, ATTEN...TION! GUARD, SLOPE...ARMS! THE PARADE WILL MOVE TO THE RIGHT IN COLUMN OF ROUTE. RIGHT...TURN!"

The Cadet Parade Commander moved as did all the other supernumeraries. When he was in front of the parade, he gave the final marching order.

"PARADE, BY THE LEFT...QUICK..MARCH!"

The band started to march and play, and the cadets of the Vernon Army Cadet Camp marched proudly behind it, through the camp and down the hill to Polson Park. This wasn't a sports parade. All arms were up, chins were up, and chests were out.

When they reached Polson Park, the scene was like a circus. Every officer and non-commissioned officer in camp was there along with what looked like the whole city of Vernon.

Military Police were everywhere, directing traffic with the local squad of the Royal Canadian Mounted Police.

The cadets looked sharp marching in, and forming up on the playing field in front of the covered bleachers.

Although he wasn't supposed to move his eyes or glance around, Douglas slowly surveyed the stands and saw Diane and her parents. The other Musketeers' girls were there as well.

The final parade carried on in the normal fashion. The Parade Commander accompanied Colonel St. Laurent on his inspection through the ranks. Although it was still very hot, Colonel St. Laurent stopped and talked to a lot of the cadets on parade, including Douglas.

"I see you've been made Guard Commander."

"Yes, Sir."

"And I understand you're the best cadet in the company?"

"Yes, Sir."

"We've come a long way since our episode with the birds, haven't we Douglas?"

Douglas couldn't stick his chest out far enough. The Commanding Officer had just called him by his first name.

"Yes, Sir."

"Are you coming back next year?"

"I wouldn't miss it for the world, Sir. Are you coming back, Sir?"

"No, I don't think I'll be back next year. Rumour has it that Brigadier W.J. Megill will be here. But I want you to know that I'm very proud of all of you."

"We're proud to be able to be here and represent Camp Vernon, Sir. There are a lot of traditions to be looked after."

"I know and from what I've seen this year, each and every one of you has looked after them. All the very best son."

"Thank you, Sir."

"No, let me thank you. The cadets in this camp are the future leaders of this great country of ours. Do you agree?"

"YES, SIR!"

The Commanding Officer continued with his inspection with the band playing softly as he moved through the ranks. Very few cadets passed out and none of Charlie's cadets had to be taken off parade.

After he finished his inspection and took the March Past, Colonel St. Laurent asked all the cadets to gather around him. He didn't like using a microphone, however, this time he did it so the visitors in the stands could hear him.

"I REALLY DID NOT KNOW WHAT TO EXPECT WHEN I WAS POSTED TO THIS CAMP FOR THE SUMMER. ONE OF MY FELLOW OFFICERS EVEN CALLED ME A BABY SITTER WHEN HE LEARNED I WAS COMING HERE.

"WELL, LET ME TELL YOU THIS. I HAVE WORKED WITH REGULAR FORCE TROOPS ALL OVER THE WORLD AND I AM UNDENIABLY PROUD THAT I WAS GIVEN THIS OPPORTUNITY TO WORK WITH YOU AND TO COMMAND CAMP VERNON. AS FAR AS I AM CONCERNED, YOU HAVE DEMONSTRATED TO ME AND ALL OF MY OFFICERS AND NCOs, THAT YOU CAN HOLD YOUR OWN AGAINST REGULAR FORCE TROOPS AT ANY TIME."

A loud cheer rose from the cadets and spectators.

"WHILE YOU HAVE BEEN WORKING VERY HARD LEARNING THE MILITARY WAY OF LIFE, I HAVE ALSO BEEN LEARNING. I HAVE LEARNED THAT YOU, THE YOUTH OF THIS GREAT COUNTRY, CAN AND WILL PROTECT THE TRADITIONS THAT WE SO DEARLY LOVE AND CHERISH.

"YOUR RESPONSIBILITY DOESN'T END THERE, HOWEVER, BECAUSE YOU HAVE AN OBLIGATION TO UPHOLD AND PROTECT CANADA'S HERITAGE. THAT HERITAGE IS THE FREEDOM OF OUR COUNTRY, THE CONSERVATION OF OUR CULTURE AND OUR SENSE OF FAIR PLAY. IT'S UP TO YOU TO SAFEGUARD OUR INDOMITABLE ASPIRATION TO ASSIST OTHERS IN OBTAINING DELIVERANCE FROM WHAT SOME HISTORIANS HAVE CALLED, 'THAT LONG DARK TUNNEL THAT LEADS TO LIBERTY AND FREEDOM.'

"FROM WHAT I HAVE OBSERVED OVER THESE PAST SIX WEEKS, THE CITIZENS OF CANADA WILL NEVER HAVE TO CONCERN THEMSELVES ABOUT OUR COUNTRY'S FUTURE. YOU HAVE PROVEN TO ME THAT CANADA WILL BE IN VERY GOOD HANDS FOR YEARS TO COME.

"I HAVE WATCHED YOU AT WORK AND AT PLAY. I HAVE SEEN YOU FIX AND DRIVE TRUCKS, SET UP COMMUNICATIONS AND ATTACK AN UNSEEN ENEMY WITH VIGOUR SECOND TO NONE. THERE WERE TIMES WHEN I WANTED TO JOIN YOU BECAUSE YOUR LAUGHTER WAS SO CONTAGIOUS. I'VE LAUGHED WITH YOU WHEN TIMES WERE HAPPY, AND I'VE CRIED WITH YOU WHEN THINGS WENT WRONG AT CAMP, OR IN YOUR HOME. I AM ELATED THAT I COULD SHARE THIS EXPERIENCE WITH YOU, SOMETIMES FROM A DISTANCE.

"YOU WERE NOT POSTED HERE LIKE I WAS. YOU VOLUNTEERED TO COME HERE OF YOUR OWN FREE WILL. WHEN YOU ARRIVED, I NOTICED THE EXPRESSIONS ON YOUR FACES. MOST OF YOU WERE PROBABLY SAYING TO YOURSELF, 'MY GOD, WHAT AM I DOING HERE?' BUT YOU STUCK IT OUT AND I SEE A DIFFERENT EXPRESSION ON YOUR FACES TODAY. I SEE EXPRESSIONS OF PRIDE, CONFIDENCE AND SELF-FULFILLMENT.

"I KNOW THAT YOU ARE PROUD. I WANT YOU TO KNOW THAT MY STAFF AND I ARE EQUALLY PROUD OF YOU.

"THANK YOU FOR JOINING ARMY CADETS AND FOR COMING TO VERNON. THANK YOU ALSO FOR THIS EXCELLENT PARADE.

"ALTHOUGH I'LL SEE MOST OF YOU OFF ON SATURDAY AND SUNDAY, MAY I TAKE THIS OPPORTUNITY TO WISH YOU THE VERY, VERY BEST IN THE FUTURE. GOOD-BYE, GOOD LUCK AND GOD BLESS YOU ALL."

When Colonel St. Laurent stepped back from the microphone, the Camp Regimental Sergeant-Major asked everyone to resume their positions.

In no time, cadets were back in their formations. A Right Dress was given and they were ready for the last part of the formal ceremony, the Advance In Review Order.

The march forward was completed with a General Salute and a Present Arms. The Commanding Officer looked as proud as a man could be, as he returned the salute. He even kept his hand up a little longer than usual, looking at the cadets.

When he put it down, the slope arms and order arms commands were given, then the Cadet Parade Commander said, "THREE CHEERS FOR COLONEL ST. LAURENT. HIP HIP HURRAY...HIP HIP HURRAY...HIP HIP HURRAY!"

The cheers were deafening as the Colonel saluted them again and walked away to the front row of the stands, where he would observe the various displays the cadets would exhibit.

Over the next hour, chosen cadets from the Driver-Mechanics, Signals and Instructor's Basic Training Companies demonstrated some of the knowledge they had learned at Vernon.

A jeep was taken apart and put back together by the D&M wing. Signals set up a remote nineteen-set display that was part of a telephone line-laying exercise, hooked into the loudspeaker system. IBT demonstrated an Advance to Contact Movement, using blank rounds.

The final display was reserved for the Guard. When everyone else was off the field, the guard marched on and completed numerous drill movements with only one word of command given at the start by Douglas.

Afterwards, they formed Two Deep and performed the feu de joie. It was completed exceptionally well. The three 'BBRRRRRRAAAAAACCCCKKKK,' 'BBRRRRRRAAAAAACCCCKKKK,' individual volleys of every rifle being fired one after another into the air were evenly timed throughout the front and rear ranks of the two guards.

The crowd really appreciated the displays and they applauded often throughout the evening.

When the demonstrations were over, the Cadet Parade Commander formed everyone up and handed the parade over to Mr. Gardiner, the Camp Regimental Sergeant-Major.

"Here's the guy who thinks we're the cat's meow," Danyluk whispered out of the side of his mouth to Bergie. "If he sees us, he's probably going to ask why we're not naked, or where my camera is."

"IT IS ALWAYS A DIFFICULT TASK DECIDING WHO THE BEST ALL-
ROUND CADET IS IN VERNON. HAVING WATCHED YOU TONIGHT
MAKES IT EVEN MORE DIFFICULT BECAUSE FROM WHAT I'VE SEEN, I
WOULD SAY THAT NINETY-FIVE PERCENT OF YOU COULD FIT INTO
THAT CATEGORY.
"OUR GUIDELINES FOR CHOOSING THE BEST CADET IN CAMP ARE
QUITE COMPLEX. HE MUST HAVE EXCELLENT MARKS, A GOOD
SENSE OF FAIR PLAY AND HE HAS TO GET ALONG WITH OTHERS
AND HELP THEM OUT. SOMEONE WHO IS TOTALLY UNSELFISH. SO IN
OTHER WORDS, WE HAD TO FIND SOMEONE WHO SITS ON THE RIGHT
SIDE OF GOD."
"MOST OF YOU HAVE BEEN TOLD THAT I AM GOD."
The hoots, whistling, and laughter coming from the ranks actually made Mr.
Gardiner smile. But it may have been a gas pain, no one will ever know.
"ACTUALLY, I'M ONLY HIS ASSISTANT AND I HOPE THAT DOESN'T
REVERSE THE IMAGE YOU HOLD OF ME. ONE OF REVERENCE,
ESTEEM ,NOTABILITY AND EMINENCE."
Cadets and visitors alike were laughing and clapping their hands.
"MY STAFF AND I HAVE WATCHED YOU ALL SUMMER.
UNFORTUNATELY, I HAVEN'T HAD THAT MUCH TIME BECAUSE I'VE
BEEN KEPT TOO BUSY WITH NUDISTS; SEX MANIACS WHO CLIMB
TREES; PEOPLE WHO LOVE CAMPING OUT ON THE PARADE SQUARE;
PEOPLE WHO LIKE BUILDING STILLS UNDER THE BARRACKS;
PEOPLE WHO LOVE PAINTING THE CANNON AND PUTTING OBJECTS
UP THE FLAGPOLE THAT BEAR NO MILITARY RESEMBLANCE TO
ANYTHING THAT I'VE EVER WITNESSED; CADETS WHO HAVE
SHAVED OFF HALF A MUSTACHE OF ONE OF OUR PROVOST
SERGEANTS......WHILE HE WAS SLEEPING....."
The cheers were loud.
"PEOPLE WHO INSIST IN LOOKING IN HOP SING'S WINDOW OR VIS-
ITING THE SILVER GRILL CAFÉ......"
The cheers became deafening.
"CADETS WHO LET THE AIR OUT OF MY TIRES; WHO HOOKED UP
MY OFFICE TELEPHONE TO HOP SING'S; WHO HAD CHINESE FOOD
DELIVERED TO THE COMMANDING OFFICER AT 0230; WHO ORDERED
THE LOCAL FUNERAL PARLOUR TO RESERVE A CASKET FOR A
CERTAIN MR. GARDINER AND LEFT MY OFFICE NUMBER; WHO CUT
ACROSS THE GOLF COURSE AND STARTED PLAYING GOLF; WHO PUT
LADDERS UP TO THE WINDOWS AT THE NURSING SISTERS'
QUARTERS; WHO BORROWED A JEEP AND WENT JOY-RIDING AT 0300;
WHO SENT A TELEGRAM TO THE COMMANDING OFFICER SAYING
THAT BRITISH LIEUTENANT-GENERAL JONATHON RAMMINGTON-
SMYTHE WILL BE ARRIVING IN CAMP; WHO PUT A SKUNK UNDER
THE OFFICERS' MESS, AND TRIP-WIRE AT THE BOTTOM OF THE

SERGEANTS' MESS STAIRS. TO NAME BUT A FEW OF THE MATTERS THAT KEPT ME BUSY DURING THE SUMMER. I WOULD MENTION MORE BUT THERE ARE LADIES PRESENT IN THE AUDIENCE."
The RSM paused to let the laughter die down.
"BUT WE HAVE DECIDED ON ONE PERSON. WILL CADET GLEN PINEHURST FROM D&M COME FORWARD PLEASE."
"SIR!" A cadet from Driver-Mechanics marched forward to the RSM. The cadet battalion went wild as he passed and the spectators in the stands stood up out of respect.
As Pinehurst marched up, the RSM spoke into the microphone again. "AND THE RUNNER-UP IS CADET DOUGLAS BRICE, FROM IBT. WILL BRICE COME FORWARD PLEASE."
"SIR!" Douglas marched forward, his heart pounding.
Charlie Company let it be known who Brice was. The cadets in all of the other companies then started yelling again.
The Commanding Officer presented the trophies to Pinehurst and Brice.
"CADETS PINEHURST AND BRICE, ON BEHALF OF ALL THE STAFF AND CADETS OF THE VERNON ARMY CADET CAMP AND THE MERCHANTS OF VERNON WHO DONATED THESE TROPHIES, MY CONGRATULATIONS ON A JOB WELL DONE."
Photographers from the Vernon News (later to become The Vernon Daily News) took pictures of them with Colonel St. Laurent and Mr. Gardiner. Afterward, when the trophies were removed, they saluted and returned to their companies. The response from the crowd could not be contained.
Douglas' knees were wobbling as he approached the Guard. Not only did he have an astonished grin, so did the company.
"You see, they accepted my recommendation," said Danyluk.
"THE BEST CADET AND RUNNER-UP TROPHIES WILL ALWAYS BE KEPT HERE AT VERNON. THEY WERE DONATED BY THE MERCHANTS OF THIS CITY AND WE THANK THEM FOR THEIR GENEROSITY," the RSM continued.
"BOTH CADETS HAVE BEEN GIVEN A MINIATURE TROPHY OF THE ORIGINAL."
Over the next fifteen minutes, trophies were presented to the best cadet in each company and for the best shot in camp. Douglas had to make two additional trips to the awards' table. It was the proudest day of his life.

The march up the hill that night appeared only to be a few steps for Douglas. His mind was fully absorbed with the presentations and the fact that Diane had witnessed it all.
When the Guard was dismissed after handing in rifles, Diane rushed up to him and put her hands around his neck. His face was red and he was smiling but words couldn't come out. He was speechless.
"Douglas Brice, you told me about being best cadet in the company but you

didn't tell me about the other awards."

Douglas was rubbing his rear end from the three royal bumps he'd received outside the weapons' stores.

"It was a shock to me also. I keep thinking someone has made a mistake. There are much better cadets here than me."

Diane still had her arms around his neck and he had his arms around her waist, when Tom approached.

"Hearing you say that tells me that you deserved them," Tom said shaking Douglas' hand.

Both Diane and Ellen gave him kisses, so now he had lipstick prints all over his face.

Ellen surprised them when she gave Douglas a bone-crushing squeeze. "Who could have told us that Diane was bringing home the second best cadet in camp?"

That night at the movie and Cadet Canteen, the Musketeers congratulated themselves. Each one of them ranked in the top 80 percent. Only twelve guys failed the course and they weren't from Nine Platoon.

The jubilation and feeling of pride made it a night to remember.

When the visitors left at midnight, B-21 looked like a stadium after a football game. The shack was cluttered as the Musketeers sat on Douglas' bunk.

Although the Officers and NCOs had already congratulated Douglas and the Guard at the Cadet Canteen, they were in the quarters also.

"Only one day to go," Danyluk remarked. "Oh, God, it's going to be nice to lie in my own bed at home and not have to listen to Sergeant Simpson screaming, 'STAND BY YOUR BEDS!'"

He knew Sergeant Simpson could hear him.

"Wrong. I've made arrangements with your mom and dad to move into your house for a year to straighten you out."

Danyluk went pale. "You're joking?"

Simpson was smiling. "I'll never tell."

"Danyluk's not going home," said Bergie. "He's getting a job as a gardener in an institution for unwed mothers. That way he can marry them all and become a polygamist."

"WHO'S GOT A DICTIONARY?" Danyluk screamed.

East was eating a banana. "No Bergie. He should be in an institution where women are unable to get pregnant. He'd solve the problem in no time."

Bergie looked at Sergeant Simpson. "What time are we up tomorrow, Sergeant?"

Simpson looked at his watch. "At five-thirty for P.T."

Bergie laughed. "Sergeant, you're wrong. They wouldn't get us up at that time on the last training day."

Sergeant Simpson put his hand on Bergie's shoulder. "There's something you have to understand, Bergie, my boy. I'm a Sergeant and Sergeants are never wrong. We're sometimes incorrect, mind you, but we're never wrong."

Simpson smiled and walked away as Douglas wrote down Simpson's phrase in his book. He started a new section called 'Simpson's Concepts.'

Danyluk was getting undressed to have a shower.

"Now see what you've done, Bergie. We'll probably have to get up at five-thirty tomorrow. When are you going to learn? There would be no P.T. if you hadn't asked."

"When am I going to learn? Here I've been protecting your ass all summer and you ask me when I'm going to learn. Well, let me tell you something, Moose........."

Wayne laughed. "They're at it again, Doug. Do you want to go and have a shower?"

Douglas chuckled. "Yeah, let's beat them to the hot water."

Sergeant Simpson was only joking. He didn't get them at five-thirty the next morning as he said he would. He got them up at five and he took delight in ripping Danyluk's bed apart.

"STAND BY YOUR BEDS!"

"Aw Jesus, Sergeant. It seems like we've just hit the sack," Danyluk complained, standing there with his usual morning erection.

"A HEALTHY BODY IS A HEALTHY MIND!"

"Sergeant, can't you just let us dirty minds rest for one day?"

Bergie couldn't take that. "SPEAK FOR YOURSELF!"

For the next hour, the cadets of Charlie Company ran, did pushups and sang songs on-the-move. Sergeants Simpson and Beckford joined them for breakfast in the mess hall, along with the other Company Sergeants and Corporals.

"Are the girls joining us for lunch?" Douglas asked.

"Yep," said Wayne. "It's visitor's day for lunch."

After breakfast, the trucks arrived to take Charlie Company over to the upper camp to hand in their clothing and equipment. The scene was reminiscent of the first day.

Wayne started his act. "Where am I? Where am I?"

Once again dust and dirt flew, and stuck to the skin of the cadets dressed in half-serge.

Although Earl had dust in his mouth, it didn't stop him from passing along information he had read.

"We've got a Pay Parade at eleven and if we go downtown, we've got to be back by five."

Wayne wiped the dirt from his face. He was covered with it. "You're on your own this afternoon, old buddy. I'm going over to Debbie's place."

Douglas nodded. "Diane and I are just going to Polson Park."

"Aren't you going over to her house?" Wayne asked.

"No, Tom and Ellen understand. We just want to be alone for a couple of hours. They're coming to the train station tomorrow, anyway."

With Pay Parade over, the inhabitants of 'ship wrecked B-21,' cleaned up themselves and their barracks. At noon, the girls arrived for lunch.

"What, steak again!" Moose licked his lips. "Why wasn't it like this at the start of camp?"

"It was, but they gave us weiners and beans because we sat with you," Bergie quipped.

Although they sat in close proximity to each other, the Musketeers separated for lunch. Debbie, Diane, and her parents sat with Wayne and Douglas and the other Musketeers sat with their girls at other tables.

As Bergie and Danyluk sat at a table across from them, Tom said, "Those two really give it to one another, don't they?"

Douglas smiled. "Camp would be boring without them, Sir."

"They're living legends, that's for sure," Wayne replied.

It didn't long for Danyluk's kitchen girl to come over to his table and give him a kiss on his cheek.

Alma slammed down her knife and fork. "And WHO is that?"

Danyluk never looked up from his plate. "Just one of my many fans. I'll tell you about her next year."

"You won't survive this afternoon, never mind next year," Alma said, giving him a slight slap.

"I'm innocent! Bergie, I'm innocent, aren't I Bergie?"

Bergie looked at him with a defiant smile. "Do I get the five bucks you owe me?"

"Naturally."

Bergie looked at Alma for a moment and then carried on eating. "In that case, he's innocent."

Alma grabbed Moose by the scruff of the neck. "You'd better be, you creep."

Danyluk glanced at Douglas' table, winking and wiping imaginary sweat from his forehead.

The mess hall was different that afternoon. With all the civilians dining with them, part of the military atmosphere had disappeared. It made the boys think of home and going back to a life that now seemed totally alien. The army took six weeks to take them out of their mothers' arms, and now the boys sensed the change that was coming.

"Will you guys miss all of this?" Tom asked.

Neither Wayne nor Douglas answered right away, but they were both nodding slightly.

"If you had asked me that three weeks ago, I would have said 'no,' " Douglas replied. "Now I don't think any of us wants to leave. We've lived in a barracks with two hundred guys for six weeks and we've bonded together through thick and thin. I think we'll miss all of that. I'll also miss Diane and the two of you."

Wayne sighed deeply. "I'll miss the comradeship." He then looked at Debbie and smiled. "And Debbie."

Now Tom was nodding and staring right through them, as if he were remembering his own military experience.

"I know what you mean."

When Tom and Ellen left, the Musketeers and their girls walked down the hill together in pairs. They were wearing exactly the same clothes as when they arrived: half-serge with their own web-belts and puttees.

The girls really got a kick out of seeing the Musketeers give an eyes-left to Hop Sing's Laundry. Although they knew nothing about drill, they gave an eyes-left as well, and that action started the group of them laughing.

Despite Military Police vehicles passing, all the pairs had either linked arms or were holding hands. The fact that it was the last day in camp must have touched the Provost 'hearts' because they drove by slowing brandishing expressions of gas pains.

One by one, the pairs split up as they neared Polson Park. Douglas and Diane entered the park and sat across from each other at a picnic table.

As he took hold of her hands, he said, "I really don't want to leave."

Diane just looked at the table. Tears started to roll down her cheeks. "I...I don't think I've ever had a better summer."

Douglas got up and moved around the table next to her. He put his arm around her, and with the other hand gently wiped the tears from her face. He was lost for words just as she was. Diane put her hand in his and they started strolling to the little stream that ran through the park.

Surprisingly, not too many people were around as they lay down under a giant weeping willow tree. Diane cuddled up next to him. He had one arm around her and one behind his head.

"Diane, we've still got two weeks left before we go back to school. Why don't I take the bus back up here and we can talk your parents into driving us down to the coast for the Pacific National Exhibition?"

Diane turned on her side and looked at him. "You mean you'll come back here in a week?"

"If I've got to peddle my bike all the way, I'll be back."

"But what about your mom, will she let you come?"

Douglas rolled over on his side. Now they were facing each other and subconsciously running their fingers through the grass carpet on which they were lying.

"My mom knows more about you and your parents than you think. I've explained everything in my letters and she understands there's another gal in my life. How about it?"

Diane sat up with excitement, a large smile brightening her face as she grabbed his hand. "ARE YOU SERIOUS?"

Douglas swallowed. "Nothing could hold me back."

Excitedly she said, "Let's go celebrate."

"Where do you want to go?"

"Where else? Let's go and have a banana-split. I'll buy."

Douglas laughed. "O.K., but let me buy?"

"You've been buying all summer. I feel like a cheapskate."

The next voice heard was Danyluk's. He and Alma had been sitting at a table, close by. "For God's sake, Doug. If she wants to buy, let her. Alma always buys my banana-splits."

Alma hit Moose with her purse. "Yeah, if I didn't, we'd never go into the restaurant. He always wants to stay in the basement, necking."

Danyluk smiled his sneaky smile. "You've got to admit necking is better than eating a banana-split?"

As they walked out of the park, Danyluk was still at it. "Doug, since they're buying, let's you and I have two giant banana-splits?"

"Sounds good to me," Douglas replied.

When they arrived at the Capital Café, although Earl and Wayne weren't there, the rest of the Musketeers were sitting at tables. Lyons and Foster were with them. The owner, Mr. Ma, bought everyone a soda on the house. Then he adjusted the jukebox so they didn't have to put in any money. It's a wonder it didn't break down, because Ebb Tide played for the next two hours.

At four-thirty when Douglas arrived back at the barracks, he was tired and sticky. The temperature was over ninety-five and he had walked Diane all the way home before he started his trek up the hill.

The barracks looked like a typhoon had hit it. Cadets were packing and the excess junk 'collected' over the summer was all over the place. The two garbage cans that usually sat in the smoking pit between huts had been brought into the barracks and they were overflowing, just like the regular garbage cans.

Even though cadets were dressed in their heavy serge pants, they were running on top of the bunks, through the aisles, out the windows and up the stairs, and some had even crawled over the walls of the Corporals' cubicles to french the beds. The cubicles weren't always locked, however, they were locked this day because the Corporals didn't want their beds frenched. Too bad, it was done anyway, but only after the beds received a few squirts from the fire extinguishers.

Douglas took off his clothes and took a towel from home out of his duffel-bag. He had the whole shower room to himself until Danyluk, Bergie and Banks joined him.

"I'm coming back in a week," he told Wayne.

"You mean we're both coming back," Wayne replied, doing his usual thing and covering his whole body with shampoo.

"Diane is going to ask Tom and Ellen to drive us back for the Pacific National Exhibition. We're going to have to set pins at the bowling alley to make some money."

Wayne held his face under the shower faucet. "Well, we've got a cheque coming for eighty dollars, but I don't think that's going to arrive for a while. We'll have to set pins."

"Haven't you guys had enough of this place?" Bergie asked. "Are you actually coming back?" He paused for a few moments and added, "Hey, maybe that's not a bad idea?"

Danyluk threw a bar of Sergeant's Soap at him. "You're out of your mind. When the truck passes the guardroom and I drop my pants and bare-ass the Provost, that's it for me."

Bergie laughed. "You'll be back with us, Moose."

"Ho! Ho! Ho! No, I won't!"

"Ho! Ho! Ho! Yes, you will!"

At supper that night, Jackson told everyone how Mr. Brewer picked him and his girlfriend up and took them back to the small village on the reservation. They had spent the afternoon horseback riding and swimming. Afterward, they went back to the village and had sandwiches, ice cream and pop.

"He told me to tell you guys that you're welcome back there at anytime." Then he reached in his pocket. "Oh, and I almost forgot. He asked me to give these to you."

Jackson took two small articles out of his pocket. They were wrapped in newspaper and he handed them to Wayne and Douglas.

"He said these are for you to remember him by."

They were miniature copper lanterns.

"What a heck of a nice guy," Wayne said.

Douglas smiled and shook his head. "You can say that again."

"What a heck of a nice guy," Wayne reiterated.

The movie that evening was The Story of Three Loves, with Pier Angeli. Because all cadets were confined to camp, B-3 was full. Most of the camp staff were there, as well.

As the projectionist changed reels, Sergeant Simpson, who never showed any emotion whatsoever, said, "You know, I didn't think I'd say this, but I'm actually going to miss you guys. Now I won't have anyone to run with."

Danyluk stood up and shook the Sergeant's hand. "Thank you, Sergeant. Just think, when you're running, I'll be in a nice warm bed."

"Yeah, and it won't be his own," quipped Bergie.

Moose laughed. "Bergie, how many times do I have to tell you, there's some of us who have it and some of us who don't. I can't help it if you ain't got it."

"I don't want it. The last time I had my nuts painted, they ached for a day," Bergie shot back.

"I'm not talking about that, you pongo." Danyluk pushed Bergie's head. "I'm talking about, how do you say it, savoir-faire?" He kissed three tips of his fingers on his right hand and pulled them away from his mouth. "That's what I've got with the dames."

Wayne's smile covered his face. "I'm really going to miss you guys."

Sergeant Beckford came over and sat between Moose and Bergie. "Have you two ever thought about joining the Regular Force?"

Bergie pointed at Danyluk. "Sergeant, he'd never make it. If he was in a battle and someone said, 'Find yourself a fox-hole,' he'd be looking around for a woman and would probably get himself shot."

Danyluk displayed his sneaky smile. "Oh, yeah? Well let me tell you something Mr. Bergie. You and I could never serve in the same regiment, because I'd be in the Intelligence Corps."

"The Soviet Army wouldn't take you in their Intelligence Corps."

Moose looked frustrated, but he was still smiling. "I'm not talking about the Red Army, I'm talking about our army, you idiot."

Even Sergeant Beckford was laughing now.

Bergie put his arm on Danyluk's shoulder. "Christ, now I'll have to join the Intelligence Corps with you or Canada will cease being any sort of a military power."

"You don't have the smarts, Bergie."

"Oh, yes I do! What's the square root of 896?"

"Let's keep sex out of this Bergie. That's all you've ever got on your mind."

When the movie ended, everyone headed back to B-21 and it wasn't long before it was Grand Central Station. The cadets from other companies were making their rounds, saying good-bye.

This night was different than other nights. No one was working on his uniform, or studying. Instead, they were putting their bunks together and hanging blankets over the sides and the ends, creating their own private tunnels.

A few cadets had gone home during the summer, so Rothstein managed to pull an empty bunk over and put it together with the other three bunks of the Musketeers. It was dark inside, but some of them had brought flashlights from home. At midnight, the lights went out without fanfare or complaint and there was sufficient light inside the tunnel to see each other.

The chatter had subsided and all of the Musketeers were still sitting on the lower bunks when Danyluk complained that the Corporals had not made a big enough deal out of their beds being frenched.

"If it weren't the last night, I'd be hauled out of bed and blamed for it."

"You're going to miss that, aren't you Moose?" Bergie asked.

Danyluk was in a somber mood, like the other six. "Bergie, you're probably right. I'm going to miss you guys, too."

Rothstein said, "Hey fellas, listen. Someone's playing a bugle. It's the *Last Post*."

The camp bugler had played it at sunset when the flag was lowered, now he was playing it again.

All chatter stopped in the barracks as cadets listened to the lonely notes of the bugle echoing through the rows of darkened huts and the surrounding hills. When the *Last Post* was finished, the bugler played *Reveille*.

For some uncanny reason, they all turned off their flashlights as the *Last Post* was being played. Wayne said, "I never thought I'd ever like that tune, *Reveille*. I used to hate it every morning, more than ever in the rain, and now I don't want it to end."

Although nothing was said, they all knew the meaning. The bugler's message was loud and clear. The camp was coming to an end, but there would be another day.

Jackson was at the end of the tunnel when he spoke to Rothstein. "What are you going to miss most of all, Rothie?"

Rothstein paused before answering him. "I think we're all going to miss the same thing. I'll miss the noise in the barracks." He laughed. "Did I actually say that? I'll miss the lineups for meals, the cold-water showers, the walk up the hill...I guess I'm going to miss everything about this place. But most of all, I'm going to miss our friendship. I wish I was in the recording business, I'd sign up Bergie and Moose and play the record every day."

"Along with the regular noise in this joint, eh Rothie?"

"You bet, Moose. I'd also record the noise."

Danyluk forced a laugh. "I know what I'm not going to miss. I'm not going to miss the command, "STAND BY YOUR BEDS!"

Bergie broke in. "You're different than us, Moose. The reason you don't like those words is because you had two to look after."

"Two to look after? What do you mean by that, Bergie?"

"Well, every morning when you stood by your bunk, so did your joint. Most mornings, it was straighter than you."

Bergie's statement had them all snickering now. He was at it again.

"Ya got to admit, it's well trained," replied Danyluk.

"Like I've always told ya, Moose. You've got two heads and only one of them knows what it's doing."

Danyluk was going to respond, but Douglas interrupted him. "Foster told me today that he and Lyons have volunteered to go on that Buffalo Four Exercise at Wainwright. He's going to be operating a Nineteen-Set and Lyons will be driving a Beep."

"What the hell's a Beep?" East asked.

"A three-quarter-ton truck. Over 175 cadets have volunteered to go from Signals and Driver-Mech. Apparently, the Regular Force is really short of personnel."

Bergie's voice was loud. "YOU SURE AS HELL WOULDN'T CATCH ME GOING THERE. IT'S GOING TO BE TWO WEEKS OF RAIN AND MOSQUITOES!"

"When do they leave?" asked Rothstein.

"They leave on Sunday and they're there for two weeks. Foster told me they're going to get trades pay."

Danyluk sat up. "Listen...someone's playing the pipes. I can also hear drums."

Their ears perked up and Jackson rushed to the window. "It's coming from the highway."

"They're at it again," said Bergie. "The pipes and drums are having a nighttime Sporran Parade. There's not too many cars on the highway at this time of night."

"What about the Military Police?" East asked.

"They're probably moving the traffic around them. Remember what I told ya.

Sporran Parades are traditional in Camp Vernon. A lot of our traditions have been forgotten, but I sure as hell hope that one remains."

Douglas moved over and sat next to Wayne on Bergie's bunk. "What traditions have gone, Bergie?"

"Well, they used to have a Cadet Headquarter's Staff Day. Chosen cadets would run the camp for a day and even eat in the Officers' and Sergeants' Messes. Whenever the Cadet Commanding Officer called for a vehicle to do some touring, it arrived."

Banks chuckled. "That sounds mint."

"Then they had Skit Day. Instead of a movie on the last day of camp, cadets performed their own show. It was organized at the start of camp and practised all summer. From what I've heard, some of the skits were a riot and very professionally performed. Our Cadet RSM at my home corps told me that Dog Company once put on the skit of *Rose Marie*. They mimed the record of Nelson Eddy and Jeannette MacDonald. He said it was funnier than hell. Another act was a Hawaiian act and from where he was sitting, the guys looked like real dames. The wolf whistles and growls were hilarious."

Rothstein sighed. "Too bad we never did the same."

Bergie was in a reflective mood again. "They're gone because people are too lazy to remember what this camp is all about. New officers come along and don't even bother to ask what the traditions are. Someone should write a book about Camp Vernon traditions. That way, they wouldn't be forgotten."

When Danyluk suggested they play a game of stuke, he was turned down. They were yawning and it was cold because all they were wearing was their undershorts.

Once by one, the blankets came down and the guys who slept on the upper bunks climbed up. It had been a long day.

Douglas lay on his back with his arms behind his head. He tilted his head and looked out the window at the full moon. It reminded him of the sixpence he got as a kid and his talk with Wayne at Glenemma.

Wayne and the rest had gone to sleep right away. Within minutes he was also asleep, but before sleep came, he retraced his camp experience from the day he got off the train.

He smiled as he rolled onto his side. He wouldn't have traded this summer for anything in the world.

About half an hour after everyone was asleep, Sergeant Beckford entered the barracks and walked up and down the aisles. He just wanted to make certain everything was all right.

He stopped a few times at various bunks on both sides of the hut, pausing and looking at particular cadets as they slept. When he reached the Musketeers' section, his pause was longer.

A Corporal, wearing only his shorts, came out of his cubicle and joined the Sergeant.

"Oh, it's you Sergeant."

Beckford glanced at him and acknowledged his presence. "Corporal Drake."

"Are you thinking the same thing I am, Sergeant?"

Beckford seemed to be in deep thought. "What's that?"

"That we're going to miss them?"

The Sergeant didn't answer right away, he just nodded slowly, let out a sigh and looked at the Musketeers.

"You bet we are," he said, still nodding slightly. "I've served with a lot of men, good men, but I've never experienced this feeling before. These kids have proven to me that this country is going to be well looked after if the politicians don't screw it up. I don't know if it's the enthusiasm of their youth, or the combination of their personalities, but I really respect these young guys."

"Are you coming back here next year, Sergeant?"

"Corporal Drake, come hell or high water, I'm going to do my damndest to return. What these kids have learned here will benefit them for the rest of their lives...but I've learned something, too. While we were teaching them, they were also teaching us. The world isn't ugly when it's looked at through the eyes of youth. Jesus, I liked what I saw here this summer. The innocence of loyalty beyond belief. Yes, I'm going to miss them...a lot."

Sergeant Beckford had subconsciously sat down on an empty bunk while he was talking with the Corporal.

"This was my first year working with army cadets. Before now, I never gave the organization a second thought. We treated them like Regular Force troops this summer, and they took everything we dished out."

"They expected discipline, Sergeant, that's why they came here in the first place."

Beckford grinned. "I know, but throughout the summer I've often wondered what these kids would be like without the benefit of being in cadets. I arrived at the conclusion that there's a fine line of direction when boys reach this age. They can go one way, or the other. This system teaches them to accept fair discipline as a way of life. I don't think they've realized that yet, but they've gained an asset that will last them the rest of their lives. The discipline factor is very important, Corporal. That, plus giving them a little rope, with proper guidance from a distance.

The Corporal yawned. "You mean don't smother them? Let them feel their way?"

The Sergeant nodded slowly. "Yeah. Boys will always be boys, Corporal. They want to be men. It's our job to let them think they are men, but that has to be done with tact, and within reason. It's important that the very thin line is breached properly. They can't be treated as children and they must have the space to, as you say it, 'feel their way.' The courses at this camp and at their home corps are designed that way. If we ever take Trades-Training away and eliminate section tactics with real weapons and blank rounds, boys won't get involved. Or I should say the majority of them won't."

"That shouldn't happen, Sergeant. Nobody wants to ruin a good thing."

The Sergeant shook his head slightly. "I hope not, but we live in a changing world, Corporal. Many changes are made without giving any thought to the outcome. If I had my way, I'd take every lad out of reform school and place him in a Special Company in every Regular Force regiment in Canada."

"Hey, that's a good idea, Sergeant. Have you suggested it?"

"It's too simple, Corporal. The sexual intellectuals can't see beyond their noses. Besides, all those goody-two-shoes theoretical philosophers wouldn't have a job. Somewhere along the line, those idiots forgot one thing. If you let the boys be boys and guide them as if they were men, then they'll grow up to be real men. It's the type of guidance that dictates the final outcome. There's no such person as a bad boy. If a boy goes wrong, someone didn't treat him as a man."

"Christ, I never looked at it that way."

"Simple isn't it. I also don't believe there's a dumb kid. The twelve cadets who failed this course, shouldn't have failed. As far as I'm concerned, they failed because their instructors let them down. Some people are slower than others, they need extra time and a lot more encouragement.

The Corporal yawned again, so Sergeant Beckford stood up.

"Good night, Corporal Drake. I hope I haven't bored you?"

"Good night, Sergeant. You taught me a lot tonight. I'm going to try and make it back, as well."

Beckford smiled. "I'm happy to hear that. I don't know if it's the greatest move for our careers, but an opportunity like this doesn't come along very often.

He looked a little sad as he left the hut, and quietly closed the outer door behind him. Only the moon watched Sergeant Beckford break the rules. He had his hands in his pockets and his head down.

"WHAT, NO STEAK?" Danyluk yelled as he passed over his plate. It was being heaped with 'real' scrambled eggs and bacon.

The cadet in front of him was complaining that after getting powdered eggs for six weeks, at least they could have the common decency to serve it on the last day. "I was getting used to that stuff."

Danyluk's kitchen sweetheart was serving. "Where were you last night, Moose?" she asked, smiling and blinking her big blue eyes.

"I had to assist the Commanding Officer plan for next year's camp."

"If you're coming up here next year, Moose, I'll wait for you."

"Ah, well, you see, er...I might, but, er....."

"MOVE IT UP FRONT!" A voice came from the back of the line.

"Saved by the bell," he said, as he shuffled along to the next girl, who was serving the toast.

"OVER HERE, GUYS!" Rothstein had saved their usual table and was waving his hands.

When they were seated, Rothstein chuckled, "Did you hear what happened last night?"

"You mean the Sporran Parade?" asked Jackson.

"No, better than that. The Orderly Officer must have had his hands full, because two girls from town were on mattresses under one of the huts. They were charging fifty cents a go."

"WHAT?" Pieces of egg shot out of Danyluk's mouth as he stared at Rothstein. "Where the hell were we?" What time was this?"

"At two-thirty in the morning. There were fifty cadets in the lineup. The girls were arrested before the fire started."

Danyluk was still interested. "What fire?"

"There was a small fire in one of the equipment huts in the upper camp. Cadets who rushed out of bed to join the girls' lineup disappeared because they thought they were hearing police sirens. Actually what they heard were fire trucks."

"Christ, why didn't the girls pick our hut?" Danyluk asked.

Rothstein continued. "Guess which company it was and who was caught on one of the girls when the Provost walked in with flashlights?" He didn't wait for their reply. "I'll give you a hint. Scheaffer's up at the Medical Inspection Room receiving a shot and getting painted with about fifty others."

Bergie roared laughing. "HAAAAA. So Casanova Genova is going to be in the news. At least we now know that Scheaffer's not a homo."

Wayne grimaced. "Can you imagine being number ten in line?"

"Number ten? I wouldn't want to be number two," Bergie replied.

Danyluk was still eating. "Oh, come on Bergie, where's your sense of adventurism? I think...SON OF A BITCH! THERE'S A DEAD FLY IN MY EGGS!"

Jackson went running for the door. "GOTCHA AGAIN!"

Although all the bunks were still together in B-21, the floors had been swept and blankets and sheets were folded and placed on the rolled-up mattresses.

"O.K., NINE AND TEN PLATOONS OVER HERE," one of the Corporals screamed. He had four rolls of pennies in his hand.

"Have you people organized the 'bare-ass' detail for each truck?"

"YES, CORPORAL," Danyluk answered. "Us Musketeers are dropping our drawers on the side of our truck and the squads are ready for the other trucks."

The Corporal smiled. "Good! Now I want everyone other than the 'bare-assers' to come here and I'll issue you some pennies."

For the next five minutes, the Corporals issued pennies to the company. When they were finished, the Platoon Sergeants arrived with copies of the *Vernon News*, containing a special segment of the summer activities. The articles in the paper also included the statistics of what it took to support the camp for six weeks. These were distributed along with platoon and company photographs.

Over the next fifteen minutes, company staff and cadets went around and shook hands, signed autographs,and said good bye to each other.

There was pandemonium in B-21. Some cadets still hadn't packed, and had to take the pin out of the hinges of their barrack-boxes because they'd lost the key or forgotten the combination. Others were running around getting everyone to sign the backs of their photographs.

Although they were excited, the cadets of Charlie Company felt a little down as they left B-21 and formed up for the last time on the road. A lot of their friends from the prairies gathered around and watched. They wouldn't be leaving until the next day.

After a short speech by their OC, they boarded the trucks and waved at their Sergeants and Corporals.

Danyluk bellowed. "ARE YOU COMING BACK NEXT YEAR, SERGEANT BECKFORD?"

"I MIGHT. ARE YOU COMING BACK?"

"I DIDN'T THINK I'D SAY IT, BUT MOST DEFINITELY!"

"THEN I'LL HAVE TO THINK ABOUT IT. JUST JOKING, MOOSE, I HOPE TO BE BACK!"

The cadets of Nine Platoon had spent some time with Sergeant Beckford and Sergeant Simpson, but there never seemed to be enough time to say the right words.

"THANKS AGAIN...THANKS VERY MUCH, SERGEANT." Douglas shouted. "SEE YOU NEXT YEAR."

Sergeant Beckford nodded. "I HOPE SO, BRICE. MAKE SURE YOU RETURN. ALL THE VERY BEST."

When the convoy started moving, all hands were waving. The Sergeants had to cover their ears, the farewells were so resounding.

As they neared the guardroom, the Musketeers and others took down their serge pants and their shorts and tucked the tails of their shirts up. Within seconds, the seven of them plus two were sitting on the wooden sideboards, bare bottoms facing the direction of the guardroom.

When they passed, some Provost had the guts to come out and 'bare' witness to the show. The sight of nine shiny 'moons' in each truck didn't bother them, but they were showered with pennies and the song *Oh Provost, Oh Provost,* as well.

It was a sight to behold, but one of the Corporals got his own back. He had made a slingshot and shot back a penny he had picked up from the ground. Danyluk's shriek was loud. At first, he thought he'd been stung by a bee, but a later review of the injury revealed a red welt, quite possibly the imprint of King George the Sixth.

Bergie quipped, "HEY, DANYLUK, DO YOU THINK PEOPLE WILL WANT TO KISS YOUR ASS, LIKE THEY DO THE KING'S RING?"

"IT'S THE POPE'S ASS THEY KISS, YOU IDIOT," Danyluk replied, rubbing his bottom.

Jackson was a staunch Catholic. "NO THEY DON'T, THEY KISS HIS RING!"

Not to be outdone, Moose said, "WHAT IF HE HAD A RING AROUND HIS ASS?"

There were more civilians at the train station than there had been six weeks earlier. A lot of girls held handkerchiefs to their eyes. Relationships that had taken six weeks to develop were now coming to an end.

After the trucks were unloaded, everyone was formed up in three ranks and then given the chance to say good-bye to their new-found friends.

The Musketeers all stayed in one location on the train platform. Diane and her parents were there and Debbie and her parents were with Wayne. The other guys, Bergie, Danyluk, Rothstein and East all had their girls beside them and Jackson had his girl along with Mr. Brewer and the kids from the village.

Both Douglas and Wayne thanked Mr. Brewer for the miniature lanterns, before they presented him with a camp plaque.

"Do I get a chance to kiss the second-best cadet in the camp good-bye?" Ellen asked as she gave Douglas a kiss on the cheek.

Diane's dad shook his hand. "I hear you're coming back in a few days. Don't worry, son, we'll take you home. Have a safe journey."

Douglas wrapped his arms around Diane. They didn't say anything for a minute, until Diane spoke.

"I'm going to be counting the days until you return. It'll be the longest wait I've ever had in my life. The minute you get home, I'm going to phone you, is that alright?"

"My line will be busy because I'll be phoning you."

"ALL ABOARD!" The Conductor shouted. "ALL BOAAARD!"

Still holding hands, Douglas and Diane slowly walked to his rail car. His duffel-bag was wrapped around his shoulder and it was heavy.

Diane stopped. "Hold on a second, Doug. My dad wants to talk to you."

Tom was running from the car with something wrapped up in his arms. He handed what looked like a small blanket to Douglas. "We've named him Colonel."

Douglas folded back the blanket and couldn't believe his eyes. They had given him the cutest black Labrador puppy he had ever seen. A lump came to his throat and he couldn't speak.

He found himself stroking the pup as he searched for words. "Thank you very much. I...I don't know what to say but to thank you. If I......"

Tom put his hand on the boy's shoulder. All four of them had tears in their eyes. "Don't even try to thank us son, we know what Major meant to you."

Diane was rooting in her purse. "Oh, I almost forgot, this is for you." She handed him a copy of Ebb Tide in a record sleeve. "Play it when you get home."

"I'LL WEAR IT OUT," he said, as he climbed up the stairs of the car holding the pup gently in one arm and trying to stop the heavy duffel-bag from pulling him back. The sound of trucks leaving and the yelling meant he had to speak louder.

"I'LL OPEN A WINDOW AND TALK TO YOU, O.K.?"

As Douglas searched for his seat, Diane scurried along the platform, straining to see him at a window. She wasn't alone, all the other girls were doing the same thing.

This time, Douglas had a lower berth on Diane's side of the platform. Forcing open the window, he stuck the upper half of his body out and held her outreached hand.

He was still holding it as the train started moving. It was noisy on the platform and he couldn't hear what she was saying. "I CAN'T HEAR YOU," he said as the train picked up a little speed. Then he smiled as he read her lips. "I LOVE YOU, TOO! IT'LL BE THE LONGEST WEEK OF MY LIFE."

Douglas stayed at the window waving and blowing kisses at Diane. Just before the train turned, he saw Lyons and Foster running. Although they were late, they had managed to wave good-bye.

When Diane was out of sight, Douglas brought in his head and arm. He was holding onto the pup with one hand, so he just used one hand to take off his tunic, tie, boots, puttees, and weights.

A group of cadets at the other end of the car started singing.

"There are rats, rats, as big as alley
cats, in the stores, in the stores.
There are rats, rats, as big as alley
cats, in the Quartermaster Stores. "

"My eyes are dim, I cannot see,
I have not got my specs with me.
I have, not, got, my, specs, with, me. "

Wayne came and sat opposite Douglas. He had been between cars waving at Debbie and her family and he had a melancholy look on his face. He took the pup out of Douglas' arms and cuddled it. "Maybe you're right," he said with a glazed look in his eyes. "Maybe we can fall in love at our age."

Douglas was going to answer him but he never got the chance because Bergie, Danyluk, Rothstein, Jackson and East arrived. Gord Cunningham was standing behind them shuffling a deck of cards and grinning.

"O.K., you guys, let's see the colour of your money."

CHAPTER XVII

"Excuse me, Sir, is everything all right?"

Colonel Forbes had joined General Brice on the dais, touching his arm lightly. Douglas still had his arm in the salute position, yet the final company had marched by and was returning to its parade position.

Douglas put his arm down. The sound of Peter Forbes' voice had snapped him out of his trance and brought him back to the present.

"I'm fine, Peter. In fact, I've never felt better."

The March Past had been completed and the parade was now standing at the attention position when the young Cadet Parade Commander marched up to General Brice and saluted.

"Would you like to address the parade before we conduct the Advance In Review Order, Sir?"

Douglas returned the salute. "Thank you. Please stand them at ease and have them stand easy. I want you to stay here in front of me."

The Cadet Parade Commander saluted, turned about and gave the necessary words of command. Then he faced the reviewing stand and stood at ease himself.

It was a very large parade square, so Douglas decided to use the microphone. "I WANT THE GUARD TO INDIVIDUALLY GROUND ARMS AND I WANT ALL OF YOU TO COME UP HERE AND FORM A SEMICIRCLE AROUND ME."

As the cadets in the guard were laying their rifles down, other cadets were running across the parade square to the reviewing stand. Shortly, they were standing in front of him.

Douglas looked at Colonel Forbes. "Peter, will you join me up here please."

Colonel Forbes stepped up next to him.

Douglas scanned the shiny faces of the cadets standing in front of him. They were young and keen and it was obvious they wanted to hear him.

"THANK YOU FOR THIS PARADE. IT IS DISTINCTLY EVIDENT THAT YOU HAVE WORKED HARD HERE ALL SUMMER.

"I HAVE TO BE HONEST WITH YOU. I DIDN'T VOLUNTEER TO COME HERE AND INSPECT YOU, I WAS ORDERED TO COME. MAYBE IT WAS FATE, I DON'T KNOW, BUT I WOULDN'T GIVE UP THIS MOMENT FOR ANYTHING ELSE IN THE WORLD.

"YOU SEE, I WAS A CADET HERE AT ONE TIME. MY FIRST YEAR WAS 1953 AND MY LAST YEAR WAS 1956. AFTER THAT, I EVEN CAME HERE FOR A FEW YEARS AS A MILITIA CORPORAL. PERHAPS TIMES

WERE DIFFERENT THEN, I DON'T KNOW. I DO KNOW, HOWEVER, THAT WHAT I HAVE SEEN TODAY HAS IMPRESSED ME IMMENSELY. YOUR DRESS AND DEPORTMENT WERE EXCELLENT, THEREFORE PERHAPS THINGS HAVEN'T CHANGED.

"THE FACT THAT I SERVED HERE PLACES ME IN THE FORTUNATE POSITION TO KNOW WHAT YOU'VE BEEN EXPERIENCING THESE PAST SIX WEEKS. THAT INCLUDES THOSE OF YOU WHO HAVE ONLY BEEN HERE TWO OR THREE WEEKS.

"WHEN I WAS YOUR AGE, THIS CAMP MEANT MORE TO ME THAN NEARLY ANYTHING ELSE IN MY LIFE. I WAS TAUGHT DISCIPLINE HERE AND I MADE MANY VERY GOOD FRIENDS. FRIENDS THAT I HAD FORGOTTEN ABOUT UNTIL I RETURNED.

"HUMAN BEINGS TEND TO BE VERY SELFISH AS THEY ADVANCE IN LIFE. I THINK YOU'RE OLD ENOUGH TO REALIZE THAT EVEN CHILDREN, AS THEY GET OLDER, DON'T SHOW THEIR APPRECIATION TO THEIR PARENTS AS THEY ONCE DID. WELL, PEOPLE IN JOBS AND PROFESSIONS DO THE SAME THING. THEY FORGET THEIR ROOTS. THEY FORGET THE INSTITUTIONS AND THE PEOPLE WITHIN THOSE INSTITUTIONS WHO HELPED THEM ADVANCE. FOR SOME REASON, THEY ONLY THINK OF THEMSELVES, NOT THE ONES WHO GAVE THEM A NUDGE AND THE CONFIDENCE TO MOVE AHEAD IN LIFE."

He paused to look at their faces. Not a sound was heard. They were clinging to every word that came out of his mouth. They fully understood everything he was saying.

"I'M NO DIFFERENT. I HAVE NOT BEEN BACK HERE IN OVER THIRTY-SOME-ODD YEARS. WHEN I THINK OF THAT, IT BOTHERS ME AND I FEEL GUILTY. I MOVED ON TO OTHER THINGS AND TOTALLY FORGOT ABOUT YOU. I JOINED THE ARMY AND WANTED TO DO WELL, SO WELL THAT I PUSHED THE PAST OUT OF MY MIND. THE PAST THAT GOT ME WHERE I AM IN THE FIRST PLACE...THE BRITISH COLUMBIA REGIMENT AND THE VERNON ARMY CADET CAMP.

"I DIDN'T THINK OF THOSE WHO WOULD COME BEHIND ME. IT DIDN'T ENTER MY MIND AND I COULDN'T HAVE CARED LESS. THAT'S NOT VERY GOOD BECAUSE I DIDN'T LEARN THAT PECULIARITY HERE. I ACQUIRED THAT SOMEWHERE ALONG THE LINE.

"IN VERNON, I LEARNED TO SHARE, TO ASSIST PEOPLE AND TO COMPREHEND THEIR FEELINGS AND APPRECIATE THEIR POINTS OF VIEW. IT WAS HERE IN THIS CAMP THAT I LEARNED HOW TO BE PART OF A TEAM. BELIEVE IT OR NOT, IT'S POSSIBLE TO BE AN INDIVIDUAL AND STILL BE PART OF A TEAM."

"DO ANY OF YOU KNOW WHAT A PERSONAL EVALUATION REPORT IS?"

Douglas looked around and saw them whispering to each other. Some of them may have known what he was referring to, but most of them didn't.

"IT'S A REPORT THAT DID NOT EXIST IN THE ARMY IN THE OLD DAYS. IT'S A RECORD THAT IS KEPT ON EACH INDIVIDUAL. IF FOR SOME REASON, A BLEMISH APPEARS ON A PERSON'S P.E.R., IT CAN SERIOUSLY AFFECT HIS OR HER ADVANCEMENT.

"THERE WERE OTHER SYSTEMS IN PLACE BEFORE THE P.E.R., BUT THIS METHOD OF APPRAISING PERFORMANCE MAKES EVERYONE A SLAVE TO IT, MYSELF INCLUDED. I NOW REALIZE THAT. THOSE OF YOU WHO HAVE TAKEN LEADERSHIP KNOW THERE IS A PHRASE WHICH SAYS, 'GIVE CREDIT WHERE CREDIT IS DUE.' UNFORTUNATELY SINCE 1968, THAT PHRASE HAS BEEN THROWN OUT THE WINDOW BECAUSE NOW, EVERYONE TAKES ALL THE CREDIT, TO IMPROVE THEIR P.E.R.

"NOW, WHY AM I EXPLAINING THIS TO YOU? I WANT YOU TO KNOW THAT PEOPLE LIKE MYSELF HAVE FORGOTTEN WHAT WAS MADE AVAILABLE TO US WHEN WE WERE YOUR AGE AT VERNON.

"THERE WERE TRADES-TRAINING COURSES. A CADET COULD TAKE DRIVER-MECHANICS OR SIGNALS. THE EQUIPMENT, PERSONNEL AND MONEY WERE MADE AVAILABLE. REGULAR FORCE, MILITIA AND CADET SERVICES OF CANADA STAFF INSTRUCTED THESE SUBJECTS. THEY WERE PROFESSIONALS, AS WERE THE CADETS WHO COMPLETED THE COURSES. THE CHIEF OF DEFENCE STAFF IN OTTAWA MADE CERTAIN THAT THE RESOURCES WERE HERE TO ENSURE THE CONTINUED EXISTENCE OF THE FINEST YOUTH TRAINING PROGRAM IN THE WORLD. THE POWERS THAT BE UNDERSTOOD THE NEED TO SUPPORT AND NURTURE THE FUTURE LEADERS OF THIS COUNTRY.

"THAT SENTIMENT DOESN'T EXIST TODAY BECAUSE YOU DO NOT HAVE TRADES-TRAINING OR THE FULL SUPPORT OF THE REGULAR FORCE AND MILITIA. THE CADET INSTRUCTOR'S LIST OFFICERS WHO TEACH YOU, ARE LIMITED, THROUGH NO FAULT OF THEIR OWN, TO ONLY PARTIAL TRAINING WITH VERY SPARSE RESOURCES.

"THE REASON WE ARE IN THIS DILEMMA IS VERY SIMPLE INDEED. THOSE WHO CAME THROUGH THE CADET SYSTEM, WHEN IT WAS SOMETHING VERY SPECIAL, COULDN'T CARE LESS ABOUT THOSE WHO FOLLOWED THEM. THOSE WHO WEREN'T CADETS UNFORTUNATELY DIDN'T KNOW ANY BETTER, NO ONE TOLD THEM.

"I UNDERSTAND NOW THAT CADETS CANNOT FIRE AUTOMATIC WEAPONS AND THERE IS A MOVEMENT AFOOT TO STOP YOU FROM FIRING LARGE-BORE RIFLES. THAT TO ME DOESN'T MAKE SENSE WHATSOEVER. APPARENTLY OUR POLITICAL MASTERS AND CERTAIN OFFICERS WHO ARE MORE CONCERNED ABOUT THEIR P.E.R.S DO NOT UNDERSTAND THAT HUNDREDS OF THOUSANDS OF CADETS WHO RECEIVED PROPER TRAINING ARE NOT THE

TROUBLEMAKERS OR THE WEAPON-HUNGRY CRIMINALS OF TODAY.

"THERE WAS A TIME WHEN THIS CAMP WAS GOING TO BE CLOSED DOWN, OR DID CLOSE DOWN BECAUSE IDEALISTIC PACIFIST PEOPLE SAID THAT ALL WE DO IS TRAIN KILLERS." (DOUGLAS LAUGHED). "ISN'T IT FUNNY HOW THE SQUEAKY WHEEL ALWAYS GETS THE GREASE? THAT SMALL BREED OF NARROW-MINDED DESPOTS, WHO WROTE TO THEIR POLITICIANS, DIDN'T HAVE AN IOTA WHEN IT CAME TO UNDERSTANDING WHAT THEY WERE RUINING. WHAT A PITY.

"RATHER THAN STANDING UP AND BEING COUNTED, SOMEONE IN OTTAWA COUNTERED BY CALLING CADET TRAINING, 'CITIZENSHIP TRAINING.' GOD, WE'VE ALWAYS PRODUCED GOOD CITIZENS, BUT APPARENTLY THE WORD SOUNDED BETTER AND WAS POLITICALLY ACCEPTABLE. ALL TRADITIONS WERE THROWN ASIDE AND I, LIKE EVERYONE ELSE WHO HAD BEEN GIVEN THIS GREAT OPPORTUNITY TO ATTEND HERE AND PARTICIPATE IN MILITARY EDUCATION THAT WAS THE ENVY OF THE WORLD, STOOD BACK AND LET IT HAPPEN. FOR THAT, I APOLOGIZE.

"THIS MORNING, I RECEIVED A TELEPHONE CALL FROM OTTAWA INFORMING ME THAT THE CHIEF OF DEFENCE STAFF, GENERAL HARLEY JASQUINELLE, HAS RESIGNED. IT WAS GENERAL JASQUINELLE WHO SENT ME HERE. PERHAPS HE HAD MORE IN MIND THAN I THOUGHT, BECAUSE IN ANOTHER TELEPHONE CONVERSATION, I WAS APPOINTED ACTING CHIEF OF THE DEFENCE STAFF."

Douglas was smiling now and he could hear the rumble of voices. Even in these times, cadets have good perception and this time they were right again.

"I PROMISE YOU, HERE AND NOW, THAT WHILE THE WORDS CITIZENSHIP TRAINING MAY REMAIN, TRADES TRAINING WILL BE REINTRODUCED THROUGHOUT THE ARMY CADET MOVEMENT. THAT MEANS REAL EQUIPMENT AND REAL STAFF WILL ONCE AGAIN PUT THE WORD 'ARMY,' BACK INTO ARMY CADETS."

Douglas had to stop talking because of the applause. The guests sitting behind him were on their feet cheering along with the cadets.

Colonel Forbes said, 'Congratulations, Sir" and shook his hand.

"IN 1953, THE COMMANDING OFFICER HERE TOOK TIME OUT OF HIS VERY BUSY DAY TO GIVE ME A HAND WHEN I TRIED TO SAVE SOME BABY BIRDS FROM FRYING TO DEATH IN THE BARREL OF THE CANNON OUTSIDE OF THE HEADQUARTERS BUILDING. I DON'T THINK HE WORRIED ABOUT HIS PERSONAL EVALUATION REPORT WHEN HE HELPED ME, DO YOU?"

"NO, SIR!" came their response.

Douglas smiled and nodded. "GOOD. PLEASE REMEMBER THAT IN THE FUTURE.

"I'LL BE TOURING THE CAMP AFTER THIS PARADE. I WANT TO TALK WITH ALL OF YOU MORE THAN YOU'LL EVER KNOW, ABOUT THE TRADITIONS THAT HAVE BEEN LOST. PERHAPS WE SHOULD DETAIL SOMEONE TO WRITE A BOOK? I ALSO WANT A SHOW OF HANDS FROM THOSE OF YOU WHO LIVE IN B-21."

Their hands went up, waving amidst the cheers.

"WOULD IT BE POSSIBLE TO GET A GUIDED TOUR OF THAT HUT?"

"YES, SIR!"

"THANK YOU FOR TODAY. THIS COUNTRY IS FORTUNATE TO HAVE EVERY ONE OF YOU."

"BEFORE WE CARRY ON, I'D LIKE TO LEAVE YOU WITH SOME WORDS OF WISDOM THAT A CERTAIN SERGEANT BILL BECKFORD PASSED ON TO HIS CADETS HERE AT CAMP VERNON A VERY LONG TIME AGO. HE SAID, 'WHEN YOU PEOPLE ARE CLIMBING THE LADDER OF SUCCESS, EVERYONE WILL CUP HIS HANDS AND HELP YOU UP. BUT WHEN YOU'RE AT THE TOP, IF YOU STEP ON A FACE, ALL OF THE HANDS WILL DISAPPEAR AND THEY WON'T BE THERE TO HELP YOU UP THE SECOND TIME.'"

Still talking into the microphone, he shook Colonel Forbes' hand again.

"THANK YOU, GOOD LUCK, AND GOD BLESS YOU."

Douglas nodded to the Parade Commander, who responded with, "RESUME YOUR PARADE POSITIONS!"

When all of the cadets had returned to their company positions, the Parade Commander ordered the guard to shoulder arms and reported to General Brice at the dais.

"SIR, MAY WE CARRY ON WITH THE ADVANCE IN REVIEW ORDER, SIR?"

"Please carry on."

The cadet then marched back to the parade. He was in the centre as he turned to face the reviewing stand and then gave the appropriate orders.

"THE PARADE WILL ADVANCE IN REVIEW ORDER. BY THE CENTRE, QUICK MARCH!"

The parade marched forward seven paces, with the band playing.

"PARADE, GENERAL SALUTE, PRESENT ARMS!"

On the second rifle movement, Douglas returned the salute as the band played the General Salute again. This time for some reason, it sounded better.

Douglas asked Colonel Forbes to join him on his tour of the camp. It gave them the opportunity to discuss training procedures as well as new cadet uniforms for the home corps and for summer camp.

When they arrived at B-21, he was given a guided tour fit for a king. He made a point of lying on a bunk where he had stayed as a youth, and for a magic moment he touched the bunks where Wayne, Danyluk, Bergie, Jackson, Rothstein and East had slept. He even felt like reaching up to turn on an imaginary radio above

Danyluk's bunk.

Looking at the floors which had been completely redone with a durable linoleum, he smiled. Many renovations had been made, including new showers and sinks.

"No more slivers, Peter?"

"Fortunately not, Sir."

When it was time for lunch, he joined the cadets from B-21 at his old table in the mess hall. Everyone laughed as Douglas recalled his stories.

When it was time to leave, he saw a cadet with an Iroquois haircut. His head had been shaved but a one inch thick strip of short hair was left down the middle.

"Who did that to you, Smoothy Stevens?"

"No Sir. It was Clipper Clemments."

Douglas laughed. "I think you're going to have second thoughts about having had that done?"

"I already have, Sir. Five days C.B. and a sunburnt head."

Colonel Forbes rolled his eyes, smiled and shrugged.

"We've lost a few good traditions and held on to some bad ones."

As they left, Douglas said, "Everything counts Peter. Thank God."

Later that afternoon, Douglas was in the Officers' Mess when he was called to the door. Wayne's son was standing at attention. He was immaculately dressed. "I, er...I..."

Douglas smiled and put his hand on the boy's shoulder. "Just relax son, I'll get my cap and I'll be right with you."

"Peter, I'm leaving now. Don't worry about a staff car, we're going to walk down the hill. I'll see you later."

"What if Mrs. Brice calls from Ottawa, Sir?"

Douglas had his cap in his hand and was heading for the door. "Please tell Diane I'll call her later and I'll be home in three days. Oh yes...and tell her I'm having dinner with a Musketeer."

Douglas briefed Wayne's son as they were walking out of camp. Although Hop Sing's Laundry was gone, they both gave an eyes-left.

E PILOGUE

Douglas Brice married Diane in the spring of 1960. They have three boys and a girl.

Although it took time, he found the other Musketeers. His best friend Wayne manages a liquor store in Vancouver. They see each other whenever they can and are still best friends.

As for Bergie, he joined the army and is a serving officer today. Danyluk became a physician and is living in Alberta. Jack East lives in Vancouver and is a prominent writer of culinary books. Earl Jackson became a lawyer and raises horses on Vancouver Island. Rothie Rothstein is a professor at a university in the United States. Don Lyons is a minister and Foster manages a bank in Toronto. All are good citizens, even though they were trained in a tough military fashion.

By the time the Musketeers' train arrived in Vancouver, Gamblin' Gord Cunningham had cleaned them out. He became an entrepreneur, made a few million and took up golf.

Eight days after they left, seven Musketeers returned to Vernon. Lyons and Foster couldn't be there, because they were in Wainwright Alberta, trying to stay dry.

Both of them were eaten alive by mosquitoes and they had the lumps to prove it when they returned with their stories.

As for the seven who went back: Well, after all, Musketeers are Musketeers, aren't they? Isn't it, 'ALL FOR ONE AND ONE FOR ALL?' Maybe it's the other way 'round. Where's Sergeant Beckford? He'd know?

AUTHOR'S NOTE

Those of us who were fortunate enough to serve in Canada's army cadet organization in the 50s and 60s were indeed a very lucky lot. Although we were still children, aged fourteen through sixteen, our military leaders, within reason, treated us like adults. Their knowledge was taught to us exactly as they had been taught, and they ensured we had the equipment.

A young person can spot weakness a mile away, therefore Ottawa made certain that instructors dealing with cadets, like their counterparts in the Regular Force or Militia, had to be properly trained. There could be no exceptions, cadets were a very important part of the military structure. Their training was just as important as anyone else's. That's why Regular Force personnel and Militia personnel assisted CSofC (Cadet Services of Canada) instructors.

At that time, it took fifteen to twenty years to become a Sergeant. The Sergeant was a mother, father, grand old aunt, a godfather and a FAIR disciplinarian. The Sergeants trained officers as well as other ranks, and because they had seen and experienced the worst characteristics of all men, during their rise up the ladder, they did their damndest to ensure that their charges were taught patience and compassion. All cadets who were instructed by them were shown how to reach for the sky with dignity and honour. The instructional system was based upon every instructor being fair, firm and friendly.

So, the Privates, Lance-Corporals, Corporals and Junior Officers had the benefit of the Sergeants' experience. When the Sergeants got promoted to Sergeant-Majors or Regimental Sergeant-Majors, Senior Officers were once again reminded that one rule stands above all: *The men come first!"*

Somewhere along the line, this rule has been bent, broken, put aside or totally disregarded. The reason is simple…personal advancement, regardless of the situation. Say nothing, or say the right thing and advancement is guaranteed.

In the 50s and 60s, people spoke up and their advice was always taken into consideration. That advice included not making silly unreasonable changes to a tried and tested Royal Canadian Army, Navy and Air Force…as well as the best youth organization in the world, the Royal Canadian *Army* Cadets.

I thank all of those Sergeants who helped all of those youngsters in the real days. For it was they who adhered to a piece of advice which is timeless but these days forgotten by so many; GIVE CREDIT WHERE CREDIT IS DUE.

Many people will say, "My God, is this man bitter, or what?"

No, this man isn't bitter. He's just frustrated because so many of the people who have made it to the top, made it BY TAKING CREDIT and nodding to mindless politicians who ruin everything except their salaries and pension plans.

It is difficult to describe the will, enthusiasm and unselfish dedication the cadets of the Vernon Army Cadet Camp displayed daily as they progressed at camp.

Although they had only a day-and-a-half off on the weekends, some of that time was spent working on their kit. From the time they arose in the morning, until they hit the sack, they worked and studied. In short, they had very little time to themselves. But they got around this by being organized.

There were very few complaints because complaining broke up the team they were a part of, and no one broke up the team.

Oh sure, there were problems, but the essence of their training, was learning how to identify and solve problems. They received all the guidance in the world from professional soldiers who were also a part of the team.

When it came to scrubbing floors, many of the Senior NCOs and Officers were down scrubbing the floors with the cadets. It was leadership by example, not, do what I say, but do what I do. This well set standard rubbed off for years to come. But then changes were made and the strength of corps started to decline. "It's just the times," was the explanation given by those who in effect were responsible for maintaining the strength of corps.

Well, I have watched the changes in the army cadet movement over the years, unfortunately all for the worse. At first glance, it appears that much forethought went into planning this transition from a near-perfect organization to a system that bears no resemblance to the original movement whatsoever. However, that is not the case at all. Only the initial part of the transition was planned, and that was by Hellyer's henchmen. The real damage was done by military politicians, officers who said a lot without saying anything at all. These officers knew the harm they were doing but were much too wrapped up in their careers to care about the destruction.

Maintaining strength in cadet corps is difficult today and I'm not too certain how Camp Vernon is run now. I do know, however, that midnight passes are a thing of the past. As well, cadets are curtailed from going into town in the evenings and I don't believe they have many Saturdays or Sundays when they can go downtown.

What a shame. Isn't it funny how some people don't seem to realize the cocoon syndrome doesn't work. If those same youngsters were in their home town, they could stroll at will. Yet, here they have the chance to explore a new area and meet new friends, but aren't given much of a chance.

Some will say that there is too much to distract cadets when they're in town. That's only an excuse to carry on a policy that has existed so long, everyone has forgotten who wrote it in the first place. But I must admit, it is safe. Safe for the sake of not having to complete Summary Investigations or Boards of Inquiry, or just paperwork in general. So 600 to 1000 cadets are hampered by a policy that protects a few who really are serious about their Personal Evaluation Report. (Like the strength of cadet corps, the number of cadets attending Camp Vernon is also going down. This is a result of money being allocated by Ottawa; a fixed budget, going to pay clerks and personnel who have replaced Regular Force troops. Money provided by Ottawa is going everywhere except where it should be going...to train cadets. Parkinson's Law rules)

In bygone days, the citizens of Vernon, including the merchants and the tourists loved seeing the cadets in town as much as possible. They only had them for six or seven weeks and they were very proud of them. Let's face it, The Camp is a part of Vernon's history. But The Camp is only The Camp when 'soldiers' are on the streets.

I don't know who changed many of the main policies of Camp Vernon. I can only assume it was some of those people I described in the introduction. I would imagine that they were raised in a cocoon themselves and believe it is the right thing to do. Wrong! Responsibility isn't taught that way. Perhaps it's already too late, but along with the return of Trades-Training, the cadets of the Vernon Army Cadet Camp should be allowed to earn the right to be young adults. They should be given a little rope. They won't hang themselves. Allow them to go into town, often.

The army cadet movement could boom in this country. Yes, there could once again be cadet corps with 150 to 200 cadets. How, you may ask? It's very simple. With a *little* tact, treat the youngsters as adults. Train the officers properly, and provide the equipment for Trades-Training. The original thought behind the army cadet movement was not to treat cadets as children. But as Sergeant Beckford would say, "Too many sexual intellectuals were put in a position of authority."

Oh yes and there's one more thing. Get someone off their fat-fanny in Ottawa to ensure that *qualified Regular Force Senior NCOs are sent to Camp Vernon.* That doesn't mean posting clerks and cooks to assume training positions. It means posting Senior and Junior NCOs from the infantry, armoured, artillery and Airborne regiments. Perhaps even a few Regular Force officers could also be posted, but it is entirely possible the politics of jealousy would ensue if that happened. Regardless of what the cadets need, the pettiness of what 'Branch' of the forces should be commanding the camp(s) continues. This policy in itself is part of the ever-spiralling eventual disintegration of the Army Cadet system. No forethought whatsoever has been given to the fact that the present method of training Cadet Instructors List Officers is, at the very least, totally insufficient to meet the needs of the original thought behind the movement. The Regular Force and the Militia appeared eager to get rid of the responsibility of training cadets. Get them back involved.

I should point out now, that if it is the intention of Ottawa to have the Army Cadet Movement mirror the Boy Scout Movement, then the present system is fine. If not, then some drastic mistakes have been made by 'people' who should never have been allowed to interfere with the original intent of what Army Cadets is all about.

It would appear that all requests for Regular Force assistance at the training level, particularly at the camps, has fallen on deaf ears. Every excuse why it can't be done has been delivered verbally or written in letter or memo form.

You can bet your life, the people who turn the requests down were never in the Royal Canadian Army Cadets. But then again, maybe they were. If the latter is the case, then we must consider, now, that it is entirely possible the whole hierarchy of the military structure in Canada, is a uniformed civil-service which bears no similarity to Canada's professional military structure of the past.

I'm certain I don't have to remind anyone that crime in Canada is increasing at a very alarming rate. Billions of dollars are being spent trying to stem the tide and many will say we're fighting a losing battle. Well, if a research team went to work, they would discover very quickly that the boys who served in the Royal Canadian Army Cadets when it meant something, are not the parents of the trouble makers, nor are they the criminals.

Without a doubt, the sexual intellectuals in Ottawa need to rethink their policies.

Sergeant Beckford made a lot of sense when he stated that boys in reform schools should be placed in special companies with Regular Force Regiments. Does anyone remember the Soldier Apprentice Program? Although that course wasn't originated for trouble makers, it certainly got lots of boys back on track.

Sergeant Beckford also said, "The best time to rock the boat is when the waters are calm."

Certain politicians and General Officers who have moved on to happy pension days did their damndest to ensure that the waters always stayed calm. The problem we have now, is that their successors are continuing the policy.

The damage done to Canada's military over the past twenty four years is totally inexcusable—particularly the damage done to Canada's Army Cadet Movement.

Recently I was listening to a radio broadcast with the veteran talk-host Pat Burns. When answering a question from the caller about which party in Canada would do the best for the country, he said, "If you hire an accountant and find he's stolen $50,000.00 from you, you would naturally fire him and go out and get another accountant. Then shortly afterwards if you find the second accountant had stolen $100,000.00 from you, would you hire the first one back? That's what the Canadian people have been doing with our two 'mainstream' parties."

I mention this because both the Liberals and Conservatives have kept our defence policies in the gutter. It is my opinion the NDP would let the policies go down the drain. Therefore, we have a real problem. But a problem that isn't insurmountable, if only our military 'leaders' spoke up and stopped worrying about their Personal Evaluation Reports.

There are those who will say the Canadian people are not in the least concerned about the military. Poppycock! The Canadian people were very concerned at one time. That's why Canada never had to take a back seat to any country in matters of the military. Look at our record in two world wars. But then came Pierre Trudeau and his henchman Paul Hellyer. Trudeau's intent was really to break up the country. To do so, he had to destroy the traditions and customs as much as possible. Given the situation we have today, you can say, he was largely successful.

My hat goes off to the navy, for those seven GRAND GENERAL OFFICERS, who told Trudeau and Hellyer to, 'shove it.' Yes, a few army and air force types did the same mind you, but it was the navy that stood up.

Who remained and what happened? Well, you be the judge. I can tell you though, that our present group of so-called, 'well meaning' senior servicemen and servicewomen (uniformed civil servants) certainly don't like speaking up to the ever-changing junior cabinet minister, called the Minister of National Defence. Why should they? It might screw up their careers or pensions.

Damn it, I'm mad. But not yet mad enough to write a book on the subject of Canada's military.. There are thousands that could do a better job than me.

At this moment I'm only concerned with one thing. More than ever, RIGHT NOW, for the betterment of this country, it's time to put the word 'ARMY' BACK INTO THE ROYAL CANADIAN ARMY CADETS.

Cordell Cross

Timeless. A Guard of later years giving the 'Eyes Right.' With flawless drill, razor creases, mirror-like-boots and the desire to reach for the top – they ensured they continued the traditions of those who came before them.